TRADITION, D
AND
IDEOLOG

TRADITION, DISSENT AND IDEOLOGY

Essays in Honour of Romila Thapar

Edited by

R. CHAMPAKALAKSHMI

S. GOPAL

OXFORD
UNIVERSITY PRESS

OXFORD
UNIVERSITY PRESS

YMCA Library Building, Jai Singh Road, New Delhi 110001

Oxford University Press is a department of the University of Oxford. It furthers the University's objective of excellence in research, scholarship, and education by publishing worldwide in

Oxford New York
Athens Auckland Bangkok Bogota Buenos Aires Cape Town Chennai Dar es Salaam Delhi Florence Hong Kong Istanbul Karachi Kolkata Kuala Lumpur Madrid Melbourne Mexico City Mumbai Nairobi Paris Sao Paolo Singapore Taipei Tokyo Toronto Warsaw

with associated companies in

Berlin Ibadan

Published in India
By Oxford University Press, New Delhi

First published 1996
Oxford India Paperbacks 2001

ISBN 0 19 5654420

Typset by Guru Typograph Technology, New Delhi 110045
Printed at Sai Printo Pack Pvt Ltd, New Delhi 110020
and published by Manzar Khan, Oxford University Press
YMCA Library Building, Jai Singh Road, New Delhi 110 001

A Note on the Contributors

The authors of the essays in this volume are members of the Faculty and former students of the Centre for Historical Studies, Jawaharlal Nehru University. Kumkum Roy has published a book on early Indian polity and society based on a study of Vedic and epic texts. Her current research continues to be in the same area with a focus on gender studies. Neeladri Bhattacharya completed his dissertation on agrarian history in Punjab in the late-nineteenth and early-twentieth centuries and has now expanded his interests to include a study of tradition and its transformation in colonial and contemporary India. Kunal Chakrabarti's dissertation is on the process of brahmanization in the indigenous religious base in early medieval Bengal and his current research interests include the analysis of myths and symbols. K.N. Panikkar's early works were in the areas of nineteenth-century British diplomacy *vis-à-vis* the princely states of northern India and peasant movements, while his current research is on the intellectual and cultural history of modern India. K. Meenakshi, an expert in linguistics in the Centre for Historical Studies, has published her work on the syntactical aspects of language, especially Sanskrit. Her current research focuses on ancient Indian grammatical works in Sanskrit and Tamil India. Her current research interests include religion, society and ideology in South India. Muzaffar Alam's early works have been on the state and society in Mughal India. His present programme of research is on culture, religion and politics in late medieval and early modern 'Muslim' empires. S. Gopal's early publications have been on British policies in India and the works of

Jawaharlal Nehru. His recent books include biographies of Jawaharlal Nehru and S. Radhakrishnan, which focus on their reflections on Indian philosophy, religion and society. Satish Saberwal, a sociologist in the Centre for Historical Studies, has published ethnographical studies on the Embu of central Kenya and of a Punjab industrial town. He has now moved to comparative long-term studies on Western Europe, India and China. Shereen Ratnagar, an archaeologist, is the author of two works on the Harappa civilization, its trade and political organization. Her current research focuses on urbanism, early states and pre-market economics, with comparative perspectives from West Asia and India. Sudarshan Seneviratne has done his early research on Buddhism and its social base in early South India and Sri Lanka. He continues to focus his research work on early social formation in Sri Lanka, through archaeology and allied disciplines, with perspectives on eco-systems and environment. Rajan Gurukkal's work was initially on the temple in early medieval Kerala and socio-political organization in early medieval South India. He has moved on to a study of early historical society, polity and ideology based on a semiological analysis of the Tamil classical texts.

Contents

Introduction 1

I. TRADITION AND TRANSFORMATION

1 Vedic Cosmogonies: Conceiving/Controlling Creation
KUMKUM ROY 9

2 Remaking Custom: The Discourse and Practice of Colonial Codification
NEELADRI BHATTACHARYA 20

II. ACCOMMODATION AND DOMINANCE

3 Texts and Traditions: The Making of the Bengal *Purāṇas*
KUNAL CHAKRABARTI 55

4 Creating a New Cultural Taste: Reading a Nineteenth-century Malayalam Novel
K.N. PANIKKAR 89

III. CONTESTATION AND AFFIRMATION

5 The Siddhas of Tamil Nadu: A Voice of Dissent
K. MEENAKSHI 111

6 From Devotion and Dissent to Dominance: The Bhakti of the Tamil Āḷvārs and Nāyanārs
R. CHAMPAKALAKSHMI 135

7 Assimilation from a Distance: Confrontation and Sufi Accommodation in Awadh Society
MUZAFFAR ALAM 164

IV. RESOURCES OF TRADITION

8 Nehru, Religion and Secularism
S. GOPAL 195

9 Tradition and Resilience: Mobilizational Energy in the Brahmanical Order
SATISH SABERWAL 216

V. STATES AND SYSTEMS

10 State and Lineage
SHEREEN RATNAGAR 245

11 'Peripheral Regions' and 'Marginal Communities': Towards an Alternative Explanation of Early Iron Age Material and Social Formations in Sri Lanka
SUDHARSHAN SENEVIRATNE 264

12 Towards a New Discourse: Discursive Processes in Early South India
RAJAN GURUKKAL 313

Appendix: Romila Thapar—A Bibliography 335

Index 339

Introduction

In 1991 some of Romila Thapar's colleagues and friends decided to put together a volume in her honour. Timed to felicitate her on her sixty-first birthday, this volume, which has been longer in the making than expected, seeks to acknowledge both the depth and range of her contribution to the writing of Indian history as well as her crucial role in building up the Centre for Historical Studies at Jawaharlal Nehru University. At the time this volume was planned Professor Thapar was about to retire from the Centre, and the recognition of an impending loss was widely shared amongst her colleagues and students. Her warm and inspiring presence did much to create an intellectual milieu at the Centre.

This volume is organized around the themes of tradition, dissent and ideology, which are in many ways central to Romila Thapar's concerns. Thapar has persistently questioned essentialist and unhistorical notions of tradition, and critiqued the search for simple continuities in the past. She has sought to demonstrate the historicity of traditions, the shifting nature and functions of rituals and practices, the changing meanings of texts and oral cultures, the links between cultural practices and the play of power, the dialectic between heterodoxy and orthodoxy as also between dissent and conformism, and the role that specific constructions of the past play in the politics of the present.

Implicit in the binary opposition between tradition and modernity is the assumption of a stagnant past and a dynamic present. It is as if tradition represents continuity and modernity expresses the power of transformation. The problems of such simple oppositions have long been recognized. Inverting the opposition and discovering forces of transformation within tradition has its problems. While this does historicize tradition, it tends to overemphasize change and underestimate the significance of continuities. The first two essays in the volume show how the discourse of continuity remains significant in legitimizing and carrying through changes within tradition.

Through a discussion of the cosmogonies within Vedic tradition, Kumkum Roy shows that traditions often regarded as sacrosanct and monolithic are subject to pressures which render them fluid and dynamic. Changes within the Vedic cosmogonies, however, were represented as extensions and elaborations on a theme rather than as innovations. These mutations not only reflected social and political transformations but were, in fact, integral to these processes.

Neeladri Bhattacharya's essay argues that a codification of custom in colonial Punjab was an act of rewriting tradition. The British conception of tradition shifted over the colonial years: if in the early colonial period Orientalists saw custom as embodied in sacerdotal ancient texts, by the mid-nineteenth-century community practices were seen as expressing tradition. But the effort to understand, interpret and codify custom subjected tradition to transformative processes. Bhattacharya analyses the multiple discourses of tradition and modernity within the discourse of custom, and the concepts and assumptions which informed ethnographic enquiries into custom. He shows how the rhetoric of custom becomes a new language of power and domination, as well as a basis for reordering society.

Transformative processes at work in the remaking of traditions can take on a variety of forms. How do cultures and traditions in conflict confront and influence each other? How is the domination of a specific tradition brought about? The second set of essays in this volume explores the dialectic of accommodation and marginalization, and the concurrent tendencies of homogenization and differentiation which characterize the complex history involved in the fashioning of dominant traditions.

The regional *Purāṇas* of early medieval Bengal evolved out of an interaction between the Brahmanical tradition and many local traditions. Kunal Chakrabarti suggests that this process involved a simultaneous emphasis on the authority of the *Vedas* and the significance of local customs. Regional *Purāṇas* acquired legitimacy by striking a delicate balance between the Vedic and local sources of authority. This task could be performed only by the local *brāhmaṇas* who were in a position to assess the points of minimum compatibility between different traditions and choose a specific combination from a range of available choices. Through this complex interaction a regional tradition was created, which then began to function as a point of reference for later vernacular texts.

K.N. Panikkar's essay attempts to show how colonialism in India sought to hegemonize indigenous culture through a controlled and guided process of acculturation in which the ideological apparatuses of the state played a crucial role. His reading of a popular nineteenth-century Malayalam novel highlights the cultural implications of 'new literacy' and examines how in the vernacular a new literary genre, the novel, acts as a vehicle for the creation of a fresh cultural taste and sensibility. This novel, *Indulekha*, not only captures the historical process of change in the nineteenth century but also underlines an emerging duality in the culture. The new culture neither fully identified with nor rejected the Western and indigenous traditions. This duality was also manifest in politics, in the ambivalences of nationalist consciousness.

If explorations into the constitution of dominant traditions inevitably lead us to histories of alternative traditions, the study of counter-cultures takes us back to narratives of power. The third set of essays in this volume shows how forces of opposition often affirm rather than displace the power of dominant ideals.

K. Meenakshi's essay brings out the radicalism of the *Cittar Pāṭalkaḷ* (songs of the Siddhas). Composed by a non-conformist but unorganized group of Tamil mystics, these songs posed a serious challenge to the Tamil *bhakti* tradition of temple and idol worship by questioning its formal structures. Although based on rationalist principles, Siddha ideals did not develop parallel or alternative structures. They were ultimately incorporated into the dominant and emotionally powerful cult of devotion.

R. Champakalakshmi looks at the making of an alternative religious tradition and its ultimate transformation into an instrument of power. The Tamil *bhakti* tradition, initially emerging as a simple devotional cult, soon offered a challenge to Brahmanical orthodoxy. Yet it ultimately affirmed the basis of Brāhmaṇism and undercut the potential strength of Śramaṇic sects. While it questioned the caste exclusiveness of Vedic *brāhmaṇas*, it made no effort to displace the *varṇa* order; while it refused to see caste status as ascriptive, it operated within the terms of caste discourse. It weakened the force of Vedic Brāhmaṇism only to become a vehicle for the spread of Purāṇic Brāhmaṇism. The tradition ultimately offered the idiom through which the Cōḷas could build their power, incorporating diverse groups with conflicting ideals into a social order.

Muzaffar Alam's essay takes us into the world of the Sufis. Through studies of Sufi visions, he seeks to understand the inner coherence of their ideas, as well as their conflicting logic. Though the Sufis questioned the larger Islamic tradition, they also endorsed it; they sought to assimilate local traditions but at the same time distanced themselves from it. While breaking with orthodox Islamic norms, they searched for an essential core of Islamic practices which could sustain their distinctive identity. This process created further differentiations within the larger Islamic and Sufi traditions, enlarging their variety. Alam shows that the Sufi trajectory in Awadh provided the cultural capital of Nawabi power, and the language to contain intercommunity conflicts in medieval society.

Specific attitudes to tradition are inscribed in ideologies of power. Some ideologies seek a rupture with the past, critiquing and rejecting tradition. Others are ambivalent towards tradition: accepting as well as disavowing it. Still others seek to draw upon the cultural resources of tradition, transforming these resources in the process of appropriation. The essays by S. Gopal and Satish Saberwal, in different ways, explore the ways by which resources of tradition are mobilized by ideologies, and the implications of such mobilizations.

Gopal shows how Nehru's secularism changes over the years: from a hard secularism, impatient with tradition and religion, it evolved into a mature secularism sensitive to the resources of tradition. Initially, Nehru's secularism was that of a rationalist. He attacked the social and political abuse of religion, advocated a divorce between religion and politics, and hoped that communalism would gradually disappear with modernization and development. Over the years he came to recognize, on the one hand, the embedded power of communalism, and on the other, the resources that traditions offered in building human bonds within a multi-religious society and in providing the sense of a shared cultural background. The mature secularism and 'scientific humanism' of Nehru's later years drew upon traditions of Indian philosophy. His effort was to 'evolve a modern state within the framework of Indian culture'.

In examining the working of the Brahmanical tradition, Saberwal looks at the variety of institutions and frameworks through which it could mobilize social energies: *jāti*, village, kingship and temple. Proposing that 'co-operative activities of relatively large scale can cohere over time only if these can draw adequate support from (a) shared ideas (as well as interests) and (b) legitimate institutions', he holds that 'such resources were short in this society'. Saberwal directs particular attention to political mobilization and to 'the process of handling information of learning from experience'. He concludes that 'the separativeness in the caste order . . . served to fragment both the normative order and the fields for possible social activity'.

The last set of essays focuses on the evolution of states and social formations. Systemic changes do not always signify a total break with the past. Thapar, in her study of the transition from lineage to state, has shown the continued survival of lineages under new state forms. Shereen Ratnagar, in her essay in this volume, describes the coexistence of tribal traditions and practices of land control at a time when the Mesopotamian state had newly emerged. Were these 'survivals' of the past, or practices which evolved within new contexts and under new pressures? How do we define the state which came into existence? In considering such questions, Ratnagar evaluates the possibility of reinstating the notion of 'Asiatic Mode of Production' in terms redefined by Godelier and Lawrence Krader.

Our narratives of the past define our social relations within society and the way social groups perceive themselves and others. Sudharshan Seneviratne shows that the dominant perception of the identity and significance of various social groups in Sri Lankan society is intimately connected to the way Sri Lankan history is interpreted and represented. The classical Buddhist texts linked the emergence of civilization in Sri Lanka with Indo-Aryan cultural groups from North India and depicted a core–periphery gradation in the cultural ecology of the island. The core—a hydraulic system of plough agriculture and advanced techniques—was seen as the centre of dynamism. Basing themselves on this region the Indo-Aryans, according to this history, unified Sri Lanka and played a crucial civilizational role. Seneviratne shifts the focus to the hilly and forested areas rich in minerals, treated in the classical Buddhist texts as 'retreat areas', and in the received history as the 'periphery'. Contrary to the view projected in classical texts, Seneviratne's alternative perspective highlights the influence of techno-cultural elements from South India in the formation of political and cultural institutions in different ecological zones—a process which was chronologically prior to the Indo-Aryan influence in the 'core' zone. This counter-history seeks to recover the history of the 'periphery'; it suggests that the material and social formation of the region was not only important but crucial to the very survival of the 'core' region.

Rajan Gurukkal links social transformations to shifts in hegemonic discourses. The Tamil heroic poems reveal an economy in which hunting–gathering, herding and shifting cultivation combined with pockets of wetland cultivation. Organized around descent groups controlled by chieftains, it was an economy based on prestation and plunder on the one hand, and redistributive mechanisms on the other. By analysing the recurrent terms, the semantic clusters, the enunciative codes, and the metaphors within the poems, Gurukkal seeks to understand the heroic discourse whose circulation was central to the cultural practices of this economy of plunder. Contrary voices emphasizing the value of peace, spirituality and order, and complaining against predatory campaigns, remained subordinate in the hegemonic discourse. While the heroic poems do reveal the tensions within society, it is a new class of literature, the *Kīlkkaṇakku* texts belonging to the fourth to fifth centuries AD, that announce a radical discontinuity within the dominant discourse. The ethic of personal conduct and morality, the stress on peace, loyalty, obedience and hard work, expressed in this new literature, all emit the values of a new social formation based on agrarian production. The social contradictions of this new order provided the historical context within which the powerful cult of *bhakti* emerged, supplanting the heroic ideology of the earlier social formation.

At a time when traditions are misappropriated in a variety of ways, historical explorations into the making of traditions become urgent. In seeking to contribute to such an effort, this volume acknowledges the inspirational role of Romila Thapar in such projects.

R. CHAMPAKALAKSHMI

S. GOPAL

I
Tradition and Transformation

1

Vedic Cosmogonies: Conceiving/Controlling Creation

KUMKUM ROY

Sacred traditions, textual and otherwise, are often formally regarded as sacrosanct. While this is portrayed as inevitable or even natural by proponents of the tradition, it is in effect deliberately established or maintained. Attempts to constitute a tradition as sacred (and hence sacrosanct), involve marginalizing or excising variations, while centralizing what are perceived to be crucial themes. As part of this process, specific constituents of traditions may be reworked, questioned, and subverted, even when they are not overtly challenged. Such contestations result in implicit if not explicit redefinitions. As such, while the formal inviolability or permanence of traditions is maintained, this is often accompanied by shifts within the framework which can substantially alter the content of the tradition. Yet, given that the appeal of the tradition stems from its perceived invulnerability, transformations are often represented as extensions or elaborations or, at most, variations on a theme rather than as innovations. Traditions, then, in spite of their apparently monolithic and constant character, are in reality subject to pressures rendering them fluid and dynamic. These are especially obvious in situations where disseminating and/or controlling traditions are interwoven with access to various forms of power.

The interweaving of tradition and context is evident from an examination of Vedic traditions. These have been consistently portrayed as *apauruṣeya* or supramundane, and by extension immutable. Yet this formal appeal to the unchanging has been accompanied by substantial transformations. It is commonly agreed that the *Ṛg Veda* pertains to the areas around the Indus and its tributaries, while later Vedic texts have a wider, more easterly focus. Assigning dates to the texts is more hazardous. Nevertheless, the priority of most parts of *Ṛg Veda* is generally accepted, and it is possible that the texts evolved over centuries, probably between *c.* 1500 and 600 BC. What is perhaps more relevant in the present context is the fact that the texts represent an attempt (or attempts) to deliberately preserve and, in the case of the later Vedic texts, often explicitly interpret what are perceived or construed as sacred traditions. As we will see, the contents of what was defined as 'traditional' as well as the forms in which it was represented were subject to change.

Changing definitions of sacral traditions have been related to a changing social order. While there have been debates on the specificities of early and/or later Vedic societies, there is a broad consensus that the former was probably less differentiated, whereas the latter was more sharply stratified. Clearly, traditions which may have been considered valuable and hence preserved in one context may have been perceived as somewhat dubious in a different situation or from different perspectives. As such, while sacral traditions were formally portrayed as sacrosanct, they were often subjected to reworkings and shifting emphases, and became the focus of lesser or greater degrees of priestly attention or control. Such transformations not merely reflected socio–political changes but were indeed integral to them. I focus on the discussion on cosmogonies within the Vedic tradition as illustrative of this relationship.

Cosmogonic speculation is probably an almost inevitable and fundamental human activity, resting as it does on attempts to contextualize and rationalize our existence. While this confers on it a certain universality, the specific forms of cosmogonic speculation that are tolerated, encouraged, or even actively propagated, vary substantially in different situations.

Vedic mythology, as evidenced in the *Ṛg Veda* and later Vedic texts, including the principal *Brāhmaṇas*, provides us with a range of cosmogonic ideas. However, while all of these are incorporated within the texts, some are simply noticed and recorded, while others are elaborated and worked out through ritual. The process of inclusion, subordination, or even exclusion of specific cosmogonic notions was, in all likelihood, a slow and complex one.

It is perhaps necessary to point out that the *Ṛg Veda* is qualitatively different from the other Vedic texts, consisting as it does of hymns addressed to a variety of deities. The hymns, by their very nature, either eulogize the attributes of the gods or goddesses, or focus on the necessity of invoking divine assistance or support. By and large, cosmogonic ideas are incidentally present as part of the stereotyped praise of gods. Apart from this, the last *maṇḍala* or book of the *Ṛg Veda*, which is commonly regarded as late, contains a number of hymns focusing explicitly, and occasionally exclusively, on cosmogonic issues. It is likely that although the compilation of this particular section of the text is relatively late, parts of it may have existed prior to the date of compilation. It is also possible that the disparate ideas regarding the nature and origin of the universe, which are brought together in this section, represent the speculations of different communities or even social groups within a single community. While the compilation was probably a step towards assimilating such ideas, the very fact that diverse cosmogonic understandings were allowed to coexist suggests that the process of assimilation had its limitations—no attempt was made to reduce the range of speculation to a single, homogeneous pattern. In other words, a variety of cosmological possibilities were accepted if not approved.

The *Brāhmaṇas*, on the other hand, are more centrally preoccupied with the nature and function of ritual, which they both elucidate and validate. Consequently, they attempt to provide a consolidated, more or less systematically developed understanding of cosmogonic processes as stemming from and inherent to the sacrifice. While elements of this understanding can be traced to the *Ṛg Veda*, the centrality accorded to it was a new development. What is more, this seems to have resulted in the displacement of earlier or alternative mythical speculations, or even their reinterpretation at a number of levels.

Perhaps the most outstanding example of such a reworking is the changing characterization of Indra in early and later Vedic mythology. As is widely recognized, Indra ranks amongst the chief gods within the Vedic tradition. Stereotyped eulogies of the deity almost invariably refer to his victories over Vṛtra. This contest was frequently interpreted in cosmogonic terms.[1] It has also been understood in terms of conflict between opposed natural forces—of rainfall and drought, or light and darkness, or even in terms of conflicts between hostile peoples. Such

[1] For example, F.B.J. Kuiper, 'Cosmogony and Conception: A Query', *History of Religions*, vol. X, 1970–1, p. 108; W. Norman Brown, 'Theories of Creation in the Rig Veda', *Journal of the American Oriental Society*, vol. LXXXV, 1965, p. 23.

interpretations are by no means mutually exclusive, as cosmogonies acquire greater weight in so far as they appear comprehensive and all-encompassing. Thus, a myth which purported to explain and integrate the natural with the social order was obviously significant. Hence, it is not surprising that Indra was most commonly invoked as the destroyer of Vṛtra (*Vṛtrahan*).[2] This was probably viewed as a means of empowering both the invoker and the invoked, who were bound together through the bond of shared perceptions.

Indra's victory was typically thought to be achieved through the use of his characteristic weapon, the *vajra* or thunderbolt. Its outcome, the destruction of Vṛtra, was commonly linked with the release of waters. Once again, this has been interpreted at a variety of levels, from being envisaged in literal terms as referring to the destruction of embankments or dams and thus releasing the pent up rivers or streams, to the liberation of cosmic waters. In any event, the notion of destruction as a prerequisite for creation/generation/regeneration, at whatever level one chooses to interpret the myth, points to an understanding of warlike, heroic valour as intrinsically creative or productive.

Occasionally, other cosmogonic acts are attributed to Indra. These include the setting up of the three basic spatial categories of heaven, earth, and intermediate space, and providing the basic sources of energy—producing fire, and setting the sun on its course.[3] These acts are not explicitly attributed to the deity's prowess, but given that this was regarded as Indra's typical characteristic, it is likely that there was an implicit understanding that this was a quality required of the creator god.

The fate of these mythical speculations in the later Vedic ritual tradition is interesting. Most of these mythic episodes are almost never alluded to in the later texts—indeed, perhaps the only theme to survive, with substantial modifications, is the Indra–Vṛtra myth. This is taken up and incorporated within a range of rituals—through prayers offered to Indra as the slayer of Vṛtra and, perhaps more significant, through the construction of the sacrifice as the device with which Indra destroys his arch enemy. In other words, the thunderbolt of the god was transmuted into a ritual device, suggesting that a literal recourse to valour was in itself inadequate for performers in the cosmic drama.

[2] U. Choudhuri, *Indra and Varuṇa in Indian Mythology*, Delhi, 1981, p. 4.

[3] F. Max Muller (ed.), *The Hymns of the Ṛg Veda*, Varanasi, 1965, II, 12.3; III, 30.9; III, 30.12 (henceforth *Ṛg Veda*).

The ritualization of cosmogonic speculation, other examples of which will be noted below, was extended to suggest that the correct performance of the sacrifice would enable the sacrificer to gain control over the dimensions of space and time.[4] In this context, the accurate performance of the ritual was valorized as virtually the sole means of controlling, if not creating, the universe.

At another level, the Indra–Vṛtra myth was invested with new, more social connotations—the destruction of Vṛtra was thought to be synonymous with the elimination of the hostile kinsman of the male sacrificer or *yajamāna*. The terms used to designate such kinsmen, *bhrātṛvya* or *sapatna*, are, once again, later Vedic, occurring for the first time in the latest section of the *Rg Veda* (the tenth *maṇḍala*). Thus there seems to have been an attempt to extend the scope of the myth to encompass tensions within kinship structures.

At the same time, the cosmic dimensions of the myth were implicitly curtailed—for instance, the *yajamāna* who imitated Indra in performing a sacrifice to destroy Vṛtra or rival kinsmen was not expected to lay claims to releasing the waters. What we have then is a shift in the emphases on various possible meanings of the Indra-Vṛtra myth—its cosmic significance was evidently whittled down, although not completely denied, while its social significance was both highlighted and modified to render it into a sanctified metaphor for the resolution of conflicts amongst kinsmen.

Indra was by no means alone in being subjected to revisionist tendencies that marginalized if not denied his cosmogonic rọle. The fate of the august deity Varuṇa was almost identical. The cosmogonic activities attributed to him were somewhat similar to those associated with Indra—and included demarcating spatial categories, regulating the movements of celestial bodies, creating the basic elements required for human existence, including fire and water, establishing the temporal units as well as the requisites for sacral activities—the sacrifice, chants, and *soma*.[5]

The means of creation attributed to Varuṇa were however unique, and rested on his ability to wield the mysterious power of *māyā*. In other words, it defined creative power as something virtually incomprehensible, and consequently irreducible to a human act.

The subsequent fate of the concept of *māyā* was complex. On the one

[4] A. Weber (ed.), *The Śatapatha Brāhmaṇa*, Varanasi, 1964, I, 5.3.2; XIII, 8.1.5.

[5] *Ṛg Veda*, V, 62.3; I, 24.10, V, 85.2, VII, 66.11.

hand, references to *māyā* as a typical attribute of Varuṇa become relatively sparse in the later brahmanical tradition, as indeed do references to the deity himself. At the same time, *māyā* continues to figure within the discourse, although the attitude towards it seems to become increasingly ambivalent, if not negative. It was understood as a force capable of creating both good and evil, or, more commonly, as being responsible for the illusion of worldly existence and perceived as the cause of human bondage. Thus, the recognition accorded to the cosmogonic significance of *māyā* was at best dubious.

Other possibilities which underwent similar vicissitudes included those associated with Soma. In the *Ṛg Veda*,[6] the deity was conceived as forming a heterosexual pair with the goddess Aditi, their union being regarded as generative, and responsible for the production of human beings in particular. This mythical understanding rested on an explicit analogy between human procreation and divine creation. It was, moreover, an analogy comprehensible in terms of human experience.

In the later Vedic tradition, the conception of the cosmogonic role of Soma underwent changes.[7] The notion of a generative fluid was retained, but this was no longer understood in simple, physiological terms. Instead, Soma was incorporated within the sacrificial framework, as a product that emerged from the offerings made by the gods, and was in turn offered to produce rain, rain-producing food, which produces semen, and hence men. Here, as in the case of Indra, we find that the ritualization of cosmogonic ideas functions as a mechanism whereby alternative, non-sacrificial understandings of cosmogonic processes are both absorbed and subsumed under tendencies to centralize the sacrifice.

The focus on the sacrifice as cosmogonic had other spin-offs too. Some of these are evident in the treatment accorded to Agni, the fire-god, and by extension the personified deity of the sacrificial fire representing a typical messenger between men and gods. In the early Vedic context, Agni was rarely associated with cosmogonic activity—indeed, more often than not, we have references to the creation of Agni from the friction between two pieces of wood.[8] However, in the later Vedic tradition, he was linked with the creator god Prajāpati—in one instance, it is his insatiable hunger which has to be appeased, and leads to creation,[9]

[6] Ibid., IX, 74.5.

[7] S.C. Vasu (ed. and tr.), *The Bṛhadāraṇyaka Upaniṣad*, Allahabad, 1933, VI, 2.9.

[8] E.g., *Ṛg Veda*, I, 31.2.

[9] *Śatapatha Brāhmaṇa*, II, 2.4.1.

whereas in another instance, he 'purifies' the sperm released by Prajāpati, and renders it fit for creation.[10] In both cases, the personified and deified (sacrificial) fire is conceived of as playing a crucial role in the cosmogonic drama. Indeed, it/he is considered to be as important, if not more important, than the creator god himself.

The notion of a cosmic sacrifice, and/or by extension of the sacrifice as a cosmic act was increasingly centred and elaborated in and around the figure of Prajāpati, an essentially later Vedic deity, who is mentioned for the first time in the tenth maṇḍala of the *Ṛg Veda*. Certain features of the Prajāpati-centred cosmogony are significant. To start with, Prajāpati is accorded explicit and complete recognition as a creator god—we have none of the uncertainties associated with Indra or Varuṇa, for instance, whose cosmogonic roles are implicit and consequently subject to question and modification. Besides, Prajāpati's position is reinforced by enumerating his creations—a typical example[11] included the material elements such as fire, deities, varieties of animals, soils, plants, spatial categories, heavenly bodies, the directions, and of course mortals. There is thus an obvious and systematic effort to encompass as much of the known or knowable universe as possible within such lists.

At another, operational level, the means Prajāpati was supposed to have adopted to perform his cosmogonic functions are discussed at length. Here we have evidence for a certain dichotomy, with some of the possibilities associated with Prajāpati being valorized at the expense of others. The *Ṛg Veda* contains incidental references to Prajāpati's incestuous links with his daughter,[12] a potentially generative relationship. However, in the later Vedic tradition, this mythical element was at once recognized and divested of its procreative possibilities. The notion of sexual intercourse in general and incest in particular was viewed with disfavour, and was thought to lead to generation only through the intervention of intermediate deities such as Rudra. What is more, it was not open to men to imitate Prajāpati.

However, other means of creation ascribed to Prajāpati were regarded as more amenable to human emulation. These included *tapas*, or austerity, with connotations of generative heat.[13] More often than

[10] R.R. Agashe (ed.), *Aitareya Brāhmaṇa*, Poona, 1979, III, 13.10.

[11] *Śatapatha Brāhmaṇa*, XI, 5.8.3.

[12] E.g., *Ṛg Veda*, V, 42.13.

[13] Walter O. Kaelber, '*Tapas*, Birth, and Spiritual Rebirth in the Veda', *History of Religions*, vol. XV, 1975, pp. 343–4.

not, we are introduced to a series of stages of cosmogonic activity—commencing from the aloneness of the single Prajāpati, who desires to proliferate or become many, and has recourse to austerities. These lead to the perception of the sacrifice, or of specific sacrifices. The performance of these yields the expected result.

The notion of the cosmic sacrifice, somewhat commonplace in the *Brāhmaṇas*, was not particularly original. Its earliest indications are present in the famous *puruṣasūkta*, which postulates the sacrifice of a primeval being resulting in the creation of the natural, social, and sacral orders.[14] What is new in the *Brāhmaṇas* is the transference of this understanding to specific rituals, which were now conceived of or portrayed as events of cosmogonic significance. What is more, the sacrificer was not merely equated with Prajāpati, whom he was thought to emulate, but was actually regarded as assisting or even supporting him. A typical statement prefacing ritual prescriptions suggested that the deity was weakened by his creative endeavours and had to be resuscitated through the ritual. The notion of rituals as a means of regeneration/restoration envisaged a cycle running from the deity to the sacrificer and back.

While the sacrifice in general was conceived of as an act imbued with cosmogonic significance, specific rituals were prescribed for ensuring cosmic harmony. These included the *soma* sacrifice and its variants, as also elaborate public rituals such as the *rājasūya, vājapeya*, and *aśvamedha*. Very often, the cosmogonic implications of the ritual were worked out at length, through commentary, chants, and component rituals. For instance, the *aśvamedha* was regarded as a means of obtaining the basic temporal unit of the year, of restoring Prajāpati, of endowing animals such as the cow, horse, and ox with their typical attributes.[15] In other words, both the sacral and the material bases of human existence were thought to be constituted and reconstituted through the performance of such rituals.

While such sacrifices were relatively grandiose and their performance was restricted to those both prosperous and willing enough to undertake them, more routine rituals were also endowed with cosmogonic symbolism. These included the daily offering to the fire, the *agnihotra*, which was regarded as a means of encompassing both space and time.[16]

[14] The motif of the cosmogonic sacrifice recurs in other hymns of the last maṇḍala of the *Ṛg Veda* also, e.g. nos 72 and 81.

[15] *Śatapatha Brāhmaṇa*, XIII, 1.2.1, 4.4.11, 1.9.3–5.

[16] Ibid., II, 1.4.11, 3.3.18.

The range of sacrifices which were endowed with cosmic significance is striking. It meant that virtually any ritual performance could be perceived as a means of restoring, if not generating, cosmic harmony. In other words, participation in the cosmic drama was now open to human beings, provided they undertook the necessary activities.

Yet, such participation was far from being universalized. In the first place, the construction of the correct sacrificial context was increasingly regarded as a monopoly of priestly experts. Simultaneously, the contents of priestly expertise became more complex if not complicated. This may have been a device to meet the threat of contestation, but in any case it meant that the authority to conduct the sacrifice as a cosmic event was carefully restricted. Thus while the concept of the cosmic sacrifice encouraged an understanding of cosmogonic activities as subject to human control, the exercise of such control was open to only a few.

To an extent, the sphere of control was widened to include the *yajamāna*, the male sacrificer or patron of the sacrifice, who was, in a sense, responsible for initiating proceedings, and was expected to be the chief beneficiary. Given the range of sacrifices referred to above, it would mean that a cosmogonic role was potentially available to male heads of the household belonging to the first three *varṇas*. It was also accessible to, and probably more frequently exercised by, men who aspired to achieve public recognition for their status—*rājās* who performed the *rājasūya* or *aśvamedha*, for instance.

Yet, there were many who were excluded from an independent role in the sacrifice. These included *śūdras*, junior members of the households of men belonging to the first three *varṇas*, and women. While they were often expected to participate in the ritual (indeed, in the case of the *yajamāna*'s wife this was virtually mandatory), they had little or no effective control over initiating the ritual process. As such, if the cosmos was envisaged as amenable to or even dependent on human intervention, such intervention was envisaged as open to some but not all human beings.

In all likelihood this would have meant that some but not all human beings were regarded as responsible for maintaining, if not creating, the cosmic order, and ensuring the prerequisites or fundamental bases of human existence. As opposed to this, other, lesser mortals were thrust into the role of recipients of the benefits of sacral activities, and were, by extension, subordinate. Thus access to or lack of access to the sacrifice as a cosmic act could have been one (but by no means the only) means of enforcing social stratification—between priests and non-priestly categories, between the sacrificers and others, and between men and women. In other words, a medley of disparate cosmogonic ideas was gradually welded together to arrive at an understanding emphasizing the sacral and social character of the process. What is more, it also incorporated and reinforced a specific definition of the sacred and the social.

As an offshoot of this, attempts were made to incorporate relatively new social institutions within the framework of cosmogonies. The treatment of *varṇa* is illustrative in this context. As is well known, the *puruṣasūkta* is the only hymn in the *Ṛg Veda* to refer to all four *varṇas*, thus constituting one of the earliest attempts to ascribe sacral origins to the institution.

Not all creation myths envisaged the emergence/existence of the *varṇa* order in its well-known sequence. In one instance, Indra was thought to have created the *rājanya* or the second *varṇa* first, followed by the *brāhmaṇa* and the *vaiśya*.[17] However, these were exceptions and, in most cases, the creation of the institution, ascribed to Prajāpati, was visualized in terms of the conventional order. What is more, such myths also raised and resolved questions regarding the functions ideally meant for each *varṇa*, carefully distinguishing their respective ritual and economic status. For instance, the fact that the *vaiśya* was believed to have been produced from the lower half of the body of the primeval being was thought to justify his oppression by those produced from the upper and hence superior organs.[18]

What is also significant is the selective appropriation of and elaboration on the *puruṣasūkta*. Apart from reflecting on the origins of the *varṇas*, the hymn contained an implicit understanding of an interdependent and relatively egalitarian relationship between the sexes. This is suggested by the statement,[19] that the *puruṣa* or primeval being created the *virāj* (feminine) and was in turn created by her. Here, the distinction between the creator and the created, between the masculine and the feminine, seems to be deliberately blurred. However, this possibility was not worked out in subsequent myths. Besides, and more important, rituals thought to be of cosmogonic significance, such as the *aśvamedha*, were also used as occasions for highlighting and sanctifying gender differences and enforcing gender stratification. Thus, while

[17] A.C. Sastri (ed.), *The Tāṇḍya Mahābrāhmaṇa*, Banaras, 1935–6, XIII, 4.17.

[18] Ibid., VI, 1.10.

[19] *Ṛg Veda*, X, 90.5.

a differentiated sexual order did not constitute a part of the original myth, it was subtly worked into its ritual enactment.

Vedic cosmogonies, then, underwent transformations at a number of levels. While a wide variety of cosmogonic speculation was recognized, only some, including the notion of the cosmic sacrifice, were privileged. These were, moreover, located within a context of increasing socio–ritual differentiation. Yet, alternative possibilities remained, even if their coexistence was somewhat uneasy. What is more, cosmogonic speculation did not come to an end with ritualization—indeed, its continued and varied development was manifest in a range of ideas—including idealistic and monistic concepts, on the one hand, and materialistic possibilities, on the other.[20] In other words, although an attempt was made to control and regulate cosmogonic speculation by locating it within an increasingly well-defined sacrificial context and relating the latter to notions of socio–political hierarchies, this met with only limited success. Cosmogonic speculation could not be confined within the limits of a ritualistic framework—instead it spilled beyond in a variety of directions. Given that the ritual framework was bound to and interwoven with a specific social order, the ability to develop or propagate alternative understandings of cosmic processes would have constituted an implicit if not explicit challenge to that mundane order as well. As such, the control and dissemination of cosmogonic theories also had a certain pragmatic relevance.

While varieties of cosmogonic ideas were not solely reflections of alternative social agendas, their social implications were obviously significant. Thus both the attempt to focus on and elaborate a single cosmogonic understanding and the existence of alternatives, point to a long-drawn and not necessarily conclusive contest between those in favour of a single, coherent, hierarchical social order and others representing more amorphous, fluid perspectives. In other words, the attempts to reduce cosmogonic speculation into an ideology of dominance was probably only partially successful.

[20] *See*, for instance, N.N. Bhattacharya, *History of Indian Cosmogonical Ideas*, New Delhi, 1971.

2

Remaking Custom: The Discourse and Practice of Colonial Codification

NEELADRI BHATTACHARYA

In late eighteenth-century Germany, Herder and the Brothers Grimm set about recording large numbers of folk ballads. Their effort was to capture the collective creativity of people within a specific culture, and, by documenting their stories, to salvage something of the past from oblivion. Samuel Johnson and James Boswell, the eminent English couple, were driven by similar intent to look for primitive custom in the western isles off Scotland, and in fact by the 1850s a serious interest in folklore and music had matured across several countries of Europe.[1] This discovery of popular culture was part of the large sweep of a wide-ranging Romanticism which celebrated the wild and the natural, the primitive and the archaic, the simple and the sublime, the spontaneous and the instinctive. It was an offshoot of the revolt against Reason and Classicism; it was part of the new current in favour of cultural pluralism.

Like many ideas and attitudes, this interest in the ancient, the popular and the distant made its way into the colonies. Its journey there was attended by all the twists and turns and paradoxes and contortions that such travels usually entail, but all the same, within a few decades of the European folklorists, colonial officials in many parts of the empire came to be preoccupied with rather similar cultural investigations and were to be found rooting about for folk traditions in far-flung provinces. While travellers to India voyaged in search of the picturesque and the

[1] Peter Burke, *Popular Culture in Early Modern Europe*, London, 1978, pt I; Richard Dorson, *The British Folklorists: A History*, Chicago, 1968.

exotic, the more curious among those already stationed to govern India developed an analogous interest in the social unfamiliar—in the customs, rituals and practices of native inhabitants.

Official interest in these matters assumed a specific structure in colonial Punjab. Conquered in 1848, almost ninety years after the British subdued the nawabs of Bengal, this region in north-west India experienced a form of colonial rule very different from the one established in the east. In Bengal the British saw zamindars as key figures in the countryside and the possible basis of Company Raj. In Punjab, peasants rather than zamindars were identified as the objects of imperial concern. Whereas the wet tracts of Bengal sustained a deeply stratified rural structure and a firmly entrenched caste order, Punjab, a drier tract, was in official discourse the proverbial land of peasant proprietors. If Cornwallis and his zamindari system epitomized British rule in Bengal, Lawrence's dream of Punjab showed a 'country thickly cultivated by a fat, contented yeomanry, each riding his own horse, sitting under his own fig tree . . .'[2]

After the British conquest, peasants in Punjab's villages suddenly became aware of colonial officials recording their folk-tales, ballads, songs and proverbs, investigating their customs and codifying customary law. The nature of property rights, marriage patterns, inheritance customs and collective rights on village commons were all being enquired into. The first set of *wajib-ul-arz* (village administration paper), prepared in the early 1850s, had identified rights and customs in each Punjab village. In the 1860s, the first series of *riwaj-i-ams* of tribal customs, as distinguished from village customs, were prepared. Numerous codes, digests and manuals, as well as more than forty volumes on the customary law of different districts of Punjab, were soon produced.

These British ethnographic texts reveal as much, or rather a bit less, about Indian custom as about the official observers—their minds, the conventions of their language, the assumptions implicit in their questions, and their conclusions. It is important to understand the concepts which framed the vision of these official ethnographers and directed their gaze, the processes through which a region's customary practices were codified, and the contexts which mediated this process. In the colonial situation the rhetoric of custom becomes a new language of power and legitimation. It is of interest to examine the specificities, the logic, the ambivalences, and the implications of this rhetoric.

[2] R.N. Cust, *Pictures of Indian Life*, London, 1881, p. 255.

FROM TEXT TO PRACTICE

The *Code of Gentoo Laws*, the first major colonial digest on Hindu law, was published in 1776. About a hundred years later, in 1881, appeared Tupper's *Customary Laws of Punjab*. These works represent two different strands of colonial legal discourse. Both are tied in their opposition to Benthamite Utilitarian Positivism, yet they are very different from each other. Against the Utilitarian disdain for tradition, they celebrated tradition; against the Utilitarian argument of practical reason and the principle of Utility, they invoked the authority of custom; against the Benthamite plea for radical reform by the state, they saw the need to conserve and build on established rules; against the aggressive utilitarian projection of British rule as an enlightened alien power, they hoped to transcend the alienness by presenting colonial rule as rooted in indigenous society. Both sought to base British rule on custom and tradition, but they were involved in very different imperial projects.

The late-eighteenth-century Orientalist tradition saw ancient texts as the source of authentic knowledge about immemorial custom and tradition.[3] The Sastras and the Koran, it believed, set out the codes of conduct of Hindus and Muslims, and defined the customary laws which mediated social relationships as well as conflicts within communities. Practices were seen as legitimate only when they conformed with the injunctions of ancient texts. So, present practice was no acceptable proof of valid custom: it could represent perversions, distortions and deformations of the original principles. Practices became tainted with the passage of time, marked with the imprint of generations; the real principles were buried under the weight of history. To preserve immemorial custom a return to the original form was essential: custom had to be purged of foreign influences and Sastric law had to be consolidated where an amalgam of practices had developed. The original authoritative texts had to be identified, translated and understood; and colonial codes had to be based on and authorized through these texts.[4]

[3] On the Orientalists, *see* Javed Majeed, *Ungoverned Imaginings*, Oxford, 1993, chs 1–3. On the late eighteenth-century discovery of Indian tradition by European scholars, *see* Raymond Schawb, *The Oriental Renaissance: Europe's Rediscovery of India and the East, 1680–1880*, New York, 1984; P.J. Marshall, *The British Discovery of Hinduism in the Eighteenth Century*, Cambridge, 1970; O.P. Kejariwal, *The Asiatic Society of Bengal and the Discovery of India's Past*, Delhi, 1988; Wilhelm Halbfass, *India and Europe: An Essay in Understanding*, Albany, 1990. On law, *see* J.D.M. Derrett, 'The Administration of Hindu Law by the British', *Religion Law and Society in India* (hereafter *RLSI*), New York, 1968.

[4] Hastings ordered that 'the laws of the Koran with respect to Mohamedans and those

Since the time of Hastings, Orientalist scholars had immersed themselves in the project of discovery and the translation of authentic sacerdotal texts, and in the preparation of definitive digests.[5] After the acquisition of *diwani* in Bengal in 1757, there had been, initially, a toleration of the diverse systems of popular justice and a fluid interpretation of the Sastras by pundits. This had created some insecurity about the ambiguous basis of justice and, concomitantly, the need for a stable foundation of legal knowledge. Flexible and conflicting interpretations of Sastric injunctions had to be replaced by the certitude of definitive digests of traditional textual knowledge.

In May 1773 eleven pundits began work on the first major digest. Their work, *Vivadarnava-setu* (A Bridge Across the Ocean of Litigation), was published in 1775. This was translated by N.B. Halhead into English as *The Code of Gentoo Laws*. Subsequently, under Jones's supervision, Jagannath Tarkapancanana produced another digest, *Vivadabhangarnava*, which was translated later into English by H.T. Colebrooke. Jones, whose object was to produce 'a complete digest of Hindu and Mussulman law', published *Al Sirajiyyah: Or the Mohamedan Law of Inheritance*, in 1792, and the *Institutes of Hindu Law: Or the Ordinances of Manu*, in 1796. Colebrooke's authoritative work, *The Digest of Hindu Law*, appeared in 1798.

The Orientalist thinking on custom, tradition and law was relentlessly attacked by Utilitarian Positivists inspired by the ideas of Bentham.[6] Mill, like Bentham, criticized any 'obscurantist' reverence for tradition and linked such traditionalism to the ruling conservative ideology in eighteenth-century Britain, which was pathologically opposed to liberal reform. The task of law, for the Utilitarians, was to

---

of the Shaster with respect to the Gentoos shall invariably be adhered to'. Derrett, 'The Administration of Hindu Law by the British', *RLSI*, p. 289.

[5] Kejariwal, *The Asiatic Society of Bengal and the Discovery of India's Past*; Derrett, 'The British as Patrons of the Sastras'. Jones was obsessed with the question of authenticity: the right texts had to be located and properly translated. *See* Majeed, *Ungoverned Imaginings: James Mill's The History of British India and Orientalism*, Oxford, 1992, ch. I; Rosane Rocher, 'British Orientalism in the Eighteenth Century', in Carol A. Breckenridge and Peter van der Veer (eds), *Orientalism and the Postcolonial Predicament*, Philadelphia, 1993.

[6] *See* Javed Majeed, *Ungoverned Imaginings* for James Mill's critique of Orientalism, and Eric Stokes, *The English Utilitarians in India* (Oxford, 1959) for a more general account. On Benthamite Utilitarianism there is now a rich scholarly literature. *See* L.J. Hume, *Bentham and Bureaucracy*, Cambridge, 1981; F. Rosen, *Jeremy Bentham and Representative Democracy*, Oxford, 1983; R. Harrison, *Bentham*, London, 1983; Gerald J. Postema, *Bentham and the Common Law Tradition*, Oxford, 1986.

define the basis of a new social and political order, rather than conserve the old regime; the valid concern of the law-maker was not the discovery of past custom—the law as it *is*—but rather the law as it *ought to be*.[7] Laws, in this view, did not express a deeper pre-given reality, an inner coherence of a pre-structured community with a collective history; they established that coherence by introducing order into a chaotic world of conflicting individual interests. Laws were exogenous, not endogenous, to a community; they provided a framework of fixed and public rules which made ordered life possible. Individuals were bound not by ties of community but by a commitment to clear, determinate, unambiguous public rules, systematized into a single universal code enacted by a proper legislative authority. The defining principles of this order were Reason and Utility, not shared traditions and custom.

The Punjab tradition reacted against this Utilitarianism.[8] There was, once again, an argument for basing law on immemorial custom and the authority of tradition, a concern for the collective life of communities.[9] But there was no return to the textual Orientalism of Jones and Colebrooke. Drawing on the English common law tradition, Punjab officials saw custom as embodied in practices rather than in ancient texts.[10] Injunctions within the Sastras and the Koran were not self-justifying:

[7] The criticism flowed from Bentham's crucial distinction between the 'expositor' of the law and its 'censor': 'To the province of the Expositor it belongs to explain to us what, as he supposes, the Law is: to that of the Censor, to observe to us what he thinks it ought to be. The former, therefore, is principally occupied in stating, or in inquiring after facts; the latter in discussing the reasons . . .' Cited in Postema, *Bentham and the Common Law Tradition*, p. 304. The law-maker, the codifier, had to be the censor, not a mere expositor.

[8] This critique, again, had 'conservative' roots. On the German sources of a conservative critique of Bentham, *see* P. Vinogradoff, *The Teachings of Sir Henry Maine*, London, 1904.

[9] For Tupper, as for Henry Maine, the group historically prefigures the individual: the individual emerges from the group at a specific stage of social development. Maine saw the family as the original form of social organization, while Tupper, drawing on Mclennan, traced the lineage of the individual to the tribe. The principles of tribal society tied the community internally; lineage linked the communities across generations. Custom was the expression of community life and its regulator. Custom had to be preserved; the forces leading to the disintegration of tribes had to be resisted.

[10] The reaction was not limited to Punjab. Henry Maine argued generally that the laws of Manu did not adequately represent local usages, and that 'the customary rules, reduced to writing, have been very greatly altered by Brahmanical expositors, constantly in spirit, sometimes in tenor'. Henry Maine, *Village Communities in the East and the West*, 1871, pp. 53ff. Elsewhere he criticized Jones's assumption that the laws of Manu were 'acknowledged by all Hindus to be binding on them'. It is probable, felt Maine, 'that at the end of the last century large masses of the Hindu population had not so much as heard

they were to be validated by practice.[11] The Punjab Laws Act of 1872 stated that the sacerdotal codes of Hindu and Muslim law were to be followed only to the extent that they coincided with, and had been absorbed within, customary practice.[12] When the riwaj-i-ams were prepared in the 1870s and 1880s, official observers were asked to carefully note the distance between actual practices and scriptures. The general tendency now was to repress the affinity between scriptures and practices, and play on the differences.

This general conception of custom was reinforced by a contextualist argument. Punjab was considered different from Bengal. In Punjab, so officials argued, Brahmans had no position of power, and customary law was 'unsacerdotal, unsacremental, secular'.[13] Hindu law which developed within the caste society of Bengal was unsuited for Punjab, where tribe and clan were defining features of the social ordering. 'Hindu law extravagantly exalts the Brahmans', wrote Tupper, 'it gives sacerdotal reasons for secular rules. . . .'[14] It derives its principles from caste rather than clan; it sees caste and not tribe as the natural order of society.

This move from text to practice was complicated. It occurred in hesitant and uncertain steps. Dalhousie's declaration in 1849 that British rule in Punjab would be based on native institutions was a statement of intent which conveyed no concrete content. How was custom to be defined and discovered? What were the sources of its authority? Such questions required time for debate. But the task of

---

of Manu, and knew little or nothing of the legal rules supposed to rest ultimately on his authority'. It was necessary to conserve the variety of local usages against their absorption by Brahmanical codes: 'The Sacred Law of the Hindus', in *Early Law and Custom.*

[11] In 1854, before issuing the Punjab Civil Code, the Judicial Commissioner M. R. Montgomery discussed 'how far those [Hindu and Muslim] codes are affected by, or merged in local custom, and in what places they altogether yield to that unwritten Code which is engraven on the minds of the people'. Preface to the abstract principles of law circulated for the guidance of officers employed in the administration of civil justice in the Punjab, Extract appended to Circular No. 37, dated 16 May 1854, From R. Montgomery, Judicial Comm., Punjab, to All Comms. in the Punjab, *Punjab Customary Law* (hereafter *PCL*), I, p. 59.

[12] *See* Tupper, 'Memorandum on the Means of Ascertaining the Customary Law of Punjab', dated 2 June 1873, *PCL*, I, p. 159.

[13] *See* 'Memorandum on the Customary Law in the Punjab' by C. Boulnois, Judge, Chief Court, Punjab, dated 28 November 1872, *PCL*, I; 'Memorandum on the Means of Ascertaining the Customary Law of Punjab' by Tupper, dated 2 June 1873, *PCL*, I.

[14] *See* Tupper, 'Memorandum on the Means of Ascertaining the Customary Law of Punjab', *PCL*, I.

administration could not wait. So a practical manual for officials was quickly put together by Richard Temple, drawing upon diverse textual sources: digests of European jurisprudence, and the great Orientalist texts on Sastric law produced by William Jones, T.A. Strange, W. Macnaghten, and H.T. Colebrooke—precisely those texts in opposition to which the specificities of customary practices in Punjab were later defined.

Fed on such digests and secure in the authority of their knowledge, officials went about arbitrating on matters of custom. In courts, when judges were called upon to adjudicate disputes over custom even before any serious enquiry had been undertaken, they had to fall back upon their own vague impressions of people's customs, supplemented by cursory enquiries and references to the Punjab Civil Code manual. Court decisions on issues of custom, tainted by such manuals, then became a source of knowledge about custom.[15] Later, in the volumes of Punjab Record, important judicial cases were compiled for ready reference. All customary law manuals quoted case law to prove a point about custom, and customs declared void by the courts could have no legal existence. Textual sources and judicial decisions remained important in the shaping of custom in the period between 1854 and 1872, when the Punjab Civil Code was in operation and the riwaj-i-ams were yet to be codified.

In a sense, textual authority was important even in Tupper's conception of customary law. His theory was not derived from the observation of practices; it was deductive. Drawing from the writings of English common-law theorists and nineteenth-century evolutionist anthropologists he outlined a general theory of the evolution of Punjab's society.[16] Indian evidence had no constitutive power in the making of this theory; the theory provided the frame through which the evidence was to be understood and ordered.[17]

[15] Commenting on the action of courts in transforming custom, Tupper wrote: 'How far is it probable that under the action of courts, indigenous custom has remained pure? The conjecture does not appear too rash, that if any of those parts of the lexis loci which the Punjab Civil Code treats in any detail were now to be analysed they would be found to be saturated with its influence.' Memorandum by Tupper, dated 2 June 1875, *PCL*, I, p. 207.

[16] Against Maine's, Tupper echoed Mclennan's theory that the small group emerges from the large, the family from the horde; but against Mclennan's view of the matriarchal origins of society, Tupper repeated Maine's patriarchal theory. Maine savaged Mclennan but appreciated Tupper. *See* Maine, 'Theories of Primitive Society' and 'The Sacred Law of the Hindus', in *Early Law and Custom*, 1883, rpt., Delhi, 1985.

[17] Tupper wrote: 'It cannot be too prominently stated that I pretend to offer nothing but a theory. In an agricultural population, which cannot now be less than ten millions, it is

The shift from text to practice was thus a problematic one. There was, without doubt, a definite change in the rhetoric of custom. If the late-eighteenth-century Orientalists in Bengal were preoccupied with the discovery of ancient sacred texts, in the late nineteenth century Punjab officials were busy enquiring into customary practices. But their enquiries into such practices remained implicated within textual processes and were structured by a variety of conceptual assumptions with which these officials operated.

OF INFORMANTS AND SOVEREIGNS

The enquiry into custom depended perforce upon local informants. This dependence had a peculiar logic. When the Orientalist investigations into Indian tradition began in the 1770s, with ancient texts viewed as the dominant founts of knowledge, pundits were recognized as the custodians of that knowledge. Considered as being learned in the Sastras, they knew the language of ancient texts and could help their British masters with those texts. After the 1793 Cornwallis Code, pundits were attached to the district and provincial courts: to the Sadr Diwani Adalat in Calcutta and to the Supreme Court. They were to answer questions posed by judges on specific disputes, and inform the court about what the Sastras had to say about the class of dispute in question.[18] Sastric education in the Sanskrit colleges in Calcutta and Banaras sought to produce experts to be consulted during litigation.[19] Pundits were involved in this way in producing colonial digests on Sastric law.

This dependence on the power of pundits created a deep imperial anxiety. While a dialogue with native informants was seen as essential

---

impracticable to exhaust all the facts; and even if I had time to examine vernacular documents in addition to the settlement reports and the *Punjab Record*, it would not have been possible to go beyond a theoretical statement of what the custom possibly would be under given conditions. This is what I mean by a theory of the subject; and I did not see how it could be exhibited in any general view by any other method.' Tupper, 'The Characteristics of Tribal and Village Custom', *PCL*, II, p. 77.

[18] Lata Mani discusses the structure of the dialogue with the pundits on the question of *sati*. *See* Mani, 'Contentious Traditions: The Debate on *Sati* in Colonial India', in Kumkum Sanghari and Sudesh Vaid (eds), *Recasting Women: Essays in Colonial History*, New Delhi, 1989, pp. 88–126.

[19] At the Sanskrit colleges the following texts were read: Manu, Mitakshara, Dayabhaga, Dayakarma (Sarigraha), Daya-tattva, Dattaka-candrika, Duttaka-mimansa, Vivada-cintamani, Tithi-tattva, Suddhi-tattva and Prayascitta-tattva. *See* Derrett, 'The British as Patrons of the Sastras', *Religion, Law and State in India*, New York, 1968, p. 238.

to the production of authentic knowledge, such extreme dependence was experienced by the British as a form of disempowerment. To assert sovereign power the masters had to transcend their crippling reliance on native knowledge-brokers and claim their own superior right to represent local tradition.

In the process, the authority of pundits was both recognized and denied. The British first persuaded the pundits to prepare the digests and then made disparaging comments on their works. Jones was dissatisfied with the work of the eleven pundits who prepared *Vivadarnava-setu*. Arriving in India eight years after the presentation of the Code of Gentoo Law to the East India Company, he set about preparing a more authoritative alternative digest of Sastric learning. Jagannatha Tarkapancanana, conversant with both the Mitakshara and Dayabhaga schools, prepared the digest *Vivada-bhangarnava* to Jones's specifications. Colebrooke translated the work but criticized Jagannatha; and later other official legal experts like Thomas Strange and F.W. Macnaghten even ridiculed him.[20] Colebrooke himself undertook to prepare a work in English which would establish a uniform and accurate basis of judgment and make English judges independent of their Hindu law officers. But he too was dissatisfied with Balam Bhatta and Citrapati, the two local informants who worked with him on the digest.

The question of knowledge became linked to a discourse of morality. The knowledge of the pundits was seen as suspect since their motives and morals were questionable.[21] In Jones's attack on the pundits a feeling of impotent anger fused with a sense of moral outrage: 'I can no longer bear to be at the mercy of our Pandits, who deal out Hindu law as they please, and make it at reasonable rates, when they cannot find it ready made.'[22] Within official discourse pundits came to be represented as self-seeking, corrupt and greedy; their works were associated with fraud and forgery.[23] Company intellectuals claimed the moral

[20] F.W. Macnaghten, *Considerations on the Hindoo Law as it is Current in Bengal*, Serampore, 1824, Preface; Strange, *Hindu Law*, London, 1830, II, pp. 175–6.

[21] *See* Macnaghten's Preface to *Considerations on the Hindoo Law*.

[22] Henry Maine disapprovingly quotes Jones's assessment of the pundits, 'The Sacred Laws of the Hindus', in *Early Law and Custom*, 1883, rpt., New Delhi, 1985.

[23] *See* Derrett, 'The British as Patrons of the Sastras', *Religion, Law and the State in India*. The authenticity of important works like Dattakacandrika was widely questioned by British legal minds in the nineteenth century. Derrett, among others, argues that this was an extremely important late-nineteenth-century work. Raghumani, the probable author of the text, was a highly respectable scholar, and was unlikely to 'forge' a text, ibid. On juridical fabrication, *see* Derrett, 'A Juridical Fabrication of Early British India: The

authority to represent and record Indian tradition even when they recognized the pundits' claim to superior knowledge and their symbolic power in society.[24]

This attitude towards the pundits seems partly rooted in Benthamite ideas. Orientalist traditionalism and Benthamite radical reformism developed in opposition to each other in India, but they also influenced each other.[25] Benthamite prejudices were silently inscribed onto Orientalist legal minds. Bentham reacted against the common law tradition within which common-law judges interpreted the spirit of tradition and applied it to new situations; talked of immemorial custom but constantly modified custom; innovated and introduced new rules but pretended—through the use of judicial fiction—that they were old. Such a system, Bentham argued, sustained a regime of despotism, corruption, falsehood, dishonesty, pretence and deception. When judges innovate, establish rules and decide law, they become despots. When, through the myth of immemorial custom and through reference to judicial fictions, judges pretend that they have invented nothing, they act with dishonesty, they deceive. Since the 'muddle' of uncertain, flexible rules was known only to legal experts and not to the public, these experts could manipulate law and were corruptible.[26] It was necessary to separate judicial and legislative functions, define the proper source of law, and establish that stable and certain legal framework by which public expectations could be made secure and public justification of judicial decisions rendered possible.

Many of these ideas resonate in the writings of Jones and Colebrooke. Their fear of the pundits' corrigibility, their reluctance to accept pundits as interpreters rather than factual reporters of tradition, their

---

Mahanirvana Tantra', in Derrett, *Essays in Classical and Modern Hindu Law*, vol. II, pp. 197–243.

[24] While Colebrooke set out to work on his project he was aware that the knowledge of the pundits had greater popular legitimacy. 'The public have, no doubt, more confidence in the Pundits than in me,' he said. Quoted in Derrett, 'The British as Patrons of the Sastras', *RLSI*, p. 251.

[25] Javed Majeed shows how Mill's Utilitarianism can be read as a reaction to the dominant conservative British ideology of the late nineteenth century. Majeed, *Ungoverned Imaginings*, Oxford, 1992.

[26] Bentham saw 'judicial fictions' as 'lies devised by judges to serve as instruments of, and cloaks to, injustice'. The use of judicial fiction by lawyers had pernicious effects: 'it has had for its object or effect, or both, to deceive, and, by deception to govern, and by governing, to promote the interest, real or supposed, of the party addressing, at the expense of the party addressed.' Quoted in Postema, *Bentham and the Common Law Tradition*, p. 273.

search for certainty, are all part of a wider sensibility of those times. Within this tradition, inventiveness in a non-legislative body was suspect: it was the possible basis of arbitrariness, caprice, dishonesty and corruption. British masters, even the Orientalists, were prone to distrust creative informants, ignore the vibrant tradition of contemporary indigenous legal discourse, and freeze Sastric learning into old texts.[27] As the British became more and more confident of their knowledge of Indian tradition and custom, consultations with pundit informants became infrequent, and finally in 1864 they were dismissed from the courts altogether, resolving the state's insecurities about the basis of its sovereign power.

The move from text to practice as the source of custom was paralleled by the move from pundits to village elders—the new local informants on custom. In Punjab, village headmen and elders were now seen as 'the custodians of village wisdom', the 'repositories of local knowledge'.[28] They were the anchor around which the community revolved: they held the community together, disciplined its members, preserved order, adjudicated disputes, sorted out conflicts over custom. If customary practices mediated relations within the community, these practices were maintained and reproduced via the mediation of elders.

This conception of the power of elders derived from notions of Indian village communities which became popular after the second quarter of the nineteenth century. It was a conception reinforced by the theory of the tribal constitution of Punjab villages. British officials generally identified two forms of villages. In one, individual ownership and independent holdings predominated, joint rights and obligations were unknown, and the village was managed by hereditary headmen. In the

[27] *See* Derrett, 'The British as Patrons of the Sastras', and 'The Administration of Hindu Law by the British'. Derrett argues that in the pre-British period pundits incorporated local practices into Dharmasastra, and reinterpreted texts. He shows that in Sastric learning, a creative seventeenth century was followed by a flourishing, though not assertive or brilliant, eighteenth century. In fact, in the 1820s, a series of learned texts were produced by pundits, in response to the scurrilous charges of Strange and Macnaghten; but these genuine Sastric works were not relied upon by courts suspicious of recent works. 'The pandit as a professor of a living science was rejected for the more or less fossilised treatises which would head the pandits list of references.' Derrett, 'The British as Patrons of the Sastras', *RLSI*, p. 255.

[28] Wilson wrote: 'Like the judges in England, the older men of the tribe are considered to be the repositories of the common law.' They are aware of the principles which govern social life, and the general spirit behind social practices. Wilson, *General Code of Tribal Custom in the Sirsa District of the Punjab*, Calcutta, 1883.

other, the village was populated by a compact body of co-sharers who claimed a lineage, real or mythical, from a common ancestor or a group of ancestors. The land of the village was equally shared amongst the male descendants of the original founder. The claim to common lineage cemented the village collectivity, and the notion of shares regulated duties and obligations, privileges and claims. The heads of co-sharing families formed a council of elders responsible for order. This patriarchal structure, where the word of the patriarch was law, prevailed in Punjab. Henry Maine focused mainly on the first type of village, whereas Punjab officials talked a lot about the second.[29] After the 1860s, when the theory of tribal origin of primitive society became popular in evolutionist anthropology, Tupper suggested that the family and the village as institutions were preceded by the clan and the tribe; therefore tribal characteristics were inscribed into village institutions as they developed, and tribal elders were refigured as village elders.

Through these elders the British hoped to discover the customs of India's tribes, and at the same time establish power over them.[30] So British officials in Punjab, particularly after the rebellion of 1857, went in search of *chaudhris* and *muqaddams* and instituted them where none existed.[31]

[29] Maine, *Village Communities in the East and the West*; and *Ancient Law* [1861], London, 1972, particularly ch. V, 'Primitive Society and Ancient Law', for his discussion on family and patriarchal power. *See also* Baden-Powell, *The Origin and Growth of Village Communities in India*, Oxford, 1899, rpt., Jodhpur, 1985. For Punjab *see* the various memorandums and records collected in *PCL*, vols I–III. For a discussion of the different conceptions of village community in India and England, *see* Clive Dewey, 'Images of the Village Community: A Study in Anglo-Indian Ideology', *Modern Asian Studies*, 6, no. 3, 1972.

[30] Tupper: 'It is through the tribe and clan that Government can gain its firmest hold on the inclinations and motives of the people. The people can be led by their own leaders. It is much easier for a foreign Government to deal with organized bodies of men, through those who can be trusted on both sides, than with miscellaneous hordes of individuals.' Tupper, 'On the Codification of Customary Law', *PCL*, I, p. 17.

[31] 'I do not wish to create the class where it does not exist. I do not wish to maintain an idle and useless class, but . . . to a government of foreigners such as our own, such men are invaluable both in war and peace, for they are the means of communication and explanation to their more ignorant brethren, and they are the depositories of all local traditions and local statistics,' wrote the Commissioner of Lahore Division. No. 535, 16 December 1858, Commissioner of Lahore Division to Financial Commissioner, Punjab, Hissar Division Records, Basta 38, Revenue Case 21, 15 January 1859. From Sirsa the Deputy Commissioner reported: 'Hitherto this class of men do not exist, nor can I learn that such ever were recognized in this district by any of the governments preceding ours;

Could village elders inform the British about customary practices? How reliable was their knowledge within imperial perception? The process of enquiry shows that their authority, like that of Bengal's pundits, was both recognized and demeaned; they were represented as knowledgeable as well as ignorant. This contrary assessment was part of the logic of sovereign power as it came to be constituted, and it created a space for imperial intervention in the making of custom.

THE ENQUIRY

The quality of any enquiry depends crucially on the machinery employed to conduct it. The colonial machinery for generating knowledge about custom was, not surprisingly, inadequate for the purpose. Revenue officials had neither the time nor the inclination to carry out exhaustive investigations. Badly paid and overworked, they had little passion for the execution of orders which came from the top.

The village record on customs was frequently stereotyped, the questions difficult, long, and badly formulated. 'It has often been merely an elaborate Persian document in the best official language', wrote Brandreth, 'drawn up by some learned Hindustani munshi, and copied for every manor of the pargana'.[32] The imperfections of the wajib-ul-arz, prepared in the 1850s by revenue officials, were widely recognized, yet the document, being a part of the settlement record, had the same legal force as the settlement and its entries had to be accepted by courts as correct.[33] Things did not radically improve when the first set of riwaj-i-ams were produced in the 1860s. The settlement officer who was responsible for collecting the mass of evidence still had no efficient machinery at his disposal. After attesting the records for Montgomery, W.E. Purser cautioned against their reliability,[34] complaining about the

but the advantage of such men in every pergunah is too great for me not to advocate its being created at once . . .' Deputy Commissioner Sirsa to Commissioner and Superintendent Hissar Division, Hissar Division Records, Basta 38, Revenue Case 169, 2 April 1859.

[32] *Settlement Report: Jhelum*, 1864, para 296.

[33] The presumption of correctness was attached to the wajib-ul-arz under Section 44 of the Land Revenue Act. Since the custom recorded on the wajib-ul-arz was considered a 'true' custom, the onus of proof in the court was on the party contradicting it. *See*, 54 *Punjab Record*, 1867; 87 *Punjab Record*, 1868; 13 *Punjab Record*, 1875.

[34] 'I think they ought to be received with much caution. In the first place this document is always prepared first by the Superintendent. He is, of course, utterly unable to go out of the beaten track, and the track in this case occasionally leads into the slough of downright nonsense.' W.E. Purser, *Settlement Report: Montgomery*, 1878, pt III, para 10.

incomprehensible language of the questionnaire: 'it is incorrect, and is couched in the most barbarous and unintelligible Hindustani one can imagine.' And he added: 'when the questions are incorrect, the answers are likely to be the same.'[35] Attempts were made to improve records. Every new scheme characteristically traced 'anomalies' and 'errors' in the past and assured 'authoritative' records in the future. But the problems remained.

The nature of codification is defined by its framework of questions. Issues which appear relevant to colonial administrators are likely to be different from those considered important by peasants. The inclusions and exclusions within the enquiry are therefore vital. The wajib-ul-arz, prepared for settlement purposes in the 1850s and concerned primarily with allocating responsibilities of revenue payment, had restricted its enquiry into village customs to a few questions. When Prinsep prepared the riwaj-i-ams in the 1860s by separating tribal from village custom, the scope of enquiry was broadened. Yet the focus was still limited, now to a set of issues on which 'custom' was deemed to deviate from Hindu and Muslim law. Tupper's scheme, built upon his evolutionary theory of the tribal origins of Punjab agrarian society and the ordering power of the principle of agnatic succession, focused on the questions of transfer of property—through inheritance, adoption and gift—and on marriage.[36] A whole range of other issues important to the lives of the people were marginalized in the enquiry.

The evidence on customary law collected in village meetings with elders was constituted through a colonial ethnographic dialogue. Colonial officials went there not just to hear the wisdom of elders but to question and cross-examine them, sort out ambiguities and contradictions, and then interpret, decide and attest the truth about custom. In these investigations there were confrontations between colonial observers and native informants on the authenticity of practices; there were also problems of intelligibility and comprehension. When a superintendent in charge of an enquiry into customary law gathered the leading men of a village and produced a long questionnaire, many elders could not understand the implications of the questions, in part because the questions were drawn up within an alien frame of reference.[37]

[35] Ibid.

[36] In 1873 Tupper was asked to draw up a series of questions for enquiries into tribal and local customs. The draft questions submitted in 1875 were approved by the provincial government. The third volume of *Punjab Customary Law* is structured around a revised version of these questions.

[37] E.L. Brandreth wrote about his experience of such enquiries in Jhelum: 'when they

Baffled villagers produced answers which interrogators helped to mould. When community elders were asked to spell out the generative schemes implicit in their practices, they found the matter altogether difficult. When generative schemes are immanent in social practice, people act according to custom without explicitly formulating the rules of custom. In such a context social practice occurs in a world taken for granted, within a structure of experience characterized by silences and languages of familiarity. The discourse of familiarity, as Bourdieu says, leaves unsaid all that goes without saying; it cannot express that which has always remained unsaid, never been articulated.[38] Persuaded to make a reflexive return on to their practice, the native informants inevitably produced a discourse on custom which could never capture the general sensibility that informed social practice. What appears to the 'native mind as familiar, as necessary, as self-evident, as a part of the course of nature' is, as many colonial officials complained at the time, difficult for outsiders to grasp.[39]

Even when the issues were understood by native informants, their answers could still be orchestrated. The oral evidence of village elders had to be verified, and alternative modes of verification employed by different officials defined different truths about custom. Thorburn's account of his investigations into custom in Bannu is revealing. Asked about their inheritance customs, the Bannuchis at first 'unanimously' declared that, according to the Sharia rule which they followed, a father

---

put their seals to the paper, no doubt they thought it very grand, though they did not know what it was about, as they could little understand the language . . . the villagers are confused by the long code of rules, and merely say "yes, yes", and put their seals to the paper, hoping it is nothing very dreadful . . .', *Settlement Report: Jhelum*, 1864, para 296.

The Settlement Commissioner of Multan and Derajat Divisions, J.B. Lyall, felt: 'If it is grotesque to propound these questions to a select assembly of headmen, it is much more so to propound them to the men of one village, most of whom, after listening to a few questions, will be so bored and stupefied that they will agree to anything to get away.' No. 33 S, dated 28 September 1875. From J.B. Lyall, Settlement Commissioner, Multan and Derajat Divisions, to the Settlement Secretary to the Divisional Commissioner, *PCL*, I, p. 188.

Purser reported from Montgomery: 'In many cases the people have no custom at all on the points to which the questions refer.' Among the Mohammedan jats, for instance, adoption was rare. 'Yet the chiefmen, when asked—"Can a man adopt?"—will be sure to say "yes" or "no" . . .' Purser, *Settlement Report: Montgomery*, pt III, para 10. To the British, keen on specifying different claims to the property of a sonless proprietor, adoption was an important issue.

[38] Pierre Bourdieu, *Outline of a Theory of Practice*, Cambridge, 1984, pp. 17–18.

[39] Tupper, 'Memorandum on the Means of Ascertaining the Customary Law of the Punjab', dated 2 June 1873, *PCL*, I, p. 160.

could gift his property to anyone, even if his male successors were alive. This evidence left Thorburn unconvinced and uncomfortable. He pursued the investigation, cross-questioned the Bannuchis, and was ultimately happy with the answers he helped produce:

> Asked for examples of the exercise of such powers [the right to transfer property to others, in preference to male heirs], not one was forthcoming. Had anyone so alienated half his land? No cases known. As with Bannuchis, so with the Isakhels and others. Thus reasoning from a series of negatives the people were over and over again driven to admit that their first replies were erroneous. . . . Here and there I shaped public opinion on most questions in the direction in which I myself and others of experience thought equitable.[40]

What was recorded represented Thorburn's conceptions of equity and justice, which in this case privileged patrilineal over other forms of property devolution—not that of the Bannuchis. Subsequently Arthur Roe, another colonial authority on customary law, discovered that 'what took place in Bannu, has taken place in other districts where custom was in its infancy'.[41]

When the assertions of elders conformed with the ideas of the observer, the authority of precedents could be questioned. Enquiring into Ludhiana's customs, Gordon Walker found the method of seeking proof through precedents problematic. Such a method made no distinction between 'norm' and 'exception'. Practices which operated in the past as exceptions could be cited to deny the norm. Moreover, argued Walker, practices which prevailed in an earlier stage of society could not be accepted as the legitimate basis for conditions which were widely different. There was no dearth of evidence that before British rule a daughter's husband was often a co-sharer, and a daughter's son could inherit property. But such practices, existing in a context where land was not in demand, could not be made a rule. They could only be considered 'exceptions', however numerous the instances of their practice, because in Walker's logic they 'interfered' with and 'departed' from 'the natural order' of agnatic succession. Walker was certain that, despite past practice, tribal feeling was opposed to any such rule. And in 'seeking proof of tribal custom regard should not be had merely to the few precedents . . . but rather to the general expression of tribal opinion. . . .'[42] The leading men were granted a certain power in selecting

[40] *Settlement Report: Bannu*, para 205.

[41] A.R. Roe and H.A.B. Rattigan, *Tribal Law in the Punjab: So Far as it Relates to Rights in Ancestral Land*, Lahore, 1895, p. 18.

[42] Gordon Walker, *Customary Law of Punjab—V: Ludhiana District*, 1885, p. 37.

from a range of past practices what they wanted codified, as long as their ideas did not violate those of the officials.

In these enquiries the administrator ethnographers were acting in opposed ways, proceeding from different assumptions. Thorburn used the rule of precedents to discount the authority of the elders; Gordon Walker cautioned against a slavish submission to the record of past practices. For Thorburn the authority of the elders was questionable, their knowledge of custom dubious. He drove them to admit that their replies were erroneous. For Gordon Walker the elders appeared as bearers of wisdom who unconsciously acted in accordance with the principles of custom, who knew the difference between the 'norm' and the 'exception'.

After the enquiry there began another phase in the redefinition of custom. The settlement officer in charge of the enquiry departed with the record of the custom. Back at his office, he was expected to scrutinize the answers, sort out the anomalies and ambiguities, and prepare the final authoritative version of riwaj-i-ams to be kept in the district office and consulted by the courts. This process of the translation of vernacular statements, and the re-reading of textualized records and systematization of evidence, provided a wide space for colonial authorial intervention in the making of custom. Clearly, the enquiry was a process through which the colonial state appropriated custom in specific ways. The nature of this appropriation and the reconstitution of custom was defined by the specific frames of reference through which local reality was perceived, the categories through which it was ordered. As we shall see, this frame was not marked by internal coherence: it was shot through with ambiguities, tensions and inner contradictions.

CONFLICT OF WILLS

It is the duty of the Government to improve Native institutions as well as to uphold them. It is possible . . . to domestic[ate] primitive law: you can redeem it from barbarism without killing it down.[43]

So said Dalhousie in 1849, and the thought reappears persistently in the late-nineteenth-century discussions of customary law in Punjab. It expresses the inner tension between the two contrary impulses which lie behind colonial projects: the will to preserve versus the will to transform indigenous custom and tradition. In the 1840s the terms of

[43] Cited in *PCL*, I, p. 12.

this debate were defined by the Conservative Paternalists, with their romantic concern for village institutions, and the Liberals and Benthamite Utilitarians, with their programme of radical modernist reform. Dalhousie sought to reconcile this opposition. But this reconciliation was not easy. How could traditional institutions and customs be upheld yet improved, redeemed without being killed? How could the Enlightenment ideal of improvement be married to an anti-Enlightenment love for tradition? Such questions continued to frame discussions on customary law in Punjab. Officials continued to grapple with the problem of specifying the nature of the colonial project and the functions and limits of state intervention.

The texture of their conceptions varied. Within one tradition of English common law thinking the object of state intervention was to discover and record existing practices, not to transform them; to systematize but not invent. This language of conservation shaped the rhetoric of Punjab officials. Codification had to be an unprejudiced act based on objective observation, untainted by Western concepts and *a priori* ideas. Custom had to be presented and codified *as it was*, not *as it ought to be*. It was as if social practices were transparent, they could be seen without conceptual filters. And what was seen could be codified.

This strong demand for some pure objectivity was difficult to sustain. The argument for codification usually ended with a plea for systematization according to some deliberate plan, a deliberate design guided by principle;[44] and the argument for uncorrupted observation inevitably slipped into a demand for *understanding* and *explanation*: 'the better the people are understood, the better will they be governed; . . . Fully to understand a people you must be able to explain its institutions as well as to recount them . . .'[45]

The function of the state was to make the natives aware of the inner coherence and underlying principles of their practices. The customs of the country, it was said, were 'by no means mere chance growth', but were 'founded on principles susceptible of ascertainment on enquiry and of statement as a fairly consistent whole'.[46] These principles could

[44] 'Codification implies the Consolidation of existing law or custom', wrote Tupper. But it was useless to collect the material into a 'shapeless mass'. The material 'must admit of systematic arrangement on a definite plan . . . There must be a deliberate design, and its execution must be guided by principle.' Tupper, 'On the Codification of Customary Law', *PCL*, I, pp. 15–16.

[45] Tupper, 'Some Punjab Survivals', *PCL*, p. 98.

[46] Tupper, 'Memorandum on Customary Law', *PCL*, I, p. 21.

be grasped through modern theories. Observed facts made sense only within such a framework of explanation. Tupper was convinced: 'If the facts of rural life in the Punjab be continuously read in the light of modern ideas regarding the origin and progress of society, there is, I think no doubt that their explanation will rapidly proceed.'[47] Once the essential principles were understood, ambiguities and confusions could be ironed out and the real practices systematized into codified rules.

The search for this inner principle of customary ordering of society led colonial officials into the hazy history of immemorial custom. Drawing from the writings of English common-law theorists and nineteenth-century evolutionist anthropologists, Tupper outlined a general theory of the evolution of Punjab society which he then used to order the evidence on custom. According to Tupper's evolutionary theory, the clan originates in the tribe, the village in the clan, and the joint family in the village (tribe—clan—village—joint family). Once the village is established, property rights pass from joint ownership by all members of the community towards individual ownership. First, a jointly owned village is divided into several *tarafs* held by coparceners, each group constituting a section of the community; then each share, each taraf, held by the coparceners is further divided into individual plots according to ancestral shares; subsequently the extent of individual ownership changes and begins to deviate from the ancestral customary share; so shares are disused and in course of time forgotten. Underlying the theory is the presupposition of an ever-increasing specialization within society and a general order of progress from collective to individual property: 'The tribe is broken up into different clans, the clans into villages, the villages into lots, the lots into family holdings. The group once simple and homogeneous, becomes complex and diversified. Broadly the theory may be deduced from the general law of evolution.'[48] The common origin of property was first assumed to be 'sufficiently established' by investigations in comparative jurisprudence 'without any special reference to Punjab customary law'. The succession of orders was then deduced through a general theory of evolution. The facts, as they were revealed through enquiries, only supported these inferences.

Proceeding from such a deductive theory, interrogation only reconfirmed the validity of its initial assumptions. The theory was

[47] Ibid.

[48] Tupper, 'The Village and Severalty', *PCL*, II, p. 54.

supposed to provide the only means of ordering an otherwise bewildering mass of evidence into a meaningful pattern. The perceived coherence of customary law was thus pre-given. Evidence which did not conform to the expectation of theory was explained in a number of ways. First, a distinction was made between the 'norm' and the 'exception'. All that could not be theoretically accounted for as the 'norm' was conveniently accommodated within a spacious term—'exception'. Second, a difference was made between the general and the particular. Theory could refer only to general characteristics. Local forms of customs were bound to vary. But within these local forms, the operation of the general principle could still be discerned. Finally, Tupper's theory sought to distinguish between those customs that had the authority of 'antiquity' and those which were 'innovations' and 'novelties'. Since each specific social practice conformed to a particular stage of society, it was possible to judge whether a set of rules was logically linked to a particular stage or was a meaningless 'survival' from the past.[49] Customs which were in accordance with and tended to conserve the older forms of society were seen to possess immemorial antiquity and had to be preserved.[50] Later innovations which tended to dissolve the original tribal form, premised upon patriarchal lineage and agnatic filiation, had to be repressed as alien intrusions.

This self-image of the officials as codifiers of immemorial custom can be distinguished from their self-image as preservers of a disappearing tradition. Customs, they felt, were changing, and traditions were collapsing, inevitably, naturally. This was an inexorable process, the logic of history. Without enlightened intervention the rot could not be stemmed. Standing amongst the ruins of tradition, the noble Englishman had to salvage the past. Codification could help preserve the authenticity of tradition, allow officials and judges to spot any attempt at innovation, whether by officials or by the people themselves. And through a theoretical understanding of the inner coherence of practices, the founding practices could be differentiated from 'intrusions' which corrupted their original form.

[49] Tupper, 'The Characteristics of Tribal and Village Custom', *PCL*, II, p. 78.

[50] So it could be said: 'The rule whatever it be, that tends to preserve tribal cohesion, community of interest in the village, and the integrity of the family, must if the theory of progress from communal to several rights be sound, always have the weight of past practice in its favour, its converse is by the hypothesis, a novelty; it may be a novelty of long standing, but still an innovation on an older state of things.' Tupper, *PCL*, II, p. 78.

Many colonial officials, however, were troubled by a radical self-doubt. Could the colonial state carry through its project of preservation? Could it really see with clarity a fleeting reality and fix its meaning with any certainty? Could it resist the imprint of a new time into an immemorial structure? In 1873 Tupper was talking of preserving custom from 'distortions' through judicial reform.[51] By 1875 he was emphasizing the transitional character of Punjab customs and the 'impossibility of re-constituting the form it bore immediately before annexation'.[52] His voice now carries notes of despair:

> with all the will in the world to preserve amid the transmutation in progress, as much Punjab custom as we can, we must admit that the outline and local colouring, as they existed before the British, cannot be wholly restored. Some portion of the outline, enough of the colouring, we may yet save to show in the new combinations which are appearing, that . . . sufficient account has been taken of the traditions of localities and the peculiar practices of tribes; for more than this it seems vain to hope.[53]

Even this much was difficult to achieve.

> What are we, as judicial officers, to do when customs are fading and changing, . . . How are we to give to the fleeting forms of custom, as allegedly before us, that precision of outline which would wear a sufficiently definite look under the scrutiny of the courts of appeal? We try to photograph a dissolving view with a bad camera, and no wonder the result is rather blurred.[54]

Beneath the audible voice of the preserver was the hidden transcript of the Utilitarian reformer. The aggressive authoritarian Benthamite tone of Dalhousie was missing in the discourse of customary law after the 1860s. But the Benthamite spirit did express itself in mellow undertones, in hesitant and surreptitious ways. Officials admitted that it was important for the state to consider 'very carefully not merely what the law is but what it ought to be'.[55] Tupper, with all his talk of preserving immemorial custom, could still argue that 'it is not absolutely unmodified Native usages which are to be upheld, irrespective of their social and political effect, simply because they have existed. We are to maintain native institutions; but the British system must be, and has been, introduced.'[56]

[51] Tupper, 'Memorandum on the Means of Ascertaining the Customary Law of Punjab', dated 2 June 1873, *PCL*, I, pp. 158–74.

[52] Memorandum by Tupper, dated 2 June 1875, *PCL*, I, p. 207.

[53] Ibid., p. 208.

[54] Ibid., p. 208.

[55] Tupper, Introduction, *PCL*, I, p. 13.

[56] Ibid., p. 11.

Yet the common law mind could not easily accommodate a reforming project. It argued for change, but it cast its argument for reform in the language of continuity. Wilson said, for instance, that customs have always changed, slowly and imperceptibly. Tribal leaders were always devising new solutions to new problems and redefining practices, even while acting according to the spirit of custom.[57] By appropriating the right to reorder custom the British were in fact acting according to tradition. Past practice sanctioned present interventions.

TRADITION, REASON AND TIME

According to the Punjab Regulation Act (Section 5 of Act IV of 1872), in order to be valid custom had to be 'reasonable, continuous, not against public policy or equity, justice and good conscience and not void'.[58] This statement reveals the diverse ways in which Punjab officials sought to define the validity of custom. These conflicting modes of legitimation were implicated in a set of contradictory discourses.

First, there is the obvious opposition between the authority of tradition and the authority of reason. If continuity is the basis of validity, tradition appears as self-justifying. Then the validity of a custom lies in the fact that it has been in long use, from time immemorial; it has been an intrinsic part of collective life, a basis of social ordering, an expression of social unity. It is not to be judged through any external criteria of transcendent, universal reason. But the reference to the reasonability of custom and to notions of 'equity, justice and good conscience' shifts the grounds of validation. Enlightenment Reason is brought in to judge the validity of tradition and custom. Tradition which violates principles of justice, equity and good conscience is unreasonable and hence invalid. Here tradition is not only represented in the language of reason but is appropriated through a framework of utilitarian, liberal, modernist thought.

But the opposition between tradition and reason is often negotiated in subtler ways within the official discourse of customary law. Village elders were seen as custodians not only of tradition but of 'village

[57] Just as common lawyers in England continuously modify custom in accordance with its essential spirit, wrote Wilson, 'so the leaders of a tribe are ready, without hesitation, to extend their tribal custom, and to decide in accordance with its principles any new question that comes before them.' Wilson, *General Code of Tribal Custom in Sirsa*, pp. 33–4.

[58] For a discussion, *see* 'Memorandum on the Customary Law in the Punjab' by C. Boulnois, Judge, Chief Court, Punjab, dated 28 November 1872, *PCL*, I, p. 144.

wisdom': they were aware of the general principles through which social life was to be ordered. Wilson says: 'the tribesmen among themselves decide any new case that may arise in accordance with the principles underlying the whole body of their tribal custom, and find no difficulty in applying these principles, though unconsciously, to altogether new sets of circumstances . . .'[59] Custom expressed a collective sense of what was reasonable, just and fair—what is seen as the collective good. Persistence and continuity of a custom, its temporal depth, reveal the intrinsic reasonableness of the general principles. Customs develop over time through a process of collective reasoning. Through practice, norms become part of the common sense of a time; and the dispositions shaped in the process define what counts as reasonable. Actions which conform to this sense are therefore reasonable. Reason in such an argument refers not to a unitary concept with a fixed natural Enlightenment essence, but to a tradition-shaped sense of reasonableness. The argument of tradition is cast in the language of reason, without being subordinated to it.

All these alternative conceptions of reason were at play in the act of codification and adjudication of customary law. They were the basis of conflicting interpretations of custom and popular questionings of the codified law.

Linked to these differing notions of reason and tradition were shades of differences on conceptions of time. The discourse of custom tended to present custom as timeless, as immemorial. The validity of custom lay in its continuity over time. But how was one to define the pastness of the past, the temporal depth of immemorial custom? Some officials saw the origins of practices as lost in the mists of immeasurable time. It was impossible to specify with certitude the antiquity of a particular practice.[60] If customs are presumed to be timeless and unchanging, then present practice was itself evidence of the antiquity of custom. But in general the time of memory was considered the necessary temporal depth of valid custom: 'a custom, to have the force of law, must have

[59] Wilson, *General Code of Tribal Custom in Sirsa*, p. 33.

[60] 'There is in this province no rule of law, which prescribes any period during which a custom in order to be valid and enforceable must have been observed. It is sufficient to show that the custom actually prevails and is generally observed in the tribe to which the parties belong and there is no necessity to go further and attempt to prove the impossible, viz. that it has been preserved in the tribe from a period to which the memory of man runneth not to the contrary, the test being the uniformity of practice.' 34 *Punjab Record*, 1907, p. 151.

existed as long as the memory of the tribe extends, i.e. the memory at least of its oldest members, . . .'[61] The memory of the elders, their oral evidence on the practices of the tribe, was therefore important.

Many officials, as we have seen, recognized that customs were not frozen in time. 'On all sides transition is in progress', wrote Tupper. In every district 'the original social combinations of tribe, clan and village will be found in varying stages of reconstitution'.[62] Customs changed alongside these mutations in the social forms of society. But these changes could not be publicly recognized within the discourse of 'immemorial custom'; for this would be to admit a rupture, a discontinuity in time. Since continuity was the basis of authority, temporal breaks were misrecognized in a variety of ways. First: the rule of precedents helped to mask changes. People could always pretend that rules were not new, or that they were implicit in existing norms.[63] Through judicial fictions, a continuity of practices was traced, innovations were hidden. Time transformed was presented as time immemorial, time that knew no rupture. In this conception the collective belief in the continuity of practices was crucial to the myth of immemorial custom, not the actual empirical facts of their immutability. Punjab officials searched for a space within this process of collective myth-making in which they could insert themselves. Through the language of immemorial custom and the rule of precedents, they sought to establish the temporal continuity of their codified laws with the practices of the past.

Second: when precedents were difficult to unearth, the argument of continuity was sustained in other ways. Elders, we are told, knew the spirit which informed customs, the 'unthought' which lay within the tradition even though they could not spell out its inner principles. Elders, it was said, confronted new situations and devised new norms but conformed to the general spirit of the tradition. While particular practices changed, the general principles of social order were maintained. In this argument, a reference to precedents was neither an adequate nor a necessary guide to action. Concrete practices of the past were not as important as the *spirit* behind the practices. This sort of common-law theory informs Wilson's discussion of the customary law of Sirsa:

[61] J. Wilkinson, 1 *Punjab Record*, 1975, p. 3.

[62] Tupper, *PCL*, II, p. 77.

[63] 'When people want a rule they pretend the rule has always existed.' Memorandum by Tupper, 2 June 1875, *PCL*, I, p. 205.

In English common law, by a fiction the judges are supposed to decide each case as it comes up strictly in accordance with precedent, and yet every new decision forms a new precedent, and so modifies the law—in fact, the judges decide each new case which comes before them rather in accordance with the principles that underlie precedents than strictly according to any particular set of precedents. . . .

Often when I have put a question to the assembled headmen [in Sirsa] regarding their custom on some particular point, and received an unhesitating answer, a call for instances and precedent has, after much racking of brains, elicited the unanimous reply, 'we never heard of such a case, but our custom is as we have said'. They were unconsciously deciding the new set of circumstances in accordance with general principles of their custom, familiar to the minds of all.[64]

Wilson felt that the British could intervene in a similar tradition-shaped way to reorder society and maintain the spirit and continuity of customary practices. Again, in this view temporal breaks in custom were denied and time was presented as a continuum—an uninterrupted flow from the past to the present.

CUSTOM AND POWER

The process of codification restructured rural power relations and was also shaped by those relations. The enquiry into custom opened up a space for negotiation and conflict over the truth of practice. If the answers of village elders were framed and directed by the questions they were asked, their perspectives were also inscribed in the records of customary law which were prepared.

Codification of customary law consolidated the coparcenary community. As we have seen, officials shared a set of assumptions about the relationship between blood and soil. The rights to soil, it was believed, were defined by relationships of blood. Descendants of the original founder of the village constituted the coparcenary proprietary body: *they* had the first claim to land. Those who failed to assert such a mythical ancestry could not be members of the brotherhood. Records of rights prepared on the basis of such an assumption inevitably repressed the rights of all those who did not belong to the dominant lineage.

During the tenant enquiry it was usual to record members of the dominant lineage as proprietors and others as tenants. 'I have thought

[64] Wilson, *General Code of Tribal Custom in Sirsa*, pp. 33–4.

it quite sufficient', wrote Wynyard from Amballa, 'if he is not one of the Bhyachara, to record him as a tenant . . .'[65] In courts, the claims of lower castes and 'non-agricultural' communities to property rights in land were routinely denied. Officials also sought to regulate transfers of land through the assumptions of agnatic theory. The myth of common ancestry defined the membership of the coparcenary body and the rights to land, but it also limited these rights. Since the proprietors held land as co-sharers, they were not to sell to outsiders. Land had to be held by, and preserved within, the community of co-sharers—the brotherhood. When land was up for sale, co-sharers had the first right of purchase, a right of pre-emption. Judges who mediated conflicts over customs argued from these assumptions. And their judgments, flowing from theoretical premises, were recognized as learned observations on practice, and came to define practice. Consider the famous judgment of 1887 on the rights of a proprietor to alienate land:

> The land came to him as a member of a village community which at no distant period held the whole of their land jointly, recognizing in the individual members only a right of usufruct, that is a right to enjoy the profits of the portion of the common land actually cultivated by him and his family, and to share in those of the portion[s] still under joint management. In such a community, the proprietary title and the power of permanently alienating parts of the common property is vested in the whole body. These communities of villages in their turn spring from a still more primitive state of society in which the proprietary unit was the tribe. . . . It is not unreasonable to presume that the absence of lineal male heirs does not confer on a proprietor privileges greatly in excess of those enjoyed by his fellows. It should only be natural, that, in such a case, the next male collateral . . . shall take the place of the lineal heirs, and that his consent to the alienation of land, which by the customary rules of inheritance would have descended to him, should also be necessary.[66]

This judgment set the pattern for subsequent ones. A picture, clearly deduced from evolutionary anthropology, is presented here as an observation of existing reality. The language of judicial discourse continuously slips from the deductive to the inductive, from the mythical to the 'real', transcending such oppositions and intermeshing them inseparably. The imagined reality of the coparcenary community became part of official and judicial common sense and imposed its own specific order into the rural world of customary practices.[67] The

[65] *Settlement Report: Amballa*, 1859, para 310.

[66] 107 *Punjab Record*, 1887, FB.

[67] Justice Plowden observed: 'I think we are justified in stating, as a principle consonant

boundaries of the proprietary community were sharply demarcated, the entry of 'outsiders' into it was legally restricted. The logic of the argument led to the Land Alienation Act of 1900, when communities classified as 'non-agriculturists' were debarred entry into the rural land market.

The colonial regime of customary law thus sharpened the opposition between the outsiders and the insiders, the 'agriculturists' and the 'non-agriculturists', the proprietary body and the lower castes. This opposition was written into the very definition of customary law. Customary law was applicable only to agriculturists; non-agriculturists were governed by personal law. The argument was that agricultural groups had a tribal past and retained a tribal constitution, with all its customary principles; whereas non-agriculturists had no tribal origin, and hence no customary law. Even when the existing practices of different groups were similar, they could not be governed by the same customary law. Differences between groups were deepened by narrativizing their histories in dissimilar ways. The authenticity of the present was denied by attributing a greater significance to the assumed divergence of past origin.

The process of the codification of custom also reordered the world of women. Agnatic theory could recognize no rights of women. Patrilineal male inheritance was officially seen as a 'natural order of succession': daughters could not succeed, nor could a daughter's or a sister's son. A widow with a male child could not inherit, and one without a child had a life interest: after her death the land reverted to the control of the husband's family, her cognates had no claim. Adoption by a sonless proprietor was necessary to retain community control over land, but adoption had to be from within the male agnates, the co-sharers within the village. Since women could not own land, they could neither sell nor mortgage it. The volumes on customary law for the different districts of Punjab recorded the existence of these customs with the expected monotony.[68]

---

with facts, that the mere circumstance that immovable property is ancestral raises a presumption that the individual in possession as owner had not unrestricted power of disposition.' Ibid.

[68] There were, of course, exceptions. Some volumes of customary law are insightful, and record contestatory evidence that allow us to question the dominant picture. *See*, in particular, the excellent customary law volumes of Sirsa, Ludhiana, Multan, and Gurgaon. On changing rights of women in colonial Punjab, *see* Prem Chowdhry, *The Veiled Women: Shifting Gender Equations in Rural Haryana, 1880–1990*, New Delhi,

The structure of customs, derived from the framework of theory, was reaffirmed through the dialogue with informants. Village elders were invariably proprietors, and they were speaking at a time when open fields were disappearing behind the expanding agrarian frontier, and land becoming scarce and valuable. The village body closed in on itself, strengthened its boundaries, resisted competition and sought to consolidate control over land. The village elders and *lambardars* who collected to give evidence on custom agreed over time on an exclusionist policy. Did the lower castes and the 'outsiders' have a right to land? In the initial enquiries answers to such questions were ambivalent. But in the later enquiries the rights of 'outsiders' were unambiguously denied. The 'outsider', as a category, crystallized in the process.

The customs recorded were male constructs. As many officials and judges recognized, the riwaj-i-am was a document 'prepared at the dictates of males only', and was particularly unreliable on questions of women's succession.[69] As the demand for land increased and prices soared, landholders became 'more and more anxious to exclude female succession', and were 'ready to state the rule against daughters as strongly as possible'.[70] Women could not come forward to talk about their rights.

In short, the discourse on custom reveals a dialogue between masters and natives. The native voice was inscribed within imperial discourse, but it was constrained, regulated and ultimately appropriated. This was a male, patriarchal voice, the voice of the dominant proprietary body speaking against the rights of non-proprietors, females, and lower castes.

At the beginning of British rule rights were ambiguous and practices fluid. In a situation of land abundance, villagers wanted additional hands

---

1994; David Gilmartin, 'Kinship, Women and Politics in Twentieth-Century Punjab', *in* Gail Minault (ed.), *The Extended Family: Women and Political Participation in India and Pakistan*, Delhi, 1981.

[69] Badr-ud-din Kureshi, *The Punjab Customs*, 1911, p. 43.

[70] 86 *Punjab Record*, 1908. Such observations were repeatedly made in judicial records. 'The record before us shows that the male relations, in many cases at least, have been clearly more concerned for their own advantage than for the security of the rights of the widows and other female relatives with rights, or alleged rights . . .' *Punjab Law Report*, 1901, p. 466. Another judge reflected on the general politics of representation: 'Such evidence, in defeasement of the rights of females, recalls to one's mind the remarks attributed in the fable to a tiger when he was shown the picture of a tiger running away from an old woman: "If a tiger had painted the picture, he would be eating the woman".' 11 *Punjab Record*, 1901, p. 79.

to work the land and pay the revenue. In practice, non-agriculturists held land, and so did women. We have extensive evidence of a daughter's husband and sons inheriting. Both the agnatic and cognatic principles operated at different levels, and in complicated ways. This complexity could not be accommodated within the dominant official theory, and ambiguities had to be ironed out into coherent, rational codes. Once a 'natural order' was defined, conflicting evidence was classed as anomalous.

Naturally, though, the official discourse was not monologic: the dominant voice could not repress all others. Through the cracks opened up by contestation, evidence of alternative practices becomes visible.[71]

THE DISCOURSE ON CUSTOM: CONCLUDING COMMENTS

The argument against Anglo-Indian law is often premised upon the assumption that the British ignored customary practices and based their law on an amalgam of Sastric learning and Western legal tradition. The gap between custom and law widened when scriptures were privileged within colonial discourse as the source of authentic tradition.[72] I have tried here to argue that the colonial relationship with native tradition was more complex, ambiguous and varied—spatially and temporally. If, in late-eighteenth-century Bengal, scriptures were seen as synonymous with tradition, in Punjab a century later custom was pitted against sacred texts. But this did not make colonial law any closer to 'tradition', it did not preserve the practices of the community uncontaminated. Understanding and codifying custom was as problematic as translating and

[71] My larger work on customs, codes and colonial order examines the evidence of such practices and the contestatory logic of their transformation.

[72] Derrett argues that British intervention fossilized Sastric learning, perverted the meaning of texts and created a 'great chasm between custom and law'. Derrett feels that Anglo-Indian law would have created fewer problems if it took cognizance of customary practices. Derrett, 'The Administration of Hindu Law by the British'. Lata Mani suggests that the marginalization of custom and the sanctity accorded to scriptures defined, in fact, the specificity of colonial discourse. Mani shows with great effect that the entire debate on the abolition of sati was structured within the terms of this discourse: while the Liberals pointed to the absence of scriptural sanction for sati, the Conservatives produced a scriptural defence of the ritual. Mani, 'Contentious Traditions'.

In such arguments the specificities of one form of colonial thinking and discourse tend to be projected as a general feature of colonial India. Imperial officials were very well aware of customary practices, but their understandings had their own specific structures.

interpreting ancient texts. Both, in different ways, subjected tradition to transformative processes.

Codification, one could say, hybridized custom: it appropriated indigenous custom through Western categories and mixed heterogeneous traditions. Hybridity is an expressive concept, and a problematic one, for it suggests an amalgamation of pure essences,[73] hybridity being premised on the notion of something originally pure. The concept seeks to transcend essentialism, only to rehabilitate it.

Tupper, in despair, spoke of the bad camera through which officials took blurred shots. There are two obvious problems with this statement. No camera, we know, can ever capture reality untransformed: the point of focus and the depth of field define the nature of the pictures produced. And is there ever only one camera, one lens, one filter through which the world can be viewed? Different officials, as we have seen, looking through different lenses, saw different realities, interpreted custom in dissimilar ways. Native tradition was not appropriated through any fixed frame of Orientalist discourse which had crystallized in the West into a congealed form. This frame was not only fractured, it was continuously reconstituted. So we need to look not only at the multiple discourses of tradition and modernity but the ways in which the elements of different traditions were incessantly recombined into new forms, new languages of power and domination. Opposing principles were sought to be reconciled within the same discourse: the romantic reverence of tradition coexisted with a Benthamite reforming zeal, the language of conservation fused with that of modernization, the principle of Authority was married to that of Reason. Categories and assumptions drawn from Western traditions reappeared, but were recast. This process revealed the inner tensions and ambiguities within colonial ideology. Codification as a process of rewriting tradition was carried through not by self-assured imperial minds confident of their strategies and goals, but by minds troubled by self-doubt and anxieties.

The discourse on custom was not just a textual process, nor simply the fruit of official imagination structured by Western thought. The nature of the dialogues with local informants was crucial to the

[73] Hybridity is one of the key concepts used by Homi Bhabha in his insightful essays on colonial and nationalist discourses. *See* Homi K. Bhabha, 'Sly Civility' and 'Of Mimicry and Man: The Ambivalence of Colonial Discourse', in *Location of Culture*; idem., 'Introduction: Narrating the Nation' and 'Dissemination: Time, Narrative and the Margins of the Modern Nation, in idem. (ed.), *Nation and Narration*, London, 1990.

remaking of custom. While the utterances of the informants were often directed and overwritten by the masters, the natives did not merely cast their answers in the frames provided by imperial officials. They sought to express their perception of tradition, and resisted imperial interpretations; they reacted to changing social contexts—to the scarcity of land and its increasing value, the pressure of population, the consolidation of rural power—and then felt the need to redefine customary practices. Etched in the codes which were produced was the patriarchal voice of property-owning elites, a voice neither directly inherited nor entirely borrowed, but something creatively produced through varied dialogues.

Not all the native voices could be easily accommodated within the imperial discourse on customary law, not all the evidence was always recognized. Codification was also a process of silencing and erasure. Imperial officials defined the terms of validity of custom and the criteria of reasonability and equity; they distinguished between the norm and the exception, between antiquated and living practices. Through their classificatory practices they sought to repress troubling evidence and fix the meanings of customs in the act of encoding them.

But can custom be so easily frozen? Do codes have the power to reorder practices unhindered? Are traditions and customary practices so malleable as to succumb to the transforming power of a codifying state? The common argument that customs are frozen through codification is premised on a simple contrast between the oral and the textual. The oral tradition is seen as fluid, open to a variety of interpretations and meanings, a range of appropriations according to the contexts. When the oral tradition is textualized the fluidity disappears, meanings are fixed: put into writing, they become frozen into codes. We now recognize that this opposition is problematic. Texts too can convey a variety of meanings; and new meanings are continuously inscribed onto texts in the process of interpretation and elaboration. Codes, like all texts, are open to multiple readings, and the same code can produce different judgments. Codification may seek to fix the meanings of practices, but the original intentions do not not always materialize in the same ways. Judicial records reveal how codes were read in conflicting ways, questioned and rewritten. The search for certainty and fixity remained elusive.

Codification does shift the terrain on which conflicts over meaning are played out. While customs remained uncodified, they were embodied in the collective knowledge of the community, remaining as the preserve of the community, interpreted and recorded within the community through its institutions. It remained, at that stage, a process through which the power relations between different castes, sexes and generations were worked out. Under the colonial regime of codes, the institutions of the state appropriated the right to interpret and rewrite custom. The custom of the community was to be decided by courts; conflicts over understanding were to be resolved through the mediation of courts.

There were, however, limits to the reach of the state. Beneath the regime of codes was the reality of uncodified practices. Inheritance rules, rights of women, and norms of marriage did not all change with codification. There were violations of rules, a public flouting of norms, a silent persistence with alternative practices. The official mind could not close itself to the pressure of this subversive evidence. Colonial officials could not continue living in a world of imagined reality, gloriously ignorant of native understanding and practices.[74] Subversion and contestation did not simply constitute a private transcript which remained hidden behind the public transcript—a code to which people submitted.[75] The private transcript persistently asserted its presence in public spaces, the language and understanding of the rulers felt the strain of contest. Challenged in courts, codified customs were reinterpreted by judges; inundated with conflicting evidence, officials acknowledged the validity of customs unauthenticated by colonial codes. In the process of this cultural confrontation, colonial structures and categories of representation were dislocated and refigured, while the public transcript imprinted itself onto the private in invisible ways.

[74] I find the theory of ideology which informs Gauri Viswanathan's fine work *Masks of Conquest* (London, 1989) problematic. Viswanathan's suggestion that it is entirely possible to study imperial ideology 'quite independent of an account of how Indians actually received, reacted to, imbibed, manipulated, reinterpreted, or resisted it' is perfectly acceptable. An author has the right to define the limits of a particular study. But Viswanathan proceeds to argue that a study of Indian reactions is irrelevant to the study of ideology because the colonizers were imprisoned within the tyrannical structure of their own representations unaware of 'how the native *actually* responds'. There is almost a suggestion that the realm of imperial imagination was sealed off from the world of the colonized. Were the two realms so hermetically sealed? Are the reactions of the natives important only as the *effects* of imperial ideologies? Did they not often force the masters to rewrite the scripts of their domination?

[75] Scott's major work on hegemony and resistance introduces the useful distinction between the public and the private transcript, but inflates the separation between the two. *See* C. James Scott, *Domination and the Arts of Resistance: Hidden Transcripts*, New Haven and London, 1990

II
Accommodation and Dominance

3 Texts and Traditions: The Making of the Bengal *Purāṇas*

KUNAL CHAKRABARTI

1

In the older Vedic literature, the word *Purāṇa* usually occurs in connection with *Itihāsa* and originally seems to have meant old narrative without any special significance as to the character of the narrative.[1] According to the classical definition, a *Purāṇa* is supposed to deal with five topics or *pañcalakṣaṇa*, namely creation of the universe, recreation after destruction, genealogy, periods of time with Manu as the primal ancestor, and the history of the solar and lunar dynasties. The *Purāṇas*, however, seldom adhere to this definition which suggests that if the definition was based on the contents of the actual texts, the present *Purāṇas* must be thoroughly revised versions of either the original texts or at least what they were ideally intended to be. The *Purāṇas* themselves state their number to be eighteen. Originally the *Purāṇas*, as in the case of the epics, were narrated by the *sūtas* or the bards. Thus in almost all the *Purāṇas* the *sūta* Lomaharṣaṇa or his son *souti* Ugrasravas appears as the narrator. However, according to the orthodox tradition, as recorded in the *Atharva Veda* and *Bṛhadāraṇyaka Upaniṣad*, the *Purāṇas* were of divine origin.[2] Even the *Purāṇas* claim that the chief speaker gathered his information, through Vyāsa, from the creator himself, which has led to the unsubstantiated speculation that originally

[1] M.A. Mehendale, 'The Purāṇas', *in* R.C. Majumdar (ed.), *The Classical Age*, Bombay, 1970, pp. 291–2.

[2] Ibid., pp. 296–7.

there was a single *Purāṇa* from which the later *Purāṇas* were derived. Later the Purāṇic material was extensively revised by the *brāhmaṇa* priests who continued to add matters of religious and social importance to the original core, so that the present *Purāṇas* have practically turned into *Smṛti* codes.

As a result the *Purāṇa* texts, as we have them now, were written at such divergent periods that it is difficult to fix their chronology with even an approximate degree of certainty. Although the word *Purāṇa* occurs in the Vedic literature, their actual existence can be traced from the *Sūtra* period. Thus references to the *Purāṇas* in some of the *Dharma Sūtras* such as *Gautama* and *Āpastamba* and in the *Mahābhārata* seem to indicate that they existed long before the Christian era.[3] R.C. Hazra, an acknowledged authority on the dating and provenance of the Purāṇic corpus, has painstakingly analysed the contents of the *Purāṇas* to show how the different sections, dealing with orthodox rites and customs in the manner of the *Smṛtis*, were added to them at widely varying periods.[4] Hazra's method may be described as a close comparative analysis of the Purāṇic material.

That is however merely to scratch the surface of the problem, for, in the great majority of the cases, the *Purāṇas* have not come down to us with their early incorporations alone; they have undergone continuous and substantial re-editions. This re-editing was done in three different ways: by adding fresh chapters to those already in existence, by substituting the latter by the former, and by writing new works bearing old titles. Hazra however argues that all these practices had a common feature, in that they came to have units belonging to different ages, and that fresh additions were not always fresh compositions, but chapters and verses transferred from one to the other, and from the *Smṛti* to the *Purāṇas*.[5] He proves the truth of his assumption by comparing almost verse by verse the contents of the eighteen *Purāṇas* and other *Smṛti* literature, and thus constructing a comparative chronology of the various sections of the *Purāṇas*.[6]

What necessitated this ceaseless revision of the *Purāṇas*? The

[3] Ibid., p. 294.

[4] R.C. Hazra, *Studies in the Purāṇic Records on Hindu Rites and Customs*, Delhi, 1975. Chapters II–IV are devoted to working out the chronology of the *Mahāpurāṇas*.

[5] Ibid., pp. 6–7.

[6] In App. I, Hazra has drawn up an exhaustive list of the numerous verses quoted by the *Nibandha* writers from the various *Purāṇas*. Ibid., pp. 265–335.

Purāṇas themselves assert that in order to keep pace with the changes in society such periodic revisions were necessary[7] to sustain their importance as works of authority. Thus the *Purāṇas*, which dealt originally only with the five topics, grew into encyclopaedic works by incorporating chapters not only on religious and social matters, but also on law, politics, poetics, grammar, medicine, music, and sculpture.[8] If the *Purāṇas* were quoted as authority in Medhātithi's commentary on the *Manusmṛti* as early as the sixth century AD, and if by the medieval period they had acquired a status equal to those of the *Smṛtis*,[9] the *Purāṇas* naturally had to be continuously revised to accommodate the needs of changing social conditions and incorporate matters which were traditionally considered to have belonged exclusively to the province of the *Smṛtis*.

Hazra has identified two principal stages in the development of Purāṇic rites and customs. He argues that ancient India saw the rise of various religious movements which may be classified as Vedic (*Śrauta* and *Smārta*), anti-Vedic (Buddhism, Jainism, Ajivikism, etc.), semi-Vedic (consisting primarily of Vaiṣṇavism, Śaivism and Brāhmaṇism), and non-Vedic (Śāktism). The recognition of the authority of the *Vedas* and the superiority of *brāhmaṇas* are the two essential constituents of the Vedic brahmanical religion. Hazra suggests that probably long before the time of Gautama Buddha there were protests against the brahmanical doctrines, and with the rise and popularity of Buddhism, Jainism, and Ajivikism these protests were institutionalized. Hazra adds that the original character of Vaiṣṇavism and Śaivism was also most probably non-brahmanical, as both the Pāñcarātras and the Pāśupatas were irreverent to the *varṇāśramadharma*. Besides, Vedic religion got into further trouble with the transfer of political authority from the *kṣatriyas* to the *śūdras* under the Nandas, the Mauryas, and probably the Andhras.[10]

[7] *kālenāgrahaṇaṁ dṛṣṭvā purāṇasya tato nṛpa* ।
vyāsa-rūpaṁ ahaṁ kṛtvā saṁhārāmi yuge yuge ॥

This is what the Fish says to Manu in *Matsya Purāṇa*, 53, 8–9, cited in ibid., p. 6, note 38.

[8] Hazra provides a glimpse of the assortment of topics dealt with in the *Purāṇas*: R.C. Hazra, 'The Purāṇa', *in* S.K. De, U.N. Ghosal, A.D. Pusalkar, R.C. Hazra (eds), *The Cultural Heritage of India*, vol. II, Calcutta, 1969, pp. 246–7.

[9] J. Duncan M. Derrett, 'The Purāṇas in Vyavahāra Portions of Medieval Smṛti Works', *Purāṇa*, vol. 5, no. 1, Jan. 1963, p. 13.

[10] R.C. Hazra, *Studies in the Purāṇic Records*, pp. 193–205.

As a result of these developments the brahmanical social order was disrupted to such a degree that we perceive an obsessive fear of the *Kali* age in all the early *Purāṇas*. In the *Kali* age the people were said to neglect their caste rules and the duties enjoined by the *Ṛg, Sāma*, and *Yajur Vedas*. The *brāhmaṇas* abandoned study of the *Vedas* and the performance of sacrifices and *en masse* took to becoming wandering mendicants. They lost their social and ritual supremacy, and people of all castes professed equal status with them. The *kṣatriyas* and the *vaiśyas* were almost extinct, and the prevailing caste was the *śūdra* who acquired political importance. The general demoralization in the *Kali* age was particularly manifest in the conduct of the women who became wicked and self-willed, joined the Buddhist *saṅghas* in large numbers and disregarded the four stages of life (*caturāśrama*), one of the indispensable preconditions of the brahmanical way of living.[11]

Thus every aspect of the fabric of the ideal brahmanical social structure was undermined. In remedy, an attempt was made to re-establish the authority of the *Vedas*, the *varṇāśramadharma* and the moral order among the women and the lower castes. This attempt seems to have been made by two sections of the people, in two different ways, namely by the orthodox *brāhmaṇas* who began to preach the performance of *Gṛhya* rites through *Smṛti* works and by the more numerous *Smārta*–Vaiṣṇavas and *Smārta*–Śaivas who introduced *Smṛti* materials into the *Mahābhārata* and the *Purāṇas* for the propagation of their sectarian points of view against the heretical religions by upholding the brahmanical social order.[12]

Hazra locates the second stage in the development of Purāṇic rites and customs from the third to the sixth centuries AD, when Vedic religion was once again threatened by foreign invaders from the north-west, identified by Hazra as the Śakas, the Yavanas, the Bāhlīkas, etc., and by the spread and popularity of Tantrism. The early *Purāṇas* are eloquent about the evils brought about by these rulers.[13] From the brahmanical

[11] Despite obvious exaggerations in the dismal picture of the *Kali* age, portrayed by the *Purāṇas*, there must have been some substance in these descriptions, for Hazra points out that the *Jātakas* confirm that with the rise of Buddhism the Vedic sacrifices and the priestly class lost their authority and with them the compulsion to follow caste demarcations, hereditary occupation, and the four stages of life, which naturally caused such acute reaction among the *brāhmaṇas*. Ibid., pp. 210–11.

[12] Ibid., pp. 206–14.

[13] Although no inscriptional evidence exists to corroborate this supposition, the *Purāṇas*, particularly *Vāyu* (99. 387–412), *Brahmāṇḍa* (III. 74.130–204), *Matsya* (273. 25–33), *Viṣṇu* (IV. 24.18–25), and *Bhāgavata* (XII. 1.38–41) are vehement in their

point of view the socio–political disruption created by the rule of such dynasties was somewhat remedied by the rise of the Guptas, but from about the beginning of the fifth century AD the Vaiṣṇavas and the Śaivas fell under the influence of Tantrism. Hazra has shown how an analysis of the Pāñcarātra *Saṁhitās* and the Śaiva *Āgamas* decisively proves that the Tāntric cult attained popularity at a very early period. The *Tantras* believed in equal opportunity of worship to all, including women and *śūdras*, and the ritual practices recommended by them were distinctly non-brahmanical in character. The spread of such ideas obviously affected the existing status of Brāhmaṇism so adversely that the authors of the *Purāṇas* could no longer remain content to introduce only those *Smṛti* topics that fell within the scope of the earlier *Smṛti Saṁhitās*, but deemed it necessary to add chapters, presumably on aspects of popular religious practices, such as *pūjā* (popular worship), *vrata* (vow), *homa* (sacrifice), *sandhyā* (daily rites), *utsarga* (gift), *tīrtha* (glorification of holy places), *pratiṣṭhā* (consecration of images), etc., which they tried to free from Tāntric influence and infuse with Vedic rituals as far as practicable. The occurrence of these topics in the comparatively late *Purāṇas*, and the way these *Purāṇas* denounce the scriptures that imbibed Tāntric characteristics tend to support this view.[14] However, the element of Vedic ritual in the *Purāṇas* progressively diminished with time and was increasingly replaced by popular material. Indeed, by the beginning of the ninth century AD, some of these texts began to recognize even the *Tantras* as a source of authority on religious matters.[15]

This is how the Purāṇic tradition came into existence and eventually

---

condemnation of the misdeeds of these rulers. Ibid., pp. 213–17. It can therefore be surmised that at least from the brahmanical point of view their rule was not perceived as conducive to the spread of Vedic religion and the social order that flowed from it.

[14] Ibid., pp. 215–26.

[15] Ibid., p. 260. Hazra points out that this tendency became so universal that by the medieval period the *Smṛti* writers, particularly of Bengal, such as Raghunandana, completely accepted the authority of the *Tantras* and drew profusely upon them on almost all matters concerning '*dharma*' (ibid., p. 264). Hazra believes that the gradual recognition of the authority of the *Tantras* by the *Purāṇas*, and the latter's absorption of the Tāntric elements enabled the *Tantras* to exercise such remarkable influence even on the *Smṛti-nibandhas* (ibid., p. 262). But Suresh Chandra Bandopadhyaya feels that Tāntric influence on religious rites and social customs was so pervasive in Bengal by Raghunandana's time that he had to reluctantly accept its authority as an indispensable part of Bengal's religious life, and thus imbibed Tāntric elements in his works directly from the *Tantras* themselves and not through the mediation of the *Purāṇas*. Suresh Chandra Bandopadhyaya, *Smṛti Śāstre Bāṅgālī*, A. Mukherji and Co., Calcutta, 1961, pp. 198–9. Whatever be the process through which Tāntric elements were assimilated, the point to remember is that the

crystallized through a process of continuous revision. Tradition, however, is, as Heesterman puts it, 'the way society formulates and deals with the basic problems of human existence', and as these problems are insoluble, they are 'attacked, formulated and dealt with each time anew under a different aspect. Tradition therefore is and has to be bound up with the ever-shifting present. Hence the irritating flexibility and fluidity of tradition.'[16] Romila Thapar has also emphasized the aspect of 'contemporary requirements' as a determinant of tradition, and consequently its renewability and the need to look at it 'in its various phases'.[17] Thus even the eighteen *Purāṇas* must have proved inadequate for brahmanical requirements at some point of time, since another group of literature, belonging to the same genre but with a different emphasis, came into being, called the *Upapurāṇas*, the formation of which, according to Hazra, should be placed approximately between AD 650 and AD 800.[18] This approximate date must not be taken to be the period of composition of the individual texts of the *Upapurāṇas*, for all of them could not have been written at the same time. Regarding the origin of the *Upapurāṇas*, the *Śiva-māhātmya Khaṇḍa* of the *Kūrma Purāṇa* records a tradition that the sages proclaimed the *Upapurāṇas* after listening to the eighteen *Purāṇas* from Vyāsa.[19] This tradition assigns to the *Upapurāṇas* a date following that of the *Purāṇas* and thus an inferior status. Indeed, the *Matsya Purāṇa* terms the *Upapurāṇas* mere subsections or supplements—*upabheda*—of the principal *Purāṇas*.[20] The *Upapurāṇas* do not, however, often look upon this characterization with the same respect as the principal or what were later called the *Mahāpurāṇas*, as a large number of the *Upapurāṇas* call themselves simply *Purāṇa* and do not try to attach themselves for the sake of authority to any of the principal *Purāṇas*.

The non-inclusion of the term *Upapurāṇa* in the *Amarakoṣa*, which defines the *Purāṇa* in accordance with the *pañcalakṣaṇa*, and the mention of the titles of the eighteen *Purāṇas* in the *Viṣṇu* and *Mārkaṇḍeya*

Tantras ultimately found their way even into the most conservative category of brahmanical texts, namely the *Smṛtis*.

[16] J.C. Heesterman, 'India and the Inner Conflict of Tradition', *The Inner Conflict of Tradition*, Chicago, 1985, p. 10.

[17] Romila Thapar, *Cultural Transaction and Early India: Tradition and Patronage*, Delhi, 1987, p. 8.

[18] R.C. Hazra, *Studies in the Upapurāṇas*, vol. I, Calcutta, 1958, p. 15.

[19] Ibid., p. 16.

[20] Ibid., p. 17.

Purāṇas without any references to the *Upapurāṇas*, tend to show that the group of eighteen *Purāṇas* had been formed before the *Upapurāṇas* came into existence.[21] After this group had been completed, there came into focus many sub-systems, arising out of the principal systems of religion, i.e. Bhāgavata Pāñcarātra and Śaiva Pāśupata, either directly, or by identifying the local deities with one or the other of the prominent deities of the principal systems. In addition to these, there were also other independent systems such as Saura, Śākta, etc. which began to rival the systems already established. These sub-systems also had their *Smārta* adherents who interpolated chapters in the *Purāṇas* already in vogue and in some cases wrote new and independent Purāṇic works in order to propagate their own views. But as the followers of the principal *Purāṇas* believed that there could be no *Purāṇa* beyond the famous eighteen, they were unwilling to assign to these new Purāṇic works a status equal to that of the *Mahāpurāṇas*. On the other hand, these new Purāṇic works had become too well known and popular to be completely ignored. The problem was resolved by maintaining the numerical rigidity of the eighteen original *Purāṇas* and assigning to the *Upapurāṇas* an independent, albeit subservient, position.[22]

Following the tradition of the *Mahāpurāṇas*, orthodox opinion tried also to limit the number of the *Upapurāṇas* to eighteen, but while in the enumeration of the *Purāṇas* there is almost complete agreement with regard to the titles, this is by no means the case with the *Upapurāṇas*. Hazra has compiled a list of over a hundred titles from the conflicting lists of the *Purāṇas*, the *Upapurāṇas* and other texts, most of which are no longer available even in their manuscript form.[23]

One of the major differences between the *Mahāpurāṇas* and the *Upapurāṇas* is that the latter are regionally identifiable. It has been claimed that even some of the additions to the *Mahāpurāṇas* have a local tinge so that the *Brahma Purāṇa* may represent the Orissa version of the original work, just as the *Padma* may give that of Puṣkara, the *Agni* that of Gayā, the *Varāha* that of Mathurā, the *Vāmana* that of Thāneśvar, the *Kūrma* that of Vārānasī, and the *Matsya* that of the *brāhmaṇas* of Narmadā.[24] In their entirety, however, none of these texts can be said to have been composed in these regions and although they partially reflect local interests, it is impossible to precisely locate their place of origin.

[21] Ibid., p. 23.
[22] Ibid., pp. 23–9.
[23] Ibid., pp. 2–13.
[24] Mehendale, 'The Purāṇas', p. 296.

The *Upapurāṇas*, on the other hand, are so overwhelmingly regional in their concerns, catering as they more or less exclusively did to local requirements, that they can be identified with a particular locale with a fair degree of certainty. Thus Hazra points out that most of the available *Upapurāṇas* were written in the areas peripheral to the brahmanical sphere of influence. For example the *Viṣṇudharmottara* was composed in Kashmir,[25] the *Kālikā* in Assam,[26] and a great majority of them in Bengal. Another curious fact about the *Upapurāṇas*, to which Hazra draws our attention, is that while the *Mahāpurāṇas*, because of their status, have undergone innumerable modifications, the *Upapurāṇas* have remained comparatively free from later redactors. In consequence, the *Upapurāṇas* are better preserved and among those that are extant there are some which are much older than many of the *Mahāpurāṇas*.[27]

While even the *Mahāpurāṇas* did not entirely adhere to the classical definition of the *pañcalakṣaṇa*, the *Upapurāṇas* were almost exclusively adapted to suit the requirements of local cults and the religious needs of sects other than those already assimilated in the *Mahāpurāṇas*, and are never in consequence particularly concerned about these five topics. They especially neglect the genealogies of kings and sages, and even when they mention them, it is only to give a stamp of antiquity to these works, and nothing is said about the dynasties of the *Kali* age. What the *Upapurāṇas* do discuss are the religion and social structure, particularly the assimilation of divergent values and practices through the reformulation of certain fundamental principles of Brāhmaṇism in the peripheral areas. They tell us about mythology, idol-worship, theism, and pantheism, festivals and ceremonies, ethics and superstitions; in short everything that constitutes the domain of religion in the widest possible sense.[28]

In deciding the date and provenance of these texts, I have accepted the suggestions of R. C. Hazra,[29] which are as presented in Table 4.1.

[25] Hazra, *Studies in the Upapurāṇas*, vol. I, p. 214.

[26] Hazra, *Studies in the Upapurāṇas*, vol. II, Calcutta, 1963, p. 232.

[27] Ibid., vol. I, p. 27.

[28] Ibid., pp. 25–6.

[29] Hazra has made a thorough textual analysis to arrive at his conclusions regarding the date and provenance of the individual *Purāṇas* and *Upapurāṇas*, and no research of comparable scholarship has been subsequently attempted to contradict them. It has therefore become customary to accept his findings on these aspects of the *Purāṇa* as authoritative in any discussion on the subject.

Table 4.1

Name	*Locale*	*Date*
Brahmavaivarta Purāṇa	Unspecifiable, but so completely remodelled in Bengal, that it can be taken to represent unambiguously the specific regional context of Bengal.[30]	Tenth to sixteenth century AD[31]
Kriyāyogasāra (claims to belong to the *Padma Purāṇa*)[31]	Bengal.[32]	Not later than eleventh century AD.[33]
Bṛhannāradīya Purāṇa	Eastern Orissa or Western Bengal (recognized by the early *Smṛti* writers of Bengal).[34]	750–900 AD.[35]
Devī Purāṇa	Bengal.[36]	Cannot be placed later than AD 850.[37]
Kālikā Purāṇa	Either in Assam or that part of Bengal that is adjacent to Assam.[38]	Tenth or the first half of the eleventh century AD[39]

(*cont.*)

[30] R.C. Hazra, *Studies in the Purāṇic Records*, p. 166. Hazra says that the *Brahmavaivarta* was first composed most probably in the eighth century AD, but from about the tenth century it began to be changed by 'the interfering hands' of the Bengal authors who recast it in its present form and contents in the sixteenth century. In the chronological table of the Puranic chapters on Hindu rites and customs, Hazra assigns the sections on Janmāṣṭamī and Ekādaśī *vrata* to the eighth to the beginning of the fourteenth centuries and the rest from the tenth to the sixteenth centuries (pp. 187–8). In other words, the *Brahmavaivarta* has been so continuously revised that even Hazra, with his textual precision, could not go beyond pointing out the outer limits of the beginning of its composition to the end of the redactions.

[31] R.C. Hazra, *Studies in the Upapurāṇas*, vol. I, p. 267.

[32] Ibid., p. 274. [33] Ibid., p. 277. [34] Ibid., pp. 344–5.

[35] Ibid., p. 344.

[36] Hazra, *Studies in the Upapurāṇas*, vol. II, p. 79.

[37] Ibid., p. 73. However, he later adds that it is very probable that the *Devī Purāṇa*, as we have it now, comes down from the sixth century AD and most probably from its latter half (p. 77). This of course does not contradict his final judgement that it cannot be later than AD 850.

[38] Ibid., p. 232. This *Purāṇa* exerted such an influence, particularly on the ritual pattern of goddess worship in Bengal, that even though it cannot be ascertained whether it was definitely composed in Bengal or not, I have to take it into consideration for my study.

[39] Ibid., p. 245.

Table 4.1 (*cont.*)

Mahābhāgavata Purāṇa	Eastern Bengal, close to Assam.[40]	Tenth or eleventh century; not later than the twelfth century AD.[41]
Devībhāgavata Purāṇa	Bengal.[42]	Eleventh or twelfth century AD.[43]
Bṛhaddharma Purāṇa	Bengal.[44]	Latter half of the thirteenth century AD.[45]

It may be observed that except the *Brahmavaivarta*, all the other *Purāṇas* were written between the eighth and thirteenth centuries, and most of them between the eleventh and twelfth centuries AD, so that the Bengal *Purāṇas* may be broadly labelled as the product of the early medieval period. Indeed, by the late fifteenth century, Purāṇic digests such as the *Purāṇa-sarvasva* were being compiled in Bengal,[46] which shows that by then these *Purāṇas* had been accepted as normative texts and it was considered worthwhile to produce abridged compendia setting out their essential message.

2

The *Purāṇas* were thus an instrument for the propagation of brahmanical ideals of social reconstruction and sectarian interests, a medium for the absorption of local cults and associated practices, and a vehicle for popular instruction on norms governing everyday existence. They combined in them the functions of both the sacred religious scriptures and the social codes of the *Smṛtis* in a form acceptable to most people. In short, the *Purāṇas* performed the delicate task of operating simultaneously at several levels, widening their scope to accommodate local elements as much as possible and involve as many people as permissible without compromising their principal objectives of establishing the brahmanical social order; in the process even running the risk of appearing to be self-contradictory, without losing their essential unity. The technique of accomplishing this task may be described as the Purāṇic process. The cumulative effect of the composition of the *Purāṇas* and the popularization of the Purāṇic religion was the construction of the somewhat imprecise category of what is popularly known

[40] Ibid., p. 277. [41] Ibid., p. 282. [42] Ibid., p. 353.
[43] Ibid., pp. 346–7. [44] Ibid., p. 455. [45] Ibid., p. 461.
[46] R.C. Majumdar, *History of Medieval Bengal*, Calcutta, 1974, p. 264. Majumdar refers to two other texts of the same nature, namely *Purāṇasāra* and *Purāṇārtha Prakāśaka*, compiled in medieval Bengal (p. 264).

today as 'Hinduism'. The impressions of two English civil servants of the early twentieth century regarding what constitutes Hinduism will serve to illustrate the point. L.S.S. O'Malley, who edited the *Bengal District Gazetteer* in 1912, describes Hinduism thus:

Considered purely as a religion . . . Hinduism may be described as a conglomerate of cults and creeds. The non-Aryan tribes who were admitted to the fold of Hinduism and the Hindus of Aryan descent reacted on one another, the former adopting the rites and customs of their conquerors, while the latter assimilated some of their less civilized cults and incorporated in their system the objects of popular devotion. The higher and the lower forms of religion still coexist side by side. At one end of the scale, therefore, is the cultured monotheist or the eclectic pantheist for whom no mysticism is too subtle. Pantheists actually form a small minority, and the great majority of Hindus are theists believing in one personal god, though they are at the same time polytheistic in their religious observances. At the bottom of the scale is a great multitude of people in a low state of religious development, some of whom have scarcely risen above mere fetishism.[47]

J.H. Hutton, who directed the Census of India in 1931, is more particular:

If the view be accepted that the Hindu religion has its origin in pre-Vedic times and that in its later form it is the result of the reaction by the religion of the country to the intrusive beliefs of northern invaders, many features of Hinduism will become at once more comprehensible, while the very striking difference between the religion of the Rigveda and that of the Dharmashastras will seem natural. . . . This would explain Hinduism's amalgamation with and absorption of local cults and its excessive multiformity, and is, moreover, in entire accordance with the manner in which it still spreads at the present day, absorbing tribal religions by virtue of its social prestige, by identification of local gods with its own, by the experimental resort to Hindu priests, and by the social promotion of pagan chiefs who are provided with suitable mythological pedigrees. Into the early Hindu beliefs spread in this manner the religion of the Rigveda has been imposed and absorbed.[48]

Despite the explicit acceptance of the theory of Aryan invasion and the expression of such value judgements as high and low forms of religion that appear contrary to our understanding and sensibility, both of them have captured the essence of Purāṇic Hinduism with remarkable accuracy. Although neither of them actually uses the term *Purāṇa*, what they have in mind is evidently the Purāṇic religion, and indeed in

[47] L.S.S. O'Malley, *Popular Hinduism: The Religion of the Masses*, Cambridge, 1935, rpt., New York, 1970, p. 2.

[48] J.H. Hutton, *Caste in India: Its Nature, Function, and Origins*, Bombay, 1980 (originally published in 1946), p. 230.

Hutton's description one can read *Purāṇa* for 'the Dharmashastras' without the slightest difficulty, particularly when both these categories of texts were the product of the same process and, in a sense, complementary to one another. Both O'Malley and Hutton view Purāṇic Hinduism as the result of an interaction between the Vedic and the indigenous forms of religion which is a continuous process, ever enlarging its scope and authority. Hence, what Hutton calls the 'multiformity' and O'Malley the 'scale' of Purāṇic Hinduism.

Purāṇic Hinduism is thus by its very nature and motivation assimilative rather than exclusive; it accommodates rather than rejects. Irawati Karve refers to this cultural process when she characterizes 'Indian society' as a 'culture by accretion'.[49] According to her, in this scheme of things, all phenomena are relative and the world of the humans as well as the gods share in this relativity. Even human values, including good and evil, have no absolute reality and have an equal right to exist. This is the source and the justification of the continuous and simultaneous existence of a multiplicity of behavioural patterns within the society. This conception of the universe is, however, so relativistic that it should lead to a society that is anarchist—a society in which there could be no agencies of control other than the individual's own. But, Karve points out, Indian society is governed by fairly strict rules of behaviour. These rules are the rules of the groups known as castes. She suggests that the coexistence of groups with different norms of behaviour and the structures governing the behaviour of the coexisting caste groups are explained by the theory of *Brahman* and *karma* respectively.[50] *Brahman*, as the Absolute, is above all attributes, and thus all other categories belong to the world of partial truths, and *karma*, as the positive and negative worth of human action, is the regulating agency of such actions of the members of the caste groups. *Brahman*, as the origin of all begins, legitimates their right to exist and *karma* ensures that they exist within the societal framework of discipline and authority. Together, they impart the requisite stability to the fluid structure of Purāṇic Hinduism and the society it presupposes.

All the *Purāṇas* acknowledge the centrality of *Brahman* and the caste-oriented social structure governed by *karma* as axiomatic in their assimilative synthesis. Within the framework of these given constants however, each *Purāṇa* has the manipulative space to choose a divine manifestation of the *Brahman* as the Absolute, depending on its

[49] Irawati Karve, *Hindu Society: An Interpretation*, Poona, 1968, p. 89.

[50] Ibid., pp. 87–90.

sectarian leaning. Once this preliminary choice has been exercised, it can then gather around its chosen deity all the diverse elements it seeks to accommodate. At the philosophical level, a perfect example of the multiplicity of Purāṇic ideation is provided by the following passage from the *Brahmavaivarta*, which recognizes Kṛṣṇa as the supreme deity:

> The Lord has nine forms . . . The six schools each assign to him a form, the Vaiṣṇavas and the *Vedas* one each, and the *Purāṇas* one also. In this way he has nine forms. The *Nyāya* and Śaṅkara call him indescribable, the *Vaiśeṣikas* call him eternal, the *Sāṁkhya* calls him the eternal god in the form of light; the *Mīmāṁsā* calls him the form of all, the *Vedānta*, the cause of all, the *Pātañjala*, the infinite, the *Vedas*, the essence of truth, the *Purāṇas*, self-willed, and the devotees, having an external form.[51]

Such adjustments in the realm of thought offered justification for accommodation at a more mundane level.

But the interesting thing to note in the characterization of the views of the various schools in this passage is that they are not merely imprecise, but are also unrelated to the specific philosophical positions of these different schools. Clearly, therefore, these names have been thrown in, not to suggest that they have literally described Kṛṣṇa in this way, but to invoke their figurative support to the recognition of Kṛṣṇa by the brahmanical authority. Brahmanical authority accepts Kṛṣṇa; therefore the entire tradition that it upholds must also accept him, disregarding whether or not they actually do so. This is the principal mechanism of the Purāṇic process, and nowhere is it more visibly evident than in their handling of the *Vedas* as symbolic authority.

Brian K. Smith has identified two criteria as constitutive of Hinduism: 1. recognition of the authority of the *brāhmaṇa* class, and 2. recognition of the authority of the *Vedas*.[52] He says that the *brāhmaṇas* are recognized as religious authorities because of their intimate, special relationship with the *Vedas*, the authoritative texts of Hinduism. The *brāhmaṇas* are the traditional bearers, purveyors, interpreters and protectors of the authority of the *Veda*, and the *Veda* exists because of the traditional function the *brāhmaṇa* has assumed for its preservation. Thus Smith arrives at the following definition of Hinduism: 'Hinduism is the religion of those humans who create, perpetuate and transform traditions with legitimizing reference to the authority of the *Veda*.'[53]

[51] *Brahmavaivarta Purāṇa*, IV. 129. 75–8.

[52] Brian K. Smith, *Reflections on Resemblance, Ritual and Religion*, New York, 1989, p. 10.

[53] Ibid., pp. 13–14.

The importance of the *Vedas* in Hinduism arises out of what Heesterman calls the inescapable need for ultimate authority.[54] The great paradox of Hinduism is however that, although the religion is inextricably tied to the legitimizing authority of the *Vedas*, in post-Vedic times the subject matter of the *Vedas* was and is largely unknown to those who define themselves in relation to it, primarily because the *Vedas* lost their doctrinal and practical relevance for post-Vedic Hinduism. Thus the *Vedas* became notional authority and came to represent not the Vedic texts, but rather the totality of knowledge. And yet the *Vedas* are preserved in all their pristine sanctity. This paradox is resolved if we look upon the *Vedas* as the key to ultimate legitimation, whereby even if they are unrelated to the ways of human life and society, one still has to come to terms with them. Smith has defined Hinduism as a process and not an essence. Consequently, it is not the essential nature of the *Vedas* that is of defining import as much as the particular relationships Hindus establish and maintain with them.[55]

Giorgio Bonazzoli describes canon as either a list of works that are accepted as normative and hence authentic or a complex of rules through which one can establish whether a work should be accepted as authentic and normative or not.[56] The *Vedas* provide the touchstone by which the *brāhmaṇas* decide which texts should be considered normative and authentic. In other words, the principal rule for determining canon in Hinduism is whether or not it is Vedic. The method through which later texts such as the *Smṛtis* and the *Purāṇas* are related to the symbolic authority of the *Vedas* has been characterized by Smith as 'strategies for orthodoxy'.[57] Smith has observed a variety of such strategies employed for constituting post-Vedic texts, doctrines, and practices as Vedic: 'reflection (this *is* the *Veda*), restatement (this is *based* on the *Veda*), reduction (this is the *simplified Veda*), reproduction (this *enlarges* the *Veda*), recapitulation (this is the *condensed essence* of the *Veda*), and even reversal (the *Veda* is *based on this*).'[58] Smith points out that by representing, through deployment of these strategies for orthodoxy, new texts, doctrines, and practices as connected in some way or

[54] J.C. Heesterman, 'Veda and Dharma', Wendy Doniger O'Flaherty and J.D.M. Derrett (eds), *The Concept of Duty in South Asia*, Columbia, p. 84. *Also see* p. 93.

[55] Smith, *Reflections on Resemblance, Ritual and Religion*, p. 28.

[56] Giorgio Bonazzoli, 'The Dynamic Canon of the Purāṇas', *Purāṇa*, vol. 26, July 1979, pp. 127–8.

[57] Smith, *Reflections on Resemblance, Ritual and Religion*, p. 20.

[58] Ibid., p. 29.

another to the *Vedas*, change is both legitimized and denied, and continuity is both affirmed and stretched.[59] It is immaterial whether the texts, doctrines, and practices, thus legitimized, have in reality anything to do with the *Vedas* or not, except the assertion of the *brāhmaṇas*.

This is a universal process in the living tradition of Hinduism, and all the post-Vedic texts, raised to the status of normative and authentic, have claimed connection with the *Vedas* in one form or another. This method of seeking legitimation through the *Vedas* is particularly relevant for those texts composed with a view to introducing brahmanical socio–religious practices in the peripheral areas where the Vedic tradition did not sufficiently penetrate to render reiteration unnecessary, such as the *Upapurāṇas* of Bengal, especially when, to begin with, they were combining the functions of both the *Purāṇas* and the *Smṛtis* in these areas. Thus it may be observed that all the techniques of establishing Purāṇic authority, as derived from the *Vedas*, underlined by Smith, were operative in the Bengal *Purāṇas*.[60] I will cite a selected few instances from among innumerable such examples. In the *Devī-bhāgavata*, Nārāyaṇa, in response to Nārada's question on the sources of *dharma*, says that *Śrūti* and *Smṛti* are the two eyes of the god and *Purāṇa* is his heart. None other than that which has been determined in these three is *dharma*.[61] Similarly, in enumerating the fruits of reading the *Rādhākavaca*, typical of the *Purāṇas*, the *Brahmavaivarta* declares that the results obtained from reading this *kavaca* are the same as that of studying the four *Vedas*.[62] Even if these instances cannot be described exactly as what Smith calls 'reflection' (this is the *Veda*), they certainly indicate an attempt to establish equivalence between the *Vedas* and the *Purāṇas*.

But the major thrust of the Bengal *Purāṇas* was to try and establish themselves as the 'restatement' (this is based on the *Veda*) of the *Vedas*. Thus the *Brahmavaivarta* says, blessed are the four *Vedas* because everything is being done according to their prescription. All the *Śāstras* are derived from these *Vedas* and the *Purāṇas* also reside in them.[63] Instances of 'reduction' (this is the simplified *Veda*) are also numerous.

[59] Ibid., p. 26.

[60] For the opinions expressed on the relationship between the *Vedas* and the *Purāṇas* in general, from complete rejection to uncritical acceptance, *see* Ludo Rocher, *The Purāṇas* (A History of Indian Literature, vol. II, pt 3), Wiesbaden, 1986, pp. 13–17, esp. fns 1, 3–9.

[61] *Devībhāgavata Purāṇa*, XI. 1.21.

[62] *Brahmavaivarta Purāṇa*, II. 56.53.

[63] Ibid., IV. 83.60–1.

For example, the *Devībhāgavata* states, in all the *manvantaras*, in every *Dvāpara* age, Vedavyāsa composes the *Purāṇas* in order to protect *dharma*. It is Viṣṇu, in the form of Vyāsa, who divides the one *Veda* into four units for the good of the universe in every *Dvapara* age. Knowing that in the *Kali* age the *brāhmaṇas* will be stupid and short-lived and thus unable to understand the *Vedas*, he composes the holy *Purāṇa Saṁhitās* in each age. In particular, women, the *śūdras* and unworthy *brāhmaṇas* are debarred from listening to the *Vedas*. It is for their benefit that the *Purāṇas* have been written.[64] The same idea has been indirectly expressed in the *Bṛhannāradīya Purāṇa*.[65] Here the *sūta* says that there are two ways to salvation—*kriyāyoga* and *jñānayoga*. The long passage seems to indicate that only the *yogīs*[66] can aspire to salvation through *jñānayoga* which involves, among other things, reading the *Upaniṣads* and repeated recitation of *praṇava* and the twelve-, eight- or five-lettered mantras,[67] presumably because this is difficult, while the common people (*mānava*) should follow the simpler procedure of *kriyāyoga* which demands fasting, listening to the *Purāṇas*, and worshipping Viṣṇu with flowers.[68] The implication is that Vedic scholarship, which is evidently superior, is for the select few and the *Purāṇas*, which are in consonance with the *Vedas* but much simpler, are for the masses.

The Bengal *Purāṇas* also claim that they are the 'reproduction' (this enlarges the *Veda*). Hence the *Devībhāgavata* declares that the half verse signifying the central thesis of the *Vedas* that the Devī had told the infant Viṣṇu lying on the banyan leaf during the great deluge, is the key to the *Devībhāgavata*. As an explanation of that key, Brahmā composed the *Bhāgavataśāstra* in myriads of verses. Vyāsa summarized it into the *Devībhāgavata Purāṇa*, consisting of eighteen thousand verses distributed over twelve sections, for the enlightenment of his son Śuka.[69] But the easiest way of linking the Purāṇic corpus with the Vedic was to claim that the *Purāṇas* were the 'recapitulation' (this is the condensed essence of the *Veda*). Thus the *Bṛhannāradīya* begins with the statement that for the good of the universe Vedavyāsa has included the quintessence of the entire *Vedavedāṅgaśāstra* in the *Purāṇas*.[70] The *Devībhāgavata* ends with the same assertion and adds that the result of reading and listening

[64] *Devībhāgavata Purāṇa*, I.3.18–21.
[65] *Bṛhannāradīya Purāṇa*, ch. 31.
[66] Ibid., 31.31. [67] Ibid., 31.90–1.
[68] Ibid., 31.44.
[69] *Devībhāgavata Purāṇa*, XII. 14.1–3.
[70] *Bṛhannāradīya Purāṇa*, 1.21.

to the *Devībhāgavata* is comparable to the fruits of reading the *Vedas*.[71] 'Reversal' (the *Veda* is based on this) is an attitude which was difficult for the Bengal *Purāṇas* to adopt, because they were operative in an area where Vedic authority itself was not sufficiently well grounded and it would have been presumptuous to challenge it from the point of view of brahmanical interests which were uppermost in the *Purāṇas*. Neverthe-less there are certain indirect suggestions, such as in the *Brahmavaivarta*, where Pārvatī tells Kṛṣṇa that she is known to him, but she does not know him, for who can know him? Not even the *Vedas* themselves, nor the Vedic scholar or interpreter,[72] which implies certain superiority over the *Vedas*. But the Bengal *Purāṇas* have permitted themselves to go only that far.

On the whole, the message of the Bengal *Purāṇas* is that they are the confirming elaboration of the *Vedas*. They enshrine the essential wisdom of the *Vedas*, but simplify, condense or enlarge it, depending on the necessity of the common people, as perceived by the *Purāṇas*. The attempt was to forge a legitimating relationship with the *Vedas* and they had deployed every possible means to achieve this. The *brāhmaṇas* composed these *Purāṇas*, but this in itself, though necessary, was not sufficient to establish their status as normative texts, unless they also ensured the sanctifying support of the ultimate authority of Hinduism—the *Vedas*. The Bengal *Purāṇas* therefore subtly insist on continuity with the Vedic tradition. Innumerable statements such as 'it is a great secret even in the *Vedas* and the *Purāṇas*'[73] or 'the four *Vedas* and the *Purāṇas* assert that Mādhava is submissive to Rādhā',[74] etc., are meant to confirm this continuity through endless repetition. Hazra cites an unidentified passage that captures the essence of this continuity in its fullest elaboration,

> That twice born [Brāhmaṇa], who knows the four *Vedas* with the Angas [supplementary sciences] and the Upaniṣads should not be [regarded as] proficient unless he thoroughly knows the Purāṇas. He should reinforce the Vedas with the Itihāsa and the Purāṇa. The Vedas is [sic.] afraid of him who is deficient in traditional knowledge [thinking] 'He will hurt me'.[75]

V.S. Agrawala interprets the crucial line '*itihāsa-purāṇābhyāṁ vedaṁ samupabṛṁhayet*' in this passage as 'the metaphysical truth of

[71] *Devībhāgavata Purāṇa*, XII. 14.25–6.

[72] *Brahmavaivarta Purāṇa*, III. 7.110

[73] Ibid., IV. 96.4.

[74] Ibid., IV. 126.63.

[75] Hazra, 'The Purāṇas', p. 268.

the *Vedas* is intended to be demonstrated in the Itihāsa-Purāṇa manner'.[76] The *Brahmavaivarta* closely follows this sentiment when it states, 'because of your ignorance you could not know him who has been ascertained in all the *Vedas, Purāṇas* and *Itihāsa* as Sarveśa'.[77] The *Purāṇas* generally, and the Bengal *Purāṇas* in particular, have incorporated nearly everything that they considered relevant in the name of the *Vedas*, irrespective of the fact that they at times, indeed quite often, might have had nothing to do with the *Vedas* or were even contradictory to them. The *Purāṇas* have however scrupulously maintained the cover of the *Vedas*, not so much out of deference to them (which of course was given) as for their own survival. Thus when the *Brahmavaivarta* says that copulation during daytime is prohibited in the *Vedas*,[78] it does not mean that it is necessarily so; it merely signifies that for some reason the *Brahmavaivarta* or more precisely, the *brāhmaṇas* who were introducing Brāhmaṇism to Bengal through the *Brahmavaivarta* and such other *Purāṇas*, consider this act to be improper, or at least wish this to be considered improper and were merely calling on the *Vedas* to witness that they endorse this stricture. We have already noted that the *Vedas* had lost their practical and doctrinal relevance for post-Vedic Hinduism and reformulations were necessary to match altered circumstances. This reformulation required the sanction of authority that could be passed off as legitimate. As Kosambi points out, the *Vedas* did not help in this since

> their text was fixed by immutable routine, so that not even a single syllable could be changed. The *Smrtis*, once written, could not be tampered with soon, or the conflict would mean loss of all authority. This meant raising new texts to venerable antiquity in some plausible fashion which would allow revision of their contents.[79]

These 'new texts' were the *Purāṇas* and the 'plausible fashion' of raising them to the status of 'venerable antiquity' was to claim for them the sanction of Vedic authority.

This process has been characterized by Mackenzie Brown as shift from sound to image of the holy word in the Hindu tradition. He writes,

[76] V.S. Agrawala, 'Editorial', *Purāṇa*, vol. I, no. 2, 1960, p. 118.

[77] *Brahmavaivarta Purāṇa*, IV. 25.67.

[78] Ibid., IV. 79.18.

[79] D.D. Kosambi, *An Introduction to the Study of Indian History*, Bombay, 1975, pp. 289–90.

Earlier, the '*artha* tradition' was subservient to the '*śabda* tradition', the narrative history facilitating and ensuring the success of the *mantra*. In the *Purāṇas*, the narrative or story literature has become the primary holy word, reincorporating the old mantric tradition under new terms. The saving story itself has taken on the character of mantric efficacy though not the mantric immutability.[80]

Once the emphasis was on meaning, it was no longer immutable, for meaning is always contextual and seldom, if ever, universal. Hence it can explain, absorb, re-create itself, and construct its own meaning, depending on the necessity. This flexibility of the *Purāṇas* helped Brāhmaṇism to penetrate peripheral areas such as Bengal, and write its own texts to suit its innovations. Thus R.C. Majumdar is mistaken in assuming a sharp distinction between the Vedic and the Purāṇic tradition in Bengal when he claims that the former was 'replaced' by the latter.[81] Bengal was never a stronghold of Vedic religion, and if the *Vedas* in Majumdar's understanding stand for the symbol of Brāhmaṇism, this was carried forward in the Bengal *Purāṇas* in their notional acknowledgement and glorification of the Vedic authority.

3

The method of invoking the authority of the *Vedas* for legitimation is a process common to all the *Purāṇas*, even if the tendency to emphasize the Vedic–Purāṇic continuum is somewhat stronger in the Bengal variants, because the need for such authentication was greater in their case. The Bengal *Purāṇas* were, however, unique, in that they were consistent in their effort to assimilate local customs in the religious and cultural ethos and practices they attempted to introduce. We have already noticed that even some of the *Mahāpurāṇas* show traces of regional interest,[82] but none so completely and systematically as the Bengal *Purāṇas* which even evolved general principles to justify such inclusions. It is the continuation of the same Purāṇic process of appropriating Vedic authority for Purāṇic innovations that they now extended to local customs, assimilating them within its fold by according them the sanction of brahmanical authority. The ideal gamut of Purāṇic Hinduism thus consists of the *Vedas* at one end of the scale, and the local at the

[80] C. Mackenzie Brown, 'Purāṇa as Scripture: From Sound to Image of the Holy Word in the Hindu Tradition', *History of Religions*, vol. 26, no. 1, Aug. 1986, p. 75.

[81] Majumdar, *History of Ancient Bengal*, vol. I, p. 508.

[82] *See* note 25.

other, with the *Purāṇas* at the centre mediating between these two poles. This process reached its perfect culmination in the Bengal *Purāṇas*.

If the *Purāṇas* are seen as an attempt of brahmanical Hinduism to extend itself into areas hitherto beyond its pale and to broaden its base of mass following, then assimilation of local customs in some form or other would appear inevitable. Indeed, in the epics, which are justly considered proto-Purāṇic, this tendency is already discernible. For example, the *Mahābhārata* says that the seven illustrious Citraśikhaṇḍin Ṛṣis unanimously proclaimed on the mount Meru an excellent *Śāstra* which was made consistent with the four *Vedas* and was meant for the populace, that it consisted of one lakh verses and dealt with the best *lokadharma* (religious duties of the people).[83] What is called *lokadharma* in the *Mahābhārata* gets transformed into *ācāra* in the more explicit Bengal *Purāṇas*. *Ācāra* is a difficult term to translate. According to H.H. Wilson, it means 'an established rule of conduct', 'custom, practice, usage',[84] but in this context it also connotes: of a specific region, at a given time, in consonance with one's stage and order of life. Thus when the *Bṛhannāradīya Purāṇa* declares,

> One who gives himself up to devotion to Hari without transgressing one's own *ācāra*, goes to the abode of Viṣṇu which is seen by the gods. O powerful sage, one who, while performing the duties declared by the *Vedas* and required by one's own order of life, engages himself in meditation on Hari, attains final beatitude. *Dharma* arises from *ācāra* and Acyuta is the lord of *dharma*. Being worshipped by one who is engaged in [the practice of] *ācāra* enjoined by one's stage of life, Hari gives everything. He who, though being a master of *Vedānta* together with the *aṅgas*, falls from his own *ācāra*, is known as *patita* [degraded], because he is outside [of *śrauta* and *smārta*] work. He who deviates from *ācāra* enjoined by his own order of life, is said to be *patita*, no matter whether he is given to devotion to Hari or engaged in meditation on him. O best of the *brāhmaṇa*, neither the *Veda*, nor devotion to Hari or Maheśvara purifies that fool who has fallen from *ācāra*. Neither visit to holy places, nor residence in sacred *tīrthas*, nor performance of various sacrifices saves one who has discarded *ācāra*. Heaven is attained by [the practice of] *ācāra*, happiness is attained by [the practice of] *ācāra*, and final release is attained by [the practice of] *ācāra*. What is not obtained by [the practice of] *ācāra*?[85]

there is no uncertainty about its meaning. One must perform the duties

[83] Cited in Hazra, *Studies in the Upapurāṇas*, vol. II, pp. 162–3.

[84] Horace Hayman Wilson, *Sanskrit–English Dictionary*, Delhi, enlarged edn, 1979, p. 87.

[85] *Bṛhannāradīya Purāṇa*, 4.20–7.

prescribed by the *Vedas*, one must demonstrate unswerving allegiance to the Purāṇic high gods Hari or Maheśvara—because these are inescapable preconditions of *dharma*. But even these are rendered ineffective if one deviates from the prevailing custom, for 'in all sacred scriptures *ācāra* has the first consideration. *Dharma* arises from *ācāra*'.[86] Thus *ācāra* receives priority over all the other components of Brāhmaṇism. In these instances of course the term *ācāra* has been used in its widest possible sense, which includes the duties of both one's stage (*āśrama*) and one's station (*varṇa*) in life.

But the term also has specific implications. This is borne out by the use of such compounds as *vṛddhācāra*[87] (practice of old men) in the same text and the meaning gets even more localized when the text says, 'complete *ācāra* [is to be practised] in [one's] own village, half [of the same] on the way [during a journey], O best of sages, there is no rule in times of illness as well as in great distress'.[88] Finally, the *Purāṇa* sheds all ambiguity and asserts, 'all the *varṇas* should perform the practices of the village [*grāmācāra*] prevailing at the time, in consonance with the ways of the *Smṛtis*',[89] and again 'the practices of different countries [*deśācāra*] should be followed by the people born in those particular countries. Otherwise one is known as *patita* and is excluded from all *dharma*.'[90] The *Bṛhannāradīya* further proclaims, 'Correct statement is truth. Those who are committed to *dharma* will tell the truth which is not contrary to *dharma*. Therefore the statements wise men make after proper consideration of time and space [*deśakālādivijñānāt*], which are in conformity with their own *dharma*, are truth.'[91] Thus it does not hesitate to designate even truth context specific and hence conditional, such is the magnitude of importance placed on local customs. The *Devībhāgavata* virtually equates *dharma* with *ācāra*. It says: 'The *dharma* of the village, of the caste, of the country and of the lineage has to be performed by all men. Under no circumstances can these be disregarded. Men of improper conduct [*durācāraḥ*] are condemned by the people.'[92]

Apart from *ācāra*, the other expression that the authors of the Bengal *Purāṇas* frequently use is *laukika* (literally, popular). The *Bṛhaddharma* apportions *dharma* into two fundamental categories—*vaidika* and *laukika*.[93] At times they seem to be independent of and yet consistent

[86] Ibid., 14.210. [87] Ibid., 24.45. [88] Ibid., 25.16.
[89] Ibid., 22.11. [90] Ibid., 22.17. [91] Ibid., 15.24–5.
[92] *Devībhāgavata Purāṇa*, XI. 1.17–18.
[93] *Bṛhaddharma Purāṇa*, III. 4.15.

with one another: 'adultery in women is prohibited in the *Vedas* and in popular custom',[94] and at other times form a continuum: 'as there is no difference between milk and its whiteness . . . similarly there is no distinction between Rādhā and Mādhava in popular perception, in the *Vedas* and in the *Purāṇa*'.[95] Significantly, however, the *Brahmavaivarta* asserts that in case of conflict between these two sources of *dharma*, popular custom must prevail. When the gods told Pārvatī, 'whatever is approved in the *Vedas* is *dharma* and anything to the contrary is the absence of *dharma*', Pārvatī replied, 'who can decide on the basis of the *Vedas* alone? Popular custom is more powerful than the *Vedas*. Hence who can renounce popular custom?'[96]

Indeed, these *Purāṇas* were written and revised over a long period of time and contributions of many authors, presumably without absolute unanimity of opinion in every matter of detail, has introduced confusing inconsistencies in them. A stray statement should not therefore be taken to represent the central argument of a *Purāṇa*. But at the same time, upholding popular customs appears to be a dominant attitude in these texts, and since it runs as a continuous thread throughout the corpus of the Bengal *Purāṇas* its importance in the Purāṇic scheme of things is inescapable. Besides, the *Vedas* constitute such an infallible symbol of sacred authority for the *Purāṇas* that if it is defied even once in favour of popular custom, this significant deviation should be given due weightage.

An example of how inconspicuously popular customs were incorporated into brahmanical proceedings will make my meaning clear. In connection with the preparation of the planting of the *Indradhvaja*, the *Devī Purāṇa* instructs that amidst the beating of drums, music of the prostitutes, blowing of conch-shells and recitation of the *Vedas* by the *brāhmaṇas* the pole should be taken to the hoisting place.[97] Songs of the prostitutes must have been a popular custom on occasions of collective festivity and was retained. So long as the primary prerequisite of brahmanical Hinduism—the recitation of the *Vedas* by the *brāhmaṇas*—was fulfilled, it did not object to entertaining a prevailing social custom. On the contrary, the practice was conferred with the seal of brahmanical authority by declaring it a part of the ritual scheme. It did not upset the

[94] *Brahmavaivarta Purāṇa*, IV. 32.25.

[95] Ibid., IV. 92.87–8.

[96] Ibid., III. 7.49–50.

[97] *Devī Purāṇa*, 12.26.

Purāṇic arrangement and at the same time it assured the local participants of continuity with the existing usage, thus paving the way for an easier acceptance of the innovations the *Purāṇas* were attempting to introduce. This has indeed been the basic technique of the *Purāṇas* in their assimilative process. To select an instance at random, the *Devībhāgavata* decrees that after defecation a *brāhmaṇa* should cleanse himself with white-coloured clay and the other *varṇas* with red-, yellow- and black-coloured clay respectively, or whatever be the practice in whichever country will suffice.[98] In the same context it later adds that in all matters, one should act according to the considerations of place, time, material, and capability.[99] Purification of the body is an essential requirement. Provided that is performed, the *Purāṇas* are willing, even eager, to accommodate local constraints.

4

In view of this explicitly stated Purāṇic need to acknowledge, and if possible, integrate regional specificities, we are confronted with an important question: the status of a normative text, such as the *Purāṇas*, in a given region. The question assumes greater significance if this happens to be a region where Brāhmaṇism came comparatively late. The question has been partly addressed, although inadvertently, in a major contemporary debate over the interpretation of the *Purāṇas* by the journal *Purāṇa*. The crux of the discussion has been the possibility, and the significance, of critical editions of *Smṛti* literature. Since a consensus exists on later human elaborations of the 'original' *Purāṇasaṃhitā* by Vyāsa, the issue was: if a Purāṇic text is edited along the lines laid down by V.S. Sukthankar for the critical edition of the *Mahābhārata*, will it violate the Purāṇic spirit? Madeleine Biardeau identified the problem as that of the application of methods of textual criticism to what is basically an oral tradition, only subsequently written down. She has pointed out that in India the spoken word is more revered than the written and more importantly, here a further distinction is drawn between *Śruti* (revealed truth which is immutable) and *Smṛti* (remembered truth which is of human composition). She believes that the latter acquires normative value only through its acceptance by the *brāhmaṇas* in a particular locale and it is this locus of authority at the local level which Biardeau

[98] *Devībhāgavata Purāṇa*, XI. 2.18–19.

[99] Ibid., XI. 2.32.

feels Sukthankar has betrayed by trying to establish the earliest text and then treating it as authoritative by virtue of its greater chronological proximity to Vyāsa. She claims that this method introduced the historical dimension into the realm of myth, where it cannot exist.[100] V.M. Bedekar defended Sukthankar's method against Biardeau's criticism on the grounds that once a tradition is committed to writing, it becomes liable to textual criticism, regardless of its origin and the text so constituted is simply a text which may or may not have been at some time some place accepted as authoritative.[101] A.S. Gupta joined issue by attempting to find a compromise between the rigour of Sukthankar and the scepticism of Biardeau. He views the entire Purāṇic corpus as a whole, with the individual *Purāṇas* representing different parts of that organism. He believes that it is possible to characterize each of these parts according to its sectarian preference, and that it is then open to an editor to treat additions not according with that bias as spurious and relegate them to notes and appendices.[102]

The details of this debate and its outcome are irrelevant to my purpose. I am only concerned with an interesting by-product of this debate, namely the mechanism of the acceptability of such a text in a given region, particularly when such a region has not long been exposed to brahmanical influence. Biardeau has expressed her opinion unequivocally:

> any epic or purāṇic story is true if the local brahmins recognize it as part of their beliefs. These brahmins are the *śruta*, the people that warrant the authority of the local tradition because they are well-versed in the *śruti*. And if such a story is recognized by the brahmins, it is attributed to Vyāsa, the mythic author of epics and Purāṇas, regardless of whether it is mentioned in any of the classical text[s].[103]

Biardeau illustrates this general proposition with an experience she had with the Śrīvaiṣṇava pundits of the Simhacalam *pāṭhaśālā* in Andhra. These pundits admitted to her that the local *Purāṇa*, relating the story of Narasiṁha and Prahlāda, was quite different from the *Skanda Purāṇa* version of the same story, though this was its avowed source. In spite

[100] Madeleine Biardeau, 'Some More Considerations About Textual Criticism', *Purāṇa*, vol. X, no. 2, July 1968, pp. 121–2.

[101] V.M. Bedekar, 'Principles of Mahābhārata Textual Criticism: The Need for a Restatement', *Purāṇa*, vol. XI, no. 2, July 1969, p. 219.

[102] A.S. Gupta, 'A Problem of Purāṇic Text-Reconstruction', *Purāṇa*, vol. XII, no. 2, July 1970, pp. 310–21.

[103] Biardeau, 'Some More Considerations About Textual Criticism', p. 121.

of this difference the local *Purāṇa* was authoritative for them, since it expressed their belief and was therefore considered superior to any other local version. Biardeau believes that there is no contradiction here since the Śrīvaiṣṇava *brāhmaṇas* saw themselves as the real source of the authoritativeness of the story without caring too much for the real origin of the tradition in time or place.[104]

For my purpose this is an important point, the significance of which was lost in the polemics of the debate, as its focus lay elsewhere. It should be noted, however, that both the critics of Biardeau concede her this point in passing. Bedekar, for example, does not deny that the traditional locus of authority was the local *brāhmaṇas* who expressed their 'subjective preference'[105] and Gupta does not dismiss the later revisions as mere corruptions, for he recognizes in them 'the desire on the part of the redactors to revise the text of the Purāṇas from time to time and keep them in line with the current religious and social ideas of their time'.[106] Thus, an inevitable condition of the *Purāṇas* seems to be to remain 'in line'. The question is therefore: in line with what and who determines this?

Coburn rightly points out that the intention of the *Purāṇas* is to 'make the original Vedic truth available in a contemporarily relevant way'.[107] Whatever be the connotation of the term 'Vedic truth', I suggest that the contemporaneity relates both to time and place because it is absurd to assume homogeneity of tradition for so large and diverse a country as India, and that too in the early medieval period. How is this conformity with time and place ensured? For an answer to this it will be useful to recall Mackenzie Brown's discussion on the general role of the *Purāṇas* in Hindu culture.[108] He argues that for the Hindus, truth is something to be discovered by each generation. But it is merely a rediscovery, because truth was fully revealed in the past by the *Vedas*. The *Purāṇas* are primarily a means of rediscovering and reinterpreting truth; and also an easier form of truth adapted to contemporary conditions:

> Implicit in this is the notion that mankind can accept only a modified form of truth. It is assumed that the revisions are made in complete harmony of the truth

[104] Ibid., pp. 121–2.

[105] Bedekar, 'Principles of Mahābhārata Textual Criticism', p. 221.

[106] Gupta, 'A Problem of Purāṇic Text-Reconstruction', pp. 306–7.

[107] Thomas B. Coburn, *Devī Māhātmya: The Crystallization of the Goddess Tradition*, Delhi, 1984, p. 37.

[108] Cheever Mackenzie Brown, *God as Mother: A Feminine Theology in India*, Hartford Vt., 1974, pp. 18–19.

contained in the *śruti*. The Purāṇas represent then an interpretation or clarification of the *śruti*, revealing the eternal, immutable truth in a comprehensible form to all mankind in his changing, historical situation.[109]

Since Gupta, Coburn, and Brown are concerned with the 'revisions of the *Mahāpurāṇas*', their explanations naturally rest with the changing needs of the 'time', although Brown is more explicit in the sense that 'historical situation' clearly includes the specificities of both time and space. They however establish the principle behind the process through which new materials were incorporated in the *Purāṇas*. However, in the case of the *Upapurāṇas*, which were evidently composed with a view to transmitting brahmanical religion in the peripheral areas, the demands of place must have received precedence over the ever-changing needs of the time. Otherwise it is difficult to explain the repeated insistence of the Bengal *Purāṇas* on the necessity to honour *deśācāra-lokācāra*. Most of these local customs must have been inconsistent with the brahmanical tradition which was being transmitted. And yet the essential features of both of these had to be retained in some form for them to appear acceptable to both. Moreover, these customs, even within a region, are hardly expected to be uniform. Thus, which of the available choices is to be accepted and incorporated in the local *Purāṇas*, with suitable modifications, if need be?

In matters of such adjustments the judgement of the local *brāhmaṇa* was crucial. For instance, in the example cited by Biardeau, there was the brahmanical version of the Narasiṁha–Prahlāda story contained in the *Skanda Purāṇa* and many local variants. For the Śrīvaiṣṇava *brāhmaṇas*, however, the version of the local *Purāṇa* was considered superior to all others. Biardeau explains this in terms of the 'authoritativeness' of the local *brāhmaṇas*.[110] This is indeed true, but how in the first place did the version of the local *Purāṇa* come about if it was neither an exact reproduction of the *Skanda Purāṇa*, nor in complete agreement with the many local variants? It is reasonable to speculate that the particular version, adopted or constructed for the local *Sthalapurāṇa*, must have been the one that carried the fundamentals of Brāhmaṇism and at the same time appeared least disruptive to the local traditions, in the assessment of the contemporary local *brāhmaṇas*. Brown rightly suggests that the Purāṇic redactions reflect the 'reality as perceived and

[109] Ibid., p. 19

[110] Biardeau, 'Some More Considerations About Textual Criticism', p. 122.

interpreted' by the redactors.[111] This reality of the redactors, or in the case of the Bengal *Purāṇas*—the authors and redactors, consisted of mediating and striking a delicate balance between brahmanical authority and the local beliefs, customs, and traditions. Thus a text could attain normative status in a given region provided it was approved, and in many instances written and rewritten, by the local *brāhmaṇas* and not by an impersonal brahmanical authority. The Bengal *Purāṇas* often repeat the epic and Purāṇic stories. But this in itself was considered insufficient. These had to be retold with a minor or pronounced revision, depending on the necessity as perceived by the local *brāhmaṇas*. This is an integral part of the Purāṇic process and a particularly important one for the Bengal *Purāṇas*.

An example will serve to illustrate the foregoing discussion on the general aspects of this process. The following is an account of the circumstances leading to the introduction of Purāṇic religion in Kāmarūpa, as described in the *Kālikā Purāṇa*.

In the olden days, everybody started going to heaven after taking bath in the water of the river, drinking its water and worshipping the deities in the *mahāpīṭha* of Kāmarūpa. Yama, out of deference to Pārvatī, could not stop them, nor could he take them to his abode. Yama went to Vidhātā and complained that people in Kāmarūpa, after performing the ritual worship, are becoming the attendants of Śiva and Kāmākhyā; he has no jurisdiction there. Brahmā, Yama and Viṣṇu went to Śiva and requested him to make an arrangement so that Yama retains his power over the people of Kāmarūpa. Śiva then asked Ugratārā and his Gaṇas to drive away the people from Kāmarūpa. When everybody, including the members of the four *varṇas* and even the *brāhmaṇas* started being thrown out, the sage Vaśiṣṭha, residing at Sandhyācala, became extremely angry. When Ugratārā and the Gaṇas came to him with the same intention, he cursed them and said, I am a saint and you want to evict me too? Therefore you, along with the Mātṛs will be worshipped in the *vāma* way. Since your Pramathas are roaming around in a state of drunkenness like the Mlecchas, this Kāmarūpa *kṣetra* will be treated as Mleccha country. I am a sage versed in the *Vedas*. Mahādeva, like an inconsiderate Mleccha, tried to evict me. He should therefore stay here bedecked with ash and bones, loved by the Mlecchas. Let the Kāmarūpa *kṣetra* be infested with Mlecchas. Till such time as Viṣṇu himself comes to this place, it will remain like this. The *Tantras* which express the glory of Kāmarūpa will be rare. Thus in the Kāmarūpa *pīṭha*—the abode of the gods—the gods became Mlecchas, Ugratārā became *vāmā* and Mahādeva came to be devoted to the Mlecchas. Within a moment Kāmarūpa became

[111] Brown, *God as Mother*, p. 20.

devoid of the *Vedas* and the four *varṇas*. Although after Viṣṇu came here, Kāmarūpa was released of its curse and began to deliver the fruits of worship again, gods and men remained oblivious of its former glory.[112]

The story admits of two significant facts about Kāmarūpa: that it was devoid of the *Vedas* and the *brāhmaṇas*, and here the gods and the goddesses were worshipped in the left (*vāma*) way, prior to the penetration of brahmanical ideology. The story also reluctantly concedes that the process of brahmanization was not completely successful in the land of the Mlecchas, despite the cleansing presence of Viṣṇu. Indeed, the story is remarkably soft on the prevailing form of religion in Kāmarūpa, as it has no word of censure for a non-brahmanical mode of worship which made one defy death, and it is only through the obviously artificial device of a curse that the text creates an excuse to condemn the left, anti-Vedic religious practice of the outcastes and finds a way of introducing Viṣṇu. This story is symptomatic of the message of the *Purāṇas*, particularly for Bengal.

Van Kooij, who has translated and edited a part of the *Kālikā Purāṇa* with an introduction, suggests that the long exposition dealing with ceremonies and rites for the worship of the goddess in her various forms has no intrinsic unity and gives the impression of being a collection of cults and practices current at the time of the final redaction of the *Kālikā Purāṇa*. However, it is possible to draw a distinction between two categories. One category closely corresponds to the general kind of worship, called common worship (*sāmānyapūjā*) in the text, as practised in large parts of India not only among the Śāktas but also among the Vaiṣṇavas and the Śaivas. The second category consists of the more special rituals in which orgiastic rites play a major role and which were kept outside the brahmanical sphere for a long time.[113] Since this first category of common ritual covers by far the greater part of the fragment on Devī-worship, Kooij takes this to be a clear indication of the *Kālikā Purāṇa's* author's concern to have the deities of Kāmarūpa propitiated by a cult form concordant with the one of the brahmanical tradition commonly accepted[114] in large parts of India of his time and thus to draw in this way the borderland of Kāmarūpa into the Hindu fold.

For the second category, dealing with the religious forms of the

[112] *Kālikā Purāṇa*, summary of 81.1–30.

[113] K.R. Van Kooij, *Worship of the Goddess According to the Kālikāpurāṇa*: Part I, A Translation with Introduction and Notes of Chapters 54–69, Leiden, 1972, p. 6.

[114] Kooij uses the expression 'usual', but this is an imprecise term and requires far too many qualifications to bring out its specific connotation. Ibid., p. 8.

heterodox communities, the author/redactor of the *Kālikā Purāṇa* is willing to allow much less room. This tradition is called the left method or *vāmabhāva*, i.e. unorthodox behaviour characterized by the use of intoxicating liquors and meat, and the stress laid on sexual intercourse.[115] It is centred around the ambivalent goddess Tripura-bhairavī, but significantly the *Kālikā Purāṇa* recommends this form of worship for the brahmanical deities when they assume their heterodox left shapes.[116] Although *Kālikā Purāṇa* sanctions these forms of worship, it warns that a person practising them does not absolve himself from his debts to seers, gods, ancestors, men and demons. In other words, it does not release him from the obligation to carry out the five great sacrifices, which is the right method or *dakṣiṇabhāva*, i.e. the orthodox behaviour.[117] But at the same time, the text recognizes that orthodox behaviour may be an obstacle for an individual who wants to attain final emancipation through the *vāma* method.[118] Moreover, the results that can be obtained by the left worshipper, such as happiness, political power, radiating body, ability to seduce women, the freedom to move about like wind, and the power to control ghosts and wild animals[119] are so alluring that compared to these, absolving one's debts pales into insignificance. Thus it seems that the *Kālikā Purāṇa* does accept the *vāmabhāva* and actually instructs that some goddesses should be honoured with both forms of worship,[120] although, as Kooij rightly points out, it remains true to the general tendency of the *Purāṇas* to stimulate

[115] *Kālikā Purāṇa*, 74. 205.

[116] Śiva is the best-known god with a heterodox nature and the *Kālikā Purāṇa* actually narrates the incident where he was refused attendance at the great sacrifice of Dakṣa because he was a bearer of skulls (*Kapālin*), (*Kālikā Purāṇa*, 61.4). Interestingly, however, this text also mentions the left shapes of most of the major brahmanical deities. For example, the left aspect of Brahmā is called Māyāmoha, Viṣṇu is Narasiṁha, Sarasvatī is Vāgbhairavī, Sūrya is Mārtaṇḍa-bhairava and Gaṇeśa is Agnivetala, who should be worshipped in the *vāma* way. Even the Bāla-gopāla form of Viṣṇu has a left shape, encased in uterus, who eats fish and meat and is ever lustful of women. Goddess Caṇḍikā of course has many left forms. *Kālikā Purāṇa*, 74.206–15. Indeed, the text could not have been more explicit when it says that from the left shape of Brahmā emanated the philosophical school of Cāravāka (*Kālikā Purāṇa*, 74.206–7) which was known to be anti-brahmanical in its attitude and was opposed to all kinds of religious observance.

[117] *Kālikā Purāṇa*, 74.128–9, 133.

[118] Ibid., 74.135. Indeed, the text goes so far as to say that whether one performs the five sacrifices or not, in the worship of the *iṣṭadeva* one must follow the *vāma* method. Ibid., 74.132.

[119] Ibid., 74.136–8.

[120] Ibid., 74.140.

the performance of brahmanical rituals and sacrifices, and attendance to the established forms of social behaviour.[121] Indeed, the text adds that those who worship through the left method do not fulfil the expectations of the other gods, while the right worshipper satisfies everybody. That is why the right method is the better of the two.[122]

Juxtaposed in this way, the text of the *Kālikā Purāṇa*, as indeed the entire corpus of the Bengal *Purāṇas*, would appear hopelessly ambivalent. But seen in the context of the force of local traditions, on the one hand, and the intentions of the purveyors of brahmanical religion, on the other, much of these inconsistencies will be resolved. The primary purpose of the authors of these *Purāṇas* was to propagate brahmanical religion in eastern India which had not merely been outside the sphere of brahmanical influence for a long time, but had developed strong local traditions. Thus the brahmanical religion had to be introduced as unobtrusively as possible and as much in keeping with the local customs as practicable. In other words, the strategy of the brahmanical religion had to be necessarily assimilation rather than imposition. Thus while not a single *Mahāpurāṇa* ever dealt exhaustively or even principally with Śakti worship, although chapters on the praise and worship of the different forms of Devī are found in some of them, the foremost preoccupation of the Bengal *Purāṇas* is the goddess, primarily because the tradition of goddess worship and its associated customs were so firmly entrenched in that region.

There was no problem in principle with the goddess cult as such, because she was already integrated with the brahmanical religion. It was however much more difficult with a near-indispensable corollary of goddess worship, namely the *Tantras*, since it disregarded the two fundamental premises of Brāhmaṇism—the infallibility of the *Vedas* and the authority of the *brāhmaṇas*. Hazra shows that till about the beginning of the ninth century AD Tāntric elements were systematically purged from Purāṇic literature and it was only later that the *Purāṇas* started recognizing the *Tantras* as a result of 'the great spread of Tantricism among the people',[123] when it was no longer possible to ignore them. Even here the Bengal *Purāṇas* had to maintain a facade and declare that only those *Tantras* can be accepted as authoritative which are not in conflict with the *Vedas*.[124] This obviously is a face-saving

[121] Kooij, *Worship of the Goddess According to the Kālikāpurāṇa*, pp. 28–9.

[122] *Kālikā Purāṇa*, 74.144.

[123] Hazra, *Studies in the Purāṇic Records*, p. 260.

[124] *Devībhāgavata Purāṇa*, XI. 1.25. Indeed, the *vāma* worship of the *Kālikā Purāṇa* is

device, for the *Tantras* are, by their very nature, external to the Vedic tradition and all that it signifies. However, the authors of the Bengal *Purāṇas* had to arrive at an intermediate position where accommodation of local customs would not render the features of brahmanical religion unrecognizable, nor the assertion of brahmanical religion would constitute such a threat to the local people that they would be persuaded to reject the entire package.

All theories of social change through cultural contact accept this process as the primary prerequisite of transmission of new ideas and order. Strasser and Randall have made the following summary of the findings of those who have studied similar assimilative processes in a number of contexts:

> In the receiving system we will always find willingness to accept and to integrate innovations in varying degrees. . . . The acceptance or rejection of an innovation *may*, first, depend upon congruence conditions. An innovation is congruent if it shows some similarity to the existing cultural elements with which the public is confident. Secondly, the acceptance may depend upon the condition of compatibility that is met if the innovation fits into the new social context without incurring destructive consequences.[125]

It is precisely to satisfy the conditions of congruence and compatibility that the Bengal *Purāṇas* have laid down separate provisions for separate groups of people. For instance the *Kālikā Purāṇa* says that the *brāhmaṇa* should offer intoxicating liquor to the goddess only once, and that too through others, while it imposes no such restriction on the *śūdras*.[126] Use of liquor is an indispensable aspect of the *vāma* worship and that has to be complied with by every member of the society, but once this insuperable requirement is fulfilled, the text is willing to make exception for different social groups. Liquor plays no part in the brahmanical *dakṣiṇa* method of worship, recommended by the *Purāṇa* to be superior to the *vāma*, and therefore, for the *brāhmaṇa* outsider, the offer of liquor is merely the ritual acknowledgement of a local practice. But the local people, the *śūdras*, were presumably used to this form of worship and hence are allowed to continue with their custom without

---

a variant of the Tāntric mode of worship. Kooij points out that the method recommended in the *Kālikā Purāṇa* agrees substantially with those of the *Kulacūḍāmaṇi* and the *Kulārṇava Tantra*, Kooij, *Worship of the Goddess According to the Kālikāpurāṇa*, p. 29.

[125] Hermann Strasser and Susan C. Randall, *An Introduction to Theories of Social Change*, London, 1981, p. 77.

[126] *Kālikā Purāṇa*, 74.124.

hasty attempts at peremptory reforms.[127] The consideration of minimum compatibility must have weighed heavily with these *Purāṇas*, for the *Kālikā Purāṇa*, despite its obvious preference for the brahmanical way of worship, suggests that when one goes to a *pīṭha* belonging to another country, he should worship according to the advice of the local people and that one should follow the prevailing form of worship in a particular region, such as in Oḍra or in Pāñcāla.[128] In other words, the text concedes that so long as the locally prevailing form of worship is not brought in line with the brahmanical way, it is safer not to disturb the existing equilibrium.

I may add that this process of tacit adjustment with local tradition through the mediation of some legitimating authority is in no way unique to the Bengal *Purāṇas*. This technique is indeed central to the complex process of reformulation and transmission of tradition throughout India in all periods. It is only when the *Purāṇas* themselves became firmly established as the source of brahmanical authority at a later date, that the *Vedas* were replaced by the *Purāṇas* as the effective symbol of mobilization, particularly at the village level. I will furnish two examples to illustrate this point.

The social anthropologist D.F. Pocock, who has worked on the beliefs and practices of a village in central Gujarat, has discussed a popular local-level text in vernacular (as contrasted with the high-profile texts such as the Bengal *Purāṇas* for example, which were written in Sanskrit and contributed to the creation of a great regional tradition), on 'The Most Glorious History of the Goddess'.[129] A typical book of this genre—thick, cheaply bound, printed in large characters and containing garish illustrations—it lays down the rules for animal sacrifice by the *brāhmaṇas*. In Pocock's translation the passage reads thus:

Although many Brahmans are meat eaters they should not openly make flesh offerings. This prohibition derives from the first part of Kalikapurana. That we are to understand that this custom is directed to Kshatriya appears from that section called Sharadatilaka which says [here follow two lines of Sanskrit

[127] One is reminded of the technique adopted by the Vaiṣṇava preachers in the tribal areas of Bengal for the propagation of their faith some centuries later. They apparently declared that the three cardinal tenets of Vaiṣṇavism were chicken curry, lap of a young woman, and chanting of the name of Hari. This was related to me in a private conversation by Hitesh Ranjan Sanyal.

[128] *Kālikā Purāṇa*, 64.34, 36.

[129] D.F. Pocock, *Mind, Body and Wealth: A Study of Belief and Practice in an Indian Village*, Oxford, 1973, pp. 77–9.

which the editor glosses in Gujarati]. Pure Brahman who follow the ordinances should make pure [*sātvik*] offerings for, when they have abandoned offerings associated with violence, these then become for other castes the highest.[130]

There is no such section as 'Sharadatilaka' in the *Kālikā Purāṇa*, but chapter 65 of the *Purāṇa* is entitled '*Śāradātantra*' which of course does not even mention the topic of sacrifices either by a *brāhmaṇa* or a *kṣatriya*. The fact of the matter is that Gujarat is a predominantly vegetarian area and the anxiety of the norm-setters to ensure that at least the *brāhmaṇas* do not violate this custom is understandable. What is interesting, however, is that it invokes a spurious Purāṇic authority to enforce this prohibition.

The other example is directly related to Bengal. There is a particular genre of local-level texts in Bengal known as the *pāñcālī*, which are composed in simple verse usually in praise of a local deity. Cheaply produced thin books, these are read aloud before an audience on an appointed day of the weak or month as a part of a ritual practised by women (*vrata-kathā*). The book that I discuss here is an intriguing variant of the texts of this kind.[131] Impressively printed and bound, it spreads over 285 pages which suggests that it was not meant to be recited in one sitting. Entitled *Śrī Śrī Padma Purāṇa* or the *Pāñcālī of Viṣahari* (Manasā), it begins in typically Purāṇic Sanskrit with the *dhyāna* and eulogy of Manasā, Gaṇeśa, the Daśāvatāra and a number of goddesses. Then follows the central narrative in Bengali which is a retelling of the Cānd Sadāgar–Lakhindar story of the popular *Manasā Maṅgala* of medieval Bengal, without any innovation, but suitably prefaced with stereotyped descriptions of the beginning of creation, the origin of the *Vedas* and time, the churning of the ocean, the sacrifice of Dakṣa, the burning of Madana, etc.; episodes utterly irrelevant for the content of the story and not mentioned at all in the original *Manasā Maṅgala*. From the style of the composition, and also from the choice of topics and their arrangement, it is clear that the author of this text was claiming for his work the status of a *Purāṇa*. It indeed says as much: 'Says *dvija* Vaṁśīdāsa that one who listens to this [text] will be absolved of his sins, as it is stated in the Vālmīki *Purāṇa*.'[132]

In both these instances the point to note is that either a *Purāṇa* is

[130] Ibid., p. 78.

[131] *Śrī Śrī Padma Purāṇa vā Viṣaharir Pāñcālī*, written by Dvija Vaṁśīdāsa in *payāra* metre, collected and revised by Purna Chandra Chakrabarti, Calcutta, n.d.

[132] Ibid., p. 165.

quoted, whether or not the citation is authentic, or the style of the *Purāṇas* is simulated, however transparent the simulation may be, to acquire the status of authority in order to either reinforce a local custom or to elevate the status of a local deity with a regional following in the divine hierarchy—a process already initiated by the *Purāṇas*. Besides, in both these instances the *Purāṇas* perform the same function for these local-level vernacular texts as the *Vedas* did for the *Purāṇas*. In orthodox Hinduism ultimate authority does stem from the *Vedas*, but in course of transmission, as the *Vedas* get further removed from the actual context, the symbol of authority gets transformed and, in the case of Bengal, it is largely appropriated by the epic-Purāṇic tradition, particularly in what may be termed the secondary elaboration of brahmanical authority at the grassroots level, for in the Bengal *Purāṇas* and in the vernacular rendering of the epics, the conditions of congruence and compatibility with regional requirements were already partially fulfilled, and their general acceptability paved the way for greater absorption in the future.

4 Creating a New Cultural Taste: Reading a Nineteenth-century Malayalam Novel

K.N. PANIKKAR

1

All over the world, transforming indigenous cultures had been an agenda central to colonial domination. Such transformations were attempted to ensure the consent of the colonized, as distinct from physical control exercised through military success and territorial conquest. The colonial state and its agencies, both through direct intervention and indirect influence, communicated and reproduced a cultural ideal, attractive and powerful enough for the local intelligentsia to internalize and in turn disseminate. The new cultural scenarios which were brought about by the Spanish in Latin America, the Dutch and the Portuguese in South and South East Asia, and the French and the British in Africa and Asia, were as much a result of interventions by the ideological apparatuses of state, as of participation and collaboration by the local intelligentsia in the process of colonial hegemonization. Culture and politics were integrated in the processes of domination, even if their conjunction was not perceived or realized by the colonized.

The cultural engineering, possible only with the effective organization of state institutions, was not undertaken in a hurry. On the contrary, it was a deliberately cautious venture. The officials of the East India Company in India, during the early period of colonial consolidation, were conscious that they had entered unknown territory, the topography of which they could not easily ascertain.[1] Any attempt at disturbing the

[1] Alexander Dow had articulated one dimension of this difficulty: 'Excuses . . . may be found for our ignorance concerning the learning, religion and philosophy of the Brahmins.

existing cultural sensibilities, they feared, might engender violent reaction. Many among them viewed the Revolt of 1857 as a confirmation of this apprehension; that popular uprising, in their perception, was essentially a conservative reaction to colonial cultural intervention.

While engaged in conquest and initial administrative organization, the Company's officials hardly had time or opportunity to gain knowledge about the civilizations they encountered. The customs, habits, traditions and social institutions of their new subjects remained an enigma to them. Their bewilderment was partly on account of cultural plurality, and partly because of their lack of access to knowledge about the subjected. Even for day-to-day administration the officials, not always conversant with the local languages, relied on the 'natives'.[2]

An easy and cautious option exercised by early colonial administrators was to draw upon pre-colonial institutional structures.[3] Warren Hastings, who was involved in setting up the administrative infrastructure in Bengal, preferred to depend upon the pre-colonial system rather than to revamp it immediately. For instance, in the case of the judiciary he laid down that,

> in all suits regarding inheritance, marriage, caste and other usages and institutions, the laws of the *Koran* with respect to Mahomedans and those of the *Shastras* with respect to Gentoos shall be invariably adhered to; on all such occasions the *moulavis* or Brahmins shall respectively attend to expound the law, and they shall sign the report and assist in passing the decree.[4]

Preliminary to the setting up of the administrative structure and formulating methods of appropriating surplus, the East India Company ascertained the resources of conquered territories through enquiries into their historical, moral and material conditions. These enquiries were not just exercises in assessing resources for revenue purposes; they marked the beginning of the collection of cultural and ethnographic data which later became the knowledge base for formulations of

---

Literary inquiries are [by] no means a capital object to many of our adventurers in Asia. The few who have a turn for researches of that kind, are discouraged by the very great difficulty in acquiring that language, in which the learning of the Hindus contained, or by that impenetrable veil of mystery with which the Brahmins industriously cover their religious tenets and philosophy'. Quoted in O.P. Kejariwal, *The Asiatic Society of Bengal and the Discovery of India's Past*, Delhi, 1988, p. 20.

[2] R.E. Frykenberg, *Guntur, 1788–1848*, Oxford, 1965.

[3] B.B. Misra, *Central Administration of the English East India Company*, Manchester, 1959.

[4] O.P. Kejariwal, op. cit., p. 23.

colonial policy. By this method the colonial state and its agencies promoted and appropriated indigenous knowledge which contributed to the political task of manufacturing consent. According to Hastings,

> Every accumulation of knowledge and especially such as is obtained by social communication with people over whom we exercise a dominion founded on the right of conquest, is useful to the state . . . it attracts and conciliates distant affections; it lessens the weight of the chain by which the natives are held in subjection; and it imprints on the heart of our own countrymen the sense and obligation of benevolence.[5]

This was actively pursued during the course of the late eighteenth and early nineteenth centuries, by bringing to life a network of cultural institutions and practices which might ensure easy access to knowledge about the colonized.

To begin with, attention was focused on textual knowledge and how it could be made available to officials engaged in bringing natives under the colonial cultural umbrella. The codification of Hindu laws and the translation of Indian epics into English, undertaken by Nathaniel Halhed, were early expressions of this quest. Francis Gladwin and William Davy followed the example of Halhed. Gladwin compiled an English–Persian vocabulary and translated the *Ain-i-Akbari*, and Davy composed a history of *The Civil and Military Institutes of Timour*.[6]

The most important contribution in this regard came from British Orientalists who, in the words of William Jones (founder of the Asiatic Society of Bengal in 1784), enquired into 'whatever is performed by the one [man] and produced by the other [nature] in Asia'.[7] The researches of the Society fulfilled two imperial needs. First, the achievements of the past helped to highlight the decadent present, which explained and legitimized colonial intervention. Second, it armed imperial rule with valuable insights into the world of the subjected. Both formed an integral part of colonial control. This was, as Edward Said has remarked, 'the great collective appropriation of one country by another'.[8]

Once the foundations of empire were laid, the focus shifted from appropriations to expropriations of indigenous cultural heritage. Unlike as in the African and Latin American countries, colonialism in India did not attempt to destroy indigenous culture; it only sought to hegemonize

[5] Ibid., p. 24.

[6] Ibid., p. 23.

[7] Ibid., p. 35. *Also see* S.N. Mukherjee, *Sir William Jones*, Cambridge, 1968, pp. 73–90.

[8] Edward Said, *Orientalism*, London, 1978, p. 84.

through a controlled and guided process of acculturation. The ideological apparatuses of the state played a crucial role in this process by actively intervening to reorder the intellectual and cultural domain of the 'natives'. The English-educated intelligentsia became the receivers and carriers of a new cultural taste and sensibility. But not they alone. Even if the expectations of cultural filtration did not really materialize, and the popular and traditional culture continued to be the way of life of an overwhelming majority of the people the influence of colonial culture did transgress the limits of the English-educated middle class. To many outside this social stratum the new cultural possibilities, though difficult to realize, were alluring. The significance of this accultured middle class lies in the fact that it became the ideal and the legitimizer of this vision.

2

The make-up of the cultural world of the middle class, drew to a great extent upon the possibilities inherent in the new literacy that colonialism introduced in India. The colonial system initiated by Macaulay and Bentinck and elaborated during the course of the nineteenth century had many facets and functions, among which its contribution to the creation of a new cultural 'common sense' figures as one of the most enduring and critical. Both in content and organization it was qualitatively different from the pre-colonial system; so too in intent, assumptions and epistemological foundations. Limitations in knowledge notwithstanding, the pre-colonial system had the distinct advantage of being indigenous; in contrast, the body of knowledge which the colonial system sought to inculcate had not evolved from within; its epistemological assumptions were alien to the Indian mind.

The new literacy was important in another way: it opened up large areas for cultural intervention by the state and its agencies. The debate about the nature of education to be imparted to Indians as embodied in the Anglicist–Orientalist controversy, in fact, reflected the cultural space which the colonial state was seeking for establishing its hegemony.[9] By then the East India Company was moving away from the Orientalist task of acquiring knowledge about the subjected to the Anglicist task of imparting knowledge to them. The concern of the state was now the construction of a colonial subject, a cultural symbol for Indians in quest of modernity. The importance of the educational policy

[9] B.K. Boman-Behram, *Educational Controversies in India: The Cultural Conquest of India Under British Imperialism*, Bombay, 1943.

initiated and evolved by the Anglicists, particularly by Macaulay and Bentinck, lay precisely in this dimension. As Macaulay said—

> I feel that it is impossible for us, with our limited means, to attempt to educate the body of the people. We must at present do our best to form a class who may be interpreters between us and the millions whom we govern—a class of persons, Indians in blood and colour, but English in tastes, in opinions, in morals and in intellect. To that class we may leave it to refine the vernacular dialects of the country, enrich those dialects with terms of science borrowed from the Western nomenclature, and to render them by degrees fit vehicles for conveying knowledge to the great mass of the population.[10]

The elaboration of this policy by the colonial rule through cultural engineering and institutional practices embedded in society a concept of literacy which privileged reading in the English language. The cultural universe opened up by this practice had its epicentre in the colonial metropolis. This in turn created within the colonized what Mannoni has called a dependency complex,[11] and Edward Shills, a sense of provinciality.[12] The cultural ideal in literature, theatre, painting, music, dress, food, conversation, etiquette and so on was now drawn from the colonizer's world. The new literacy thus tried to transform India into a cultural province of the colonial metropolis and neo-literate Indians into cultural compradors.

The development of printing during the colonial period played a central role in disseminating the cultural content of this new literacy. Its cultural possibilities were realized by the printed word, by 'setting up new networks of communication, facilitating new options for the people, and also providing new means of controlling the people'.[13] By facilitating easier access to literary products, print contributed to the making of a new cultural taste and sensibility, and thus a new cultural personality.

The cultural impact of the new literacy was not confined to English literates. There was a spillover effect on vernacular readers. The new cultural essence invariably found its way into the Indian languages, and through them to a larger audience. The growth of printing facilities in

[10] H. Sharp, *Selections from Educational Records, Pt I, 1781–1839*, Calcutta, 1920, p. 116.

[11] O. Mannoni, *Prospero and Caliban: The Psychology of Colonization*, Ann Arbor, 1990, pp. 39–48.

[12] Edward Shills, *The Intellectual Between Tradition and Modernity: The Indian Situation*, The Hague, 1961.

[13] Natalie Zemon Davis, *Society and Culture in Early Modern France*, London, 1965, p. 190.

these languages during the course of the nineteenth century furthered this process, for the new cultural taste could thus enter the arena of 'popular' reading. The catalogue of the Registrar of Books of the Bengal, Bombay and Madras Presidencies, which lists the publications for each year, reflects the new concerns in vernacular literatures. Two trends were evident by the beginning of the twentieth century; first, a groundswell in the publication of pamphlets, tracts and other popular genres in the vernacular languages; second, their receptivity to the colonial cultural discourse.

The incorporation of colonial cultural elements is very marked within textbooks in the Indian languages produced by the government, Christian missionaries, voluntary organizations and private individuals. These books, both in diction and content, guide the impressionable minds of children to a cultural universe alien to their life experience. It appears that colonialism, like fascism, believed in catching them young. This was not always achieved through a dismissal or denigration of indigenous culture, but by locating the cultural ideal in the achievements of Western society. The West therefore, loomed large in the cultural productions promoted by colonial rule. For instance, in textbooks and other reading materials for children, a shift to the 'Western' was pronounced, both in texts and illustrations. A good example of this is some of the Hindi books prescribed in the schools of the North Western Provinces. In one of them a popular Indian tale is illustrated with the sketch of a boy wearing a coat, trousers and top hat. This was not an aberration, but an expression of the larger colonial project, which sought to make India meaningful only when related to the West.

The written word as a cultural factor became increasingly important and influential during the course of the nineteenth century. The context in which this happened was the vernaculars' access to print technology and the consequent commodification of vernacular literature. The importance of this development was not limited to the physical presence of the 'book' in the market-place, and thus to its easy accessibility, but also in the new relationship it forged between reader and book. Printed matter now penetrated the readers' private world, 'mobilizing their sentiments, fixing their memories and guiding their habits'.[14] The transition from earlier group reading and listening to individual reading was an immediate and important consequence. Since books could now

[14] Roger Chatier, *The Cultural Uses of Print in Early Modern France*, Princeton, 1981, p. 233.

be possessed by individuals, the need for group reading and public recitals began to decline. Increasingly, reading became a private activity, enabling the reader to go back to the book again and again to internalize its contents. The availability of printed literature contributed to a change in attitude towards leisure itself. Leisure in the past had been defined mainly in terms of participation in group activities, be it gossip within the family or with friends, or sports and games in the locality. Now the educated middle class found in reading an entirely different way of spending leisure time. Leisure activity became increasingly individual, a means by which the cultural world of the West came within grasp and in turn facilitated its internalization.

New literary genres like the novel were a product of this process; they emerged simultaneously with the educated middle class being drawn into the colonial cultural world. Although prose was not unknown in Indian literatures, 'its potentiality and possibilities as an effective instrument of communication', both literary and non-literary, was realized only during the course of the nineteenth century.[15] The emergence of the novel as a popular literary form was also part of this process. The first novel in Bengali, *Alaler Gharer Dulal*, by Pearey Chand Mitra, appeared in 1858, followed by Bankimchandra Chatterji's *Durgeshnandini* and *Kapalakundala* in 1865 and 1866 respectively. In Marathi, Baba Padmanji's *Yamuna Paryattan* appeared in 1857, and in Gujarati *Karan Ghelo* by Nanda Shankar Tiliya Shankar Mehta in 1866. In the South-Indian languages, novels were written much later. The first novel in Malayalam, *Kundalata* by Appu Nedungadi, was published in 1887; in Tamil *Piratapa Mutaliyar Carittiram* by Samuel Vedanayakam Pillai in 1879; and in Telugu *Rajasekhara Charitra* by Kandukuri Viresalingam Pantulu in 1880.[16]

Why the novel came into being as a popular genre during the second half of the nineteenth century is a question many have attempted to answer. Its imitative or derivative character has often found uncritical acceptance.[17] Modern literature in the Indian languages itself is seen within the rubric of 'western impact and Indian response'—as the title of the Sahitya Akademi sponsored history of nineteenth-century literature suggests.[18] The influence of English on early novels in India is

[15] Sisir Kumar Das, *A History of Indian Literature*, vol. VIII, New Delhi, 1991, p. 70.

[16] Ibid., pp. 197–216.

[17] *See*, for instance, K.M. George, *Western Influence on Malayalam Language and Literature*, New Delhi, 1972.

[18] Sisir Kumar Das, op. cit. The sub-title is 'Western Impact: Indian Response'.

unmistakable, but this literary form was not generated exclusively here by external stimulus; it was rooted in the intellectual needs and aesthetic sensibility of the burgeoning middle class. Naturally, the contradictions, ambiguities and uncertainties of the middle class in their social and cultural life, which arose out of the mix of a hegemonizing colonial culture and contending traditional cultures, formed the contexts in which a literary sensibility found expression in the nineteenth century. The cultural perspective of the middle class was neither entirely hegemonized by the colonial nor confined within the traditional, but was posited in a dialogue between the two. They looked beyond the Western and the traditional; neither received their unqualified approval. The dialogical possibilities of the novel as a literary genre created the new space for incorporating this cultural ambience.

3

What follows is an attempt to read one of the early Malayalam novels, *Indulekha*, published in 1889, in the context of the cultural situation engendered by colonialism, and to explore the ways in which it contributed to the making of a cultural taste in Kerala.

By the time *Indulekha* was published, print technology was well entrenched in literary production; yet *Indulekha* was the first expression of its immense potential in Kerala. Highly acclaimed by discerning readers and informed critics, its popularity was so overwhelming that the first edition was sold out within three months and several imitations vainly tried to emulate its success. To the author this came as a pleasant surprise, because 'Malayalis who had not till then read any book like an English novel so suddenly liked and enjoyed' reading his book.[19] By 1971 the novel had gone through sixty editions with the print order for each edition ranging from 1000 to 6000.

The author of the novel, Oyyarath Chandu Menon, was born in 1847 in a Nair family of north Malabar. Like many of his contemporaries, he received both a traditional and a Western education. Beginning in a vernacular school where he learnt Sanskrit, he moved to the Basel Mission school at Tellichery and acquired proficiency in English. Subsequently, he passed the uncovenanted civil services examination and began his official career as the sixth clerk in a small cause court in 1864. After three years he was promoted as the first clerk of the sub-collector's office, where he had the good fortune to receive the

[19] O. Chandu Menon, *Indulekha*, Preface, 2nd edn, Kottayam, 1971, p. 23.

patronage of William Logan, the celebrated author of *Malabar Manual*. Eventually Menon rose in the official hierarchy to retire as the sub-judge of Calicut in 1897.[20]

Robert Darnton is of the opinion that 'despite the proliferation of biographies of great writers, the basic conditions of authorship remain obscure'.[21] In the case of Chandu Menon, of whom there is no good biography, in fact nothing more than a bare outline of his life is known, it is more difficult to ascertain the conditions in which *Indulekha* was written. However, Chandu Menon has recounted the circumstances in which he took to writing the novel while he was a *munsif* at Parappanangadi. Among other things, his account reflects how a new literary taste, and through that a new cultural taste, was developing among the vernacular intelligentsia.

Parappanangadi being a small *mofussil* town where the demand of official duties was relatively light, Menon had considerable leisure to read a large number of English novels. This new-found love of literature in him supplanted the normal leisure time activity of *vedi parayal* (gossip) among friends and members of the family. Consequently, Menon's 'circle of intimates' felt somewhat neglected. To offset this, he says he 'attempted to convey to them in Malayalam the gist of the stories of novels' he had been reading. Initially they were not particularly interested in these stories of English romantic encounters, but they soon developed a 'taste' for them. One of them, Menon says, 'was greatly taken with Lord Beaconsfield's *Henrietta Temple*, and the *taste then acquired for listening to novels* translated orally, gradually *developed into a passion*' (emphasis added).[22] Inspired by this interest in Beaconsfield's novel, Menon decided to translate it, but he soon gave it up as an impossible task. Instead, he undertook to write a new novel 'after the English fashion'.[23] His reasons for doing so were:

Firstly, my wife's oft-expressed desire to read in her own language a novel written after the English fashion, and secondly, a desire on my part to try whether I should be able *to create a taste among my Malayalam readers* not

[20] P.K. Gopalakrishnan, *O. Chandu Menon*, Thiruvananthapuram, 1982.

[21] Robert Darnton, *The Kiss of Lamourette: Reflections in Cultural History*, London, 1990, p. 125.

[22] *Indulekha*, translated into English by W. Dumergue, Preface, 1st edn, p. x. All quotations in this essay are from Dumergue's translation, 1965 edn, Calicut.

[23] The author of *Kundalatha*, the first novel in Malayalam, was also influenced by a similar urge. He regretted that those who are ignorant of English are not acquainted with novels in English. His attempt was to write a story on the lines of English novels. Appu Nedungadi, *Kundalatha*, Preface, 1st edn, Calicut, 1887.

conversant with English, for that class of literature represented in the English language by novels, of which at present they have no idea, and to see whether they could appreciate a story that contains only such facts and incidents as may happen in their own households under a given state of circumstances [emphasis added].[24]

The story of *Indulekha* is set amidst the social and ideological changes of Malabar in the nineteenth century, these changes being a consequence of the administrative, economic and social policies of the colonial government. A social phenomenon of far-reaching significance, arising out of the agrarian policy of the Company, was the emergence of an affluent class of intermediary tenants almost exclusively drawn from the Nair community.[25] The bulk of the English-educated middle class came from this social stratum; they had the necessary financial resources as well as social vision to send their wards to educational institutions which imparted English education.[26] The opportunities were thus opened up in government employment and professions, and a new worldview, informed by the individualism and liberalism, was imbibed from Western thought. This then led to critical introspection about various prevailing social institutions and practices. The reform and change initiated by this class sought to transform those existing relationships, in the social and domestic spheres, which curbed individual liberty and upward mobility. What attracted most attention was the matrilineal family and marriage system which the Nairs had followed, probably since the ninth century. *Indulekha* reflects these concerns as well as the tensions to which they gave rise.

The universe of the novel is a Nair *taravad* (household) in which forces of change and continuity struggle for supremacy. The *karanavan* (patriarch), Panchu Menon, who exercises control over the resources of the family, and by virtue of that over the lives of its members, represents the force of continuity. He is affectionate and sincere, but, being strongly anchored in traditional ideology, is indifferent to the aspirations of the younger generation in the family and insensitive to the changes occurring around him. The novel opens with an allusion to a dispute between Panchu Menon and Madhavan, the hero of the novel, over the education of the children in the family. Madhavan wants one of the boys to be sent to Madras for an English education, which the karanavan is not prepared to agree to. The dispute is not just over the

[24] *Indulekha*, p. xvi.

[25] K.N. Panikkar, *Against Lord and State*, New Delhi, 1989, p. 28.

[26] *Report of the Malabar Tenancy Committee, 1927–28*, Madras, 1928.

distribution of resources within the family; it symbolizes a struggle between the status quo and change. This is the curtain raiser to the central concern of the novel: an exploration of the different ways in which Malabar society was trying to grapple with the cultural situation in the nineteenth century.

The plot of the novel, conceived by Chandu Menon on the lines of English storybooks, is rather simple. It revolves around the love between two cousins in a Nair taravad, Madhavan and Indulekha, whose marriage is traditionally sanctioned in the matrilineal system. The intervention of a Nambudiri Brahmin who, enamoured of the reported beauty of Indulekha, seeks her hand in marriage, gives rise to misunderstanding and a temporary separation of the lovers. The story predictably ends in the happy marriage of the lovers.

If *Indulekha* had only narrated this love story, as many of its puerile imitations did later, it would not have been a literary event of any consequence, nor demanded continued attention thereafter.[27] The novel went through so many editions and has been at the centre of literary discussions not only because of its narrative excellence, but also because of its significance as a social and cultural statement of the times. The love story is only the necessary skeleton; the flesh is provided by the contending cultural sensibilities inherent in the colonial society of Malabar which it represents. *Indulekha* transcends the limits of a storybook on the lines of English novels and reflects the struggle for cultural hegemony in civil society.

Chandu Menon conceived the three main characters in the novel—Madhavan, Indulekha and Suri Nambudiripad—to reflect the main contending cultural traits in Malabar in the nineteenth century. Madhavan is English educated, socially progressive, politically alive, and at home with European customs, manners and knowledge. He is adept at lawn tennis, cricket and other athletic games. At the same time he is not an anglophile, nor contemptuous of Indian tradition; rather, he is well grounded in it. He has 'profound critical knowledge' of Sanskrit literature, he can appreciate the nuances of traditional art forms and recite Malayalam poems from memory with ease. The evolution of his character represents an intellectual process which comes to terms with the contradictions of colonial hegemony, namely the coexistence of consent and contestation. Located in this milieu, Madhavan is not a

[27] *Indulekha's* success had led several aspirants for fame to try their hand at writing novels. None of them made an impact on the reader. George Irumbayam (ed.), *Nalu Novalukal* (in Malayalam), Trichur, 1985.

static character symbolizing the accultured Indian of Macaulayan vintage. That part of his make-up is indeed quite evident, but he goes beyond it to embody the elements of a newly emerging national consciousness.[28]

A combination of the indigenous and colonial cultures is more sharply and elaborately etched in the character of Indulekha. She has been brought up by her uncle, a Dewan Peishkar who was 'well versed in English, Sanskrit, Music and other accomplishments'. Under his tutelage Indulekha's cultural attainments are of a high order. She is

thoroughly grounded in English; her Sanskrit studies included the works of the dramatic authors; and in Music she not only learned the theory of harmony, but also became an efficient performer on the piano, violin and the Indian lute. At the same time her uncle did not neglect to have his charming niece instructed in needle work, drawing and other arts in which European girls are trained. In fact his darling wish was that Indulekha *should possess the acquirements and culture of an English lady*, and it can be truly said that his efforts were crowned with the success due to a man of his liberal mind and sound judgement, so far as this could be compassed within the sixteenth year of her age [emphasis added].[29]

Chandu Menon was conscious that this picture of Indulekha was too idealized to be true of nineteenth-century Malabar: 'some readers may object that it would be impossible to find a young Nair lady of Indulekha's intellectual attainment in Malabar'. He believed however that there are 'hundreds of young ladies in respectable Nair Taravads who would undoubtedly come up to the standard' of 'Indulekha in beauty, personal charms, refined manners, simplicity of taste, conversational powers, wit and humour'.[30] The only quality not possessed by them, which distinguishes Indulekha, is her knowledge of English. The justification for this was as follows:

One of my objects in writing this book is to illustrate how a young Malayalee woman, possessing, in addition to her natural charms and intellectual culture, a knowledge of the English language would conduct herself in matters of supreme interest to her, such as choosing of a partner in life. I have thought it necessary that my Indulekha should be conversant with the richest language of the world.[31]

Her English accomplishments notwithstanding, Indulekha, unlike Madhavan, does not consider the Nair system of marriage devoid of

[28] *Indulekha*, pp. 2–4.

[29] Ibid., p. 10. [30] Ibid., p. xx. [31] Ibid.

merit. The conversation between Indulekha and Madhavan on the man–woman relationship prevalent among Nairs encapsulates the discussion then raging in society about marriage reform. Madhavan feels that men suffer untold misery on account of the freedom and opportunities which the women of Malabar enjoy. Disapproving of the freedom enjoyed by women in marital affairs, Madhavan observes: '. . . in Malabar, the women don't practice the virtue of fidelity so strictly as do the women of other countries. Why in Malabar a woman may take a husband and cast him off as she pleases, and on many other points she is completely at liberty to do as she likes.[32]

Madhavan's allusion to the impermanence of Nair marriage is obviously nuanced against women. He overlooks the fact that the impermanence is more on account of the libertine male than the freedom-loving woman. Yet Madhavan's argument echoes the patriarchal demand for establishing what is 'natural' and ideal in man–woman relations. Indulekha's defence of Nair women strives to reconcile patriarchal rights and female freedom:

What, did you say that Malayali woman are not chaste? To say that a woman makes light of the marriage tie, is tantamount to saying that she is immoral. Did you then mean that all or most of women in the land of palms are immoral? If you did, then I for one certainly cannot believe him. If you intended to signify that we Nairs encourage immorality, because, unlike the Brahmins, we do not force our womenfolk to live lives worthy only of the brute creation by prohibiting all intercourse with others, and by closing against them the gates of knowledge, then never was there formed any opinion so false. Look at Europe and America, where women share equally with men the advantages of education and enlightenment and liberty! Are these women all immoral? If, in those countries, a woman who adds refinement of education to beauty of person, enjoys the society and conversation of men, is it to be straightaway supposed that then men whom she admits into the circle of her friends are more to her than mere friends?[33]

Indulekha's spirited defence reflects the gender equality that Nair women had enjoyed for centuries, which was likely to be upset by the reforms contemplated by the government and supported by the educated middle class. Whether this practice, which had evolved as a part of the cultural tradition, needed to be changed was a matter of doubt among many. In the evidence and discussion of the Malabar Marriage Commission and the public response to its recommendations, this uncertainty found varied expression. Chandu Menon, who was a member of the

[32] Ibid., p. 40. [33] Ibid., p. 41.

Marriage Commission, argued in a note of dissent that Nair marriages had validity both in law and religion, and that no legislative interference was needed in this matter.[34] The Madhavan–Indulekha conversation was in many ways a precursor to the debate among the educated middle class, generated by the marriage reform proposal. Indulekha's arguments can perhaps be identified with the largely unstated opinion of women, which did not altogether match the patriarchal urge to control women's sexuality and independence.

The character of the 'fickle-minded and libertine' Suri Nambudiripad has multiple functions and meanings in the plot. His escapades are not intended as purely comic interludes in an otherwise serious novel, but as the expression of a cultural ethos with which the middle class in Malabar was contending. In almost every aspect—in looks, in knowledge, in character—he is contrasted implicitly if not explicitly with Madhavan. While Madhavan is 'remarkably good looking', Nambudiripad is 'neither good looking nor elegant'. 'When he laughed his mouth stretched from ear to ear, his nose, though not deformed, was far too small for his face, and, instead of walking, he hopped like a crow.' Madhavan is cautious and respectful towards women, whereas Nambudiripad is arrogant and condescending. He looks upon women only as objects of sexual pleasure, regardless of age or marital status. He is enamoured of every woman he meets, whether a young girl like Indulekha or an elderly woman like her mother or an attractive girl like her servant. Reflecting the traditional Nambudiri attitude, he believes that it is his right to marry any woman in a Nair family to whom he takes a fancy.[35]

Even in traditional knowledge, within which Nambudiris are generally well grounded, Suri Nambudiri cannot match the accomplishments of Madhavan or Indulekha. Despite his 'madness' for Kathakali and pretensions to scholarship in Sanskrit literature, he can hardly remember or recite even a few lines of poetry. His efforts at this provide comic relief. Indulekha recites with great ease the poems which he struggles to remember.

Another dimension of Nambudiripad's character is his contempt for the new cultural situation, arising more out of ignorance than reflection or understanding. Consequently, he is trapped in sexual obsession. He believes that English 'destroys romance and hinders all love making'.

[34] *Malabar Marriage Commission Report*, Memorandum by O. Chandu Menon, Enclosure C, Madras, 1891.

[35] *Indulekha*, pp. 95–6.

Even Panchu Menon, whose fealty to traditional ideologies led him to welcome the Nambudiripad, finds him an 'unmitigated fool, destitute of intellect and intelligence'.[36]

Chandu Menon's reservations about the proposed legislative intervention notwithstanding, *Indulekha* underlines the growing awareness about the iniquity of the Nair–Nambudiri marriage alliance. The new generation resented sexual exploitation by Nambudiris and questioned the ideological dominance which sanctioned it. Indulekha's rejection of Suri Nambudiripad is a powerful statement of this cultural consciousness. Yet, ideologies hardly fade so quickly. That is why Nambudiripad is able to marry one of Indulekha's cousins, despite his clumsy and offensive mannerisms.

4

Apart from being a means to contrast the feudal and the modern, the Nambudiripad episode has yet another function in the plot. It is used as a device to take the story outside the 'region' to the wider arena of the nation. Madhavan, under the false impression that Suri Nambudiripad has married Indulekha and taken her with him, seeks solace in travel which takes him to Calcutta, the centre of nationalist activity at that time. At Calcutta he befriends those who are active in the Indian National Congress and participates in their meetings. This sojourn provides the context for an extended discussion on religion, the colonial state and the Congress movement, which takes up about a sixth of the novel.

The participants in the discussion, apart from Madhavan, are his father Govinda Panikkar and his cousin Govindan Kutty Menon. They represent three different strands of thought. Govindan Kutty Menon is an atheist and liberal reformist, Govinda Panikkar is a theist who values belief in and reverence for spiritual preceptors, and Madhavan is a critical rationalist and supporter of the Indian National Congress. Their discussion broadly covers two main issues, first, the place of religion in human life and second, the nature of the Congress movement in the context of colonial rule.

The discussion on religion reflects the intellectual ferment which stirred Indian society during the religious and cultural regeneration of the nineteenth century. All three strands of 'renaissance' thought are articulated during the discussion: a defence of religious tradition, a rational critique of religious practices and an atheistic attitude towards religious faith.

[36] Ibid., p. 191.

The conversation opens with a critique of the non-conformist attitude of young men, which Govinda Panikkar attributes 'solely to the ideas and mode of thinking adopted in consequence of English education'. The influence of education is such that reverence, faith and love for spiritual preceptors and family elders, and belief in god and piety, has ceased to exist. The educated youth, according to him, have scant regard for the good old practices of the Hindus and think that the Hindu religion is altogether contemptible. He has no doubt that the acquisition of knowledge and culture are 'utterly worthless, if they came into conflict with faith in things divine'.[37]

This opening statement leads to an animated discussion on god, religion and ideology, from which three distinct positions emerge. Holding that 'the origin, preservation, growth and decay of the whole world are due to natural forces', Govindan Kutty refuses to believe that there is any supreme power which can be called God. As for religion, he thinks that it is 'simply a fabric of each man's brain' and that 'as human knowledge increases, faith in religion must decrease'. Madhavan, on the other hand, is 'firmly convinced that there is a God', but fails to see any connection between temples and God.[38]

The views of these young men, who are 'wonderful examples of the times', are shocking to Govinda Panikkar who believes that any departure from the faith of his forefathers is undesirable. Realizing that any attempt to convince the young radicals on god and religion would be a difficult task, he confines his defence to the need for temples. Temples, he argues, were meant as a reminder of 'the admiration and homage due to the Almighty', since people are likely to ignore 'His presence in every place, even the most secret'. Madhavan interprets his father's argument to mean that there is no 'essential connection between temples and God', and that 'temples are nothing but symbolical institutions founded by pious individuals for the benefit of those who have no natural inclination to piety'. He not only questions the connection between temples and God, but also the relevance of temples for true believers. Acknowledging that God is present throughout the world and that the powers of creation, preservation and destruction are vested in him, Madhavan feels that it would be 'a gross mockery to go to a temple and pretend that the image set up therein was my God and worship it and prostrate myself before it'.[39]

Opposition to idolatry was a major idea around which religious reform in the nineteenth century was organized and propagated. Since

[37] Ibid., pp. 299–300. [38] Ibid., pp. 301–2. [39] Ibid., pp. 303–4.

there is no authorial intervention, Chandu Menon's views on the subject are not clear. But Govinda Panikkar's defence of idolatry appears weak when compared with the forceful articulation of the anti-idolatry argument by Madhavan. This is reinforced by the discussion on the role of religious leaders in perpetuating superstition. The incident of an ascetic living for ten days on seven pepper berries and seven neem leaves narrated by Govinda Panikkar is dismissed by Madhavan as the trick of an impostor: for, it was not done under verifiable conditions and hence not acceptable.[40]

The critique of religion and religious practices, though undertaken in the context of tradition, did not involve its rejection. Instead, it led to an exploration of the relative relevance of tradition and modernity. Steeped in Western thought and influenced by the ideas of Charles Bradlaugh and Darwin, Govindan Kutty Menon is contemptuous of the knowledge contained in traditional texts, which he dismisses as 'crammed with incongruities and impossibilities'. Citing from the works of Darwin and Bradlaugh, he seeks to establish that the scientific and rational ideas which European thought contained are totally absent in the Indian tradition, represented by the Puranas and other ancient texts.

An altogether different view, sensitive to the importance and strength of tradition, is articulated by Madhavan, who argues that Govindan Kutty Menon's contempt for traditional knowledge is more due to ignorance than a proper understanding of the contents of those ancient texts which contributed considerably to the advance of European thought and ideas. He reminds Govindan Kutty Menon that the atheism the latter has adopted from Bradlaugh was very much in existence in the Sankhya system of Kapila.[41] That there were atheists in India comes as a surprise to both Govindan Kutty Menon and Govinda Panikkar, suggesting how both the 'modernists' and the 'traditionalists' are equally ill-informed about their own past. The entire discussion is so conceived as to underline a cultural–intellectual perspective, advocated by Madhavan, which is in favour of the new, without renouncing the old.

Reminiscent of what happened to the intellectual concerns of the nineteenth century, the engagement with religion and tradition shifts to the realm of politics. The discussion covers two interrelated dimensions of political reality: the nature of colonial rule and the character of the Congress movement. All the three discussants share the colonial view on the benevolence of British rule, but their assessment of the possible benefits from the Congress movement are sharply different. They

[40] Ibid., pp. 305–7. [41] Ibid., p. 322.

believe that the British government is far superior to earlier regimes—'like our old rulers [not] guilty of injustice, irregularity and oppression'[42]—and would eventually lead India to progress. Madhavan expresses this common conviction in unambiguous terms:

> The fact is that the establishment of the British Empire has been productive of indescribable benefits to this country. In no other nation do we find intellectual capacity so fully developed as it is in the English, and the statesmanship they display is one proof of this fact. Another proof lies in their impartiality, a third in their benevolence, a fourth in their valour, a fifth in their energy and a sixth in their endurance. It is through the preponderance of these six qualities that the English have succeeded in bringing so many countries of the world under their domination and protection, and the subjection of India by a people endowed with such vast natural ability is the greatest good fortune that could have befallen us.[43]

This assessment of British rule provides the necessary context to envision the possible ways in which the Indian polity might develop. One of them, the liberal reformist view articulated by Govindan Kutty Menon, advocates gradual change and reform introduced by the British government. To facilitate this process, Indians could prove themselves socially worthy of political advancement by changing their 'imperfect and disgraceful customs and institutions', raising India to a state of equality with England. Popular assemblies, self-government and enfranchisement could only follow, not precede this. In the absence of this necessary improvement, the Congress is 'worthless' and nothing but 'pompous bombast', a 'vain agitation and waste of money'. It is 'altogether contemptible'.[44]

Articulating the moderate view and emphasizing the positive role of the Congress, Madhavan attributes to it an instrumentalist function which is to bring to 'maturity and perfection' the indescribable benefits afforded by the British by striving 'to instill into the English greater faith in us, greater affection and greater regard for us, and thus to persuade the English government to make no difference between us and Englishmen'.[45] Such an objective could be achieved neither by resorting to violence nor by lapsing into inactivity, but by making every legitimate effort to raise India's position higher and higher. Such efforts, he believes, would be rewarded by the establishment in India, as in England, of a free government.[46] With Govindan Kutty Menon almost

[42] Ibid., p. 342. [43] Ibid., p. 346. [44] Ibid., p. 337.
[45] Ibid., pp. 339–40. [46] Ibid., p. 343.

agreeing with Madhavan's contention, a resolution of the conflict between the social and political reform is posited.

This long and laboured discussion, as argued by many literary critics, would appear to be unconnected with the plot, but is in fact integral to the theme of the novel. Baffled by this supposedly unnecessary detour, some have criticized it as 'a stone blocking the unhampered progress of the plot'.[47] If the discussion on atheism and the Congress were to be left out, as in some of the later editions, perhaps it would not have done any harm to the story. Chandu Menon's stated intention of writing a 'story book' would also have been fulfilled. But then Chandu Menon was attempting more than narrating a story. He was making a cultural and political statement, and integrating into the plot the vital issues Indian society faced at that time.

Indulekha is not merely a story set in the context of colonial history. It collapses and encapsulates the historical process of nineteenth-century Malabar into a literary genre consciously borrowed from the English. The novelty of the new genre and the possible attraction of a love story do not fully account either for its popularity or for its importance. Its significance and success are to a great extent rooted in its ability to capture the cultural and political experience of the intelligentsia, nuanced by the contradictions, ambiguities and uncertainties inherent in it.

By internalizing colonial cultural values and political ideas, the intelligentsia fulfilled a legitimizing role for colonialism. This dimension is effectively projected in *Indulekha* through an emphasis on the modernizing potential of English education and the benevolent, liberal character of British rule. The characters, conversations and authorial interventions unmistakably articulate this early consciousness. Madhavan and Indulekha are forceful representations of this colonial ideal. At the same time, a disjunction between the cultural consequences of English education and the liberalism of British rule is also posited. Govinda Panikkar, for instance, is a cultural critic of English education but a political supporter of British rule. He holds that English education subverted tradition and encouraged atheism, but at the same time initiated the beginnings of a liberal polity in India.

Despite the influence of English education, Madhavan and Indulekha are not colonial cultural stereotypes. Their personalities are a complex

[47] M.P. Paul, *Novel Sahithyam. Also see* P.K. Balakrishnan, *Chandu Menon, Oru patanam*, Kottayam, 1971, pp. 112–17 (both in Malayalam).

admixture of the Western and the indigenous, reflecting the cultural introspection embodying the intelligentsia's alienation from the struggle against colonial culture. They were neither completely hegemonized by the colonial nor fully distanced from the traditional. Thus their identity was rooted in a new cultural taste, anchored in both the Western and the indigenous without fully identifying with or rejecting either of them. In the field of politics as well, this duality is evident; the acceptance of British rule on the one hand and the transition to national consciousness on the other. The capturing of this historical process is what makes *Indulekha* an unusually interesting work of fiction.

III

Contestation and Affirmation

5

The Siddhas of Tamil Nadu: A Voice of Dissent*

K. MEENAKSHI

tēvar kallum āvarō?
cirippataṉṟi eṉ ceyvēṉ!
Shall the stone be God?
What shall I do but laugh!

This couplet may be mistaken for some modern rationalist's criticism of blind religious faith. It may however be interesting to learn that it is from one of the poems of a Tamil Siddha called Śivavākkiyar who is believed to have lived in the ninth century AD.

Thousands of such songs expressing radical ideas were composed by a group of mystics called the Siddhas (Tamil: Cittar). Composed in folk-song metre, Siddha songs are widely popular among people of all strata of society and hence are often sung even by those who do not understand their essential meaning and context.[1]

However, to date no single critical edition of these songs has been attempted, nor any serious study made of the Siddhas or their poetry.

*The translations in this essay are by Kamil Zvelebil, Jesudasan and Jesudasan, and K. Kailasapathy; some are mine.

[1] Beggars sing songs like *nanta vanattilōr āṇṭi* (Kāṭuveḷiccittar, 4) while begging without even understanding the high philosophical truth hidden in such simple verse. A music concert or a *bharatanatyam* dance will not be considered complete without a piece from Pāmpāṭṭicittar or Paṭṭinattār such as snake dance with the song *nātar muṭi mēlirukkum nākappāmpē*.

A few edited collections of Siddha poems have however been published, the earliest of these being the *Periya Ñānakkōvai* of Ramalinga Mudaliar (1899) in two volumes.[2]

No authentic or historical material is available on the life of the Siddhas, although most sources agree that there were eighteen Siddhas. Mystics from a number of countries, e.g. China, Egypt and Sri Lanka, and different religions (Piru Muhammadu was a Muslim) are also included in the traditional list of Siddhas.[3]

Many of the Siddhas belonged to low caste groups such as shepherds, temple drummers, artificers, robbers, potters, fishermen and hunters. In the caste order they were well below the *brāhmaṇas* and *Vēḷāḷas* (agriculturists), who, along with the *Vaṇigar* (merchants) constituted the higher castes in early medieval and medieval South India, i.e. sixth to seventeenth centuries AD.[4] However, one or two *brāhmaṇas* and *Vēḷāḷas* are also listed among the Siddhas.

It would be extremely difficult to provide a definitive chronology of the Siddhas or their precise dates. It may, however, be noted that Tirumūlar, the earliest of them, is believed to have lived in the second half of the seventh century AD. Attempts have also been made to date the others in the ninth to tenth centuries and after, primarily on the basis of the style and content of their songs.

Siddhas in their songs used not the classical, refined or literary language but that spoken by the common man, adopting the folk-song style. For instance, the poems of Pāmpāṭṭi-c-cittar or 'the snake-charmer Siddha' are modelled on the songs of the professional snake-charmers. It may be suggested, in this context, that the language of the Siddha poems is similar to that of the Tāntric texts, which has been described variously as 'twilight language', 'intentional language', etc.,[5] and is equally applicable to Siddha poems.

The majority of the Siddha poems seem to be composed in a metrical

[2] Other editions are: M.V. Venugopalapillai (ed.), *Cittar ñānakkōvai*, Madras. Originally published in 1947 and reprinted in 1956. Aru Ramanathan (ed.), *Ñanakkovai ena vaḷankum cittar pāṭalkaḷ*, 2 vols, Madras, 1987. Orig. pub. 1959.

[3] Aru Ramanathan, 1987.

[4] K. Kailasapathy, 'The Writings of the Tamil Siddhars', *in* Karine Schomer and W.H. McLeod (eds), *The Sants—Studies in a Devotional Tradition of India*, Berkeley Religious Studies Series, Berkeley, California, 1987; rpt., Delhi, 1987, p. 391.

[5] Mircea Eliade, *Yoga, Immortality and Freedom*, trans. from French by Williard R. Trask, Bollingen Series LVI, Princeton, 1958. Originally published in French as *Le Yoga, Immortalite et Liberte*, Paris, 1954, p. 249.

form known as *cintu*. Akappēy cittar, Kutampaiccittar, Iṭaikkāṭṭuc-cittar, Aḻukaṇi cittar and some other later Siddhas employed this metre in their poems. *Kummi*, a poem composed in a metre meant for the *kummi* dance, and *kaṇṇi* are some of the other metrical forms used,[6] and these forms remain popular to this day. *Kaṇṇi* (two-line stanzas) used by the Siddhas seem to share similarities with the *doha* verses one encounters in Tāntric literature.[7] Such 'pithy stanzas are initiatic lyrics in which the mystic, with a terminology understandable only by his brethren, sings of his ecstasies and hints in devious terms at his laborious and blissful conquests'.[8] This remark about Tāntric literature is equally appropriate for the poems of the Tamil Siddhas. Zvelebil aptly describes the language of the Siddhas. He says that the diction is often enigmatic, mysterious, hidden, full of ambiguous symbols and double meanings but the language the text employs in its syntax and lexicon is more often than not almost vulgar. At any rate, it is simple colloquial idiom, close to the speech of the masses. However, the meanings of the verses are not easily comprehensible to the uninitiated.[9]

The Siddhas were those who 'understood liberation as the conquest of immortality.[10] Some Tamil texts describe Siddhas as those who have attained knowledge.[11] They draw a distinction between the Siddhas and the *bhaktas*; the former have been described as those who have realized the Supreme Being and the latter as those who strive to see Him through the path of *bhakti* (devotion).[12] It is generally believed that those who have attained *siddhi*, 'magical power', by practising *aṣṭāngayoga* are Siddhas.[13]

Siddha non-conformism is often expressed in their external appearance and attitudes. They resembled madmen, roaming about at will,

[6] Kailasapathy, 1987, p. 403.

[7] Ibid., pp. 405–6.

[8] Guiseppe Tucci, *Tibetan Printed Scrolls*, Rome Libreria Dello Stato, 1949, p. 226, as cited in Kailasapathy, 1987, p. 406.

[9] Kamil V. Zvelebil, *The Poets of the Powers*, London, 1973, p. 21.

[10] Eliade, 1958, p. 302.

[11] *Tirumantiram* of Tirumular, vs. 1446; *Cittar civañānam eytiyayvare, Tiruvācakam*, 614.

[12] Campantar, 463; Cuntarar, 7768, T.P. Meenakshisundaram, 'Cittar' in *Tamil Kalaikkaḷañciyam*, Madras, 1960, vol. 4; pp. 643–4.

[13] *Cornta en yokattār cittar camātiyōr, Tirumantiram*, 1447; *yokacamāti ukantavar cittare, Tirumantiram*, 1490.

scantily clad, and eating whatever they were given. Paṭṭinattār picturesquely describes them in one of his songs:

There is the loincloth for my dress,
And for my pillow the outer porch,
To eat areca nuts and leaf,
Cool water to drink.
For the cool mist there are rags,
There is rice in every house,
Just beg and eat.[14]

Roaming about like a ghost,
Lying down like a corpse,
Eating whatever is available,
Like a stray dog.[15]

Mystics in many cultural traditions have emphasized the necessity of detachment. The Siddhas also emphasized this aspect, achieving their isolation and worldly detachment through their crazy behaviour that invited the censure of their fellow humans. The state of detachment is a necessary ingredient of Jainism, Buddhism and also Upaniṣadic thought. The Pāśupata doctrine also lays emphasis on such a state. 'He should go about like an outcaste [ghost?] [*preta*].' 'He should appear as though mad, like a pauper, his body covered with filth, letting his beard, nails and hair grow long, without any bodily care. Hereby, he becomes cut off from the respectable castes and conditions of men *and the power of passionless detachment is produced*'[16] [emphasis in the original].

The Siddhas are believed to have written some medical texts, their system known as *cittavaittiyam* or Siddha medicine. Among the Siddhas, Tēraiyar, Pokar, Roma Rṣi, and Puli Pani are reputed to have been great healers. The Siddhas' preoccupation with medicine and alchemy is understandable and may be attributed to their quest for perfect health and immortality. Their goal, the attainment of immortality, salvation, and perfect health in this life, is common to all Tāntric Siddhayoga.

Though some Siddhas (Pāmpāṭṭiccittar for instance) speak contemptuously about the body, the Siddhas generally reflect the idea that the body is a necessary instrument for achieving their goal and it should therefore be well preserved. 'The body is no longer a source of pain and temptation but the most reliable and effective instrument of man in his

[14] *Paṭṭinattār Tiruppāṭal Tiraṭṭu Potu*, 15.

[15] Ibid., 35.

[16] David N. Lorenzen, *The Kapalikas and Kalamukhas: Two Lost Saivite Sects*, Delhi, 1972, p. 188.

quest to conquer death and bondage. Since liberation can be gained even in this life, the body must be preserved as long as possible, and in perfect condition'.[17] Tirumūlar asserts this point time and again:

Mistakenly I had believed the body to be imperfect,
But within it I realized the Ultimate Reality.[18]

Elsewhere Tirumūlar describes the divine nature of the human body and says it is the actual abode of God:

The mind is the sacred chamber,
The physical body is the temple,
For my gracious Lord the mouth is the tower gate,
The enlightened ones know the soul to be Śiva's *linga*,
The guileful senses are truly lamps that illuminate.[19]

The Siddhas were all basically theists and believed in a transcendental God. However, they were not devotees in the sense of idol-worshippers. In this context it may be mentioned that the recurrent use by the Siddhas of the term *civam*, a neuter form of an abstract noun signifying goodness and auspiciousness is very significant. Instead of the common term *civan* (masculine noun), their choice of the abstract noun civam makes it clear that they believed in an abstract idea of Godhead. In the North Indian *bhakti* tradition, this abstraction has been described as *nirguṇi bhakti*.

Siddhas in general were anti-ritual, anti-ceremonial, anti-caste and opposed to orthodoxy. They were rebels to the core. At the same time, there is emphasis on right conduct, moral behaviour and character in almost all the Siddha texts, which is absent in the poems of the *bhakti* poets. The Siddhas insist more on purity of character than external purity. Tirumūlar states that it is the duty of the kings to punish those who swerve from their duties.[20] Śivavākkiyar, a powerful poet, employs such expressions as *cālākkar*[21] for 'wicked men', *poyyar*[22] or 'liar' for hypocrites, and their worship as *caṟpaṇai*[23] or 'hypocrisy' in his poems. Some Siddhas decry hypocrisy in the name of Siddhism and also denounce the habit among some Siddhas of consuming opium.[24]

[17] Zvelebil, 1973, p. 31.
[18] *Tirumantiram*, 725.
[19] Ibid., 56.
[20] Ibid., 247.
[21] Śivavākkiyar *Pāṭal*, 242.
[22] Ibid.
[23] Ibid.
[24] Kāṭuveḷiccittar *Pāṭal*, 24; Śivavākkiyar *Pāṭal*, 516.

THE TAMIL SIDDHAS

1. Tirumūlar

Chronologically, Tirmular was probably the earliest of the Siddhas, assigned to the second half of the seventh century. He was the greatest exponent of Tāntric Yoga in South India.

Tirumūlar's work known as *Tirumantiram*, consists of 3000 quadrains divided into nine *tantras* that discuss *tantra, āgama, mantra*, and *yoga*. He refers also to *bhakti* and sings the glory of Śiva. Though he sings the glory of Śiva, he stresses the need to realize God within. Internalization of God, according to him, is superior to the external ceremonial worship of God.[25] In contrast to *bhakti* literature, there is an almost total absence of any cult of a local deity in his poems.

2. Śivavākkiyar

The next great Siddha in point of time is Śivavākkiyar, who may have lived in the ninth century. He was a powerful poet, a great mystic, and foremost of the Śivayogis. His *Śivavākkiyar pāṭalkaḷ*, consisting of 526 quadrains, is perhaps the longest written by a Siddha, next only to Tirumūlar's *Tirumantiram*.

He is one of the greatest rebels against the brahmanical order of things. He denounces the *brāhmaṇa*, the authority of the *Vedas*, and the *Āgamas*. He scoffs at idol worship and temple ceremonies, and is strongly opposed to the caste system and all forms of orthodoxy. He mocks local customs and his attack on all these is very blunt and direct. Though his poems are similar to those of Tirumūlar, they were ignored and perhaps even suppressed by the established tradition that laid stress on temple worship and ritual. Whereas the *Tirumantiram* has been included in the Śaiva canonical texts (*Paṉṉiru Tirumuṟai*), Śivavākkiyar's *Pāṭalkaḷ* seems to have been destroyed. Even as late as the end of the nineteenth century AD, W. Taylor observes, 'I was told the ascetics [*Paṇḍāram*] of the Śaiva class seek after copies of the poem [i.e. *Civavākkiyar Pāṭal*] with avidity and uniformly destroy every copy they find'.[26]

Śivavākkiyar's poem has also been charged with being vulgar. Though there is an element of unsophisticated bluntness in his poems

[25] *Tirumantiram*, 1823.

[26] *A Catalogue raisonne of oriental manuscripts*, 2 vols, Madras, 1857–62, cited in Zvelebil, 1973, p. 20.

taken as a whole, there is no vulgarity in his poems as they do not result in an unwholesome excitement of the mind as do some verses of the *Tiruppukaḻ* of Arunagirinathar.[27]

3. Paṭṭinattār

Paṭṭinattār is more popular than either Tirumūlar or Śivavākkiyar. It is believed that there were two poets bearing the same name. One, whose poems are included in the *Tirumuṟai*, is the earlier and probably lived in the tenth century; the other, the greatest Siddha, lived probably in the fourteenth or fifteenth century. There are striking differences in their poems. While the earlier poet uses literary Tamil and his poetry is in the high style, the later one, the Siddha, frequently adopts common colloquial speech in the manner of the folk-song.[28] The earlier Paṭṭinattār has sung the glory of the temple, and the importance of visiting and worshipping in many temples. He shows clear affinity with the *bhakti* hymnists. Though he is not counted among the 63 canonized Śaivite saints, his poems were included in the eleventh book of the Śaiva canon. The later poet, like any other Siddha, is a man in revolt against brahmanical customs and rituals.

4. Pattiragiṛiyār

A contemporary and pupil of Paṭṭinattār, according to popular legend, he was a king who renounced his kingdom and was converted to Siddhism by the latter. His name appears to be a Tamilized form of Sanskrit Bhartṛhari or Bhadragiri. He composed 237 stanzas which go under the name *Meyñānappulampal* or 'Lamentations (craving) for True Knowledge'. His lamentations show utter frustration and disgust, and a longing for peace and deliverance. In his ideas about religion, ritual, and caste, he is nearer to Śivavākkiyar than to Paṭṭinattār, his *guru*.

THE LATER SIDDHAS

The four Siddhas dealt with above are said to have belonged to the hymnal period, i.e. from the sixth to the tenth centuries. It is generally believed that the later Siddhas lived in the sixteenth and seventeenth centuries. Nothing definite is known about them. Even their names are a mystery and seem to be derived from a special refrain associated with

[27] A.V. Subramanya Iyer, *The Poetry and Philosophy of the Tamil Siddhars*, Chidambaram, 1969, p. 49.

[28] Zvelebil, 1973, p. 26.

their poems such as those of Pāmpāṭṭi, Akappēy and Kutampai, *āṭu pāmptē* (dance of snake), *akkappēy* (the human mind addressed as a ghost) and *kutampāi* (addressing a girl wearing an ear-ring) respectively. They, like early Siddhas, were believers in *yoga* and protesters against the then existing religious practices and social life.

5. Pāmpāṭṭicittar

The most popular and well known of all Tamil Siddhas is Pāmpāṭṭicittar (The Snake Charmer Siddha). His poem has the refrain *āṭu pāmpē* 'O Snake, do thou dance' concluding each stanza of his poem. His work consists of 129 verses. He is perhaps the most outspoken of all the Siddhas, ridiculing idol worship, the *Vedas*, the *Āgamas* and other scriptures and denouncing caste. He is egoistic and boasts of the immense power of the Siddhas.

6. Iṭaikkāṭṭuccittar

According to tradition, he belonged to the Iṭaiyar or cowherd caste. His poem, composed in 130 stanzas, is in the form of a dialogue between two shepherds, Tāṇṭavarāyakkōnār and Nārāyaṇakkōnār. He stresses that God is within and need not be sought elsewhere and he denounces *japa, tapa*, *manṭra*, etc.

7. Akappēycittar

His poem is in the form of an address to the human mind which is characterized as ghost (*pēy*). His work consists of 90 stanzas presenting mystic and yogic ideas in the simplest language possible.

'He picturizes the development of the Universe to a total nihilism resulting in accepting Pure Void (*cūnyam*) as the only reality.'[29] Unlike other Siddhas he believes that even *yoga* will not bring salvation,[30] and believes that realized souls do not aspire even for salvation (*mōṭcam*).[31]

8. Kutampaiccittar

In his poem, the Siddha addresses Kutampai, 'a girl wearing an ear-ring'. This poem consists of 32 stanzas. Each stanza concludes with the refrain *Kutampāi*. In this poem, the Siddha describes the condition of a realized soul, summarizing the outlook and the philosophy of the Siddhas admirably in simple and symbolic language. The ultimate reality

[29] Zvelebil, 1973, pp 109–10.

[30] Akappey cittar *Pāṭal*, 35.

[31] Ibid., 82.

as conceived by him is *veṭṭaveḷi*,[32] 'plain, clear light' or '*uyar veḷi*'[33] 'the highest light'. *Veḷi* or '*light*' (also 'void) is the term generally used by the Siddhas for the Ultimate Reality. According to him realized souls do not require or hanker after worldly possessions and material comforts.

9. Kāṭuveḷicittar

His poem consists of 34 stanzas. It is in the form of an address to his own mind. This poem is largely concerned with advice on moral subjects. He denounces drinking liquor and consuming opium[34] which suggests that the Siddhas were in the habit of drinking and consuming opium.

10. Aḷukuṇi or Aḷukaṇiccittar

His work has 32 verses. It may be more appropriate perhaps to call him *aḷakaṇiccittar*, 'a Siddha who has composed his verses with beautiful figures of speech' than by his traditional name, as his Tamil is rich in beautiful figures of speech with great emotional appeal.

The Siddhas' attitudes towards society and religion are best expressed by Śivavākkiyar:

> What does it mean—a pariah woman
> What is it—a brahmin woman!
> Is there any distinguishing mark
> (number) in flesh or skin or bone?
> Do you find any difference
> When you sleep with a *paṛiah* or
> brahmin woman?[35]
>
> In bricks and in granites,
> In the red—rubbed *lingam*,
> In copper and brass
> Is Śiva's abode
> That is what you say
> and you are wrong.[36]
>
> What is temple! What are bathing pools!
> Oh slaves, you worship in temples and bathing tanks!

[32] Kutampaiccittar *Pāṭal*, 1; Kāṭuveḷiccittar *Pāṭal*, 10.
[33] Kutampaiccittar *Pāṭal*, 11.
[34] Kāṭuveḷiccittar *Pāṭal*, 29.
[35] Śivavākkiyar *Pāṭal*, 38.
[36] Ibid., 34.

Temples are in the mind and bathing
pools in the mind.[37]

Then and now you ate no fish, are there
not fish in the water you bathe and drink?
Then and now you ate no venison
Is not the thread on your bosom
made of deerskin?[38]

Then and now, you ate no mutton,
Do you not perform your sacrifices
with sheep's flesh?[39]

The chanting of the four *Vedas*
The meticulous study of the sacred scripts,
The smearing of the holy ashes,
And the muttering of prayers,
Will not lead to the Lord!
Let your heart melt within you, And if you
can be true to yourself,
Then you will join the boundless light,
And lead an endless life.[40]

You dumb fools performing the rituals,
With care and in leisureliness,
Do Gods ever become stone?
What can I do but laugh.[41]

The songs of Śivavākkiyar quoted above illustrate his attitude and mode of his expression, and the same can be found in the writings of almost all the Siddhas. Their poems are a grand remonstrance against virtually everything that was held sacred. The Siddhas were implacable opponents of the caste system and the respectability to which it gave rise.[42]

Socio–religious Background of the Tamil Siddhas

In early historical Tamiḻakam (*c.* 200 BC to AD 200), tribal forms of religion and worship prevailed in different *tiṇais* or ecozones. The worship of the folk deities with offerings of blood and toddy went on side by side with the performance of Vedic sacrifices, the latter mainly confined to the *marutam* zone or the plains (river valleys) where the three ruling families—Cēra, Cōḻa and Pāṇṭiya—rose to power. Buddhists and Jains

[37] Ibid., 33.

[38] Ibid., 154. [39] Ibid., 155.

[40] Ibid., 36. [41] Ibid., 126.

[42] Subramanya Iyer, 1969, pp. 47–8.

were found in considerable numbers in different parts of Tamil Nadu, particularly the coastal region and trading centres, following their practices without any hindrance.[43]

It would appear that the Buddhists and Jains gained influence and considerable following and patronage in the post-third-century AD period, i.e. during the period of the Kaḷabhras, who are believed to have subverted the earlier Tamil polities of the Cēras, Cōḷas and Pāṇṭiyas. The popularity of Jainism and Buddhism created a situation of conflict and rivalry for royal patronage. The sectarian movements of the Śaivas and Vaiṣṇavas in the post-sixth century AD period, represent a sharp reaction to the 'heterodox' religions, from which they claim to have released the country and 'revived' brahmanical religion. Even members of the ruling class like Mahendravarman, the Pallava ruler of early seventh century AD and prominent *bhakti* saints like Tirunāvukkaracar, popularly known as Appar, are believed to have originally been followers of Jainism and subsequently to have returned to the brahmanical fold, i.e. Śaivism. It was in this period that the Tamil region witnessed the growth, on the one hand, of an intensive emotional *bhakti* to Śiva or Viṣṇu and on the other, of an outspoken hatred of Buddhists and Jains.[44]

Amongst the Āḻvārs, Tirumankai (eighth century AD) was the greatest opponent of Buddhists.[45] Tirumankai's hymns express a direct antagonism to both the Jains and Buddhists. Toṇḍaraṭippoṭi's intolerance of Buddhism and Jainism[46] was nearly as great as that of Tirumankai. Tirumaḻicai attacks not only Jains and Buddhists but also Śaivites.[47] Tiruñānacampantar was the greatest opponent of Jainism. During his time it is believed that the Pāṇṭiya country was dominated by Jain influence, and that it was Campantar who converted the king and his subjects to Śaivisim after foiling all their conspiracies against him and vanquishing them in debate.[48] The Pallavas and Pāṇṭiyas, it is claimed, contributed to the success of the 'revivalist movement' by extending their patronage to either Śaivite or Vaiṣṇavite sects. Subsequently, the Cōḷas became the great force behind this revival of brahmanical religion.

Bhakti poets are said to have visited temples and 'sung' the glories of the presiding deities of these temples. As the Nāyanārs and Āḻvārs

[43] K.A. Nilakantha Sastri, *A History of South India*, 4th edn, Madras, 1975, pp. 422–3.

[44] Ibid., p. 423.

[45] *Periya Tirumoḻi*, II, 1, 5; 6; I, 5.8.

[46] *Tirumālai*, 7, 8.

[47] 'The Jains are ignorant, the Buddhists have forgotten God; the Śaivites are small men', *Nānmukan Tiruvantāti*, 6.

[48] Nilakantha Sastri, 1975, p. 424.

employed popular speech in their soul-stirring compositions, their songs became very popular. The temples at which these *bhakti* poets sang acquired sanctity. These poets are said to have undertaken a tour of all the important centres of pilgrimage in South India, singing and dancing, thus creating a sacred geography for the movement.

The construction of temples began roughly during the Pallava–Pāṇṭiya period, i.e. seventh to ninth centuries, and gained momentum and reached its culmination during the Cōḷa period (ninth to twelfth centuries). The Cōḷas are known to have constructed a large number of temples. Though the earlier ruling dynasties instituted grants for worship at and maintenance of temples, it was during the Cōḷa period that temples were institutionalized, becoming thereby the centre of all social and economic activities.

The temples, which were centres of huge *brahmadeya* or *brāhmaṇa* settlements as well as non-*brahmadeya* settlements, acquired a position of central importance in the local government;[49] and as 'landed magnates'[50] and 'big employers',[51] the temples played a crucial role in the organization of society and economy.

In the process of development of the temples as the institutional base of brahmanical Hinduism, *brāhmaṇas* and other landowners who controlled temple property, and *brāhmaṇa* priests who officiated at services, emerged as a dominant group. As such, it has been argued that the *bhakti* movement was essentially a temple movement seeking to propagate the ideology of upper caste landowners.[52]

This leads to an important question as to whether the *bhakti* movement was really a protest movement. If so, then another question arises, namely what were *bhakti* poets protesting against? Were they against casteism, or rituals or ceremonials of the temples? It is said that the *bhakti* poets were largely drawn from the lower castes. As devotees, no distinction was made amongst them and no caste hierarchy was observed. As a member of the family of the devotees (*toṇṭar kulam*) everybody was considered equal.

[49] Kesavan Veluthat, 'The Temple Base of the Bhakti Movement in South India', *in* Krishnamohan Srimali (ed.), *Essays in Indian Art, Religion and Society*, Indian History Congress Golden Jubilee, vol. 1, Delhi, 1987.

[50] D.N. Jha, 'Temples as Landed Magnates in Early Medieval South India (AD 700–1300'), *in* R.S. Sharma (ed.), *Indian Society: Historical Probings*, New Delhi, 1974, pp. 202–16.

[51] R. Nagaswamy, 'South Indian Temple as Employer', *Indian Economic and Social History Review*, II, 1965, pp. 367–72, cited in Veluthat, 1987, p. 155.

[52] Veluthat, 1987, p. 155.

It may be mentioned that in the corpus of *bhakti* literature there is not even a single instance reflecting hostility to caste or the existing order as in the writings of the Siddhas or the works of the *sants* of North India. However there are some references in the legends woven around the life of the devotees to the conflict between the devotees and the *brāhmaṇas* (as their masters or temple priests) when the former were denied permission by the latter to visit the temples and have a *darśan* of their favourite deity enshrined in these temples. Such instances are very few (e.g. Nandanār a Śaivite devotee, and Tiruppāṇāḻvār a Vaiśṇava saint). Chronologically these are later legends and they only to go show the devotee's wish to participate in worship in a temple, i.e. an individual's aspiration to attain salvation, i.e. equality only in the religious sphere.

The *bhakti* period witnessed the construction of a large number of temples and the introduction of the Āgamic mode of worship in these temples. With the introduction of Āgamic worship the *brāhmaṇas* engaged in priestly functions in temples acquired high ritual status, while the others, ritually less pure, came to be assigned lower ranking, leading to the emergence of a hierarchy around the temple based on brahmanical caste relations.[53]

In the early phases of the *bhakti* movement, we notice the intolerance of the *bhakti* poets towards heterodox religions, leading to rivalry for royal patronage. As the popularity of Buddhism and Jainisim waned, the movement virtually became a part of the establishment by the beginning of the tenth century. The role of the Āḻvārs and the Nāyanārs and their peregrinations ended. They were replaced by the Ācāryas who were *brāhmaṇas* and ritualists.[54] It is moreover claimed that the *bhakti* movement helped in the consolidation and extension of classical Hindu society[55] associated with *varṇāśramadharma*. All these would point to the fact that the *bhakti* movement was not a protest against caste consciousness. Nor was it against the ritual or ceremonial as these elements were a product of the same *bhakti* cult. In view of the evidence being contrary, we may conclude that it was not a protest movement though some elements of dissent are noticeable.

To sum up, the *bhakti* movement resulted in the emergence of

[53] Burton Stein, *Peasant, State and Society in Medieval South India*, Delhi, 1980, p. 84.

[54] M.G.S. Narayanan and Veluthat Kesavan, 'Bhakti Movement in South India', *in* D.N. Jha (ed.), *Feudal Social Formation in Early India*, Delhi 1987, p. 372. Reprinted from S.C. Mallick (ed.), *Indian Movements: Some Aspects of Dissent, Protest and Reform*, Simla, 1978.

[55] Narayanan and Veluthat, 1987, p. 348.

brāhmaṇas and other members of the upper castes as powerful groups and in the construction of a large number of temples with the introduction of the Āgamic mode of worship, which in turn brought into being elaborate rituals.

This was the social context within which the Siddhas composed their poems. The early Siddhas were contemporaneous with the hymnists and the later ones lived after the *bhakti* period.

The Siddhas of North India

The Siddhas of Tamil Nadu were not an isolated or unique body of non-conformists but an integral part of a pan-Indian tradition. All Yogins who have attained perfection by practising *yoga* were called Siddhas. The Buddhist Sahajiya Yogins of much renown were honoured with the epithet 'Siddhācārya' and the apostles among Nāth Yogins are also called Siddhas.[56]

The Nāth cult is essentially a Yogic cult and appears to represent a particular phase of the Indian Siddha cult. Nāth Yogins were non-conformists. They strongly opposed caste distinction and held ritual purity in contempt. They were basically monotheists and believed in the all-pervading Godhead as Paramasiva or the invisible Satguru.

The Nāth Yogis, a type of Śaiva ascetics who bear resemblance to the ancient Kāpālikas, are also known as Gorakhnāthi Yogis after the name of their foremost Guru Gorakhnāth, and also as 'Kān phaṭa Yogis' on account of their slit ears.[57] It is of particular interest to note that in almost all the lists of Tamil Siddhas, Gorakhnāth appears as one of them. The Nāths are generally considered to be nine in number, though some of their names also appear in the list of eighty-four Siddhas.

Both the Siddhas and the Nāths were exponents and propagators of Tāntric or Haṭhayoga. The most important feature common to all schools of esotericism is the culture of the body (*Kāya sādhana*) through the process of Haṭhayoga. They practised this Yogic *sādhana*, as they believed that they could make the body perfect (*siddhadeha*) and immutable, thereby attaining an immortal spiritual life. Escape from death through the perfection of the body was regarded by these yogins as the highest achievement. Their overriding goal is *jīvanmukti* or

[56] Shashibhushan Dasgupta, *Obscure Religious Cults*, Calcutta, 1976 (Orig. ed., 1946), p. 202.

[57] Charlotte Vaudeville, *Kabir*, vol. I, Oxford, 1974, p. 86.

liberation in life, and it is this state of liberation that connotes immortality. As a pre-eminently Śaivite school, the state of *jīvanmukti* according to this belief is virtually the same as the attainment of the state of Maheśvara.[58]

In general the Siddhas challenged the established religious and social order, and denounced the exterior manifestations of religious practices such as elaborate sacrifice, idol worship, and pilgrimages to holy places. Like the Tamil Siddhas, they also employed a language that could be understood only by the 'initiated'.

The Voice of Dissent: Its Various Forms

The earliest trace of heterodoxy and criticism in the history of religious thought is to be found in the *Araṇyakas* and the *Upaniṣads*. The religion of the *Samhitās* and the *Brāhmaṇas* was pre-eminently sacrificial in its practical aspect, with innumerable accessories of ceremonies and rituals accompanied by the recitation of Vedic hymns. It is in the *Upaniṣads*, for the first time, that one notices the dissenting voice against the performance of sacrifice. The *Upaniṣads* raise the question whether these sacrifices and rituals are capable of leading the sacrificer to a state of immortality, thus denying the efficacy of Vedic sacrifices. Maitreyi, the wife of the famous sage Yajnavalkya, exclaims, 'What shall I do with that which will not make me immortal?'[59] The stress in the *Upaniṣads* is on the realization of *Brahman*, i.e. identity between the individual soul and the Supreme Being, which it is claimed, could be achieved by meditation. Thus, in the *Upaniṣads*, ritualism and sacrifice began to be replaced by meditation.

The Pūrva Mīmāmsa school is the only one (among the brahmanical schools of thought) that strongly supported the sacrificial ritual. The Yoga school of thought emphasizes the need for yogic *sādhana*, which is essentially a process of disciplining the mind within a moral context. From the very nature of *yoga* proper, it is evident that it has no scope for idolatry, ritual, or ceremonial.

The Tāntric schools (both Hindu and Buddhist) are antagonistic to the orthodox school throughout. The Hindu *Tantras* have the same kind of apathy towards caste distinction or *vạrṇāśramadharma* of the *brāhmaṇas* as the Buddhist *Tantras* have against monasteries. The principal emphasis of the Tāntrics was on the practical side of religion, i.e. on

[58] Dasgupta, 1976, p. 221.
[59] *Bṛhadāraṇyaka Upaniṣad*, 24.

yoga. They discouraged much reading and scholarship, such knowledge being of little use to them.[60]

These schools are theistic. The severest attack on the *brāhmaṇas* and their rituals came from the atheists, of whom the Cārvākas, Buddhists, and Jains deserve special mention. The Cārvākas (materialists) are generally spoken of as Lokayatas in early texts. The Cārvākas resolutely defied the authority of the scriptures. According to them, religion is nothing but a ruse devised by cunning priests to earn their livelihood.[61]

The Buddhists were strongly opposed to the caste system and the *varṇāśramadharma* of the brahmanical religion. It is well known that the heterodox religious faiths, such as Buddhism and Jainism, were against sacrificial religion. The Sahajiyas (Buddhist) held that *sahaja*, 'nature', is the *mahāsukha* 'perfect bliss', and this 'nature', according to them is neither definable nor accessible to our mind nor expressible by speech. As the Brahman is to be realized within, so also, this sahaja nature is to be understood within (*svayamvedya*). According to the *Upaniṣads*, when one realizes the self as Brahman there is neither the knower (*jñāta*) nor the knowable (*jñeyam*) nor the knowledge (*jñāna*). This Upaniṣadic principle has been adopted by the Sahajiyas in speaking of the sahaja state. In Tāntric parlance sahaja is practically identical with *mahāsukha*, 'perfect bliss'. This state is largely considered to be a kind of Absolute or Transcendent Reality and as such is equated with the 'void' or *sūnya*.[62] It may be mentioned that the Tamil Siddhas have also expressed exactly the same idea and the term they employ for the Transcendent Reality is veḷi or veṭṭa veḷi which denotes 'void'.

Sant, meaning 'one who knows the truth' or one who has experienced Ultimate Reality is the designation given to the poet–saints belonging to the distinct though related devotional *bhakti* cults—the first is the sectarian group of Vaiṣṇava poet–saints who flourished in Maharashtra from the thirteenth to the eighteenth centuries AD—devotees of the God Viṭṭhala or Viṭhoba; the second is the group of poets of the Hindi-speaking area from the fifteenth century onwards—the believers in a Supreme God conceived as beyond all qualifications *nirguṇa*.[63]

The Sants refused to accept the authority of the *Vedas*, rejected the

[60] Dasgupta, 1976, p. 68.

[61] Ibid., p. 69.

[62] Vaudeville, 1974, p. 125.

[63] Karine Schomer, 'Introduction: The Sant Tradition in Perspective', *in* Schomer and McLeod (eds), *The Sants*, p. 3.

priestly prerogatives of the *brāhmaṇas* and opposed the outer forms of devotion and propagated the devotion which is generally known as nirguṇi *bhakti*. They were against caste hierarchy and the great majority of the leading figures in the tradition were from the lower castes.

In many ways the Sants are closer in spirit to the 'heterodox' religious traditions of India—the Buddhists, Jains, and the esoteric Śaivite traditions of the Nāth Yogins—than they were to the 'orthodox' Vaiṣṇava devotional religion. We notice a striking similarity between the ideas of the Sants and theme of the Tamil Siddhas. The northern Sants led by Kabir 'reject the *Veda* altogether and make fun of all Vedic teaching, rituals and knowledge. The brahmin's pretensions to perfect purity and his obsession with pollution are turned into ridicule by Kabir'.[64]

Protests, conflicts, dissent and criticism are not uncommon in the religious history of India. Such a critical approach to religion began to appear for the first time in the *Āraṇyakas* and the *Upaniṣads* in North India and continued to provide a parallel tradition throughout. Such trends can be noticed in South India too, but there is no evidence of the continuity of a counter tradition as in the case of North India.

In the Tamil Sangam texts of the early historical period there is no evidence of the universalization of godhead. In the Sangam situation the multiple folk and popular forms of worship are reflective of different eco-situations and their specific cult needs coexisting with northern

[64] Vaudeville, 'Sant Mat: Santism as the Universal Path to Sanctity', *in* Karine Schomer and McLeod (eds), 1987, p. 24.

Hey Pandit! Beware of that water
You are drinking! BI S'abda [47]
Oh Fools, you bathe in the river morning and evening
What will the toad which is in the
river morning and evening attain [117]
Oh, fools you bathe daily saying 'Pollution' 'Pollution' [*tumai*]
Don't you know that your body
itself is formed by the accumulation of *tumai* [menses] [464]
You drink water and spit it
in order to cleanse from *eccil*
When the mouth remains where does that *eccil* go?
Is it not the mantra you
recite your mouth's *eccil* [saliva?] [456]
You call the water in your mouth *eccil*.
How is it then, that which you
munch in your mouth
you call *Veda* [39]

Sanskritic forms derived from Vedic and epic-Purāṇic traditions. The *bhakti* period (seventh to eleventh centuries) is marked by rivalry and hatred towards the Jains and Buddhists, and the emergence of the *bhakti* cult of the Purāṇic Śaiva and Vaiṣṇava sectarian movements. It has been mentioned earlier that the *bhakti* movement led to the 'revival' of brahmanical religions and the emergence of *brāhmaṇas* and members of the other upper castes as powerful groups. 'By feigning to admit the low born into their ranks and treat them on a par with the higher groups, these sects wanted to take the edge away from the Jain propaganda that only Jainism stood for a society of equals. In practice, however, the *śūdra nāyanār* continued to suffer as ever, from social disabilities.'[65] It is thus rightly argued that the *bhakti* movement was 'counter-productive'.[66]

Hostility to caste consciousness is a normal feature of Tāntric worship. Tāntric worshippers show antagonism to orthodoxy. Several sources attest to the presence of Kāpālikas and similar Tāntric ascetics in South India. The most important South Indian source is *Mattavilāsa prahasana* (a farce) written by the Pallava ruler Mahendravarman. Appar, a Nāyanār, and a contemporary of Mahendravarman, refers to Kāpālikas, Pāśupatas, Mahāvratas, and Śaivites.[67] Another Śaivite *bhakti* poet Campantar mentions certain other temples known by the name Kārōṇam[68] (Skt.: Kāyāvarohaṇa), evidently named after the birthplace of Lakulisa, the founder of the Pāśupata sect.[69] It is believed that the Kāpālikas originated in South India or the Deccan.[70] They were influential in south India between the eleventh and thirteenth centuries.[71]

The Kālāmukhas were an important sect originating in Mysore from the larger and more ancient body of the Lakulīśa Pāśupatas in the eighth century, and spread to Tamil Nadu and Andhra Pradesh in the ninth and tenth centuries. The early Siddhas, who are believed to have lived in the hymnal period, were also contemporaries of the Kāpālikas and the Kālāmukhas who were Tāntric worshippers. Tirumūlar, the earliest of

[65] C.V. Narayana Ayyar, *Origin and Early History of Saivism in South India*, Madras, 1936, pp. 122–206, cited in R.N. Nandi, 'Origin and Nature of Saivite Monasticism: The Case of Kalamukhas', *in* R.S. Sharma, 1974, p. 197.

[66] Veluthat, 1987, p. 157.

[67] *Tēvāram aṭankanmuṟai*, vs. 4358.

[68] Campantar, *Tēvāram*, vs. 1971.

[69] T.P. Meenakshisundaram, 1965, p. 65.

[70] Lorenzen, 1972, p. 53.

[71] Nandi, 1987, p. 190.

the Siddhas, is believed to have come from Kashmir, and the earliest work on Tāntric *yoga* in Tamil was written by him. We notice a striking similarity between the Siddhas of Tamil Nadu and the Nāth Yogis, Sahajiyas, and the Sants of North India in their attitude towards society and religion. All of them believed and practised Tāntric Yoga in order to attain their goal, i.e. immortality in this life. Siddhism is not a phenomenon unique to Tamil Nadu, but what is interesting is its sudden appearance there and the lack of evidence of its continuity. It is also curious that their ideas had hardly any influence on society despite the writings of powerful Siddhas such as Śivavākkiyar. *Bhakti* poets were successful in getting patronage from the rulers and were also able to captivate the common people with their soul stirring songs and create a mass following; the Siddhas, on the other hand, were unable to influence either the rulers or the people and thus were marginalized. They were considered religious *pañcamas* (outcastes) by the orthodox. The religious orthodoxy of the *bhakti* tradition proved to be more influential with the kings and upper castes as its supporters. The Siddhas' fiery onslaught on social inequality and ritualism was therefore unable to make an impact or to shake off the influence of the *bhakti* cult, nor were their yogic teachings influential. Tāntric worship was not a monopoly of the Siddhas but was also undertaken by the Kāpālikas and Kālāmukhas. The extinction of these sects may be attributed to their marginalization as 'unconventional' religious practitices and to their absorption or integration into the mainstream of the *bhakti* tradition.

APPENDIX

The author's translation in English of Select Songs of Śivavākkiyar

1

How many flowers you plucked and threw in the past?
How many *mantras* you muttered in vain?
How much water you threw when you roamed about as a fool?
How many Śiva temples you went round?
ñānis who realized where God dwells,
Who can understand their excellence?
Those who realized Him do speak nothing but of Him
Do not salute wherever they see a temple or god [26]

2

You break the stone into two
Stamp on the one you place at the entrance,
Place a wreath and pour water
On the stone you instal for worship,
Tell which stone is appropriate for god [420]

3

The deity fashioned out of wood and stone,
The deity fashioned out of leaf stalk of plantain or coconut tree,
The deity fashioned out of cloak or turmeric or cowdung,
All these are nothing but bright light [511]

4

Adorning a planted stone with a few flowers as if it were god,
What is that *mantra* which you
mutter going round [it],
When the God is within you, does the
stone ever speak?
Will the cooking vessel or ladle
know the taste of curry? [497]

5

Stone, silver, copper, iron
out of the alloys of these base metals
different shapes were fashioned and
forms shaped of almighty gods
and in praising them
Do you think one will attain
perfect happiness?
no, no, no, no [528]

6

On fools, you do *Pūjā* repeatedly,
When the *Pūjā* itself is within you where
Did it accept *Pūjā*?
Did the beginning accept *Pūjā*?
Did the end accept *Pūjā*?
What was that which accepted *Pūjā*
Tell what it is [35]

7

Brick, black stone, red linga,
Copper and the other base metals
You say Śiva resides in these metals
After you realize yourself
The omnipresent god will sing and dance within you [34]

8

If a buffalo and a cow mate,
the young ones [born of this]
are born with the features of the species.
If the reciter of the
Vedas [brahmin] and a *pulaicci* [low caste woman] mate
How is it that the children
born of such union
show no difference? Tell [458]

9

Loin-cloth, sacred thread, and tuft
Were all these born along with you?
Did the four *Vedas* which you forget,
appear in your mind? [188]

10

Even f the four *Vedas* you
recite till you get tired,
Even if you smear the sacred
ash all over the body and babble
foolishly, the Supreme Being will not be there,
When you are able to tell the
truth by melting your heart and unite with it
Then only you can merge with that broad light [86]

11

You recite the four *Vedas*, you do not know *ñāna*,
Oh sinners, like the ghee mixed in milk, you do not know,
When Śiva whose neck has the mark of poison is within,
What you speak of Kālan [Yama],
That does not exist even in dream [15]

12

Sāma and other *Vedas* and all the *Śāstras*
Even if you recite well, you do not understand Śiva [19]

13

By reading the scriptures repeatedly you have become blind,
Oh fools, you look at the sun directly while you pray,
Knowing Him if you meditate on him,
Every one will become pure as mentioned [525]

14

Reciting the *Vedas* will be a waste in the world.
Is it necessary to run to distant places to worship
When *ādināthan* is within us
Is there any need for cow worship or the *Veda* [504]

15

Wearing earrings you bathe in each and every lake,
You do not remove the filth in your mind like the frogs
If you are capable of placing
Śiva, the holder of skull, in your mind,
you will be the happiest one [491]

16

Oh poor people, you go in search of bathing *ghats* in order to bathe,
Which place is suitable for bathing
tell after knowing it clearly.
After you realize that which is within you as *tīrtha*
That which is *tīrtha* is only the five lettered Śivāya [63]

17

Oh wicked ones, you run in search of *tīrtha*, *linga* and *mūrti* (deity),
You realize that *tīrtha* and *linga* are within you,
Once you realize that tīrtha and linga are within you,
You yourself become *tīrtha* and *linga* [480]

18

Oh poor ones, you keep away from *eccil*!
Is it not the semen [*eccil*] which transforms into pure body?
Is not honey, the bee's saliva,
Is not flower contaminated by the bee's saliva?
Is not milk mixed with the saliva of the calf. [479]

[*eccil*: 'Saliva, spittle, anything defiled by contact with mouth, refuse of food, leavings, excretion form the body as faeces, urine, semen, etc.]

19

You drink water and spit it in order to remove *eccil*,
When the mouth remains, where does that *eccil* go?
Is not the *mantra* you recite the *eccil* of the mouth?
When you realize the Supreme Being,
What is that which you think *eccil*? [456]

20

The water which springs in your mouth, you say *eccil*,
How do the *Vedas* you munch in your mouth, become a blessing
You who drink water to remove the *eccil* of your mouth
Tell how this *eccil* of your mouth goes? [39]

21

It is the monthly cycle [*tumai*]
Is it not the *tumai* [menses], [which]
When it stops, shapes into a body?
What is *nādam*, *Veda*, or good family?
These are created by the *brāhmaṇa* who recites the *Vedas* [131]

22

You take bath daily in the river
saying *tīṭṭam* [impurity]
Is not the body itself formed out of accumulation
of *tīṭṭam* [menses]? [463]

23

Oh, the village folk, all of you join together
placing the copper inside the chariot and draw it
Ādicittanātar who is beyond comprehension
see how people ridicule Him [237]

24

The slothful sluggards say that He is far, far away,
But the Supreme Being is spread everywhere on earth and heaven,
O poor dumb ones, running stunned and suffering through
villages, cities, and forests.
He is right there within you, stand still and understand Him [14]

25

He is not Hari, He is not the Lord Śiva,
He is the Ultimate cause
In the beyond of beyond

Transcending the Blackness, Redness, and Whiteness,
He is not big, He is not small, Try to understand,
He is Infinite Distance, transcending even quiescence [*turiya*] [9]

26

Milk does not return to the udder, nor butter to the butter-milk;
Nor the life within the sea-shell, if it breaks, to its body;
The blown flower, the fallen fruit, do not return to the tree;
The dead are not born, never, never, never [46]

6 From Devotion and Dissent to Dominance: The Bhakti of the Tamil Āḻvārs and Nāyanārs

R. CHAMPAKALAKSHMI

The *bhakti* of the Tamil Āḻvārs and Nāyanārs has been the theme of many scholarly works studying the concept and its impact from various standpoints, namely *bhakti* as a cult under the broad rubric of the development of religion in South India, or as an important element in the sectarian Purāṇic religions, or as the focus of a debate on the nature of bhakti as a protest/dissent against caste hierarchy, status, and privileges. Recent studies have examined the concept, its origins, varied contexts as well as its content, both metaphysical and emotional. Works that dwell upon the rich poetic and aesthetic appeal of *bhakti* literature are also known. Despite the availability of an impressive volume of published literature on the subject, fresh insights may still be gained from a study of the *bhakti* hymns, the nature of the concept and its social impact, its ideological significance, and institutional developments in early medieval Tamiḻakam.

This essay* is an attempt to study *bhakti* as a concept evolving first in the hymns of the Vaiṣṇava Āḻvārs, subsequently in those of the Śaiva Nāyanārs, growing into an instrument of protest or dissent against

*This essay is a revised version of one of the two lectures delivered at various Indian Universities under the UGC National Lectures Scheme in 1979 and a paper presented at the 31st International Congress of Human Sciences in Asia and North Africa, Tokyo, 1983. See Proceedings of this Congress published in 1984 (Tokyo), vol. II, ed. Yammo Tatsuro.

brāhmaṇa orthodoxy, existing social norms and inequalities, developing into an ethical/moral principle capable of evolving new value systems, and thus providing the basis for the emergence of a dominant ideology[1] that was to ultimately become the ruling ideology at the hands of powerful dynasts and elite groups, with immense capacities to sustain and revitalize itself during situations of crises.

1

You people
who have gone there to worship,
the name Irunkuṉṟam
has spread far and wide
on this great bustling earth
it boasts fame in ages past
for it is the home of the dear lord
who eradicates delusions
for people who fill their eyes
with his image

[*Paripāṭal*, 15, trans. Norman Cutler, 1993.][2]

Addressing mortals on the earth the poet of this verse from the *Paripāṭal*, a Cankam classic, praises Mālirunkuṉṟam (Tirumāliruñcōlai or Aḻakarmalai near Maturai) as the best of all earth's mountains as it is the god's abode on earth. The *Paripāṭal* introduces us to a new era in Tamil culture, a new milieu to Tamil religion and worship, namely the temple, which was to become one of the major symbols of South Indian tradition. *Bhakti* or devotion appears here for the first time as the central concept, which was to be later developed more fully by the Āḻvārs (and Nāyanārs), and elaborated in the exegesis of the Vaiṣṇava and Śaiva canonical texts of medieval times. The work also brings into Tamil religion the idea of an absolute or universal godhead—Māl/Māyōn/Viṣṇu and Murukan—and his abode, the temple, which was to become the most innovative focus of Tamil life and culture.

The *Paripāṭal* is classified as one of the eight Cankam anthologies (*eṭṭuttokai*), but yet stands apart from the others on account of its religious content and character, somewhat alien to the anthologies. Dated by all serious students of Cankam literature somewhere between the

[1] In this essay 'dominant ideology' is used strictly in its dictionary sense/meaning.

[2] *See* A.K. Ramanujan and Norman Cutler, Bardwell L. Smith (ed.), *Essays on Gupta Culture*, Delhi, 1983, pp. 177–214.

period of the anthologies and the *bhakti* or hymnal literature, i.e. in about the fifth–sixth centuries AD,[3] it has more in common with the late Cankam collection, *Kalittokai*, and the epic *Cilappatikāram*. Together these works belong to a transitional phase in Tamil religious and cultural traditions. Standing on the threshold to a new form of poetry, i.e. the *bhakti* hymns, the *Paripāṭal* shows evidence of Vedic, Upaniṣadic and Purāṇic influence, and as has been admirably shown by Friedhelm Hardy's study[4] of emotional Kṛṣṇa *bhakti*, reveals the meeting point of northern Sanskritic devotional themes with the *akam* (interior/love) as well as *puṟam* (exterior/war) themes of Cankam literature. It marks a new synthesis and leads to the intensely powerful emotional *bhakti* in Āḻvār poetry, which derives its principal motifs from the Māl (Viṣṇu) hymns of the *Paripāṭal*.

Bhakti as a concept may also be recognized in another late Cankam text, the *Tirumurukāṟṟuppaṭai* (guide to Murukan), which speaks in exaltation of the idea in relation to the worship of Murukan. Like the *Paripāṭal*, it also speaks of the specific association of a place/places and shrines for the deity. Significantly, Śiva, one of the central deities of the Purāṇic religion, receives only marginal attention and is grouped as one of the five great gods in the *Kalittokai*,[5] none of them being the pre-eminent one. Śiva, it may be pointed out, was not one of the *tiṇai* deities of the Cankam, as Māl and Murukan were of the *mullai* (forest) and *kuṟiñci* (hilly) *tiṇais* or eco-zones.

The *Paripāṭal* and *Tirumurukāṟṟuppaṭai* would thus seem to represent the transition from the worship of tribal or folk deities of the anthologies to the universalization of godhead and the evolution of formal religious systems, which under the Pallavas and Pāṇṭiyas of the seventh to ninth centuries AD became crystallized as the Purāṇic Vaiṣṇava and Śaiva religions. It was a new regional synthesis of Purāṇic forms in which the northern Sanskritic elements assumed a dominant position while the local or folk cults and their deities either got

[3] The chronology for Early Tamil Classics adopted in this essay are based on the following works:

Kamil V. Zvelebil, *The Smile of Murugan: On Tamil Literature of South India*, Leiden, 1973. Idem., *Tamil Literature, A History of Indian Literature*, Jan Gonda, vol. X, Wiesbaden, 1974; George L. Hart III, *The Poems of Ancient Tamil: Their Milieu and Their Sanskrit Counterparts*, Berkeley, 1975; Friedhelm Hardy, *Viraha-Bhakti: The Early History of Kṛṣṇa Devotion in South India*, Oxford, 1983.

[4] Friedhelm Hardy, 1983.

[5] *Kalittokai*, vs. 26 and 94. *See* R. Champakalakshmi, *Vaiṣṇava Iconography in the Tamil Country*, New Delhi, 1981, p. 42.

completely merged or remained major components of the Purāṇic pantheon. The concept of *bhakti*, drawing largely upon the *akam* or love theme of Cankam poetry, was systematically developed initially by the Āḻvārs and subsequently by the Nāyanārs to carry these Purāṇic forms to the Tamil masses in their own idiom, namely an 'intensely human religious awareness'[6] and in the vernacular, namely Tamil.

The idea of the temple as the focus of this devotional cult emerges in the above two works, but is again crystallized and promoted in the *bhakti* hymns. This is not to say that shrines or centres of worship were unknown to the Cankam Tamils. Such cult centres did exist, as is known from the references to *kōyil* and *nakar*, apart from the *kantu* (pillar) and *potiyil* (common place)[7] for purposes of worship. What was absent was the institutionalization of such centres for the promotion of a formal religious system.

Āḻvār and Nāyanār *bhakti* brings several strands together, the typical Cankam Tamil humanism, anthropocentric religion, emotional and sensual character of worship, and the northern brahmanic/Sanskritic concept of a transcendental absolute (monotheism), together with several mythological structures. The *Purāṇas* and *Āgamas* would seem to have provided the major myths and iconographic forms that find constant mention in the hymns. Under sectarian Purāṇic influence, the brahmanical religion became polarized into the Vaiṣṇava and Śaiva. While Viṣṇu, the first major deity of this religion was the Māl/Māyōn of the Cankam milieu, Śiva, as has been pointed out, was only of marginal importance in the same milieu and is not even mentioned in the *Tolakāppiyam*, the earliest known grammar, which systematically explicates all important concepts and symbols. It was Murukan, the god of love and war of the Cankam *kuṟiñci tiṇai*, who provided a major component to the Śaiva pantheon, as the son of Śiva. With Koṟṟavai, the deity of the *pālai tiṇai* (arid zone) being identified with Durgā and as the consort of Śiva, the basic elements in Purāṇic Śaivism had become established in the Tamil region by the seventh century AD.

Bhakti thus arose as a sophisticated expression, i.e. in singing the praise of god and as an emotional seeking of union with the absolute, symbolized by the temple image. The development of this concept is traceable through various stages in Āḻvār poetry, dominated by emotional Kṛṣṇa *bhakti*. The three early Āḻvārs who have been dated in the

[6] F. Hardy, 1983, pt III.

[7] *Paṭṭinappālai*, 49, 57; *Puṟanāṉūṟu*, 51, 78.

pre-seventh-century period, i.e. about fifth to sixth centuries AD, express a simple form of devotion[8] and appear to be more preoccupied with the intellectual than the emotional aspects of *bhakti*. The early Āḻvār *bhakti* has also been characterized as a special form of theistic *yoga* derived from the *Bhagavad Gītā*,[9] a relatively calm expression of adoration, service, and loyalty; a personal experience of intimacy with and dependence on god. The three early Āḻvārs seem to follow the *āṟṟuppaṭai* (guide) poems of the Cankam, which praise the patron by describing his country, applying the nature landscape—the beauty of the temple and its environment—to the praise of god. While the temple is the centre of their religion in a generic sense, they refer to Vēnkaṭam (Tirupati), Mallai (Māmallapuram), and Tirukkōvalūr as three important locales of Viṣṇu worship.[10] Their geographical environment is thus confined to northern Tamiḻakam, with Vēnkaṭam as the spiritual centre.

The development of *bhakti* reaches its culmination in Nammāḻvār (seventh century AD), in whose hymns the intensely powerful emotional *bhakti* supersedes all other religious attitudes and methods.[11] The notion of complete trust and surrender (*prapatti*) clearly emanates from Nammāḻvār, although it is more fully developed only in the Śrīvaiṣṇava theology of the twelfth to thirteenth centuries.[12] With Tirumankai Āḻvār (eighth century) *bhakti* acquires yet another meaning, through the concept of pilgrimage (*tīrthayātra*), which, it has been suggested, was intended to help in resolving emotional tensions. It also signifies the change from the poetic landscape to the landscape of the South Indian temple through the concept of pilgrimage.[13] It is only in the *Tirumaṭals* of Tirumankai that something like a systematic theory of *bhakti* has been recognized.[14]

Bhakti acquires yet another meaning, namely devotion to the true

[8] K.A. Nilakantha Sastri, *Development of Religion in South India*, Madras, 1963, p. 45.

[9] F. Hardy, 1983, pp. 282ff.

[10] The three early Āḻvārs were born in Kāñcīpuram (Poykai), Māmallapuram (Pūtam), and Mayilai (Pēy), and their hymns are devoted to the three Vaiṣṇava centres Vēnkaṭam, Māmallapuram, and Tirukkōyilūr. *See* R. Champakalakshmi, 1981, ch. 12 and the three Antātis of the first three Āḻvārs in the *Divyaprabandham*.

[11] F. Hardy, 1983, pp. 309ff. On *bhakti* in general and Nammāḻvār's *bhakti* in particular, *see* A.K. Ramanujan, 'Afterword' in his *Hymns for the Drowning: Poems for Viṣṇu by Nammāḻvār*, Princeton, 1981, pp. 103ff.

[12] N. Jagadeesan, *History of Srivaishnavism in the Tamil Country (Post Rāmānuja)*, Madurai, 1977, chs III and IV.

[13] F. Hardy, 1983, p. 400.

[14] Ibid., p. 388.

bhaktas and becomes more complex with Tirumankai and others like Kulacēkara and Toṇṭaraṭippoṭi, who followed him.[15] These Āḻvārs claim to be devotees of true *bhaktas*, 'carry' them on their heads, or claim to be the 'dust of the feet of the devotees' (*Toṇṭar-aṭi-p-poṭi*). Mathurakavi, who also belongs to the later phase of the Āḻvār movement emphasizes 'reverence to the ideal bhaktas'. Thus the notion of a community of *bhaktas* would seem to emerge along with the concept of pilgrimage.

Periyāḻvār or Viṣṇucitta (ninth century AD) creates a whole series of mythical folk-songs, through which *bhakti* is brought home, in a variety of ways, into the day-to-day existence of the people. In the poems of the mother and child likened to Yasoda and Kṛṣṇa,[16] composed by this *brāhmaṇa* Āḻvār, folk art and sentiment become interwoven with *bhakti*. In the hymns of Āṇṭāḷ, his foster daughter and the only lady saint among the Āḻvārs, the eroticism of Kṛṣṇa *bhakti* attains a new intensity in her love for Kṛṣṇa and her 'marriage' to god Ranganātha of Śrīrangam as expressed in the *Tiruppāvai* and the 'dream' poem *Nācciyār Tirumoḻi*.[17]

The idea of temple service as hereditary and professional, recurs in the hymns of both Viṣṇucitta and Toṇṭaraṭippoṭi,[18] echoing the Āḻvār concept of service to god/temple. In the hymns of Kulacēkara, *bhakti* itself becomes an ideal and an institution. In these later Āḻvār hymns Śrīrangam emerges as the new geographical and spiritual centre in the lower Kaveri valley[19] and continues so through the period of the later *ācāryas* of Śrīvaiṣṇavism to this day.

The *Bhāgavata Purāṇa* of the late-ninth and early-tenth centuries AD[20] marks the culmination of the *bhakti* ideal in its emotional form and renders in Sanskrit the religion of the Āḻvār.[21] It integrates all the different strands, Tamil and Sanskrit, but preserves its southern character as it derives its content and mythology from the vernacular sources, namely Āḻvār *bhakti* poetry, although it adopts the Purāṇic literary structure. This text even adopts the *Advaita* position, probably in response to the non-dualism of Śankarācārya, to reconcile *bhakti* with

[15] Ibid., pp. 371ff.

[16] *Periyāḻvār Tirumoḻi*, II and III.

[17] *Tiruppāvai* expresses the girl's desire to win Kṛṣṇa's favour and *Nācciyār Tirumoḻi* describes her (Āṇṭāḷ's) marriage with Viṣṇu as Ranganātha.

[18] *Tiruppallāṇṭu*, 8.1. and *Tiruppaḷḷiyeḻucci*.

[19] F. Hardy, p. 441.

[20] R. Champakalakshmi, 1981, p. 41; F. Hardy, 1983, pp. 48ff; For different dates taking it back to fifth century AD, *see* T.S. Rukmani, *A Critical Study of the Bhāgavata Purāṇa* (with special reference to *bhakti*), vol. LXXVII, Varanasi, 1970, pp. 9–14.

[21] R. Champakalakshmi, 1981, chs 3 and 6.

brahmanical orthodoxy.[22] Thus, it is said, the Āḻvār religion was finally made available to the rest of the Indian subcontinent through this *mahāpurāṇa*.[23] It also stands at the very beginning of a millennium of intensive speculation on Vaiṣṇava *bhakti* and the different schools of monistic and dualistic philosophies that arose in various parts of South India, and even Bengal and Mathura.[24]

The *bhakti* of the Śaiva Nāyanārs, like that of the Āḻvārs derives from both the religious humanism of the Cankam works and the influence of the northern Sanskritic traditions. However, there is no evidence in their hymns of a systematic development of the concept, as in the Āḻvār hymns. Theirs, indeed, is a given or received tradition, secondary and derivative,[25] equally emotional but less erotic than the Kṛṣṇa *bhakti* of the Āḻvārs, particularly of Nammāḻvār and Āṇṭāḷ. Like the *Divyaprabandham* (sacred collection) of the Āḻvārs, the *Tēvāram* of the Nāyanārs also represents a new synthesis of northern brahmanical traditions and regional Tamil traditions.[26] It also derives its theism, image worship, and temple-centred religion from the *Purāṇas* and *Āgamas*.

The meaning of the word *tēvāram* has proved elusive, and varied interpretations have been provided with no single interpretation being entirely satisfactory. It is derived from *Devagṛha* or god's house, and from *vāram* as a song addressed to a deity, hence *tēvāram*. It is also said to mean 'private ritual worship',[27] and is applied to the hymns because of their association with temple worship. Significantly, the word has also been used in a Jain context in a ninth-tenth century inscription, which refers to a niche (a shrine in sculpted relief) on a rock enshrining a Pārśvanātha image.[28]

Like the Āḻvār hymns, the *Tēvāram* adopts both the *akam* and *puṟam* structures, although it has been pointed out that it has affinities with the

[22] Krishna Sharma, *Bhakti and Bhakti Movement: A New Perspective*, Delhi, 1987, pp. 131ff.

[23] F. Hardy, 1983, pt V—*Bhāgavata Puṟāṇa*.

[24] Krishna Sharma, 1987, pp. 296ff.

[25] R. Champakalakshmi, 'Urbanisation in Medieval South India: The Role of Ideology and Polity', Presidential Address, Ancient India Section, 47th Session of Indian History Congress, Srinagar, 1986.

[26] Indira Viswanathan Peterson, *Poems to Śiva: The Hymns of the Tamil Saints*, Delhi, 1991, p. 5.

[27] *See* Francois Gros, Introduction ('Towards Reading the Tevaram'), *in* T.V. Gopal Iyer (ed.), *Tevaram, Hymnes Sivaites du Pays tamoul*, vol. I, Pondicherry, 1984, p. xxxix; Dorai Rangaswamy, *Religion and Philosophy of the Tevaram*, I, Madras, 1958, pp. 27–35.

[28] R. Champakalakshmi, 'An Unnoticed Jain Cavern near Madurantakam', *Journal of the Madras University*, vol. XLI, nos 1 and 2, Jan.–July 1969, pp. 111–13.

puṟam[29] rather than *akam*, for as *puṟam* or 'public poetry' it is used to praise a god manifesting himself in particular places and to celebrate a particular community. As heir to the *puṟam* tradition, the *Tēvāram* hymnists are said to describe the heroic deeds of Śiva, locate them in specific centres (the *aṭṭavīraṭṭānam* for eight heroic deeds) and the transfer of the Cankam idea of the king with sacred power to the deity in the temple—e.g. *iṟaivan* and *perumān*, or lord in the *kōyil* or temple. Śiva thus becomes the local hero to fit into the indigenous concept of the divine. Śiva sometimes even manifests himself at a shrine to protect it from major catastrophes like the cosmic flood.[30] While, in general, the *akam* conventions are less relevant to Śiva *bhakti vis-à-vis* the *bhakti* of the lover-god Kṛṣṇa, Māṇikkavācakar, the fourth important Śaiva saint incorporates *akam* themes in his *Tirukkōvaiyār*.[31]

Campantar's hymns (seventh to eighth centuries AD) are considered the most successful from the *bhakti* point of view,[32] as they, apart from their emotional significance, also establish Śiva as the local god and the transcendent deity. Campantar's hymns are also significant as extolling the idea of pilgrimage. On his peregrinations to various Śaiva shrines composing melodious Tamil hymns, he is said to have been accompanied by crowds of fellow devotees. A *pāṇar* or musician called Tirunīlakaṇṭa Yāḻppāṇar set his hymns to music (*paṇ*) and accompanied him on his journeys. Campantar also visited many Śiva shrines with his elder contemporary Tirunāvukkaracar (Appar), both of them drawing a large following of devotees.[33]

2

There has been a general assumption among historians and sociologists that the concept of *bhakti*, as expressed in the Āḻvār and Nāyanār hymns, initiated a movement of protest and reform particularly aimed at caste hierarchy and *brāhmaṇa* exclusiveness in Tamil society. This view represents an inadequate understanding of the hymns, the chronological position of the hymnists, both Vaiṣṇava and Śaiva, and the later

[29] I.V. Peterson, 1991, pp. 24, 34–6.

[30] *See* David Shulman, *Tamil Temple Myths: Sacrifice and Divine Marriage in the South Indian Śaiva Tradition*, Princeton, 1980, for myths relating to Śiva temples.

[31] *Tirukkōvaiyār*, 352–400. On the Theme of 'Separation on Account of a Prostitute'.

[32] I.V. Peterson, 1991, pp. 38–9.

[33] The stories of the Śaiva saints used in this chapter are from K. Vellaivaranan, *Panniṟu Tirumuṟai Varalāṟu*, 2 vols, Annamalainagar, 1972 and 1980.

hagiographical accounts about the hymnists and other *bhakti* saints, some of whose historicity is not beyond doubt. It also points to a lack of clear perspectives of the historical processes that made *bhakti* a major ideological force in the restructuring of economy and society with the brahmanical temple as its focus.

There was, admittedly, an element of protest or dissent in the Āḻvār and Nāyanār poetry, representing an attempt to provide avenues of social acceptance and even mobility to the less privileged castes and economic groups. A certain reformatory zeal characterizes some of the *bhakti* saints like Tirunāvukkaracar and Nammāḻvār, and the later *ācāryas* or religious teachers like Rāmānuja, who followed them. Yet, the movement itself does not reflect a popular character or a broad social base till at least the twelfth century AD. A related question is whether social reform was indeed the end result of the movement, and, if so, what kind of social change was achieved. An answer should be sought in the very contents of the *bhakti* hymns, the social groups propagating them, their objectives and, above all, the ideological implications of *bhakti* for the ruling families. Hence, if the hymns are read as registering a protest, it is important to see what they were protesting against or dissenting from. The hymns themselves provide ample evidence of the nature of protest or dissent, the social background of the hymnists who expounded *bhakti*, and their attitude to caste hierarchy.

The *bhakti* hymns are dominated by three major themes. Foremost among them is the idea of devotion to a personal god, i.e. *bhakti*, which has been discussed above. The second is a protest against orthodox Vedic Brāhmaṇism and the exclusiveness of the *brāhmaṇas* in their access to divine grace and salvation, i.e. an elitism in the religious sphere. The third is a vehement denunciation of the Jains and Buddhists as non-believers, heretics, and hence as 'heterodox'. It is the second theme, namely protest against orthodox Vedic Brāhmaṇism, that needs to be examined from the point of view of the social base sought by the exponents of *bhakti*. Hints of the struggle between the Tamil hymnists and orthodox Vedic *brāhmaṇas* are found in the poetry of Nammāḻvār, Toṇṭaraṭippoṭi, and Mathurakavi, and in the hagiography of the twelfth to thirteenth centuries, as, for example, in the story of Tiruppāṇāḻvār.[34]

In Toṇṭaraṭippoṭi, the antagonism to the Caturvedins (*brāhmaṇas* well versed in the four *Vedas*), who represented the *brāhmaṇa* establishment controlling the temple, is expressed in the following verse:

[34] F. Hardy, 1983, pp. 436–8.

You [= Viṣṇu] manifestly like
those 'servants' who express their love for your feet,
though they may be born as outcastes, more than
the Caturvedins who are strangers and without
allegiance to your service.

[*Tirumālai*, 42]

Mathurakavi (ninth century) says that the Caturvedins, the lords of the four *Vedas*, regarded him as vile and that he accepted only Nammāḻvār (a *Śūdra*), whose hymns represent a Tamil rendering of the *Vedas*, as his lord/teacher.[35] These are expressions of the solidarity of the *bhakta* community with their Tamil *Veda* against the orthodox Vedic *brāhmaṇas*. Hence, the opposition seems to be against orthodox religious attitudes. It stemmed primarily from the need to defend the *bhakti* tradition not by denying the superiority claimed by orthodox *brāhmaṇas* but by hailing the devotee's status as higher than even that of the *brāhmaṇa*.[36] In other words, to be a *bhakta* was more important than being a *brāhmaṇa*. Toṇṭaraṭippoṭi states emphatically that even those who recite the *Vedas* and know the six *angas*, if they speak ill of the devotee of Viṣṇu, are equal to the *pulaiyar* (outcastes). He further holds that even the Caturvedins become slaves if they are not devotees of Viṣṇu, whereas, even those actually born among the *kuṭis*, who work on the lands of others, are better than the *brāhmaṇas* (if they are *bhaktas*).[37] A similar idea is expressed much more directly in a hymn of Nammāḻvār, which says:

The four castes uphold all clans
go down, far down to the lowliest outcastes of outcastes [*caṇḍāla*]
if they are the intimate henchmen of our lord
with the wheel in his right hand,
his body as dark as blue sapphire
then even the slaves of their slaves are
our masters.

[*Tiruvāymoḻi*, III, 7.9]

The *Bhāgavata Purāṇa* only reiterates this position when it says that even a *caṇḍāla* or a *svapaca* (dog eater), who is a true devotee, is better than a 'virtuous' *brāhmaṇa* who has turned away from Viṣṇu's feet.[38]

The story of Pāṇāḻvār, a minstrel of low caste, being carried to the

[35] *Kaṇṇi-nuṇ-Ciṟu-t-tāmpu*, 4, 8.

[36] F. Hardy, 1983, p. 493.

[37] *Tirumālai*, pp. 39 and 43.

[38] *Bhāgavata Purāṇa*, VII. 9 and 10; X.23.

temple by a *brāhmaṇa* (*munivāhana*) implies such a struggle between the hymnists and the brahmanical temple establishment. The relation between the *bhaktas* and the *varṇa* system is represented here as one of tension, and its resolution lay not in the negation of caste but in an attempted synthesis as narrated in the hagiography.[39] If anything like a direct rejection of caste can be recognized in the Śaiva hymns, it is only in the hymns of Tirunāvukkaracar, popularly known as Appar, as in the following verse:

O rogues who quote the Law Books:
Of what use are your *gotra* and *kula* [clan]
Just bow to Māṟpēru's lord as your sole refuge.
[*Tirumāṟpēru*, v, 2.3]

Appar would worship even the 'leper with rotting limbs, the outcaste, even the foul *pulaiyan* who skins and eats cows, even these men, if they are servants of him who shelters the Ganges in his long hair' (Poem 211 in I.V. Peterson, 1991, p. 263).

Working on the early historical Tamil classics, Hart has pointed out that there were several kinds of *brāhmaṇas* in the Tamil area, each showing varying degrees of assimilation of the indigenous culture.[40] This is also reflected in the rivalry shown by the *bhakti* saints, some of whom were *brāhmaṇas*, against the Caturvedins or Vedic scholars and the *brāhmaṇas* who were temple authorities. That the Smārta *brāhmaṇas* (Vedic scholars and performers of Vedic sacrifices) are treated as superior to the Ādi Śaivas or Śaiva *brāhmaṇas* and *gurukkaḷs* or temple priests[41] is a well-known fact of Tamil society, and this may be traced to the process of acculturation and assimilation referred to by Hart and clearly recognizable in the *bhakti* hymns.

A major aspect of this process of acculturation relates to the creation of temples at various centres by royal and chiefly patrons, which meant, apart from new shrines, also the conversion of local cult centres into shrines of Śiva. The priests of such local cult shrines were evidently integrated into the new order of worship based on the *Āgamas* and the priestly group called Śiva-*brāhmaṇas* in the ninth to twelfth centuries would seem to be such newly initiated temple priests.[42] This class of temple priests later came to be distinguished from the more orthodox

[39] K. Zvelebil, 1973, pp. 190–9; F. Hardy, 1983, p. 478.

[40] G.L. Hart III, 1975, pp. 51–8.

[41] C.J. Fuller, *Servants of the Goddess: The Priests of a South Indian Temple*, Cambridge, 1984, ch. 3.

[42] R. Champakalakshmi, 'Ideology and the State in Medieval South India', Mamidipudi Venkatarangiah Memorial Lecture, Andhra Pradesh History Congress, Srisailam, 1989.

Smārta *brāhmaṇas* and Vaḍamas, i.e. followers of Vedic and Smṛti rites, with an inferior rank among the *brāhmaṇa* subcastes.

The caste and occupational background of the *bhakti* saints, if examined closely, would provide a useful insight into the nature of the 'movement'. The first three or early Āḻvārs (fifth to sixth centuries), whose historicity is uncertain, would seem to be elitist or scholarly and may be described as the Cāṉṟōr of the early Tamil texts. They were the first to come under northern, Sanskritic influences. Nammāḻvār, who stands between them and the later Āḻvārs of the eighth to ninth centuries AD was of the *Vēḷāḷa* community and hence a *śūdra*.[43] Along with Tiruppāṇāḻvār, the low-caste minstrel, he represents the two non-*brāhmaṇa* saints, whose hymns register protest against caste stratification in matters of worship and salvation. The stories of their birth are deliberately camouflaged in the later hagiographies, and hence their *Vēḷāḷa* and Pāṇa associations might well represent a conscious attempt to provide a low caste background and to create the myth of the social/religious revolt, when the *varṇa* system had become well-established or consolidated.[44] The birth of Tirumalisai Āḻvār is associated with the sage Bhārgava and an *apsara*, and being born as a mass of flesh he is said to have been abandoned in a bush, but due to the grace of Viṣṇu he was revived and brought up by a *Vēḷāḷa*. Tirumankai was a chieftain of Kaḷvar (robber) clan, Kulacēkara was a Cēra king, while Periyāḻvār, his foster-daughter Āṇṭāḷ, Toṇṭaraṭippoṭi, and Mathurakavi were *brāhmaṇas*. Even Nāthamuni (late tenth century), the first of the *ācāryas*, who 'discovered' the hymns through Nammāḻvār's *Tiruvāymoḻi* was a *brāhmaṇa*.[45]

The Śaiva *bhakti* saints, whose number came to be fixed at sixty-three by the twelfth century AD, were drawn from various social strata, from the *brāhmaṇa* to the *paṟaiya*. However, it is necessary to distinguish between those saints who composed devotional hymns propagating the *bhakti* cult and those who came to be canonized and included in the hagiographical works of the eleventh to twelfth centuries, namely *Tiruttoṇṭar tiruvantāti* and the *Periya purāṇam*. Even as early as the ninth century AD the *Tiruttoṇṭattokai* of Cuntarar, one of the *Tēvāram* trio, lists all the sixty-two Nāyanār before him. Some of them are known even to the first two hymnists, as, for example, Kannappa, the hunter

[43] F. Hardy, 'The Tamil Veda of a Śūdra Saint: The Śrīvaiṣṇava Interpretation of Nammāḻvār', *in* Gopal Krishna (ed.), *Contributions to South Asian Studies*, vol. 1, pp. 42–114.

[44] K. Zvelebil, 1973, 190–9; F. Hardy, 1983, p. 478.

[45] F. Hardy, 1983, pt 4.

(Appar, VI, 310; Campantar, III. 327), Caṇṭīśa (Appar, V. 73.5), Kōccenkaṇ, the Cōḷa king (Appar, IV. 40–65; Campantar, VII. 9, III. 276, 277; Cuntarar, VII. 98, and even Tirumankai, *Periya Tirumoḻi*, 6.6.8), Kulacciṟai, the Pāṇṭiya minister (Campantar, III. 378), and Tirunāḷaippōvār, the outcaste (Cuntarar, VII. 39.3), and others.

Only seven of the sixty-three Nāyanārs are credited with hymns, the most important among them being the *Tēvāram* trio. Appar, Campantar, and Cuntarar (seventh to ninth centuries) and Māṇikkavācakar, along with whom they constitute the group of four or Camayakkuravar Nālvar. Campantar and Cuntarar were *brāhmaṇas* and Appar, a *Vēḷāḷa*.[46] Māṇikkavācakar was a philosopher, an Ādi Śaiva *brāhmaṇa*, and the son of a minister at the Pāṇṭiya court in the ninth century AD. His avowed aim was to discredit Buddhism.

The Śaiva canon (*Tirumuṟai*) includes hymns composed by Kāraikkāl Ammaiyār, the lady saint (fifth to sixth centuries AD), by the Cōḷa king Gaṇḍarāditya (tenth century) and Karuvūr Tēvar, the royal preceptor of the Cōḷa Rājarāja I (eleventh century) apart from Cēramān Perumāḷ (ninth century), a Cēra king and friend of Cuntarar. However, their hymns do not form a regular part of the ritual singing in the temples. Only the hymns of Appar, Campantar, Cuntarar, and Māṇikkavācakar were assigned a special ritual status in the temples even as early as the tenth century AD. These four were the first to be apotheosized and worshipped from the tenth–eleventh centuries.[47] The rest came to be canonized only in the twelfth-century hagiographical work, i.e. *Periya Purāṇam*. Thus, with the exception of the seven hymnists and Kōccenkaṇ, a pre-imperial Cōḷa king, the other canonized saints are of doubtful historicity and the chronological muddle that surrounds them would lead to the suspicion that many of them were fictitious[48] and were added to make the number sixty-three, the number being directly borrowed from the sixty-three Salākapuruṣas of the Jain *Purāṇas*. Significantly, the historicity

[46] Campantar was a *brāhmaṇa* of Kauṇḍinya *gotra* from Sīrkāḻi (I.8.11), Cuntarar, a *brāhmaṇa* from Tirunāvalūr, calls himself the servant of the servants of the *brāhmaṇas* of Tillai (VII.9.1), and Appar was a *Vēḷāḷa* from Tiruvāmūr. *See* K. Zvelebil, 1975, pp. 138–44.

[47] Rājarāja I's inscriptions in Tanjavur refer to the making of the images of Śaiva saints. See, *South Indian Inscriptions*, vol. II. The *Tirumuṟaikaṇṭa Purāṇam*, dealing with the discovery of the hymns associates a Cōḷa ruler, identified with Rājarāja I, with the apotheosis of the three saints, Appar, Campantar, and Cuntarar. *See* K. Vellaivaranan, vol. 1, 1972.

[48] There are references to former sages and devotees as those 'who seek the lord's feet' and those 'who sing only of Śiva', etc. who are shadowy figures.

of even Tirumūlar, the greatest of the Tamil Siddhas, whose work *Tirumantiram* serves as the basis of the entire *Śaiva Siddhānta* canon, and whose canonization in the *Periya Purāṇam* was crucial in integrating the Siddhas into Śaiva tradition, cannot be established. The curious story of his origin making him a northern Siddha who came to south India and became a cowherd through an act of transmigration, may be taken as a pointer to the anxiety of the hagiographers to include people of low origins among the sixty-three Nāyanārs. This is true also of the stories of Kaṇṇappar, the hunter, and Nantan, the untouchable, apart from the potter, the washerman, the weaver, and the others of a similar social background who figure among the Nāyanārs.[49]

Those who collected the hymns and composed the hagiographies belonged to the *brāhmaṇa* caste, upper strata, and ruling families. Nambi Āṇḍār Nambi who collected the Śaiva hymns under the royal patronage of Cōḷa Rājarāja I[50] was an Ādi Śaiva *brāhmaṇa* and Cēkkiḻar, the author of the *Periya Purāṇam*, was a *Vēḷāḷa* and a minister in the court of Kulottunga II.[51] The propagators came primarily from the upper strata or castes, but the movement acquired a popular character with the canonization of members of the lower castes, untouchables, and unprivileged social groups. Interestingly, the *brāhmaṇa* remained the only medium through whom initiation into religion and salvation could be effected, as is revealed by the story of Nantan, the untouchable, whose purification through brahmanical rituals was necessary before salvation.

The third major theme in the *bhakti* hymns is their opposition to the Jain and Buddhist religions. The Āḻvār hymns express a profound reaction to the Jain and Buddhist ideologies, a feature much more pronounced in the hymns of the Nāyanārs, some of whom give vent to their animosity in unequivocal terms. Tirumankai's hymns, in which a systematic theory of *bhakti* can be recognized, reveal clear indications of the rejection of the Jain way of life and perception of the uselessness of their austere penance and self-mortification as a means of attaining salvation.[52] Tirumankai's *Periya Tirumaṭal* (7–9) says:

> But we know only from hearsay that person
> X at such and such a time obtained exactly
> this [*mokṣa*], by eating rotten fruit and dry leaves

[49] Vellaivaranan, vol. 2, 1980; K. Zvelebil, 1973, pp. 192–3.
[50] K.A. Nilakantha Sastri, *Cōlas*, Madras, 1975, rpt., p. 637.
[51] Ibid., p. 676.
[52] F. Hardy, 1983, p. 389.

by torturing his body . . . by exposing himself to
the heat of the sun. . . . We shall not correct
such people with stupid small minds who say
these things without being able to prove them.
[Trans. F. Hardy, 1983]

Toṇṭaraṭippoṭi expresses this opposition more directly by saying that it should be the duty of a devotee to chop off the 'heads' of the Jains and Buddhists if they speak ill of the lord (Viṣṇu). [*Tirumālai*, 8.]

Appar, one of the *Tēvāram* trio, laments his past associations with the Jains and expresses his gratitude to Śiva for having redeemed him from the sin of such association (IV, 39—Tiruvaiyāṟu; 100.1—Kacci Ēkampam; 102–Tiruvārūr). He says that the Jains are wicked, full of wiles and do not understand the truth, i.e. greatness of Śiva. The story of his persecution by the Jains and by their royal patron, identified with the Pallava Mahendravarman I[53] evoked Appar's response in several hymns, among which the following oft-quoted lines are significant:

We are slaves to no man
nor do we fear death
Hell holds no torment for us
We know no deceit
We rejoice, we are strangers to disease
We bow to none.
[V. 312.1, trans. I.V. Peterson, 1991]

Campantar was a crusader, and his denunciation of the Jains and Buddhists was instrumental in bringing about their decline at the royal court of the Pāṇṭiyas. He constantly refers to 'the false doctrines of the heretic Jain and Buddhist monks' (I, 75.10). The Jains, as also the Buddhists, are 'worthless, wily rogues, scantily clad, wicked' (I, 69; 130). At the Pāṇṭiya court, claims Campantar boastfully, the fire that the Jains aimed against him was instead directed by his prayer to afflict the Pāṇṭiya king as a disease, and by curing the king he established the superiority of Śaivism. (III.1.309; II.11.202). Campantar ridicules Jain names ending with the suffixes 'Sena' and 'Nandi' (III.4), and their habits of plucking out their hair, eating food standing, mutilating the good Sanskrit of the *Āgama* and *Mantra*, loudly declaiming (them) in the corrupt Prakrit tongue (III.2.297). Every tenth verse of his *patikam* (= *padya*) systematically abuses the Jains and the Buddhists. In Cuntarar's view, god condemned the stupid Jains and the stinking Buddhist monks

[53] I.V. Peterson, 1991, pp. 292–3.

to ignorance (VII.90.0). The metaphor of the human body as the temple (Appar, IV.76.4) and the emphasis on the use of the senses in the apprehension of the divine through acts of devotion also provided the much-needed justification of human existence, as against the Jain idea of self-mortification for salvation.

Thus the enemy was not brahmanical or Purāṇic religion but Buddhism and Jainism, 'alien' to Tamil culture. Hence, it is represented in their hymns that kings who had been seduced by the false doctrines of the Jains and Buddhists, were being rescued and brought back to the fold of the true religion.[54]

The *bhakti* hymnists were, at the same time, not negating the importance of the *Vedas* as scriptures. On the contrary, they were trying to provide the status of the *Vedas* to the Tamil hymns. This is nowhere as clearly stated as in the hymns of the most celebrated Śaiva saints Appar and Campantar. To Appar, Śiva was Sanskrit of the north and southern Tamil (VI.301.1), and it was he who gave the four *Vedas* to the world (I.100.9). To Campantar, Śiva was the *Veda* and the sacred word (II.148.1), the *brāhmaṇa*, who knew the four *Vedas* (II.147.1) and the six sacred sciences. It was through Śiva's grace that the *Vedas* were revealed to the young Campantar (I.75.11) who, hence, became well versed in them (I.4.11). Appar and Campantar hail as sacred the places where the *brāhmaṇas* lived, performed Vedic sacrifices; places which were filled with Vedic chants and the smoke of sacrifice (Appar, V.157; VI.216; Campantar, 312.1). Śiva chose such places as his abode, i.e. the temple. Several such settlements on the banks of the Kaveri are thus praised by Appar and Campantar; places which acquired temples to Śiva at various points of time under the Cōḷas between late ninth and twelfth centuries AD.[55]

The idea, hence, was to establish the Tamil hymns, both Vaiṣṇava and Śaiva, as scriptures, i.e. *maṟai*, equal to the *Vedas*, to invest the hymns with authority. In this respect, the Śrīvaiṣṇava teachers (*ācāryas*) were more successful in relating the Sanskrit Vedic tradition to Tamil Vaiṣṇava doctrine and practice[56] than the Tamil Śaivas. The latter could not directly relate their tradition to the Vedic Śruti or revealed literature. However, it has been shown that the Śaiva *patikam* exhibit a close

[54] Campantar, II.202–11, on the Pāṇṭiya king; I.V. Peterson, 1991, p. 12.

[55] *See* S.R. Balasubramaniam, *Early Cōḷa Temples*, Delhi, 1971; *Middle Cōḷa Temples*, Delhi, 1975; *Later Cōḷa Temples*, Faridabad, 1979.

[56] K.K.A. Venkatachari, *The Maṇipravāḷa Literature of the Śrīvaiṣṇava Ācāryas: 12th–15th Century AD*, III, Bombay, 1980.

similarity with the Sanskrit *stotra* or poems of praise, and their affinities with early Sanskrit litanies have been stressed (Campantar, II, 148.1). The 'Śatarudrīya' hymn in the *Yajur Veda* is said to be the most influential model of the *patikam*.[57]

It is significant that no commentaries were written on the *Tēvāram*, although the theologies of the Śaiva Siddhānta treated it as scripture and looked up to the Āgamic tradition rather than orthodox Vedic tradition as their metaphysical source.[58] The Śrīvaiṣṇava philosophers, on the other hand, not only wrote in Sanskrit but also evolved a scriptural tradition, in which both Āḻvār *bhakti* hymns (as *Drāviḍa Veda*) and their own philosophical formulations based on the *Vedānta* were related through powerful arguments, and thereby established the authority of the *Divyaprabandham*. The philosophy thus evolved by them represents the *ubhaya Vedānta*, i.e. both the Sanskrit and Tamil philosophical traditions.[59]

The sense of a community evolving around a sectarian theistic cult comes through strongly in both the Vaiṣṇava and Śaiva hymns. In the Śaiva context, the image of a community supersedes that of social hierarchy, the members of the community sharing their love/devotion for Śiva and his sacred shrines. Through ritual singing of hymns (*pāmālai* or garland of verses), ecstatic dancing, 'seeing' (*darśana*) and helping fellow devotees to gain Śiva's grace, it is said, the sense of communitas[60] increasingly binds or brings together people of varying social backgrounds. In the *puṟam* tradition, the hymns are regarded as public poems[61] calling the community to witness, giving a public dimension to the ways in which participation in this experience is made possible for all. Śiva is looked upon as a close kin, father, mother, uncle, aunt, lord, family, friend, etc. (Appar, VI.309.1).

The concept of pilgrimage added to the movement's growing strength by chalking out the sacred, cultural geography of that community dotted

[57] I.V. Peterson, 1991, p. 26; for the *Śatarudrīya*, *see* C. Sivaramamurti, *Śatarudrīya. Vibhūti in Śaiva Iconography*, Delhi, 1986.

[58] I.V. Peterson, 1991, pp. 53, 90; *also* Jean Filliozat, 'The Role of the Śaivāgamas in the Śaiva Ritual System', *in* Fred W. Clothey and J. Bruce Lony (eds), *Experiencing Śiva: Encounters with a Hindu Deity*, Columbia, 1983.

[59] F. Hardy, 1983, p. 480.

[60] I.V. Peterson, 1991, pp. 44–5; 'Communitas' is Victor Turner's term in the *Ritual Process: Structure and Anti-Structure*, Chicago, 1969.

[61] A.K. Ramanujan, 'Form in Classical Tamil Poetry', in *Symposium on Dravidian Civilisation*, ed. Andrée F. Sjoberg, pub. no. 1, Asian Series, Austin, 1971, p. 97; *also* A.K. Ramanujan and N. Cutler, 1983.

by Śaiva shrines. The Tamil countryside, the Tamil *paṇ* or music, communal singing and dancing derived from the early indigenous rituals of worship at Murukan shrines (*Paripāṭal*, 19), add a regional dimension to the movement. It has been mentioned earlier that the Tamil god Murukan gets a place of primacy in the Śaiva pantheon.

The emphasis in *bhakti* literature on ritual worship as highly meritorious and the temple as the house of god and the iconographic descriptions of the Purāṇic deities (Śiva and Viṣṇu) are closely related to the teaching and ethos of the *Āgama* and *Tantra*, which laid stress on temple and image worship.[62] It was not always a case of the hymnist 'seeing' an icon or sculpture in a specific locale and describing it in his poems,[63] but the reverse is true of many sculptural representations, which seem to be inspired by the hymns. The hymns were meant to popularize Śiva's forms either through complete descriptions or episodic allusions to Śiva's feats, thereby paving the way for introducing them in the temples, which were built subsequent to the hymnal compositions from the tenth to thirteenth centuries.

The most notable iconographic forms of Śiva constantly referred to in the *Tēvāram* are Śiva as a Yogi, i.e. Dakṣiṇāmūrti, Naṭarāja, Bhikṣāṭana and Rāvaṇānugraha (humbling of Rāvaṇa), and above all Lingodbhava.[64] The last one was particularly useful in establishing the cosmic character of Śiva, as the cosmic pillar or column of light, i.e. the *linga*, the beginning (head) and end (feet) of which could not be discovered even by Brahma and Viṣṇu, a theme which also at once subordinated the other two of the brahmanical trinity, Brahma and Viṣṇu to Śiva.

On the basis of the *brāhmaṇa* and *Vēḷāla* background of the hymnists, it has been suggested that the hymns indicate the closeness of the *brāhmaṇa* and *Vēḷāḷa*.[65] Undoubtedly, such an interpretation draws its inspiration from Burton Stein's theory of a *brāhmaṇa–Vēḷāḷa* alliance to demonstrate the peasant basis of society and polity (state) in medieval South India.[66] Further supportive evidence of this relationship is located in the cult leadership and the Śaiva sect's core constituency which were provided by the *Vēḷāḷas* or non-*brāhmaṇa* agricultural community and in the fact that although the Śaiva hymns and the *Śaiva Siddhānta* canon were composed and compiled by *Vēḷāḷas* and *brāhmaṇas*,

[62] Jean Filliozat, 1983.

[63] I.V. Peterson, 1991, pp. 95–6.

[64] *Tēvāram* Appar, V.209; Campantar, I.100.9; I.132.1.

[65] I.V. Peterson, 1991, p. 44.

[66] *See* B. Stein, *Peasant State and Society in Medieval South India*, New Delhi, 1980.

the heads of the sectarian Śaiva *maṭhas* were invariably *Vēḷāḷas*.[67] Even the language of Śaiva scriptures, i.e. Tamil and of the Vaiṣṇava scriptures, i.e. Tamil, Sanskrit, and Maṇipravāḷa, are said to closely relate to the differences that developed in the cultural milieu and caste orientation after the period of the *bhakti* saints, the Śaivas becoming predominantly *Vēḷāḷa* and the Vaiṣṇavas predominantly *brāhmaṇas*.[68] Such a view ignores the developments in Vaisnavism, especially after Rāmānuja, when the social base of Śrīvaiṣṇavism was widened to allow *śūdra* participation in temple rituals and administration after the reforms introduced by him in major Vaiṣṇava centres.[69] It also fails to see the parallel growth of a Smārta tradition after Śankarācārya, the *Advaita* philosopher, leading to the evolution of a *maṭha* organization in which the cult leadership was confined to the *brāhmaṇa* caste, particularly, of the orthodox Vedic scholars.

Śankara's *Advaita*, or non-dualism, had its roots in *Vedānta* or Upaniṣadic philosophy and represents a brahmanical philosophic thrust to the opposition to 'heterodoxy'.[70] His attempts to root out Buddhism and to establish Smārta *maṭhas*, particularly the one at Kāñcīpuram, were more in the nature of an emphasis on the importance of the Sanskritic/normative aspects of the brahmanical order and the upholding of the Smṛti tradition.

Śankara looked upon Śaiva and Vaiṣṇava worship as two equally important aspects of brahmanical religion. In a limited sense, his supreme *Brahman*, the universal soul, could be seen in either of the supreme godheads—Śiva or Viṣṇu. Indeed, Śankara scarcely addressed himself to the masses, his following being generally confined to the higher castes and the intellectual elite. Hence, temple worship played a secondary role in his scheme of religious experience. Monastic organization and preservation of Sanskrit scriptures were the two major aspects of the Śankara school, and although, according to tradition, these organizational efforts date from the time of Śankara himself, i.e. ninth

[67] M. Rajamanickam, *Śaiva Samaya Vaḷarchchi*, Madras, 1972 (2nd edn), chs 9, 11; R. Champakalakshmi, 'Growth of Urban Centres in South India: Kuḍamūkku Paḻaiyāṟai, the Twin City of the Cōḻas', *Studies in History*, vol. I, no. 1 (1979), pp. 15 (note 94) and 20.

[68] I.V. Peterson, 1991, p. 54.

[69] B. Stein, 'Social Mobility and Medieval South Indian Hindu Sects', *in* J. Silverberg (ed.), *Social Mobility and the Caste System in India: An Interdisciplinary Symposium*, Paris, 1966, pp. 78–94.

[70] *See* David N. Lorenzen, 'The Life of Śankarācārya', *in* F. Reynolds and D. Copps (eds), *The Biographical Process*, Paris, pp. 87–107.

century AD, there is hardly any reference to them in the more authentic epigraphic records till the post-thirteenth-century period,[71] that is, the fourteenth century onwards, in which a fresh wave of Sanskritization took place in South India, including Tamil Nadu, which may well be associated with the expansion of Vijayanagar authority.

Philosophical systems, such as that of Śankara and others, were successfully challenged by the 'institutional coherence and synthesis' attained by the *bhakti* tradition due to organized and collective action on the part of the ruling and landed elite of the Cōḷa period. These philosophical schools worked on a different plane, i.e. metaphysical theory and Sanskritic orientation, whereas the *bhakti* tradition worked at a popular level, with a local Tamil orientation.

The *Vēḷāḷa–brāhmaṇa* base of the Śaiva movement should be seen not as a mere caste phenomenon, and this may be perceived in the elitist character of the *Vēḷāḷa* landowners, i.e. agriculturally dominant *Vēḷāḷas*, who alone gained control over the temple and *maṭha* administration and landed property from the twelfth century, as against their sharing of a part of the control over temple lands and administration with the *brāhmaṇas* in the pre-twelfth-century period, i.e. tenth to twelfth centuries. As landowning members of the *Sabhā* of the *brahmadeya*, the *brāhmaṇas* played a predominant role in the period from the seventh to ninth centuries AD till the temple superseded the *brahmadeya* as an instrument of agrarian expansion and integration.[72]

The twelfth-century situation was one in which the *Vēḷāḷas* and other non-*brāhmaṇa* castes were gaining social importance *vis-à-vis* the *brāhmaṇas*, and hence the *Vēḷāḷas* achieved greater control over the temple and the *maṭha*, by giving a popular character to the Śaiva *bhakti* movement through the hagiographical tradition incorporating all lower castes into the Nāyanār list and thereby acquiring a wider popular base *vis-à-vis* other sects. It was this tendency that brought into Śaiva temple ritual and pantheon a series of local, popular, and folk forms in the post-twelfth-century temple tradition, the apotheosis of all the sixty-three Nāyanār being of central importance. The lower categories of agricultural classes and craftsmen, who were professionally and socially differentiated from the higher agricultural groups even among the non-*brāhmaṇas*, retained their earlier association with the 'subsidiary' elements in the brahmanical, particularly the Śaiva, pantheon. Hence, the lower castes among the non-*brāhmaṇas*, who professed allegiance

[71] R. Champakalakshmi, 1979, pp. 14–15.
[72] R. Champakalakshmi, 1986.

to Śaivism, still continued to follow rituals and worship centring on local and tutelary deities rather than major Purāṇic gods. Evidence on this point, which is crucial to an understanding of later-day Śaivism, is scanty, indirect, and largely inferential, based on later social developments and the fact that temples for the goddesses and 'minor' deities increasingly received patronage and centrality in the post-Cōḷa period.[73]

The notion of temple service manifesting itself in the Āḻvār and Nāyanār hymns is often likened to a feudal relationship,[74] i.e. between the god and the devotee, which is perceived as deriving from the chieftain–bard or patron–client relationship of Cankam society, and which is said to provide the model for the landlord–tenant or labourer, king–subject and the lord–servant relationships. Further, the references to *attāṇicēvakam* (royal service) in the later Āḻvār poetry are taken to indicate a court model underlying temple ritual and the old meaning of *bhakti*, namely loyalty.[75] The idea of Śiva as patron–king permeates the verses of Cuntarar, the Śaiva poet (VII, 34). The term *aṭiyār*, constantly used in the hymns to denote the servants of the temple, may also imply the idea of service and loyalty.

However, neither the theory of the *brāhmaṇa–Vēḷāḷa* alliance as the basis of a peasant society nor that of the feudal basis of Tamil society explains the complex processes through which resource mobilization and redistribution were achieved in early medieval Tamiḻakam, in which the temple enabled royal and chiefly families to establish their political presence and social dominance by intruding into the peasant regions known as *nāḍu*s. The temple, as the house of god, was of central importance not only for the development of the cult but its equation with the palace (*kōyil*) was also of crucial institutional significance in assisting the process of the simultaneous expansion of divine and royal authority by establishing the symbolism of the cosmos/temple/territory.[76]

3

Bhakti, it has been shown, is a crucial element in the evolution and spread of Purāṇic religion, which emerged by the sixth century AD as a universal and formal system in the Indian subcontinent as a whole. In

[73] B. Stein, 'Temples in Tamil Country, AD 1300–1750', *in* B. Stein (ed.), *South Indian Temples: An Analytical Reconsideration*', New Delhi, 1978, pp. 11–46.

[74] M.G.S. Narayanan and Veluthat Kesavan 'Bhakti Movement in South India', *in* D.N. Jha (ed.), *Feudal Social Formation in Early India*, pp. 347–75.

[75] F. Hardy, 1983, p. 460.

[76] R. Champakalakshmi, 1986.

the Tamil region, as elsewhere in South India, the expansion of Purāṇic religion is intrinsically linked with local and popular traditions and their interaction with brahmanical religion in a two-way process. It was a synchronic and at times diachronic evolution, which it would be too simplistic or facile to explain as the interaction between the 'Great' and 'Little' traditions, and one requiring a multidimensional model for correct explication.[77] It is the beginning of such a process that is seen in the *Paripāṭal* and *Tirumurkāṟṟuppaṭai* and reflected more fully in the *bhakti* hymns, in which the concept of *bhakti* progresses and simultaneously the Vaiṣṇava and Śaiva pantheons emerge.

The growth of *bhakti* into a dominant ideology may be historically demonstrated through the Pallava–Pāṇṭiya (seventh to ninth centuries) and Cōḷa periods (ninth to thirteenth centuries). The first two major brahmanical ruling families of the Pallavas and Pāṇṭiyas adopted Purāṇic religion, the northern normative Sanskrit tradition and together with their *brāhmaṇa* ideologues established the Purāṇic religion as the vehicle of propagating a 'cosmological world-view'. To some extent the three early Āḻvārs, who belonged to the Tirupati, Kāñcīpuram, and Māmallapuram regions, would seem to have inspired the Purāṇic temples, both rock-cut and structural, and their narrative sculptures which the Pallavas executed in their capital Kāñcīpuram and port-city Māmallapuram. Rājasimha's *magnum opus*, the Kailāsanātha temple, at Kāñcīpuram, derives most of its iconographic forms directly from the Śaiva *Āgamas*.[78] However, the most remarkable iconographic form, which they seem to have innovated, is the Somāskaṇda image, which appears as the cult object in the principal shrine, which combines Śiva with Murukan and Koṟṟavai (Durgā), the Cankam *tiṇai* deities. Their land grants[79] to the *brāhmaṇas* (*brahmadeya*) and the temples they built for Śiva and Viṣṇu, were directly inspired by the northern *Dharma Śāstras* and Purāṇic and Āgamic forms of ritual and worship. It is significant that no canonical temples, with the exception of the Parameśvara Viṇṇagaram in Kāñcīpuram,[80] owe their existence to the Pallavas or Pāṇṭiyas till the ninth century AD. In other words, no such temple was

[77] F. Hardy, 1983, p. 11.

[78] R. Nagaswamy, *Kailāsanātha Temple at Kāñcīpuram*, Madras.

[79] T.N. Subramanian, *Thirty Pallava Copper Plates*, Madras, 1966.

[80] Tirumankai Āḻvār refers to Parameśvara Viṇṇakaram in his hymns (*Periya Tirumoḻi*, II.9). On the basis of the chronology of the canonical temples, i.e. ninth century onwards, B.G.L. Swamy dates the *Tēvāram* trio to the tenth century AD. *See* B.G.L. Swamy, 'The Date of the Tevaram Trio': An Analysis and Reappraisal', in *Bulletin of the Institute of Traditional Cultures*, Madras, 1975, pp. 119–79.

built in the centres 'sung' by the hymnists, and the vernacular *bhakti* hymns did not inspire their temples of the seventh and eighth centuries.

The hymnists were propagating *bhakti* in a situation of conflict and rivalry with non-orthodox sects like the Jains and Buddhists whose influence and dominance in royal and urban centres had been established in the pre-seventh-century period. This is attested to by the epics *Cilappatikāram* and *Maṇimēkalai*[81] (fifth–sixth centuries) and early archaeological evidence from Puhār or Kāvērippaṭṭiṇam.[82] The establishment of a Jain Sangha, known as the Drāviḍa Sangha, at Madurai in AD 470[83] and the patronage presumably extended to the Jain and Buddhist sects by the Kaḷabhras, who are believed to have subverted the early historical Tamil polities of the Cēra–Cōḷa–Pāṇṭiya ruling families,[84] also point to their ascendancy. These two sects drew their followers and support in the early historical period primarily from the merchant and artisan communities, and the general decline in trade by the third to fourth centuries AD, particularly maritime trade, would seem to have forced these sects to turn to other avenues of material support. The acquisition of landed property by the Jains and Buddhists is recorded in the early Paḷḷankōyil copper plates[85] (AD 550) of the Pallavas and also indirectly attested to by the references to *paḷliccandam* lands in early medieval brahmanical records, which exclude them from the land grants made to the 'orthodox' sects. More importantly, the Pāṇṭiya copper plates of the eighth century[86] record the restoration of lands to *brāhmaṇas* from those who 'appropriated' those lands. The Kaḷabhras, who presumably patronized these sects and made land gifts to them, are referred to in these records as *kali* or evil kings. *Bhakti* would, therefore, seem to have emanated and spread in a context of rivalry for social dominance and royal patronage as seen in Kāñcīpuram and Madurai, which were the centres of such conflict and change. Presumably, *bhakti*, by throwing open the path of salvation to all, irrespective of caste and

[81] These two works, written by a Jain and a Buddhist respectively, refer to the cities of early Tamiḻakam as teeming with Jain and Buddhist followers and monasteries.

[82] Kāvērippūmpaṭṭiṇam Excavations reported in *Indian Archaeology: A Review*, 1961–2, 1963–4; Clarence Maloney, 'Archaeology in South India–Accomplishments and Prospects', *in* B. Stein (ed.), *Essays on South India*, New Delhi, 1976, pp. 1–40.

[83] P. B. Desai, *Jainism in South India and Some Jaina Epigraphs*, Sholapur, 1957.

[84] N. Subrahmanian, *Sangam Polity: The Administration and Social Life of the Sangam Tamils*, Madras, 1966, p. 29.

[85] T.N. Subramanian, 'Pallankoyil Copper Plate', in *Transactions of the Archaeological Society of South India*, Madras, 1958–9.

[86] T.N. Subramanian, *Ten Pandya Copper Plates*, Madras, 1967.

social hierarchy, imbibed the ideals of the non-orthodox creeds, namely birth and caste as no obstacles to salvation, and thereby succeeded in rooting out 'heretical' sects. Hence, the seventh–eighth-century religious developments are depicted in brahmanical records as well as in the hymns as a revival of orthodox forms, which inevitably led to serious sectarian rivalry, particularly in royal and urban centres. Royal 'conversion' was the symbol of this change and hence central to this conflict. The stories of conflict and persecution leading to royal conversions and change in patronage are referred to in the *bhakti* hymns, and more systematically narrated in the hagiographical literature of the eleventh and twelfth centuries. Epigraphic evidence as well as sculptural and architectural evidence have been cited to prove that the consequent changes led to the conversion of Jain into Śaiva temples under royal patronage.[87] Of the two non-orthodox sects, Buddhism declined, leaving very few traces behind in certain urban centres (Kāñcīpuram),[88] while Jainism became subordinate to Purāṇic religions. Yet, Jainism survived as a significant factor in South Indian religion, and hence repeatedly evoked strong reaction among the Purāṇic sects. Its survival may be attributed to its adoption of the institutional and ritual forms of the Purāṇic religion, namely temple worship.

The second major impact of *bhakti* ideology was more significant as it induced messianic expectations among the lower orders of *varṇa*-based society, presumably by providing a delusion of equality among the low castes, which in reality remained beyond their access even in the ritual area as revealed by the story of Nantan, the untouchable. With its messianic appeal, *bhakti* also became amplified into an ethical (moral) system capable of sanctioning and integrating new values, which the older, particularly northern/Sanskritic norms, could not provide, into a coherent and viable synthesis. Correspondingly, it led to the expansion of the temple's role in restructuring society and economy, and facilitating the advance of those branches of knowledge concerned with ritual display, namely the sciences of architecture, sculpture, painting, the fine arts such as music, dance, and allied crafts—in short

[87] K.R. Srinivasan, 'South India', *in* A. Ghosh (ed.), *Jaina Art and Architecture*, vol. II, New Delhi, 1975; R. Champakalakshmi, 'Religious Conflict in the Tamil Country: A Reappraisal of Epigraphic Evidence', *Journal of the Epigraphical Society of India*, vol. IV, 1978; *also* C.V. Narayana Ayyar, *Origin and Early History of Saivism in South India*, Madras, 1974 (rpt.).

[88] R. Champakalakshmi, 'Urban Configurations of Tondaimandalam: The Kāñcīpuram and Madras Regions 600–1300 AD', School of Social Sciences Series, No. 2, New Delhi, 1988 (in print).

iconography, religious and political, and art as efficient ideological apparatuses.

The temple-based *bhakti* was also capable of developing into a transcendental norm and hence acquired a centrality providing a focus for the achievement of uniformity among various sects, given their differences. Several non-conformist elements and religious sects observing extreme forms of rites could also be integrated through the *bhakti* ideology. Through the *maṭha* organization attached to temples from the ninth century AD the Kālāmukha–Pāśupata sects became an integral part of Śaiva temple religion.[89] They are believed to be anti-Vedic and anti-caste in origin, a fact known even to the Vaiṣṇava teachers of the eleventh and twelfth centuries such as Yāmunācārya and Rāmānuja. However, epigraphic evidence indicates that they favoured the study of the *Vedas* and *Varṇāśrama* in defence of social orthodoxy.[90] The Virasaiva sect, which seems to have been a reformist schism of the Kālāmukha sect in Karnataka,[91] was undoubtedly influenced by the Tamil Śaiva *bhakti*. Vīraśaivism originated both as a counter to Jain ascendancy and also as an anti-caste movement in Karnataka.[92]

Another dimension of the progress of the movement is the interaction of the *bhakti* tradition with the Siddha philosophers, which became a mutually beneficial influence. The Siddhas were an unorganized group of wandering mendicants who generally preferred the seclusion of hills and the periphery of civilization. Although the Tamil Siddha school represents an important and interesting offshoot of the pan-Indian tāntric-yoga movement, Tamil Siddhism shows features such as anti-Brāhmaṇism and even anti-ritualism.[93] Tirumūlar, one of the canonized *bhakti* saints, was the greatest of the Tamil Siddhas, who laid emphasis on the importance of Śiva and Murukan worship, the latter being the

[89] These sects are known to the hymnists. *See* Appar IV. 20 and 21 (Tiruvārūr).

[90] Romila Thapar, 'Renunciation: The Making of a Counter Culture', in *Ancient Indian Social History: Some Interpretations*, New Delhi, 1978, p. 75; David N. Lorenzen, *The Kāpālikas and Kālāmukhas: Two Lost Śaivite Sects*, 2nd rev. edn, Delhi, 1991, pp. 148–9.

[91] David N. Lorenzen, 'The Kālāmukha Background to Vīraśaivism', *in* S. K. Maity, et al. (eds), *Studies in Orientology*, Agra, 1988, pp. 278–93.

[92] *See* A.K. Ramanujan, *Speaking of Śiva*, Baltimore, 1973; *see* C.N. Venugopal, 'Lingayat Ideology of Salvation: An Enquiry into some of its Social Dimensions', *Religion and Society*, vol. XXIX, no. 4, Dec. 1982; K. Ishwaran, *Religion and Society Among the Lingayats of South India*, New Delhi, 1982.

[93] Kamil Zvelebil, *The Poets of the Powers*, London, 1973; David Shulman, 'The Enemy Within: Idealism and Dissent in South Indian Hinduism', *in* S. N. Eisenstadt, Reuven Kahane, and David Shulman (eds), *Orthodoxy, Heterodoxy and Dissent in India*, Berlin, 1984, pp. 32–6.

Tamil deity *par excellence*. His canonization has, therefore, a special significance in the integration of the Siddha element into *bhakti* tradition. His analogy of the human body and the temple of god, and the idea of the body as a fit instrument for the soul (= icon = god) in pursuit of self-discipline and quest for god, provided a convenient alternative to the icon in the temple. His canonization took place in the twelfth century as a part of the attempts to resolve the societal and ideological crisis of the times due to the claims for greater non-*brāhmaṇa* participation in temple ritual and temple administration consequent upon the enhancement of economic status among some artisanal and craft groups, particularly weavers. It was a successful attempt of the twelfth-century Śaiva protagonists to include an important anti-brahmanical and non-orthodox element in the traditional Śaiva order.

It has been shown earlier that both the Vaiṣṇava and Śaiva saints shared a common animosity aimed at the rooting out of the Jain and Buddhist sects. They however remained exponents of a parallel movement throughout. This is indeed established beyond doubt by the deliberate choice of Śaivism by the Cōḷas after Parāntaka I (907–55), for Śaivism proved to be a more efficacious instrument of acculturation for acquisition of a wider popular base both during the period of the Nāyanārs and subsequently due to royal patronage of the cult of the *linga*, which was of central importance in the process of acculturation. The incorporation of Murukan, Durga, and the equation of the phallic symbol or the aniconic *linga* with the folk worship of the pillar and tree were the most significant factors in the elaboration of the popular base of Śaivism. Śaiva iconography evolved in direct relation to the specific requirements of the ideological needs of Cōḷa power.

Cōḷa royal measures to adopt and propagate *bhakti* were significantly directed towards the expansion of agrarian order, its integration and the restructuring of economy and society, and enhancement of political power. The building of canonical temples from the ninth century AD by the late Pallavas and the early Cōḷas, the sacred geography of the hymns and the pattern of distribution of *bhakti* centres with temples would indicate that while both the Vaiṣṇava and Śaiva temples were built uniformly in the different sub-regions of the Tamil macro-region, the Śaiva temples superseded both in number and importance the Vaiṣṇava ones from the latter half of the tenth century AD. The sacred geography of the *Tēvāram* and *Divyaprabandham*[94] shows the following pattern of

[94] George W. Spencer, 'The Sacred Geography of the Tamil Śaiva Hymns', *Numen*, 17, Dec. 1970, pp. 232–44; F. Hardy, 1983, pp. 256–61.

distribution of the Vaiṣṇava and Śaiva temples. Vaiṣṇavism had its major centres in Toṇḍaināḍu and Pāṇḍināḍu, with a few centres including Śrīrangam in Cōḷanāḍu. On the contrary, Śaiva centres had their greatest concentration in the Cōḷa region (Kaveri valley) and in and around the Pallava and Pāṇṭiya capitals of Kāñcīpuram and Madurai. The total number of Vaiṣṇava centres would scarcely be a third of the total number of religious centres that emerged in early medieval Tamiḻakam, i.e. between the seventh and thirteenth centuries AD. The temple and its proliferation indicate the spatial and chronological spread of agrarian settlements and the emergence of urban nuclei.

The collection and organization of the hymns and the ritual of hymn-singing in temples were also made under direct royal initiative and patronage. The Vaiṣṇava hymns were collected in the late tenth century AD by Nāthamuni. The Śaiva hagiology received particular attention in the periods of Rājarāja I (985–1014) and Kulottunga II (1133–50). Closely linked with the collection of hymns was the apotheosis of the Śaiva hymnists and the installation of their images in Śiva temples from the period of Rājarāja I. Some of the remarkable Cōḷa frescoes at Tanjavur depict the stories of two of the Nāyanārs, while the *Periya Purāṇam* stories are sculpted in the narrative panels of the twelfth-century Śiva temple at Dārāsuram.[95] With the exception of Tirumankai, their Vaiṣṇava counterparts remained unrepresented in Cōḷa art. The deification and inclusion of the Āḻvārs in Vaiṣṇava temple worship was a later development and the direct result and more positive expression of the later Śrīvaiṣṇava movement founded by Rāmānuja in the twelfth century AD, when Vaiṣṇava hagiologies also began to be composed. Thus the Śaiva movement was intensified and consolidated even at the expense of Vaisnavism.

The shift in favour of Śaivism under the Cōḷas led to either a neglect of Vaiṣṇava institutions or a more active persecution of the latter under Kulottunga II. In the twelfth century it led to a societal crisis unsettling the existing social structure considerably. It is against this background that the reformatory zeal and activities of Rāmānuja may be viewed. Rāmānuja, a teacher–reformer, spent his formative years in Kāñcīpuram, and subsequently shifted to Śrīrangam, Tirupati, and Melkōṭe (Karnataka). His liberal measures to widen the social base of

[95] R. Champakalakshmi, 'New Light on the Cōḷa Frescoes at Tanjore', *Journal of Indian History*, Golden Jubilee Number, 1973, pp. 349–60; J.R. Marr, 'Periya Purāṇam Frieze in Tārācuram; Episodes in the Lives of the Tamil Śaiva Saints', *Bulletin of the School of Oriental and African Studies*, vol. XLII, pt 2, 1979, pp. 268–89.

Vaiṣṇavism involved a reorganization of rituals and incorporation of non-*brāhmaṇa* elements into Vaiṣṇava worship, thus creating avenues of status enhancement for the artisanal groups, including weavers (*kaikkōḷas*), who were among the principal beneficiaries.

Stories of the persecution of Rāmānuja by a Cōḷa king (Kṛmikaṇṭha identified with Kulottunga II) and attempts to eliminate Vaiṣṇava worship from the Chidambaram temple[96] may also be interpreted as evidence of this crisis, when sectarian ideology and rivalry seem to have taken a violent turn in the twelfth century AD. Śaiva ideology was in crisis and an anxiety to re-establish Śaiva supremacy is implied in these developments. The Śaiva religious network seems to have viewed as a serious threat the Vaiṣṇava attempts at extending their social base and assigning greater participation to *śūdras* in temple worship.

The twelfth century represents a crucial period for both the Śaiva and Vaiṣṇava sectarian movements, for we find them constantly drawing upon the *bhakti* tradition of the hymns of the Nāyanārs and Āḻvārs to strengthen their hold. In a sense the composition of the monumental hagiological work, namely the *Periya Purāṇam* by Cēkkiḻār, a minister of Kulottunga, was indeed an attempt to revitalize the Śaiva *bhakti* tradition by harking back to the earlier *bhakti* hymnists, although the ostensible purpose of the hagiography, as claimed by the Śaivas, was to supersede the Jain *Jīvakacintāmaṇi*. The Śaiva–Vaiṣṇava sectarian rivalry, together with the remnants of Jain influence, would explain the special care with which the Śaiva hagiological works and the *Śaiva Siddhānta* canon came to be codified between the twelfth and thirteenth centuries with royal support. The Śaiva protagonists also resorted to the organization of a monastic network, the *maṭhas* emerging as the custodians of *bhakti* literature and the *Śaiva Siddhānta* canon. *Maṭhas* proliferated all over the Tamil country and emerged primarily in weaving and trading centres and received royal patronage, merchant endowments, and also gifts from the newly emerging trading and craft organizations.[97] The non-*brāhmaṇa* Śaiva lineages of the Mudaliyār Santāna[98] emerged as a direct consequence of this ideological crisis. Monasteries henceforth became a decisive force in the forging of institutional base for the Śaiva religion and post-Cōḷa dynasties, particularly Vijayanagar and their military chiefs, had to come to terms with this new force in establishing authority relationships.

[96] K.A. Nilakantha Sastri, 1975, pp. 644–5.
[97] R. Champakalakshmi, 1988.
[98] Ibid., 1979, p. 15.

Another important development that may be seen as a consequence of this societal crisis is the emergence and crystallization of the vertical division of Right and Left Hand castes which became a paradigm,[99] for providing space within the traditional hierarchical order for the various craft groups and lower agricultural orders. Once again it was the *bhakti* tradition which was evoked to provide norms of validation to the newly emerging economic groups. In the medieval South Indian context, all the emergent institutions and urban forms, including the *nagaram*, merchant 'guilds', and craft organizations, were merged into a single systemic relationship. Diverse economic and ethnic groups were thereby accommodated as a substantial component within the same structure, i.e. the temple society, by seeking validation within the norms of the traditional order of ritual ranking. Claims to an enhanced ritual status by economically more powerful craft groups such as the weavers (*kaikkōḷas*) were also met by the expanding temple ritual and even participation in the gift giving and administrative functions of the temple.[100] Thus Tamil society emerged in the form of a tripartite division of *brāhmaṇas*, *Vēḷāḷas*, and the Right and Left Hand castes.

[99] Arjun Appadurai, 'Right and Left Hand Castes in South India', *Indian Economic and Social History Review*, 11, nos 2–3 (June–Sept. 1974), pp. 216–59.

[100] Vijaya Ramaswamy, *Textiles and Weavers in Medieval South India*, New Delhi, 1985, pp. 58–9.

7

Assimilation from a Distance: Confrontation and Sufi Accommodation in Awadh Society*

MUZAFFAR ALAM

The relationship between religion and society in medieval India has often been viewed without much regard for its complexities. To many modern historians, all social acts in medieval times were determined by the religious affiliations of the participants. Several scholars have also forced upon medieval man their own modern 'rationality', and have therefore explained his actions in ways which make these appear anachronistic—on account of the material and 'secular' framework from which they have been interpreted. In both these extreme positions, one emphasizing religion and the other using the lens of secular materialism, much evidence has been ignored or left unattended. Upon occasion, the import of detail has been blown out of proportion. Within these formulations, diametrically opposed views of community relationships, suggesting the existence of only conflict or only amity—have also been postulated.

No serious historian today can doubt the untenability of such interpretations of the past, and it seems plausible to assert that the truth lies somewhere in between. This is not merely to conjecture towards a safe position, but to address the need to confront all the available data and evaluate it after considering the standards of the time and the

*An earlier version of this paper was presented at a Seminar on 'Regional Varieties of Islam in Medieval India', at the University of Heidelberg, in July 1989. I have benefited in its revision from the comments of Neeladari Bhattacharya, Richard Eaton, Francis Robinson, and Satish Saberwal.

cultural as well as intellectual matrix of the people under scrutiny. For this purpose it is necessary to examine the specificity of the situation, and see how and in what forms religious ideas entered society.

Keeping this in mind, I examine here the inter-relationship between social conditions, state policies and a specific Sufi ideology in late-seventeenth and early-eighteenth-century Awadh. I try to see if a given social and political alignment has a bearing on the prevailing religious ideology, and whether this religious ideology, in turn, receives nourishment from the prevailing politics. I also ask if the contents and meanings of a religious doctrine, and of a dominant power position, remain unchanged in varying social settings. And finally, I try to probe if, with all its complexities (i.e. conflict and the emphasis on distinct religious identities), medieval society did manage to achieve a certain balance of community relations. Embellishing and enhancing these arguments is a detailed account of the life and teachings of a local Sufi. My account of his views and career tries to go beyond illustrating the arguments, towards being a consideration of the role of the Sufi in medieval politics and society. Naturally, I am aware of the limitations of this effort and submit, not just as a matter of ritual, that the generalizations offered here are subject to further research and study.

SOCIAL CONFLICT AND POLITICAL ALIGNMENTS

A very large portion of land and rural property in the Mughal province of Awadh was in the control of Hindu Rajputs. The fact that, frequently, the districts in their control formed a contiguous block added to their power and strength in the countryside. One such block was Baiswara, the stronghold of the Bais Rajputs, around Lucknow and Awadh (Ayodhya); this area was noted for zamindar and peasant uprisings in the seventeenth and early-eighteenth centuries. Another block consisted of the Gaurs, who were in control of a large area around Khairabad, to the north-west of Lucknow. Then, in the trans-Ghagra region, in Bahraich, the Raikwars and the Janwars had concentrated land possession, while in Gorakhpur the Bisens, the Surajbansis and the Sombansis dominated, accounting for almost 70 per cent of the revenue of the district.[1] The association of the land with Rajputs and their domination in the province was so conspicuous that, to an early-nineteenth-century

[1] Compare Abu'l Fazl, *Ā'īn-i Akbarī*, English translation by H.S. Jarrett, revised by J.N. Sarkar, Calcutta, 1949, rpt., Delhi, 1978, pp. 184–90; C.A. Elliot, *Chronicles of Oonao*, Allahabad, 1862, pp. 67–73.

British observer, many of the Mughal *pargana* boundaries appeared to have been fixed on the basis of the possession by one or the other of their individual clans.[2]

The Muslims, namely the Afghans, the Shaikhzadas (the Saiyids and Shaikhs) and some local Rajput converts, also occupied a high position in the province. The Muslim zamindaris covered roughly 11 per cent of the total revenue of the province, concentrated largely in *sarkārs* Awadh and Lucknow.[3] They acquired added social and cultural, if not political and economic, strength from the fact that the Muslim *madad-i-ma'āsh* holders (land-revenue grantees) occupied a very distinct position in the province.[4] A number of madad-i-ma'ash holdings in land extended over more than two to three hundred *bīghas*, while the influence and power of the grantees, in certain cases, entirely encompassed two or three parganas.[5] Awadh was also one of those Mughal *ṣūbas* from where the Muslims supplied the rank and file of the Mughal state service. Lucknow, Amethi, Bilgram, Daryabad, Gopamau, Kakori, Malihabad, Rudauli and Shahabad were among the important towns (*qaṣbas*) of Muslims who were in the service of the Mughals, in the province and outside, all over the empire.[6]

In all, the Muslims in Awadh, in terms of influence and strength, were next only to the Rajputs.[7] Even though the Muslims were not numerically so strong and their zamindaris not so large and widespread, they had enough power in villages and towns to be able to promise and provide substantial political support at the local level.

The Rajputs thus posed the most potent threat to the Mughals in Awadh. In the second half of the seventeenth century, when the local power-mongers were rich and strong enough to strike, the difficulties both for the local Muslim gentry (zamindars and madad-i-ma'āsh holders) and Mughal state officials were increasingly accentuated in the countryside. A petition of the *qāẓīs*, the Saiyids and the *mashā'ikh*,

[2] Elliot, *Chronicles of Oonao*, p. 149.

[3] *Ā'īn-i Akbarī*, Jarrett's tr., pp. 184, 187–90.

[4] Compare Shireen Moosvi, 'Suyurghāl Statistics in the *Ā'īn-i Akbarī*', *Indian Historical Review*, vol. II, no. 2, January 1976, pp. 282–9.

[5] M. Alam, *The Crisis of Empire in Mughal North India*, Delhi, 1986, pp. 110–11.

[6] Ghulam Husain Siddiqi Firshori, *Sharā'if-i Uṣmānī*, Deptt. of History, Aligarh, MS no. 63, pp. 68, 137, 146–7, 232, 235–6, 255–7, 269, 282, 283; Murtaẓā Husain Ilahyār Usmani Bilgrami, *Hadīqat-ul Aqālīm*, Lucknow, 1879, p. 131; Muhammad Ali Haider 'Alavi, *Taẓkira-i-Mashāhīr-i Kākorī*, Lucknow, 1927, p. 96.

[7] Lalji, *Mir'āt-ul-Awẓā'*, Maulana Azad Library, Aligarh University, *Ẓamīma, Fārsia Tārikh*, no. 60ff, 74b–75b.

submitted in 1662 on their behalf by one Qazi Maudud, the qāẓī of pargana Asoha in Baiswara in sarkār Lucknow, illustrates the reality of Rajput dominance in the province. The petition states:

> it is well known that Baiswara was a region of infidelity and all the 21 *parganas* are under the possession of the Bais and among those in 6 *parganas* (Asoha, Harha, Dalmau, Moranwan, Sainpur and Ranbirpur) the *qāẓīs*, exist, while in the remaning 15 *parganas* there are no *qāẓīs*, nor there is any mosque and any arrangements for *aẕān* [call for prayers] and the congregational prayers. This petitioner is residing in *pargana* Asoha which is also under the possession of the Bais, while it is well known to all concerned that earlier the ancestors of this petitioner had held the office of *qāẓī* for all the *parganas* and they had always been in war with the Bais zamindars. This way about eighty years have passed and [now] the control over these parganas has to be given up by the petitioner . . .[8]

Aurangzeb's decision to deal with 'the rebels' strongly, in particular by promoting the Muslim zamindaris, further aggravated the problem. A number of Saiyid settlements were razed to the ground by the Rajputs, notwithstanding the Mughal military expeditions against them.[9] The Rajput zamindars' clashes with Muslim revenue grantees were a major source of disturbance in the villages. Our sources record several such instances which I have discussed at length elsewhere.[10] In one case the Saiyids of Khairabad, for example, had to flee to the territory of the Bangash Afghans across the Ganga in Farrukhabad. For years they wandered homeless. They returned home only after the Gaur Rajputs of the region were finally reconciled by Safdar Jang, the second nawab of Awadh (1739–56).[11] In another case a revenue grant for the maintenance of the *k͟hānqāh* of the eminent sixteenth-century Awadh Sufi Saiyid Jahangir Ashraf at Jais had to be shifted, in 1714, to a safe area from a village where the keepers of the k͟hānqāh had begun to encounter serious trouble from 'the infidels' of the surrounding habitats.[12]

[8] National Archives of India, 2618/6. I owe this reference to Dr S.Z.H. Jafri.

[9] Bhupat Rai, *Inshā-i-Roshan Kalām*, Kanpur, n.d., pp. 3–4, 6, 14, 27.

[10] Alam, *Crisis of Empire*, pp. 117–21.

[11] Sahib Rai, *K͟hujasta Kalām* (a collection of letters of Muhammad Khan Bangash), India Office Library, London MS, pp. 165–6. *Also see* Shiv Dās, *Shāhnāma Munawwar Kalām*, British Museum Or. 26ff, 736–74a for Singha Gaur, the zamindar of Katesar's atrocities on the revenue grantees of Laharpur and Kheri in sarkār Khairabad; *'Ajā'ib ul-Āfāq* (a collection of letters of Chhabele Ram, Girdhar Bahadur and the Saiyid brothers), British Museum Or. 1779, 60ff and some *Ak͟hbārāt* of Farrukh Siyar's reign for conflicts between the zamindars and the madad-i ma'āsh grantees in Daryabad.

[12] Jais Documents, transcripts, Deptt. of History, Aligarh; *See also* Rafat Bilgrami,

In many of these cases the fight was over the nature of share in local power. Still, religious identities received added nourishment in an atmosphere wherein the battle lines were often drawn between the followers of two diverse faiths.

There seems to have been, among the different sections of the Muslims, an awareness of the need to help each other to strengthen their position. While a Muslim madad-i-ma'āsh was generally in the neighbourhood of a Muslim zamindari, a Muslim *qānūngo* counted the building of mosques and *madrasas*, establishing the tenets and practices of Islam, and promoting conditions for congregational (*Jum'a* and *'Īd*) prayers among the important social services rendered by him and his family. Late in the seventeenth century a Muslim qānūngo staked claim to greater resources on account of his being a Muslim, so that he could overcome the difficulties created for him by the Hindu *chaudhurīs* and qānūngos.[13] As the Rajput zamindars' revolts implied a serious threat to the state, certain state authorities also encouraged this trend. Muslim zamindars and other long-term landholdings, such as *altamghā*, were created in the midst of the Rajput caste bastions. In pargana Unnao, a Bais stronghold, efforts were made to promote the Saiyids as zamindars who had enjoyed eminence and had substantial kinsfolk in the pargana.[14] In western Awadh, along the road leading from Lucknow to Delhi, Afghans acquired large areas in altamqhā and later built and encouraged extensive Muslim settlements with urban and rural holdings in Pali, Shahabad, Sandi, Sirrah, Sandila, Malihabad and the other parganas in sarkārs Khairabad and Lucknow.[15]

The religious divines, the keepers and promoters of religious symbols (*Sha'ā'ir-i-Islāmī*), profited the most as landholders in the existing situation. Unlike ordinary zamindars, they seem to have been exempted from routine levies even on their zamindari holdings, which they often now combined with their erstwhile madad-i-ma'āsh. To ensure a smooth flow of revenue, some of these grantees were encouraged to

---

'Some Mughal Revenue Grants to the Family and *Khānqāh* of Saiyid Ashraf Jahāngīr', *Medieval India: A Miscellany*, II, Bombay, 1972, pp. 299–335.

[13] *Kaghazāt-i-Pargana Lāharpur*, Documents pertaining to Pargana Laharpur, Sarkar Khairabad, Lucknow University Library.

[14] *Inshā-i-Roshan Kalām*, pp. 7, 36.

[15] Compare Munshi Muzaffar-ud-Din Khan, *Nāma-i Muzaffarī*, 2 vols (in Urdu), Lucknow, 1971, vol. I, *passim* for the establishment and spread of the Afghan holdings in and around pargana Shahabad in Awadh. The book contains the texts with some photo reproductions of a large number of the documents.

acquire Rajput villages on *ijāra*.[16] Again, a number of new Muslim madad-i-ma'āsh centres seem to have been encouraged in the midst of these Rajput bastions. The rise in the fortune of Shaikh Pir Muhammad, an ancestor of the mystic family of Salon, is one such case. The Shaikh, a theologian and a mystic, was in close touch with Aurangzeb, who favoured him and his son, Shaikh Muhammad Ashraf, with rich grants in 1676 and 1679 respectively.[17] A measure of their privileges is reflected in the fact that, by the beginning of the eighteenth century, almost all offices pertaining to religious and quasi-religious departments had become hereditary.[18]

A greater acceptability of Muslim orthodoxy, and the subsequent association of the Mughal state with it, lent added strength to the claim of religious divines. It is difficult to establish—though this has been attempted—that a section of orthodox Sunni '*ulamā*' under the leadership of the Naqshbandi saint Shaikh Ahmad Sirhindi, as well as his sons, grandsons and disciples, influenced the course of Mughal politics.[19] Yet it is significant, nonetheless, that since Jahangir's time some of them (*mīr 'adls* and qāẓīs) were exempted from prostrating themselves or bowing before the emperor seated on the throne (*sajda-i-t'aẓīmī*). It is also noteworthy that Shaikh Ahmad Sirhindi had claimed a status spiritually on par with the first Caliph of Islam. The Shaikh's claim had agitated the Sunni orthodoxy, who brought the matter to the notice of Jahangir. The Shaikh's imprisonment showed their strength and appeased Muslim traditionalists who had resented the Shaikh's claim in no uncertain terms.[20]

[16] M. Alam, 'Changes in the Position of the *Madad-i-Ma'āsh* Holders in Awadh', *Proceedings of the Indian History Congress* (*PIHC*), Jadavpur, 1976.

[17] S.Z.H. Jafri, 'Two *Madad-i-Ma'āsh farmāns* of Aurangzeb from Awadh', *PIHC*, 1979, pp. 302–14.

[18] Alam, 'Changes in the Position . . .'

[19] For such a view, *see* K.A. Nizami, 'Naqshbandī Influence on Mughal Rulers and Politics', *Islamic Culture*, XXXIX, 1965, pp. 41–52. *See also* Mohammad Yasin, *A Social History of Islamic India, 1605–1748*, Lucknow, 1958, pp. 148–58. For an opposite opinion, *see* Irfan Habib, 'The Political Role of Shaikh Ahmad Sirhindi and Shah Waliullah', *Enquiry*, 5 December 1961, pp. 36–55; *see also*, S. Nurul Hasan, 'Shaikh Ahmad Sirhindi and Mughal Politics', *PIHC*, 8th Session, Annamalainagar, 1945, pp. 248–54, and Yohnan Friedmann, *Shaykh Aḥmad Sirhindī: An Outline of His Thought and Study of His Image with Posterity*, Montreal, 1971, pp. 77–86.

[20] Shaikh 'Abd-ul-Haq Muhaddis Dehlavi and Shaikh 'Abd-ul Jalil Ṣiddiqi resented Sirhindi's extravagance, excessive self-esteem and his religious views. Cf. Friedmann, *Shaykh Ahmad Sirhindī*, p. 8892. For Sirhindī's imprisonment and release, see *Tūzuk-i Jahāngīrī*, edited by Syud Ahmad (Saiyid Ahmad Khan), Ally Gurh (Aligarh), 1864,

Also significant is the fact that the Mughal endeavour to reform the *suyurghāl* administration in the seventeenth century was never carried out. Shahjahan is reported to have ordered an investigation into the affairs of the madad-i-ma'āsh holders, but he could not carry it through and had to replace the order by a new one in 1644, to the obvious benefit of the grantees. Aurangzeb's concessions to orthodox elements, as well as the conditions attending the reimposition of *jiziya* in 1678 and the royal order of 1690 which made the madad-i-ma'āsh completely hereditary, all showed the increasing pressure the 'ulamā' began to exert on the state.[21]

It is a matter of conjecture, however, whether Muslim elites endowed with additional favours and privileges could actually meet the strength of Rajput zamindars. What seems of greater interest is that a section of Awadh's Muslims, affected by this situation seemed to be longing to acquire power against the Rajputs through inexplicable divine sources, and by arousing the memory of past heroes. If, on the one hand, Shaikh 'Abd-ur-Rahman Chishti, together with his effort to adapt Hindu rituals to Muslim orthodoxy, tried to authenticate the legend of Saiyid Salar Mas'ud Ghazi as the Prince of Martyrs—as the foremost of those who laid their lives while 'Islamizing' India—the wandering and half-mad Muslim dervishes, on the other, saw the fantasy vision of a messiah possessed with invincible 'spiritual' power.[22] In his *Mir'āt-i-Mas'ūdī*, Chishti developed an extremely colourful story of Ghāzī Miyān. He based his account on an obscure and vulnerable history, but interestingly asserted that it was authentic and that his hero, Ghāzī Miyān himself, had confirmed its veracity; and moreover that this was corroborated by Sanskrit sources in the possession of a brāhmaṇa of Bahraich. Chishti thus sought not simply to remind his readers of the incredible bravery of the martyr; he also emphasized that the commonly venerated *pīr* was actually a most important 'Islamizer', and that this fact was established from the Hindu authorities as well.[23] Clearly, past glory was

---

pp. 272–3, 308, 370. For mīr 'adl and qāẓī's exemption from *sajda* before the emperor, see *Tūzuk-i Jahāngīrī*, p. 99.

[21] For details, *see* Shaikh Abd-ur-Rashid, 'Suyurghāl Land under the Mughals', in H.R. Gupta (ed.), *Essays Presented to Sir Jadu Nath Sarkar*, Punjab University, 1958, pp. 313–22. Cf. Satish Chandra, 'Jizya and the State in India during the 17th Century', *Journal of the Economic and Social History of the Orient*, vol. XII, pt III, 1969.

[22] Muhammad Raza Ansari, *Tazkira Ḥaẓrat Saiyid Ṣāḥib Bānsawī*, Lucknow, 1986, p. 45.

[23] S.A.A. Rizvi, *History of Sufism*, Delhi, 1978, I, pp. 312–14.

invoked to neutralize the effects of the ground reality, namely the successive triumphs of the dominant Rajput clans.

It was with the not-so-insignificant strength of Muslims that Aurangzeb expected to sustain a policy of confrontation against the Rajputs. But confrontation only exacerbated the social problem. While, on the one hand, it strained the imperial treasury, on the other the Rajputs gained little from their unabated war against the Mughals. Indeed, in the face of the intensified imperial drive against them, they found their powers exhausted, with no prospect of recovery. In addition to this, their internal organization was severely impaired by an unending kin-and-clan war. Rajput holdings had to be guarded against ever-threatening encroachments from the countryside. Thus, all sections of society, including the state, the local Muslim landholders and the Hindu Rajputs, appeared to be looking for a way out.

We get some idea from a local legend of what the Rajputs, in general, then preferred. According to this legend, in the early eighteenth century, when the Mughal governor Burhān-ul-Mulk (who also happened to be the first independent ruler of Awadh) took stock of agriculture in the province, he decided to enhance his revenue. But before he did so, he visited Baiswara, summoned the Rajput leaders, placed before them on one side a heap of *pān* (betel) leaves, and on the other a heap of bullets. The pan obviously symbolized friendship, the bullets hostility. Burhan-ul-Mulk then bade the Rajput to take up one of the two. According to this legend, one after another the Rajputs came forward and took up the pān. One Chait Rai was the exception. He picked up the bullets, but managed only to wage a sham fight against the nawab.[24]

The nawab reciprocated the gesture with generosity. Many Rajputs were received into high favour, many others now began to enjoy administrative and military (*faujdārī*) power over their zamindaris. Still others were virtually autonomous in their inherited territories, combining the neighbourhood. This policy of wooing the powerful Rajputs was continued and extended by Burhan-ul-Mulk's successors, Safdar Jang and Shujā'-ud-Daulah.[25]

With all this the nawabs not only ensured stability in the countryside, they also found in the Rajputs some of their most trusted allies in times of crisis. Burhan-ul-Mulk and Safdar Jang could afford to spend half their time in Delhi, manoeuvring high Mughal politics in their own

[24] Elliot, *Chronicles of Oonao*, p. 73.

[25] Alam, *Crisis of Empire*, pp. 212–19.

favour, both in the province and at court.[26] A large contingent of Rajput zamindars was in Safdar Jang's retinue during the nawab's struggle against the Jats and the Marathas.[27] In 1765 when Shuja'-ud-Daulah, defeated by the English East India Company's troops at Buxar, fled along the banks of the Ganga to Farrukhabad, Achal Singh, the *ta'alluqadār* of Dondia Khera in Baiswara, proved to be a good friend and supporter. A large number of the Bais, who commanded a quarter of the revenue of Baiswara, joined the crestfallen nawab at Farrukhabad.[28]

The nawab–Rajput alliance could well have been to begin with, a pragmatic adjustment; it had a precedent and could also have been inspired from earlier examples in Mughal history. But while it is true that this Mughal practice was backed by a political ideology clearly defined by Abu'l Fazl and reiterated later in royal edicts and administrative documents, it received a serious setback in the wake of an atmosphere of confrontation in the late seventeenth century.[29] Its revival in Awadh in the early eighteenth century was in itself a notable achievement, but this was not a straightforward renewal. For, together with conciliating the Rajputs, the nawabs tried also to counterbalance this by encouraging the Shaikhzadas and non-Rajput Hindus in Awadh's army and bureaucracy. The Shaikhzadas formed a significant component of the local ruling group.[30] They provided a strong social base to nawabi rule, which in turn ensured safety of their honour and property both against the dominant internal Rajput zamindars and the foreign Marathas. Thus, in the eighteenth century many Muslim establishments, like the ones at Salon and Jais for instance, grew enormously in fortune. The pīrs at Salon, who began their career with a grant of 200 bīghas under Aurangzeb, came to be virtually the 'maliks' of the entire qasba, even if they called themselves mere 'fakirs'.[31]

But by co-opting these local Muslims, the nawabs did not intend to

[26] Ibid., pp. 243–6, 280–8.

[27] *See*, for instance, W.C. Benett, ***A Report** on the Family History of the Chief Clans of the Roy Bareilly District*, Lucknow, 1870, pp. 44–5.

[28] Elliot, *Chronicles of Oonao*, p. 76.

[29] For a discussion of religion and politics under the Mughals, *see* my paper 'The State Building under the Mughals: Religion, Ideology and Politics', *in* T. Aricanli et al. (eds), *The Political Culture and the Economy of the Ottoman, Safavid and Mughal Empires* (forthcoming).

[30] Alam, *Crisis of Empire*, pp. 232–7.

[31] Donald Butter, *Topography and Statistics of Southern Districts of Awadh and Sultanpur*, Calcutta, 1839, rpt., Delhi, 1982, p. 139.

'Islamize' the state in a narrow sense, indeed, several Hindus, notably the Kayasthas and the Khatris, held important offices. Atma Ram, a Khatri, had been associated with Burhan-ul-Mulk, since the latter's early days at the Mughal court. He was eventually made the *dīwān* of Awadh. His three sons, Har Narayan, Ram Narayan and Pratap Narayan, all held important offices. Har Narayan was Burhan-ul-Mulk's *vakīl* at the court of Delhi. Among Atma Ram's grandsons, Lachmi Narayan, Shiv Narayan and Jagat Narayan rose to notable positions. Lachmi Narayan also served as the nawab's vakīl at Delhi. The family of Atma Ram retained an eminent position throughout the eighteenth century.[32] Nawal Rai, a Kayastha, was a close confidant of Safdar Jang, the second nawab, and was virtually the ruler of Awadh in the 1740s when the nawab was mostly busy in Delhi court politics. How many of his family members and associates gained eminence under Safdar Jang is not known. He is mentioned, however, by a Kayastha chronicler of the early nineteenth century as 'the promoter and supporter of his community and friends . . .'[33] A number of other Hindu officials' names figure prominently in our sources. In addition the nawabs encouraged and promoted non-Rajput zamindaris in some Rajput strongholds.[34]

By integrating the aspirations of both the dominant Rajputs on the one hand, and the Muslims and non-Rajput Hindu elites on the other, the nawabs tried to achieve a political balance. Unlike the Mughals, the Awadh nawabs had no Abu'l Fazl to give a theoretical foundation to their policy or even to explain it within some theoretical frame. But this did not mean that theirs was merely a blank, pragmatic arrangement. The balance in the new political alliance received inspiration and sustenance from the prevailing religious philosophy. The emphasis in religious circles was on an open and non-combative interaction, and, in order to avoid conflict, on integration and assimilation within certain limits. Awadh's political culture had a bearing on the religious culture of the region, and an appreciation of the connection between the two requires an analysis of the religious climate.

[32] A.L. Srivastav, *First Two Nawabs of Awadh*, Agra, 1954, pp. 79–80, 89, 98, 101, 169, 224, 232. From Firshori's account in *Sharā'if*, Atma Ram appears to have hailed from Allahabad. He was initially encouraged and patronized by an Awadh Shaikhzada. Ruh-ul-Amin Khan of Bilgram, when the latter was in the service of the governor of Allahabad. Cf. *Sharā'if-i-Uṣmānī*, p. 233.

[33] Bahadur Singh Bhatnagar, *Yādgār-i Bahādūri*, MS, UP State Archives, Allahabad, 6.475a.

[34] Alam, *Crisis of Empire*, pp. 238–9.

THE RELIGIOUS CLIMATE

Awadh has been a traditional stronghold of the Sufic doctrine of *Waḥdat-ul-Wujūd* (Unity of Being), which promoted a belief in the essential unity of all phenomena, however diverse and irreconcilably conflicting they might appear. Muhammad Ashraf Simnani popularized the use of the expression 'Hama Ūst' (literally: All is He), thus emphasizing the belief that nothing exists outside God's boundaries.[35] Rudauli (in Barabanki district) was another major Sufi centre where this doctrine received unusual nourishment. The khānqāh of Shaikh Ahmad 'Abd-ul-Haq (d. 1434) has been mentioned as the 'clearing house' of Hindu *yogīs* and *sanyāsīs*. Shaikh 'Abd-ul-Quddus (1456–1537) was among the eminent Sufis associated with the khānqāh. His *Rushd Nāma*, which consists of his own verses and those of certain other Rudauli saints, and which identifies Sufi beliefs based on Waḥdat-ul-Wujūd with the philosophy and practices of Gorakhnath, received inspiration from the syncretistic religious milieu of Rudauli. Some of these verses, with slight variations, are included in Nath poetry as well as in the *dohas* of Kabir.[36]

This philosophy and associated sentiment found fascinating expression in the mid-sixteenth century, in the *Ḥaqā'iq-i-Hindī* of 'Abd-ul-Wahid Bilgrami (1510–1608), wherein Bilgrami sought to reconcile Vaisnav symbols as well as the terms and ideas used in Hindu devotional songs with orthodox Muslim beliefs. According to Bilgrami, Krishna and other names used in such verses symbolized the Prophet Muhammad, or 'Man', or sometimes the reality of human beings (*ḥaqīqat-i-insān*) in relation to the abstract notion of the oneness (*aḥadiyat*) of the Divine Essence. *Gopīs* sometimes stood for angels, sometimes for the human race, and sometimes for the relation of human reality to the *wāḥidiyat* (relative unity) of the Divine Attributes. Braj and Gokul signified the different Sufic notions of the world (*'ālam*) in different contexts, while the Yamuna and the Ganga stood for the sea of *waḥdat* (unity), the ocean of *ma'rifat* (gnosis), or the river of *ḥadṣ* (origination) and *imkān* (contingent or potential existence). The *murlī* (Krishna's flute) in the *Ḥaqā'iq-i-Hindī* represented the appearance of entity out of non-entity, and so on and so forth.[37]

[35] *Laṭā'if-i Ashrafī*, Patna, MS, 126–36ff.

[36] Rizvi, *History of Sufism*, I, pp. 335–43.

[37] Compare Mir 'Abd-ul-Wahid Bilgrami, *Ḥaqā'iq-i-Hindī*, Aligarh, MS. Hindi translation by S.A.A. Rizvi, Banaras, 1957, *see also* S.A.A. Rizvi, *Muslim Revivalist Movements in Northern India in the Sixteenth and the Seventeenth Centuries*, Agra, 1966,

The support for the doctrine of the Unity of Being, and the associated philosophy and practice of generous accommodation to local beliefs and customs, continued in Awadh through the seventeenth century. Some of the best interpreters and defenders of the doctrine came from the region. Shaikh Muhibb-ullah (d. 1648), who settled in Allahabad, and Shaikh 'Abd-ur-Rahman Chishti (*c.* 1683) deserve special notice. The reputation of some of the treatises Shaikh Muhibb-ullah wrote to expose and elaborate on the doctrine brought him in close contact with prince Dara Shukoh. His *Risāla Taswiya* (Treatise on Equality) evoked a storm of opposition in the orthodox circle, and later, under Aurangzeb—who is reported to have taken strong exception to its contents—it was ordered to be burnt in public.[38] Shaikh Muhibb-ullah undertook the study and training of yoga from a brāhmaṇa after the brāhmaṇa had perfected under him (Shaikh Muhibb-ullah) a grounding in Islamic Sufism.[39]

In another case, Shaikh 'Abd-ur-Rahman Chishti, a descendant of Shaikh Ahmad 'Abd-ul-Haq of Rudauli, translated with explanatory notes a Sanskrit treatise on Hindu cosmogony under the title of *Mir'āt-ul-Makhlūqāt* (Mirror of the Creatures). This is in the form of a dialogue between Mahādeva and Pārvati, handed down by Muni Bashisht. 'Abd-ur-Rahman sought to explain at some length certain Hindu legends, and made a plea for them to be adapted to Muslim ideas and beliefs. He also prepared a recension in Persian of the *Gīta*, entitled *Mir'āt-ul-Ḥaqā'iq* (Mirror of the Realities), presenting it as an ideal exposition of the doctrine of Hama Ūst.[40]

A change from the earlier centuries is, however, noticeable in the seventeenth century, even though there was not much enthusiasm in Awadh for the ideal and doctrine of *Wāḥdat-ush-Shuhūd* (Unity of Perception), enunciated and emphasized by Shaikh Ahmad Sirhindi (1564–1624), the famous Naqshbandi theologian saint of Mughal India who was better known as *Mujaddid-i-Alf-i Ṣānī* (the renovator of Islam of the second *Hijra* millennium). Apparently Awadh, unlike other parts

pp. 60–2. For Bilgrami's biography, *see* Mir Ghulam'Ali Azad Bilgrami, *Ma'aṣir-ul-Kirām*, edited by Maulavi Abd-ul-Haq, II, Hyderabad, 1913, pp. 247–8; *see also*, 'Abd-ul-Qādir Badāonī, *Muntakhab-ut-tawārīkh*, Calcutta, III, pp. 65–6.

[38] Mohammad Ikram, *Rūd-i Kauṣar*, rpt., Delhi, n.d., pp. 440–2; Rizvi, *Muslim Revivalist Movements*, pp. 335–6.

[39] Rizvi, *Muslim Revivalist Movements*, p. 340. For an interesting discussion on the theme, *see* Shah Muhibb-ullah, *Maktūb Banām Mullā Jaunpūrī*, Maulana Azad Library, Aligarh, *Zakhīra-i Aḥsan*, no. 297.7737, *Fārsī Taṣawwuf*.

[40] Charles Rieu, *Catalogue of the Persian Manuscripts in the British Museum*, III, London, 1883, p. 1034.

of Upper India, had no important propagandist of Sirhindi's doctrine. Still, there were cases of resistance to the ideology of *Wāḥdat-ul-Wujūd*. In Jaunpur, Mulla Mahmud and his disciple, independent of Sirhindi, waged a fairly effective opposition to the doctrine of the Unity of Being early in the seventeenth century.[41] Earlier, in Sikander Lodi's time, Jaunpur had seen in Qazi Shahab-ud-Din Daulatabadi an important precursor of the 'ulamā', namely Shaikh 'Abd-ul-Haq Muhaddis Dehlavi who endeavoured to clean Indian Islam of impurities and innovations by reviving and promoting theological study.[42]

An early warning against the implications of the doctrine of Waḥdat-ul-Wujūd came from Awadh, suggesting its acceptance in a modified form. Shaikh Nizam-ud-Din of Amethi (d. 1517), according to one report, snatched *Fuṣūṣ-ul-Ḥikam* (Bezels of Wisdom), the famous treatise written by 'Abd-ur-Rahman Ibn al-'Arabi (propounder of the doctrine), from the hand of the son of a Sufi and gave him another book. The Shaikh, a Chishti saint, wanted his disciples to read more on orthodox Sufic treatises.[43] Shaikh Muhibb-ullah is also reported to have taken pains to highlight the correct import and significance of Ibn al-'Arabi's works to clear 'the prevalent misunderstandings' about the doctrine. In his important work entitled *Manāẓir-i Ak͟hasṣ-ul-K͟hawāṣ*, he considered the doctrine to be fully appreciated only by a select few. As regards the implications of the doctrine, he made a plea for peaceful coexistence. But even as he did so, he maintained a distinction between good and evil and warned his followers against taking the bitter for the sweet.[44]

All this indicated that Sirhindi and his ideology may have created ripples in Awadh. But their limitations, indicated in some measure by the attitude of some of the eminent disciples of Shaikh Muhibb-ullah, should not be overlooked. Aurangzeb, before proclaiming the public destruction of the Shaikh's treatise, *Taswiya*, reportedly sought an

[41] Mulla Mahmud, considered essentially a 'rationalist', made his impact on the intellectual history of India because of his contribution to Graeco–Arab logic and philosophy. As a theologian he emphasized scholasticicism (*kalām*) over mysticism and interiorization of beliefs (*taṣawwuf*), M. Rahman 'Ali, *Tazkira-i 'Ulamā'i Hind*, Lucknow, 1914, p. 221; Ikram, *Rūdi-i-Kauṣar*, pp. 391–2.

[42] M. Ishaq, *India's Contribution to the Study of Health Literature*, Urdu tr. by S.H. Razzaqi, Lahore, 1976, pp. 134–5; Aziz Ahmad, *An Intellectual History: History of Islam in India*, Edinburgh, 1969, p. 68.

[43] M. Mujeeb, *Indian Muslims*, London, 1967, pp. 306–7.

[44] Rizvi, *Muslim Revivalist Movements*, p. 340.

explanation of its contents and approached two Awadhi personages for this purpose. The one, Mir Saiyid Muhammad Qannauji, who was in the imperial service, denied all association with the Shaikh, but the other, Shaikh Muhammadi, virtually challenged the emperor's decision, even as he gave an evasive answer. Muhammadi did not deny having been the Shaikh's disciple; he said it was difficult for him either to repudiate, confirm or explain the theme of the treatise. He said: 'I have not yet reached that elevated mystic stage which the Shaikh had acquired, and from which he talked. The day I reach that stage I would write a commentary, as desired. However, if His Majesty has decided to reduce the tract to ashes, much more fire is available in the royal kitchen than can be had in the house of the ascetics who have resigned themselves to God.[45]

It is not off the mark to conclude, basing ourselves on what we know about the history of the region, that Awadh did not come under the direct influence of Sirhindi. It is also true that it could not escape—as noticed above—some of the social and political implications of narrow sectarian ideas, largely under the impact of the Delhi regime. What is noteworthy is that, in the midst of intense community conflict, the message of the Awadh Sufi retained its verve.

THE FOUNDATION OF A SUFI CENTRE

The rehabilitation of non-sectarian politics in the nawabi regime had the full and reinvigorated backing of local religious leaders, though their perspective was different. Earlier, Shaikh 'Abd-ur-Rahman Chishti had applauded the Mughal policy. The reason he gave was that the policy, if combined with due regard for Islamic injunctions, eventually led the

[45] Shahnawaz Khan, *Ma'āṣir-ul-Umarā'*, Calcutta, 1805, III, pp. 604–11. See also its English tr. by H. Beveridges, II, Calcutta, 1952, pp. 129–34. Sher Khan Lodi, *Mir'āt-ui-Khayāl*, Calcutta, 1246 AH, pp. 326–36. Ghulam 'Ali Azad Bilgrami, *Ma'āṣir-ul-Kirām*, Introduction by Maulavi Abd-ul-Haq, pp. 15–16; An eighteenth-century Awadh version of Shaikh Muhammadi's answer to Aurangzeb is worth noting for an understanding of Awadh's religious climate. Shaikh Muhammadi, according to Mulla 'Abd-ul-'Ali of Firangi Mahal, retorted that 'if by any chance I am unable to give the meaning of the Holy Quran, will you then deny its [validity] too?' The emperor then asked the Shaikh to repent for what he said and did. The Shaikh was then ordered to leave the imperial domain. Subsequently he moved to a mosque, and when the emperor claimed that the mosque was also within the territory, the Shaikh reminded him of his arrogance. For a mosque was the house of God and therefore only His property. Later the Shaikh was imprisoned in Aurangabad fort where he died in 1696; Ansari, *Tazkira*, pp. 67–9.

people of diverse ethnic and religious stock to submit to Islam.[46] Among the late-seventeenth and early-eighteenth-century Sufis, in whose life and teachings the echoes of the new policy were unmistakable, the career of an illiterate Qadiri Sufi, Saiyid Shah 'Abd-ur-Razzaq of Bansa, was singularly remarkable. Shah 'Abd-ur-Razzaq was not merely an eyewitness to the devastating implications of the policy of confrontation—he himself had inherited and experienced the suffering it had brought to his family. His fascinating career, ideas and approach to the social and religious questions of the period are of considerable value.

This Saiyid Shah 'Abd-ur-Razzaq Bansawi, the founder of a Qadiri Sufi centre at Bansa, Lucknow, came from a family of zamindars established in Awadh by the Muslim rulers of Delhi. The family was originally from Badakhshan and encountered untold hardships following Rajput raids on their zamindari and possessions in the seventeenth century. Bansawi's grandmother was one of only two ladies who survived these raids. She was carrying his father when she, along with her sister-in-law, was escorted to safety by one Rasul Khan, an old associate of the family, in a village of his zamindari (named Rasulpur, after him, in the neighbourhood).[47] Bansawi's father, Saiyid 'Abd-ur-Rahim, who lived in the time of Jahangir (1605–26), Shahjahan (1626–58) and Aurangzeb (1658–1707), was born to the lady in Rasulpur.[48] Saiyid 'Abd-ur-Rahim also had a difficult time with the powerful neighbouring Rajput zamindar of Daryabad. Young Bansawi was made captive by the kinsmen of the zamindar when he was barely seven.

In their teens, zamindars' children in Awadh mostly spent their time studying and training. But Bansawi had, at this age, to leave for the Deccan in search of a reasonable livelihood and a respectable position, apparently with the objective of reinstating his family to its earlier honour and dignity.[49]

For about twelve years Bansawi stayed in the Deccan. During this period he returned at least once to Awadh, to be married. As he had received no formal education, he failed to obtain a high position in the state service. He remained just an ordinary trooper. Later, his family

[46] Rizvi, *History of Sufism*, II, p. 369.

[47] Mulla Nizam-ud-Din Firangi Mahalli, *Manāqib-i-Razzāqiya*, p. 4; Nawab Muhammad Khan Shahjahanpuri, *Malfūẓ-i Razzāqī*, Lucknow, 1313/1896, pp. 6–8.

[48] *Malfūẓ*, pp. 6–8.

[49] Cf. Ansari, *Tazkira*, pp. 43–287. Ansari quotes from Mir Baqar 'Ali Razzaqi's unpublished 'Manāqib-i Razzāqī'.

responsibility brought him back to Awadh, where too he served as a soldier, first under one Shah Muhammad Yusuf, a local Shaikhzada in charge of the troopers, and then under a Mughal military commander of the province. The Mughal paid him poorly, and irregularly to boot. Disgusted and tired, Bansawi then decided to give up the service, to settle finally in Bansa, the village of his maternal grandfather 'Abd-ul-Malik Qidwa'i, and establish there the well-known Sufi centre of eighteenth-century Awadh.[50]

Bansawi, it is reported, acquired high Sufic position through exceptional ways. He introduced and founded a branch of the Qadiri *silsilā* in which he had received *khilāfat* (legitimacy to initiate novices) from a little-known Sufi of the order, Mir 'Abd-us-Samad Khuda-numa of Ahmedabad. Later, according to his hagiographers, he obtained khilāfat in both the Nizamiya and the Sabiriya branches of the Chishtiya silsila in a miraculous way, directly from the great Sufi masters, who had long passed away, and had then founded these orders.[51] Again, according to one tradition (spread obviously after he had acquired eminence), upon his birth a *majzūb* predicted his fame far and wide. Bansawi is reported to have had visions and performed miracles even as a boy. He set himself free, the tradition goes, from the clutches of the kinsmen of the Rajput zamindar of Daryabad, unhurt and unnoticed, with the phenomenal help of 'Ali (the famous companion and cousin of the Arabian Prophet), who was the fourth pious caliph and who is believed to have been the fountainhead of nearly all the Sufi orders. His disinclination towards, or rather his deprivation from, formal learning has also been explained in Sufic terms. Bansawi himself related the story of a vision he had received while he was still young on the futility of formal education. The story goes that once, on his way from his village to a madrasa in Rudauli, he was left alone by his attendant, who had gone to meet his relatives in the nearby hamlet to arrange food for Bansawi. In his absence, the young and hungry Bansawi felt lonely and depressed. A dervish then mysteriously came to his rescue. The dervish gave him food, and with it a grand idea. Elated and enlightened, Bansawi now realized what he—and for that matter all young Muslims of his class and potential—ought to strive towards. The follow-up to this was, significantly, his decision to discontinue education and leave for the Deccan,

[50] *Malfūz*, p. 22; *see also* Nawab Muhammad Khan Shahjahanpuri, *Karāmat-i Razzāqiya*, Hardoi, 1319 AH, p. 6.

[51] *Karāmāt*, p. 6; *Malfūz*, p. 28. Such a miraculous Uwaisi method of acquiring *rushd* and khilāfat was not so rare in the Islamic world.

not in search of employment but, according to tradition, to meet the same dervish. The dervish had apparently promised to meet him again, but only in the Deccan.[52]

Bansawi was a visionary of exceptional quality. As he heard and related stories of the unusual events surrounding his birth and childhood, he saw himself as the One in possession of extraordinary social power and influence, with a mission to set in order the entire social scene. He had risen too high to now think only in terms of the interests of his own house or narrowly of his community. He believed he existed to ameliorate the general predicament of society. Education at a formal school or college (*maktab* or madrasa) appeared to him a sheer waste of his time and abilities.[53] A trip to the Deccan, the new Mughal power centre, and to the state service which had attracted many adventurers from his region must have promised sufficient fortune to fulfil this mission. But the problems of Mughal rule in the Deccan, the uncertainty and plight of state service and his own experience with it, all led him to a state where he found within extraordinary Sufic accomplishment a sure and guaranteed path to the world of his vision.

Besides personal dissatisfaction, the increasing difficulties of Mughal imperial administration are likely to have convinced him of the futility of state service. Details of his family history and personal life, the existing relations between ancient landholders on the one hand and the relatively new Muslim zamindars and holders of revenue grants of different denominations on the other, the persistent tension and threats to the *shurafā'* in the countryside even as they received support from the state—all indicated the helplessness of the Muslim elites.

However, the memory of unusual powers among the early saint–soldiers who had conquered the region, as we have seen earlier, remained strong. Tales of a local Rajput raja's surrender to unarmed and unassuming Sufis nourished this memory. In the town and villages where descendants of these Sufis lived, such stories assuaged bruised souls. According to an eighteenth-century account Malik Muhammad Jaisi, the oft-cited Sufi Hindavi poet, commanded immense respect in the court of the raja of Garh Amethi. Once, however, on the day of Lord Krishna's birthday, Jaisi was denied access to the raja on the plea that the latter, along with his brāhmaṇa priests, was busy with prayers relevant to the occasion. Infuriated and insulted, Jaisi then protested that

[52] *Manāqib*, pp. 8–9, Muḥammad 'Abd-ul Bari, *Fuyūẓ-i Haẓrat Bānsa* (in Urdu), Lucknow, n.d., pp. 51–3.

[53] *Malfūẓ*, p. 22.

the time when he had sought an interview with the raja was inauspicious for prayers, and claimed that the brāhmaṇas who performed them had either no adequate knowledge of astrology and therefore miscalculated the time or had misguided the raja. Scared and embarrassed, the raja and the brāhmaṇas eventually conceded to Jaisi's claim and sought his forgiveness.[54]

Another story with details of an encounter between the raja of Tiloi and a Chishti Ashrafi Sufi of qaṣba Jais is far more fanciful. In one of the Rajput raids early in the seventeenth century the raja of Tiloi, it is said, captured and took off with all the cattle of the residents of the qaṣba from their grazing grounds. The shurafā' of the qaṣba, who were particularly affected, appealed to Shah 'Inayat-ullah, an ancient Sufi and the *sajjāda-nashīn* of khānqāh Chishtiya Ashrafiya, to intervene and recommend to the raja that he should release their cattle. The Shah accordingly reached Tiloi to meet the raja. Sensing the purpose of his visit, the raja refused to meet him and instructed his attendants to tell him that he, the raja, was asleep, and that he, the Shah, could come to meet him some other time. Dejected, the Shah returned, but when he visited Tiloi again according to instruction, the same excuse was repeated. In a huff the Shah then cursed the raja and left for Jais, saying: 'as the Rāja kept sleeping for so long, may his eyes remain closed now'. The legend goes that the raja lost his eyesight subsequently. Later, the raja repented and apologized to the Shah for his misbehaviour. The Shah then blessed him, praying that he be endowed with unusual bravery and the strength to overpower all the other rajas of the area, even though blind. Tiloi then emerged, as the followers of the Shah and many others believed, to become the most powerful *rāj* in the region.[55]

Besides providing a kind of consolation to the hapless descendants of these legendarily 'triumphant' Sufis, such stories also indicate an attempt to assert their own superiority over the others. Bansawi may have known that through the Sufic way he could reinstate himself and his followers to some degree of their erstwhile 'high' position. But then Bansawi also had a much nobler mission before him. My aim here is not to establish that Bansawi made a cool and calculated assessment of the prevailing situation and planned to excel in Sufic power in a bid to resolve the problems of his society and community. Far from this, my attempt is simply to see the birth and growth of an individual's ideas

[54] Maulavi 'Abd-ul-Qadir, *Tārīkh-i Jā'is*, MS, Abd-ul-Ali Collection, Nadwat-ul-Ulama, Lucknow, pp. 15–16.

[55] *Tārīkh-i Jā'is*, pp. 53–6.

within their surroundings. It seems that while Bansawi looked for a job commensurate with the reputation of his family, he intended to solve his worldly difficulties. Simultaneously he also showed his anxiety to achieve something divine, inexplicable and inaccessible to ordinary souls. And this, according to tradition, was the real motive of his wanderings.

He searched for it everywhere, at a Sufi's hospice and a sadhu's *maṭha*, and was delighted to get anywhere that seemed close to his destination—towards the ability to provide remedies to all that ailed human souls and society. Again and again, he repeated to his disciples a story on the attitudes of an ascetic which he had come across on a visit to Allahabad. A sadhu, said his story, while at his deathbed, called in his favourite *chelā* (disciple) to tell him the secrets of alchemy. The chelā, instead of being excited, coolly refused to listen and said that he had not accepted the sadhu as his master for such inconsequential miraculous powers. He sought to learn and be a part of the *Ism-i A'ẓam* (The Great Name of Divinity).[56]

With Ism-i A'ẓam, it was believed, one could turn even the wheel of the universe. In his repeatedly expressed admiration for the ascetic chelā, Bansawi showed, perhaps, what he himself thought his destination ought to be. What Bansawi sought to achieve with the power of Ism-i A'ẓam is evident from a perusal of his ideas and attitudes.

INTEGRATION AND IDENTITY: A SUFI TRAJECTORY

Bansawi's teachings and attitudes embodied, in large measure, the message of a pragmatic balance in social relationships. He tried to reduce to a minimum the conflicts between diverse groups and communities, without undermining their claims to their distinct individual slots in the whole. All through his life he encouraged by his words and actions a liberal and reconciliatory approach to local Hindu religious rites and social practices. His stance towards accommodating these to the life pattern of an average Muslim had some obvious qualifications. He fully appreciated the necessity and importance of maintaining the great orthodox tradition of Islam. His 'syncretism' notwithstanding, he remained eventually a protagonist of orthodox Sufism and saw to it that its dominance and supremacy was refurbished through his pronouncements and deeds.

In Awadh many of the Hindu customs, festivals and ceremonies had become a part of Muslim social life. Mulla Nizam-ud-Din mentions

[56] *Manāqib*, p. 14.

sehrā for the bride and bridegroom approvingly. A number of other purely Hindu rituals had come to be tolerated at various levels in the life of an average Muslim. The *bhakti-bāz* song and dance sequence which depicted the life of Narsimha Avatar and Lord Krishna[57] was one such local ceremony, commonly patronized and staged both by Hindu and Muslim upper classes at celebrations and festivities. At no stage did Bansawi directly discourage this practice. Two of his major disciples who had permission from him to initiate novices into the order and train them (*khalīfas*), namely Mir Muhammad Isma'il and Shah Muhammad Ishaq Khan, and also his son Shah Ghulam Dost Muhammad, had a special liking for this. And it was in the full knowledge of their preceptor, Bansawi himself, that they once watched *bhaktiyas* performing the life of Krishna, apparently with avid interest, in a wedding party at the residence of one of Bansawi's disciples (*murīds*). As this was an occasion of joy and merriment, Bansawi allowed it to go on, even though the senior host wanted his family members and friends to stop, in deference to his pīr.[58]

Clearly there a plea for tolerance is implicit in Bansawi's act. He tolerated and showed interest in a social practice, which was violative of the *sharī'a*, on the strength of his own assessment of social realities. In Sufi terms he had justification for this in *mushāhada* (observation, contemplation) and *ilhām* (divine inspiration). But since he was an orthodox (*ba-shar'a*) and not a heterodox (*bī-shar'a*) Sufi, he appreciated the limits of his authority. According to the established Sufic norms, the act of a Sufi based on ilhām was not necessarily to be followed by others, in particular when it was overtly in contravention of the dictates of sharī'a.

Bansawi thus intended only to emphasize the exigency of tolerance. He never insisted upon his disciples acting or thinking exactly as he did. Far from this, he showed due regard for a strict observance of sharī'a. He conceded the viewpoint of his famous theologian disciple Mulla Nizam-ud-Din, the founder of the eighteenth-century madrasa curriculum (*dars-i-niẓāmī*), who had accompanied him to the wedding. Not only did he keep the Mulla away, he also—as this same theologian in his account of the saint would have us believe—reasoned that he wanted the Mulla nowhere around the scene 'lest the common Muslim should take his presence as a *sanad* (allowed in the sharī'a)'. On another occasion,

[57] Compare Masud Husain Rizvi Adeeb, *Lucknow kā Shāhī Stage*, Lucknow, 1968, pp. 46–50.

[58] *Malfūẓ*, pp. 145–7; *Karāmāt*, p. 21; Ansari, *Taẕkira*, pp. 467, 271–3.

while watching an animal fight between a buffalo and a pig—which the Ahirs used to organize as part of their Diwali celebrations—Bansawi advised the Mulla and his nephew Mulla Kamal-ud-Din, also an illustrious theologian and jurist, to stay away from the other viewers.[59]

Apparently Bansawi advocated a difference in the attitudes and actions of an *'ālim* (theologian) and a Sufi with reference to the sharī'a. He appreciated the limitation of the law-oriented worldview of a theologian. He saw himself as a Sufi who, guided by his own observations, had the power to act not always strictly according to the law. Indeed, a Sufi can appear, on occasion, as having violated the dictates of law. Bansawi preferred a measure of ambiguity in his stand. He realized that any argument over the legality of his actions might eventually weaken his position. The theologians' association with him may or may not have been to their spiritual benefit, but their silence over his position certainly guaranteed its acceptability among literate Muslims. In general, within the Muslim community the sharī'a had been the principal reference point, even if only as lip service. A more straightforward resistance to it would have been self-defeating; it would have antagonized many of those otherwise prepared to concede an equivocal stance.

It was not that Bansawi was any less concerned with either the destiny of the faith or the integrity and cohesion of the community. While watching and participating in Hindu religious festivals, this Sufi was motivated not only by an urge to establish rapport with the followers of local cults, he also sought to demonstrate the truth of his own faith. This is amply borne out from the details, for instance, of Sufi–yogi encounters.[60] Here it is interesting to note evidence in a *malfūẓ* (conversations) collection of another eighteenth-century Sufi, Khwaja 'Ali Akbar Maududi Chishti. To the question of whether a Muslim could attend a Hindu *melā*, Maududi's reply was in the negative. He then elaborated to the effect that several Sufis, including Bansawi, visited Hindu fairs and places of worship to see for themselves the mortality and transience of this world, and to experience a sort of specimen of the Day of Judgement. Maududi then related the Quranic story of the Prophet Moses' encounter with the Pharaoh's magicians, which took place on a day of festivities (*yaum-al-zīnat*) among the infidels. Moses participated in the festival with the aim of defeating the magicians and

[59] *Malfūẓ*, pp. 52–3.

[60] Compare Simon Digby, 'Hawk and Dove in Sufi Combat', *Pembroke Papers*, 1, 1990, pp. 7–25; M. Alam, 'Competition and Co-existence: Indo-Islamic Interaction in Medieval North India', *Itinerario*, 1, 1989, pp. 37–59.

establishing the truth of the message.[61] This provided evidence of legitimacy for later missionaries to visit places of worship or gatherings of infidels, if their objective was similar.

The meanings of the faith, its achievements and the cohesion of the community were, however, completely different for Bansawi. The closer a Muslim's contact with his non-Muslim neighbours and the greater his ability to show care and concern for them, the greater the glory of the faith. Religion to him meant bliss for *all.* Bansawi demonstrated this through his Bairagi friends, Chait Ram and Paras Ram. The Bairagis had become almost his formal disciples.[62] It is proper here to consider details of the events which reveal how Bansawi related himself with the great Hindu gods Krishna and Ram. In a Krishna bhaktī dance-drama organized by Chait Ram at his residence, to celebrate the appointment of one of his chelās as his successor, Bansawi reportedly fell into a trance, claimed the Lord was present, and thereby moved the entire audience—which obviously consisted mostly of Hindu followers of the Bairagi. After the play was over, Bansawi retired to rest under the shadow of a nearby banyan tree. Some of the chelās then asked their Bairagi master if they could also have vision of the Lord. The master replied: 'We can give you all that we have got from our *gurus* [preceptors]. But we have no power to show you the Lord. Only if that gentleman who has just left this place wished, you can have the Lord's *darshan.*' The chelās then approached Bansawi and were thus blessed by the Sufi to have Lord Krishna's vision.[63]

The Sufi's Islam did not prevent him from being the most blessed *bhakta* of the Lord. What is equally significant is that the Bairagis' religion did not stand in the way of their seeking the Lord's darshan through a Muslim. Bansawi's life illustrates this remarkable achievement in medieval Awadh culture. In one instance even his eminent theologian disciples, Mulla Nizam-ud-Din, his brother Mulla Muhammad Raza, and their nephew Mulla Kamal-ud-Din, were blessed by their Bansawi pīr to see the Lord with his gopīs on their way from Lucknow to Bansa. The Mullas initially mistook them for an ordinary man and his women. But as they came close, the Lord approached them and said: 'Convey our *salām* [greetings] to your *pīr.*' The Mullas were dismayed, and were also unhappy over the man's open flirtation with women. Only

[61] *Tazkira,* p. 205, Ansari cites *Latā'if-i Maudūdī*, compiled by Maududi's disciple Khwaja Hasan Maududi (d. 1835).

[62] *Malfūz*, pp. 74–8.

[63] *Karāmāt*, pp. 20–1; *Malfūz*, pp. 74–5.

later, when they related their experience to Bansawi, did they learn that the man and women were not ordinary souls. They had actually been favoured with a darshan of Lord Krishna and his gopīs.[64]

In another case, Bansawi is reported to have had a vision of Lord Ram and Lakshman. Once, as Bansawi himself narrates, during his stay in the Deccan, he lost his way in a jungle, late one evening. As it became dark and he was getting jittery, he noticed a tall, handsome man. The man came near and asked him about his home town. To Bansawi's reply that he was from Lucknow the man exclaimed, 'Our Lachhnau', adding, 'then you are my guest'. He disappeared, and in a few moments two handsome gentlemen emerged, bearing sweetmeats (*halwa sohan*). They then instructed the bears and the lions of the jungle to keep watch over their guest that night. They left after a while, promising to come again in the morning to lead Bansawi to his home. Bansawi spent the night comfortably, protected, as the gentlemen had instructed, by jungle beasts; and the following day, two young cowherds led him safely back home.[65]

In all these three instances, whether they actually happened and were narrated by Bansawi or were ascribed to him later in the eighteenth century by hagiographers, there is unmistakable evidence of a Sufi effort to maintain social order. Bansawi accepted, in a measure, the religious beliefs of the Hindus and supported their myths and memories. Strictly and theologically an un-Islamic act, it had nonetheless a noble mission. Bansawi tried to drive home the message that Ram, Lakshman and Krishna, as they were believed to be protectors and promoters of Hindus, were also his friends, and thereby the well-wishers of all of his disciples and followers. No two individuals experience truth the same way, but they must show due regard for each other's beliefs, despite their disagreements.

It is difficult to say if Bansawi believed in the multiplicity of truth. He certainly emphasized the multiple manifestations of the same truth and made a plea to blend conflicting phenomena, howsoever irreconcilable they might appear at first instance to the naked eye. The famous line of Kabir—'*Kabira: bali wah mūrakh ke jo māti mahjid jāi*' (O Kabir: May I sacrifice my life to the fool who visits the mosque in a state of intoxication)—often sent him into a trance.[66] In this line the poet, Bansawi said, had made a plea for the acceptance of what to an average soul

[64] *Malfūz*, p. 126.
[65] Ansari, *Tazkira*, p. 298.
[66] *Karāmāt*, pp. 15–16.

seemed incompatible. Saying prayers in a state of intoxication was unlawful, according to the theologians. But the Sufi, who believed in reconciling the irreconcilables, saw in Kabir the ideal. If this proved unattainable, or incomprehensible, his advice was to remain engrossed in prayer. Here again he sought support in Kabir's '*Tu Rām Rām bhaj, jag jhagran de*' (You keep repeating the name of Ram, even as the world quarrels).[67] Kabir here had suggested that peace should prevail through prayers. Ram bhakti would eventually end the world of hatred.

About the final value of Ism-i A'ẓam (the Great Divine Name), the Sufi had no doubt. His aim was to serve humanity with it. At a feast on the occasion of Janmashtami (Lord Krishna's birthday) at Paras Ram's house, the host got panicky when he realized the food was not enough for those invited. He approached Bansawi for help. The latter directed his son to inscribe the name of Ghaus-i-A'zam at the door of the kitchen, and this Muslim ritual, far from polluting a Hindu kitchen, is reported instead to have averted a crisis.[68]

With all this, Bansawi disapproved of any stance which even remotely implied an insult to the sharī'a. Such was his attitude to the bī-shar'a (*malāmatī*, majẕūb, *qalandar*, etc.). But since this had come to stay with medieval Indian Islam, he, unlike the ordinary orthodox, did not declare it absolutely anti-Islamic. Instead, he tried to integrate bī-shar'a Sufism into his own brand of orthodox Sufism in a bid to bring the former under the hegemony of the latter. This is illustrated from his dealings and relations with Shah Dosi and Shah Daula, the two best-known majẕūbs in Awadh at that time. Shah Dosi lived in Lucknow with considerable command, popularity and fame attached to his supernatural power and miracles. Bansawi made special efforts to win his friendship and to bring him under his influence, even as he showed due respect to his ego and claims to miraculous power. He accepted a piece of limestone as an auspicious gift from Shah Dosi and willed it to remain as part of his legacy at his k͟hānqāh. He saw to it that he and the majẕūb should remain a model for Sufi Islam in the region.[69] In another case, over a brief meeting he made Shah Daula of Rudauli declare, 'the secrets which *Rāghav* [Rām] declined to reveal have now been divulged to him by Rajāk [Razzāq]'.[70]

[67] Ibid., pp. 24–7.

[68] Manāqib (MS Mīr Baqar 'Alī).

[69] *Karāmāt*, p. 29. The majẕūbs took Bansawi as a *jāgīrdār* and themselves as his *kārinda*, *Manāqib* (MS, Mir Naqar 'Ali). For some more details on Bansawi's encounters with majẕūbs, see *Karāmāt*, p. 303; Ansari, *Taẕkira*, pp. 81–2, 230–1.

[70] *Malfūẓ*, p. 128.

What mystic path Bansawi traversed, and how sublime was the destination he aimed at, have not been my concern. But it was noted that, his yearnings for the ultimate Sufic communion with divinity apart, he was no less anxious for mundane things to be in harmony with each other. The Sufi in Bansawi did not live beyond this world. He was fully sensitive to the politics around, and it would not be wide of the mark to say that he, like other elites, had no small role in the post-imperial Mughal political configuration within the province. Interestingly, he tried to discipline, wherever possible, even the majẕūbs who would otherwise roam unfettered, pronouncing rewards and punishments upon all they encountered. Once a majẕūb disciple of his, in a spiritually 'intoxicated state', promised to give the imperial throne of Delhi to anyone who would prepare the *chillum* of his *huqqa*. When these utterances were reported to Bansawi, he remarked, 'with little control over one's ancestral zamindari, it is easy to claim to reward the kingdom of Delhi!'[71] More than exposing the hollow claim of the majẕūb, Bansawi emphasized the necessity of managing the immediate surroundings via this caustic utterance. A Sufi in Awadh, within the existing conditions, if he claimed power, must first manage the zamindari or the immediate legitimate resources of his followers.

Bansawi's information and interests were not limited to Awadh. According to his biographer, Bansawi had predicted developments at the court of the Mughal emperor Farrukh Siyar (1712–19). He had foreseen the death of the emperor and, subsequently, also the tragic end of the ascendancy of Saiyid 'Abd-ullah and Saiyid Husain 'Ali Khan, the famous king-makers of the early eighteenth century who plotted the deposition of the ill-fated emperor. Bansawi also claimed that the Qutb (the highest in Sufi spiritual hierarchy) of Delhi, who had a soft corner for Farrukh Siyar, had come to Bansa in Awadh and sought Bansawi's intervention in support of the emperor.[72] Bansawi watched the fateful development, apparently disinterestedly.

Bansawi's stand implied his support to the Saiyids, the chief patrons at the Mughal centre of the local Shaikhzadas, from amongst whom Bansawi had come. He was inclined to hold the emperor responsible for the malaise and lent an ear of credence to the version of court politics

[71] *Karāmāt*, p. 31.

[72] Manāqib (MS, Mir Baqar 'Ali); Ansari, *Takira*, p. 242. For factional politics at the court of Farrukh Siyar, *see* Satish Chandra, *Parties and Politics at the Mughal Court*, 2nd edn, Delhi, 1972, pp. 86–167; Z.U. Malik, *Reign of Muhammad Shah*, Bombay, 1977, pp. 22–38.

as given by an Awadh Shaikhzada author, Mir Saiyid Ghulam 'Ali Azad Bilgrami. In Bilgrami's view, the end of the ascendancy of the Saiyids and not the emperor's assassination was the tragedy. This is most forcefully evident in an elegy that Mir 'Abd-ul-Jalil Bilgrami, an eminent poet of Awadh, wrote on the death of Saiyid Husain 'Ali. The assassination of Husain 'Ali Khan seemed to the poet like the martyrdom of Husain, the grandson of the Prophet of Islam, which cast the world of Muslims into untold misery and suffering. While Saiyid Husain 'Ali Khan was identified with Husain of Karbala, the Mughal enemies of the Saiyid represented to Bilgrami, the barbarity of the killers of the great martyr.[73] Interestingly, a major Delhi poet, Mirza 'Abd-ul-Qadir Bedil, had a diametrically different view of the event. Bedil condemned the role of the Saiyids outright and characterized it as an act of unabashed treachery (*namak ḥarāmī*).[74]

Of greater significance is the fact that Bansawi perceived himself as the Qutb-ul-Aqtab (the chief of the Qutbs), which in some measure implied the region's assertion of its claim to superior power and authority. Bansawi thus, perhaps, pleaded for and foresaw what was to come under the nawabs.

The Sufi was not enthusiastic about politics: yet he was not completely detached either. The case of Bansawi, in my view, was not an aberration. At almost every stage in the history of Islam in India, Sufis showed concern for, if they did not directly interfere, in the country's political vicissitudes. Early in the thirteenth century the position of the Turkish rulers seems to have followed upon the support of the Sufis. If, on the one hand, they prayed for the stability of the Sultanate and recommended for political favour the cases of their followers and disciples, they also, on the other, came into open conflict with various *sulṭāns*, and thus had a role in the rise and fall of one or the other. Sultan Iltutmish (1206–36) earned laurels from the Chishtis, while Ghiyas-ud-Din Tughlaq had serious differences with Shaikh Nizam-ud-Din Aulia, principally because the Shaikh refused to return the money he had accepted from his predecessor, Khusrau Khan. The Shaikh had distributed this money to the poor, to whom, he asserted, it rightfully belonged. The Shaikh's illustrious disciple Khwaja Nasir-ud-Din Chiragh-e Delhi openly clashed with Muhammad bin Tughlaq, but had no hesitation in

[73] *Ma'āṣir-ul-Kirām*, II, pp. 253–86.

[74] Ibid., II, p. 149 for Mirza Bedil's opinion and chronogram (*Sādāt ba-wai namak harāmī kardand*), followed by a detailed account by the author, Mir Ghulām 'Ali Azad Bilgrami, to rectify the Mirza's negative image of the Saiyid brothers on pp. 154–73.

blessing the coronation of his successor, Firoz Tughlaq.[75] There is ample evidence of the Sufi's involvement in power politics in the Deccan under the Bahmanis and their successors.[76] Later, under the Mughals, the Naqshbandis, arguably, and the Roshniyas, indisputably, had an overt part in political matters.[77]

Certainly the Sufis, unlike the political elites, were not motivated by any immediate personal material gain or glorification.[78] Often with their own vision of power and authority, they assessed the situation and took firm positions. Their vision and judgement varied with persons, and over the centuries. There were serious differences among them, from one order (silsilā) to another, and sometimes even within an order.[79] A very powerful section of them sought to promote a healthy and positive interaction between the diverse and sometimes conflicting traditions and social practices. Bansawi's endeavour was to link his followers to the chain of such Sufis. This Sufic practice had the support, even though not invariably, in the ideology of Waḥdat-ul-Wujūd. The ideology nourished, and was in turn sustained by, the political compulsions of the rulers. These compulsions forced the rulers to adopt a generally liberal and pragmatic approach.

In the period under consideration, community consciousness often prevailed to blur the other identities; still, the society was not always divided strictly on community lines, even in times of conflict. Muslim rulers lavishly favoured one section of Rajput Hindus in the midst of

[75] *See*, for instance, Simon Digby, 'The Sufi Shaykh and the Sultan: A Conflict of Claims to Authority in Medieval India', *Iran*, XXVIII, 1990, pp. 71–81. For an opposite view, *see*, K.A. Nizami, 'Early Indo-Muslim Mystics and their Attitude Towards the State!', *Islamic Culture*, XXII, 1948, 4 and XIII, 1949, 2.

[76] Compare Richard M. Eaton, *Sufis of Bijapur: Social Roles of Sufis in Medieval India 1300–1700*, Princeton, 1978; Muhammad Suleman Siddiqi, *The Bahmani Sufis*, Delhi, 1989, pt 3, and also 'The Sufis in History in the Bahmani Deccan', my review of the book *Islam and Modern Age*, Delhi, 1990.

[77] Friedmann, *Shaykh Aḥmad Sirhindī*, for a discussion on the Naqshbandis role in Mughal politics; Ashraf Ghani, *Production and Domination: Afghanistan, 1747–1901* (forthcoming), Columbia University Press, Chapter, for a discussion on the Roshniyas' role in Pashtun's struggle for empire.

[78] But on occasion material consideration would also influence the Sufis' attitude. For one such discussion, *see* Iqtidar Alam Khan, 'Shaikh Abd-ul-Quddus Gangohi's Relations with Political Authorities: A Reappraisal', *Medieval India: A Miscellany*, IV, Delhi, 1977, pp. 73–90.

[79] Digby, 'The Sufi Shaykh and the Sultan . . .'; also his 'The Sufi Shaikh as a Source of Authority in Medieval India', *in* Marc Gaborieau (ed.), *Islam and Society in South Asia*, Paris, 1986, pp. 57–77.

their fierce fights against others. The Rajputs too saw as their enemies only those of the Muslim gentry whom they believed to be the Muslim ruler's agents, appropriators of their ancient rights and privileges. Again, as there was no homogeneous Hindu community, the followers of Islam entertained diverse notions of piety and spirituality. The Sufi's insistence on his own experimentation with truth (*ṭarīqa*) threatened a clash with the theologian's codified sharī'a; they rarely matched with each other without obvious compromises. Sharī'a and ṭarīqa, and for that matter Islam, thus acquired a variety of forms and meanings. To a Mujaddidi Sufi in Delhi, a shī'a appeared a renegade; a Qadiri Sufi in Bansa in Awadh could experience divinity in a Hindu ensemble with Hindu Bairagis. Along the multiple religious traditions, there existed diverse and variegated manifestations of medieval political culture. If one tradition tended to encourage distance or conflict across religious or sectarian lines, another induced amity. There was no single dominant tradition. Separate religious identities remained, with no single serious or comprehensive effort to provide an alternative basis for social existence. This of course is not to underrate the fact that Waḥdat-ul-Wujūd, the ideological support for resilient Islam, remained generally the most acceptable Sufi doctrine in Awadh in our period. It influenced and added to the dynamics of political and social alignments.

IV
Resources of Tradition

8

Nehru, Religion and Secularism

S. GOPAL

The idea of a secular India is today under siege, and doubts are being raised even about its roots. Distinguished sociologists and political scientists argue that secularism cannot endure in India because it is an alien cultural ideology, imposed on a country to which it is not suited, primarily by India's first prime minister, Jawaharlal Nehru. It is contended that Nehru believed there was no religious understanding of the cosmos and expected it would yield to a more rational approach as a scientific temper and economic growth gained ground.[1] But this is to oversimplify and thereby misinterpret Nehru's views on religion as well as the basis of secularism in India.

In youth and early middle age, Nehru was a conventional believer, and some of his public utterances would have done credit to a religious chauvinist. Speaking at Jhansi in 1921, for example, at a meeting over which the Sankaracharya of Puri presided, he called on Hindus to support the khilafat campaign, because 'if the English succeeded in destroying the Muslim religion, they will try to destroy your religion, our religion, the Hindu religion'. He then, while commending non-violent non-cooperation, conceded that if 'there is anybody who unsheathes his sword to save his country or his religion, you cannot call him a coward'.[2]

[1] T.N. Madan, 'Secularism in its Place', *Journal of Asian Studies*, November 1987, pp. 747–59; A. Nandy, 'The Politics of Secularism and the Recovery of Religious Tolerance', *in* V. Das (ed.), *Mirrors of Violence*, Delhi, 1990, pp. 69–93.

[2] 13 June 1921. *Selected Works of Jawaharlal Nehru* (henceforth *SW*), First Series,

But thereafter, in the mid-twenties, a reading of Marx and Bertrand Russell led him to reject dogma and the dogmatic mentality, and to perceive the social and political abuse of religion. The growing communal rancour in India reinforced this attitude, and he saw the need for scotching 'our so-called religion', for secularizing the intelligentsia at least and for proceeding on secular lines in politics. 'How long that will take I cannot say but religion in India will kill that country and its politics if it is not subdued.'[3]

Nehru had by this time no use for conventional or organized religion and gave up temple-going and participation in rituals. A mild agnostic who prided himself on a pagan outlook and approved of the ancient practice of an altar to the unknown God, he had scorn for priests and theologians who took firm positions on what was bound to be unknown, quarrelled fiercely with each other and testified to the truth by breaking heads. The founders of the world's religions had been among the greatest and noblest of men whom humanity had known, but those who came after them had been far from great or good. Religion, meant to make people better, in fact had made them behave like beasts; instead of bringing enlightenment, religions had often tried to keep people in the dark; they had not broadened people's minds but frequently made them narrow-minded and intolerant. Many great and fine deeds had been performed in the name of religion, but in its name millions had also been killed and every possible crime committed. Preaching elevation of the immortal soul had gone alongside reducing the mortal body to ashes.

Nor was Nehru impressed with talk of the other world. There was enough work to do in this world without bothering about the next. 'There is too much', he told Indians on his return from Europe at the end of 1927, 'of what is called religion in our life and politics. The less we talk of and worry about the next world, the more good we are likely to do our fellow countrymen and country'.[4] Those whose actions were prompted by hopes of going to heaven after death were like children whose behaviour was inspired by promises of being rewarded with jam puffs.[5] The

---

vol. 1, Delhi, 1972, pp. 177, 183. The speech was delivered in Hindi and the only report we have is the English version prepared by police reporters; hence there may be distortions, but the text we have generally represents Nehru's viewpoint at this time.

[3] To Syed Mahmud from Geneva, 15 July 1926, *SW*, First Series, vol. 2, Delhi, 1972, p. 235.

[4] Statement to the press, Colombo, 19 December 1927, *SW*, First Series, vol. 3, Delhi, 1972, pp. 1–2.

[5] Letter to his daughter from jail, 20 January 1931, *Glimpses of World History* (henceforth *Glimpses*), Allahabad, 1933, pp. 37–8.

methods of reason and of science were sufficient for clear thought and correct action in this world, and left no room for the authoritarianism and encouragement of superstition and backwardness associated with religions. In the West, such rejection had taken the form of a struggle for freedom of conscience, but in India this had not seemed to be necessary because in the early days there had been no compulsion and men and women had been free to believe what they liked. But gradually the rites and obscurantism of a degraded religion became dominant and reduced the people to slaves of the 'sacred books', customs and conventions. The chains of retrograde ideas and outworn prejudices were far worse than the chains which tie up bodies, and men and women, though unaware of these invisible bonds, were in fact held in their terrible grip.[6]

Religion not only fettered the mind; it also allowed itself to be exploited by political and economic interests. But getting rid of religion in India did not seem to Nehru to pose a serious problem. He knew, of course, the causes that contributed to the continuous strengthening of the religious element in Indian politics: the social backwardness among all sections of the Indian people, the uneven nature of economic development in and between various parts of India, the advantage taken by the British of the prevalent social disharmony and their support of conservative elements, the Hinduized outlook of Indian nationalism and the widely accepted concept of Hindus and Muslims co-operating as two distinct communities rather than acting together as Indians. But he believed that religion in politics would disappear of its own, as had happened in Europe, with the spread of education and with industrialization replacing religious strife with economic conflicts. So, for the time being, he thought it sufficient to incorporate in the Resolution on Fundamental Rights, at the Karachi Congress in March 1931, clauses asserting that every citizen of India should enjoy freedom of conscience and the right to freely profess and practise any religion subject to public order and morality, that all citizens were equal before the law, irrespective of religion, creed, caste or sex, that no disability attached to citizens for these reasons in regard to public employment and in the exercise of any trade or calling, and that the state should observe neutrality in regard to all religions.

These provisions constitute the core of secularism as we understand it today. The Resolution did not suggest that all religions had an element of truth or that all religions were true, but insisted that religion should

[6] Letter to his daughter, 28 June 1932, *Glimpses*, p. 241.

have no role in public affairs and the state should be equidistant from all religions and not support any. The clauses were drafted in line with the thinking of Nehru rather than that of Gandhi. Once the leading political party in India was committed to this secular attitude, Nehru expected communalism to become a non-event. The masses had not been affected by it, and the communal parties, both Hindu and Muslim, derived their support from the feudal and upper classes, defensive of vested interests, seeking office and employment from the British and pandering to myth and passion in their efforts to secure a base among the people.

To Nehru these parties seemed pygmies with feet of clay, who would lose relevance once the masses were provided with an ideology which would replace religion and who would fade into nothingness once the British were pushed out. He, therefore, in accordance with his favourite strategy of indirect approach, ignored the communal problem and concentrated his energies on the campaign against imperialism and on the necessity of giving the national movement an economic orientation. The vast majority of the Indian people, whatever their religion, bore the common burdens of hunger and poverty and if attention were given to the alleviation of these conditions, the curse of religion in politics would ipso facto diminish. Religious minorities should be of no political significance; the only minority which mattered and which had to be resisted was that of the rich exploiters in the town and the countryside.

Life, however, as Nehru himself often acknowledged, is different from and larger than logic. Communalism might have been a bodiless ghost but it was a ghost which, in the penultimate decades of the Raj, refused to vanish and continued to thirst for blood. So, setting aside his view that the Hindu–Muslim problem was an artificial contrivance which was not of vital concern to the masses, Nehru decided, during the latter half of 1933 when he was out of prison, for the first time, to face the issue squarely and to make a frontal attack on communalism as a cover for political reaction. He condemned the Hindu Mahasabha for its reactionary and anti-national policy of co-operation with the Government and support of vested interests. This criticism applied equally of course to Muslim communal organizations, but Nehru rebuked them in milder terms. They seemed to him at least middle class and representative in some degree of the Muslim viewpoint; and its leaders behaved with greater dignity than those of the Hindu Mahasabha, who spoke only for capitalists, landlords and a few princes and their hangers-on. Nehru also thought it understandable that the Muslims, being economically and educationally backward, would be apprehensive about the future.

'Honest communalism is fear; false communalism is political reaction.'[7] To distinguish between shades of communalism and to contend that it could sometimes be honest and therefore, presumably, legitimate, was to embark on a dangerous course. It at once jeopardized the position of the many Muslims in the Congress who participated in the national movement; and Nehru made this worse by stating that no other organization could successfully challenge the claim of the communalists to speak for the Muslims and that their aggressively communal character gave them an advantage over Muslims who were committed to nationalism.

What explains this attitude in the thirties which ran counter to Nehru's general position and to his later efforts to combat the growing influence of the Muslim League? To some extent his slant in favour of Muslim communalism at this point was a reflection of his distaste for the efforts of M.A. Ansari and other Muslims in the Congress to reach a political settlement of the communal problem. To Nehru it was a futile endeavour to seek mutual adjustments, through formal negotiations and informal conversations, with Muslim communal leaders; unity conferences would never succeed because the British could always outbid the Congress, and the Muslims in the Congress were constantly on the retreat and continuously offering concessions to which there could be no end. Far better, it seemed to Nehru, to accept that the Muslim minority in general was afraid for the future, and to exorcize this fear not by encouraging communal leaders but by granting linguistic and cultural safeguards on the lines of the Karachi Resolution and focusing attention on economic issues.

At a deeper level, Nehru's attitude was born of his conviction, which he shared with Gandhi, that the communalism of the majority community was far more dangerous than that of any minority in India. For Hindu communalism could masquerade as nationalism and could well degenerate into the Indian version of fascism. But if the Hindus rejected communalism and treated the minorities with generosity and as of equal status as themselves, irrespective of their religion, then there would be no scope for the communal virus to flourish among the minorities. It was the Hindu majority which had the greatest opportunity for divorcing religion from public life and for firmly entrenching this position.

All this seemed airy theorizing as, in the mid-thirties, communal rioting continued to scar the face of the country; and Nehru, languishing

[7] Interview to the press, 29 November 1933, *SW*, First Series, vol. 6, Delhi, 1974, p. 164.

helplessly in prison, was plunged in gloom. 'What a disgusting savage people we are. Politics, progress, socialism, communism, science—where are they before this black religious savagery.'[8] But a chance for him to appeal directly to the people came in 1936, with him out of jail and election announced for the provincial assemblies with a wider franchise than before. Nehru undertook a country-wide campaign and in all his many speeches played down the communal issue, held up independence and better economic conditions as the first priorities and concentrated his fire on the alien rulers, the capitalists and the landlords. Speaking in the United Provinces on the same platform as Jinnah, Nehru referred to communalism as no more than a nuisance which made people petty-minded and hid from view the major problems. In his presidential address at the Faizpur Congress in December 1936 he did not refer to communalism at all.

The results of the elections validated Nehru's assessment that communalism was a shallow, skin-deep aberration. It had obviously not spread widely even among the middle classes. The electorate was still limited, with stringent educational and property qualifications; but even in the constituencies reserved for Muslims, the Muslim League could gain only 108 out of 482 seats, and 0.321 million out of 7.319 million Muslim votes. Nor could the League win enough seats to form the government in Bengal, the Punjab and the North-West Frontier Province, where the majority of the people were Muslims. So it was logical for Nehru to support the refusal of the Congress to form coalition minorities with the Muslim League in the provinces where it had obtained clear majorities. Historians, basing themselves on hindsight, have criticized this decision; but it would have been suicidal for the Congress to throw away its credentials as a national, secular organization and, functioning as a Hindu party, to join hands with a Muslim communal party which had poor support even in a restricted electorate. It made better sense to move forward from the electoral successes of 1937 to an appeal to the masses rather than turn backwards and search for political agreements at an elite level. Nehru was particularly eager to approach the Muslim masses. They had been too long doped with communal poison and were suspicious of the Congress; but he thought he saw a ferment among the younger Muslims and the rank-and-file which should not be ignored. Nehru believed that there was more freedom in social relations among Muslims than among the Hindus and,

[8] Diary entry, 17 April 1935, *SW*, First Series, vol. 6, Delhi, 1974, p. 348.

perhaps because of this, would accept a new thought if convinced of it. So in 1937 he initiated a Muslim 'mass contacts' campaign. This was an effort to implement his theory that the masses had no communal problem and could be led by an economic programme to forget this side-issue. But the opportunity was squandered. The 'mass contacts' campaign had some success in parts of the United Provinces, Bihar, Bengal and the Punjab, but generally failed to make headway in the rural areas. Nehru's effort was broken by the lukewarm attitude of the right wing of the Congress rather than by the opposition of Jinnah and the Muslim League.[9]

In fact, greater momentum was attained by Jinnah's counter-campaign, in reply to what he regarded as Nehru's challenge, to strengthen the position of the League among the Muslim masses by appealing to God and the Koran and alleging that Islam was in danger. Taking advantage of the error of the Congress in accepting office with little power in the provinces, Jinnah slid easily from attacking the Congress, representing majority opinion, to denouncing it as representing Hindu opinion. He complained of general harassment of Muslims in provinces with Congress ministries without clearly specifying his charges. Nehru had gradually and reluctantly to change his opinion that there was no real strength behind the League. Jinnah's demand that his party be recognized as the authoritative and representative organization of the Muslims was still unacceptable; but it was no longer enough merely to allay the fears of the minorities in matters of culture, language and religious observances. Nehru was now willing to consider, in any scheme of provincial redistribution, the grant to important groups and minorities of territories within which they would have full opportunities for self-development. But the League, having little interest in non-political matters, paid no attention; and by the beginning of 1939 Nehru was forced to acknowledge that the communal problem had acquired a new and serious aspect. The fear of the Muslims that they might be swamped by the Hindu majority had widened considerably. Particularly in the United Provinces, there was more general ill-will among the Muslim masses towards the Congress than at any time before,[10] and fascist elements were becoming stronger in both the communal parties. Even so, Nehru still remained hopeful that economic issues would wither the

[9] Mushirul Hasan, 'The Muslim Mass Contacts Campaign', *in* Mushirul Hasan (ed.), *India's Partition: Process, Strategy and Mobilization*, Delhi, 1993, pp. 132–58.

[10] Nehru to Rajendra Prasad, 7 July 1939, *SW*, First Series, vol. 9, Delhi, 1976, p. 471.

communal problem if the provincial governments gave priority to such measures as the annulment of rural debt and the arrears of rent; but the Congress ministries were too conservative to move in such matters. By the time war broke out and these ministries resigned, Nehru had to accept that much ground had been lost. Even civil war seemed possible to him now.

The situation compelled Nehru to turn his attention to negotiations, by which he had never set much store, with the League. His slender hopes for success were based on the League's commitment to independence; and it struck him that the League's attainment of a mass basis might prove helpful in bringing pressure to bear on its reactionary leadership. If the Congress and the League could work together in dealing with the British Government in the war crisis, the communal grievances might fall into perspective. But Nehru, as he himself recognized, was not the man for such negotiations. 'I must confess to you', he wrote to Jinnah after a round of talks with him,

> that in this matter I have lost confidence in myself though I am not usually given that way. But the last two or three years have had a powerful effect on me. My own mind moves on a different plane and most of my interests lie in other directions. And so, though I have given much thought to the problem and understand most of its implications, I feel as if I was an outsider and alien in spirit.[11]

Nor was Jinnah interested during the war years in negotiations with the Congress. He was preoccupied in building up mass support with the co-operation of the British, which was now readily available. Nehru, on his part, became more concerned with giving assurances to other religious minorities, the Christians and the Sikhs, that the Congress was committed to secularism and that legitimate minority interests could be protected by a constituent assembly in which such questions would be settled not by a majority vote but by common consent, and differences referred, if necessary, to arbitration not by the British but preferably by the League of Nations.

However, much of these war years was spent by Nehru in prison, and he was able to think more deeply on his own attitude to religion. He was still critical of the way in which religions imprisoned truth in dogmas and encouraged empty ceremonials and practices. They had discouraged their followers from trying to understand the unknown and their philosophy of submission to supernatural powers frowned on social

[11] Nehru to Jinnah, 18 October 1939, *SW*, First Series, vol. 10, Delhi, 1977, p. 359.

effort. Organized religion, allying itself to theology and often more concerned with its vested interests than with matters of the spirit, tended to close and limit the mind and to encourage a temper the very opposite of that of science. Reversing Voltaire's epigram, Nehru suggested that if there were a God it may be desirable not to look up to Him. But his agnosticism and detestation of priests and their behaviour had never meant shutting himself off from the higher values. The influence of Mahatma Gandhi, with his emphasis on morals and ethics in public life, was alone sufficient to ensure this. In his autobiography, written in the mid-thirties, Nehru conceded that religion was more than blind belief and reaction; there was something else in it which catered to a deep inner craving of human beings. He quoted with approval John Dewey's statement that religion was whatever introduced genuine perspective into the shifting episodes of existence, and any activity pursued for an ideal end because of conviction of its general and enduring value. He was also in sympathy with Romain Rolland's definition of religion as a fearless search for truth at all costs with single-minded sincerity, for it presupposes faith in an objective to human effort higher than the life of existing society and even higher than the life of humanity as a whole.[12]

The extensive reading of Indian philosophy in Ahmadnagar fort from August 1942 strengthened this inclination to see elements of value in the higher reaches of religion. The Buddha, of course, with his total commitment to finding the truth and his indifference to the other world, appealed to both in the romantic and the rational sides of Nehru's nature. Reading Asvaghosha's *Buddhacharita* (written about AD 100) and coming across the Buddha's reply to the deputation that had come to beg him to return home, 'I would enter a blazing fire, but I would not enter my home with my goal unattained,' Nehru recorded that when he read this sentence 'a thrill passed through me, almost an electric shock'.[13] But even the other schools of Indian philosophy attracted him as tracing the adventure of ideas. He was confirmed in his earlier feeling that religion supplied some deeply felt inner need of human nature and the vast majority of people all over the world could not do without some form of religious belief. It gave a set of values to human life, and though some of these values were outdated and even harmful, others were still the foundation of morality and ethics. Without some faith in spiritual tenets beyond the scope of the physical world, some reliance on moral

[12] *An Autobiography*, London, 1936, Indian edn, 1962, p. 380.

[13] Entry in prison diary, 11 November 1943, *SW*, First Series, vol. 13, Delhi, 1980, p. 282.

and idealistic conceptions, there would be no anchorage or purpose in life. Whether we believed in God or not, it was impossible not to believe in something: some ideal or distant objective draws us on, though reason may find little substance in it. All human beings have a philosophy of life, vague or precise.

Nehru was also no longer as scathing about the other world as he had been. He now acknowledged the significance of the vast unknown surrounding us. Life did not consist entirely of the visible world; it was continually touching an invisible world which no thinking person could ignore, and the normal methods of science were not adapted to deal with it. But mysticism irritated Nehru as vague, flabby and wallowing in a sea of emotional experience. He was more attracted by metaphysics which required hard thinking and, though based on premises which were assumed to be self-evident, thereafter required the application of logic and reason; but he was never fully at ease with it.

Nehru was still an agnostic, but a Hindu agnostic. He had grown up in an environment which took for granted the *atman*, a future life, the karma theory of cause and effect, and reincarnation; he had been affected by them and was favourably disposed towards these assumptions. But he did not believe in any of these theories as a matter of religious faith and they did not affect his life. He had a sense of mysteries, of unknown depths, as well as a desire to understand them; but he did not posit a God, and the idea of a personal God was alien to him. However, he could to some extent intellectually appreciate the concept of monism and was attracted towards the Advaita Vedanta philosophy. The diversity and fullness of nature stirred him and produced a harmony of the spirit, and he felt at home in the old Indian and Greek pagan and pantheistic atmosphere but without the conception of a god or of gods. He was also more impressed by what was essentially the Hindu idea that a human being could by self-effort rise to great heights rather than by the Christian notion that a superior power took the form of a human being.

Nehru had of course alongside been attracted, since the twenties, to Marxism. But he found now that, while he could accept much of the Marxist philosophical outlook without difficulty, it did not satisfy him completely or answer all the questions in his mind; 'almost unawares, a vague idealist approach would creep into my mind, something rather akin to the Vedanta approach'. It was not a difference between mind and matter but rather of something that lay beyond the mind. Nehru still, while not ruling out intuition and other such methods of sensing truth and reality, clung to the anchor of precise objective knowledge based on reason and experiment; but he now saw much in common between the latest conclusions of science and the fundamental ideas underlying the Vedanta.[14]

Of greater immediate and practical significance was Nehru's understanding of India's heritage. He had always been aware that religious bigotry had little role to play in India's composite culture. In the early thirties he had pointed out to his daughter that Mahmud of Ghazni, who destroyed the Somnath temple, was hardly a religious man and was no more than a successful soldier. More representative was Akbar, who might be considered to be the father of Indian nationalism, for at a time when there was little of nationality in the country and religion was a dividing factor, Akbar had deliberately placed the ideal of a common Indian nationhood above the claims of separatist religions. But such success as he attained in this endeavour was not due entirely to his own efforts. Akbar was a product of his times. The spirit of synthesis was aboard, and Akbar responded to it and became in fact its chief exponent.[15]

These scattered thoughts became a full-fledged analysis, over ten years later, in *The Discovery of India*. Nehru now worked out in detail, by a study of the country's long history, that the unity of India was an emotional reality rooted in history rather than a mere geographical creation or an imposed standardization of externals. Beneath the shared intellectual and cultural life among the educated was a common popular culture of philosophy, history, myth and legend. Existing traditions were accepted, adapted and changed to meet new circumstances and ways of thought, and at the same time new traditions were developed. Every challenge of incursion of foreign elements was dealt with successfully by absorption and a new synthesis. Islam had come to India as a religion centuries before it came as a political force, and it had been received with the usual tolerance. When later the rulers happened to be Muslim, the essential continuity of Indian life was not vitally affected and the new rulers rarely interfered with the ways and customs of the people. A composite culture developed in such fields as architecture, food, dress and music. Even the two religions, Hinduism and Islam, influenced each other.

In Nehru's view, the stable continuity ensured by the gradual growth of a varied culture resulted in a mellowness and gentleness which no

[14] *The Discovery of India*, Calcutta, 1945, pp. 13–23, 622, 625–6.

[15] *Glimpses*, pp. 159–60, 317–18.

amount of misfortune had been able to rub off. But this did not mean, as was often suggested, otherworldliness. The staying power of Indian culture was derived from a sound instinct for life. India had achieved an equilibrium between external activity and inner development by stressing both an acceptance of life and a detachment from it. The Buddha was the noblest example of this dual approach. Every period, during which civilization had flourished in India, witnessed an intense joy in life and nature, a pleasure in the act of living, the development of literature and the arts, and a highly sophisticated inquiry into relations between the sexes. Even in the earliest times, wrote Nehru—and the sentence is worth quoting because it obviously represents his ideal—Indians were 'a light-hearted race, confident and proud of their traditions, dabbling in the search for the mysterious, full of questions addressed to nature and human life, attaching importance to the standards and values they had created but taking life easily and joyously, and facing death without much concern.' Joy in the present and harmony with life and nature did not shut out the search for deeper knowledge; and this combination lay, as Nehru saw it, at the heart of the endurance of India's identity. Seeking the answers to essential questions was obviously the task of a small minority; but most people had some sense of purpose, of cause and effect, and of hope. Epics, legends and traditions carried value to all levels of cultural development, held together a variegated society and provided a common background of ethical living.

Writing during a dark phase of Indian nationalism, Nehru was optimistic about the future. He was confident that, with greater opportunities, the inner failure which, rather than external attack, causes the decay of civilizations, could be arrested and changes moulded in line with the Indian heritage. The past of India, with all its cultural variety, belonged to all her people whatever their religion. If all Indians had been converted to Islam or to Christianity, their culture would still have remained the same. It was a living culture, with a firm foundation of principles but with a dynamic outlook. The spirit of inquiry directed to logical reasoning prepared the ground for scientific method. The philosophical ideal was the stress on truth, beauty and goodness rather than on the acquisition of power and wealth. The general approach was one of the full acceptance of life, with asceticism the goal of but a limited few. The Indian heritage led naturally to scientific humanism even while it provided for the anchorage of faith. Their culture would in the future enable the Indian people to face life with the temper and approach of science, allied to philosophy and with reverence for all that lies beyond.

Coming out of prison in 1945, Nehru was forced to recognize that, whatever the long perspective eloquently outlined in *The Discovery of India*, in the last phase of the national struggle the dark shadow of communalism enveloped the scene. Gone was the buoyant optimism of the mid-thirties when he had asserted: 'The day on which India achieves her freedom, communal differences and jealousies will get solved of themselves.'[16] Jinnah might have thought of the demand for a separate Muslim homeland as a tactical move, but the Muslim masses had become so inflamed that the situation after the war, especially after the Calcutta killings of August 1946, was beyond control. Even had Jinnah wished to steer events, they had got out of hand and moved of their own momentum towards partition. Nehru and the Congress accepted the creation of Pakistan as a political necessity and not as recognition of the validity of the two-nation theory on the basis of religion. After the fierce frenzy of the riots of 1947, followed soon after by the murder of the Mahatma, independent India sought to move away from a sharp descent into savagery and to put together the broken pieces of national identity; 'We are building', Nehru asserted in a broadcast to the nation, 'a free secular state, where every religion and belief has full freedom and equal honour, where every citizen has equal liberty and equal opportunity.'[17] With a large Muslim minority remaining in India, the categories of secularism as defined in the Karachi Resolution of 1931 became all the more important, for they form the only possible basis of a democratic, multi-religious society. The essential principles of national cohesion are not opposition to religion but the divorce of religion from politics and public life, the separation of the state from all faiths, the insistence on religion as a private matter for the individual with no bearing on civic rights and duties, and freedom for the profession of diverse forms of religious worship, provided they do not create problems of law and order. To act in any other way, as Nehru never tired of repeating, would be barbarous and medieval. But while these principles are the products of scientific, rational thinking and are integral parts of a civilized outlook, Nehru stressed that they were also inherent in India's composite culture. They were not, as has recently been contended, a gift to India of West European Christianity. They drew strength from their own logic but they also make India's historical experience meaningful. Nehru's analysis in *The Discovery of India* is corroborated by recent scholarship. Till about the middle of the eighteenth century, religion did not

[16] Speech at Amritsar, 31 May 1936, *SW*, First Series, vol. 7, Delhi, 1975, p. 270.

[17] Nehru's broadcast from Delhi, 20 October 1948, *SW*, Second Series, vol. 7, Delhi, 1988, p. 151.

dominate public affairs in India but was almost one of several factors in a society, with 'a predominantly syncretic culture' and with no 'pervading sense of social separateness'.[18] Such tension and riots as occurred thereafter were the result of religious divisions coinciding with economic antagonisms or of local economic change being mixed up with religious disputes. Communalism as a distinct phenomenon emerged only from the middle of the nineteenth century.

This was also in tune with Nehru's thinking on religion in these years. An adherence to basic values, a commitment to ethical conduct and a sneaking sympathy for the Vedanta philosophy—these were all parts of Nehru's outlook throughout his many years as prime minister, and dispose of the contention that he was seeking to bind free India in the straitjacket of a Western ideology. The same trends of thought which surfaced in *The Discovery of India* may be seen in even sharper focus when he undertook a rethinking of first principles in 1958. Rationalism seemed to him inadequate for it appeared to deal with the surface of things without uncovering the inner core. More compelling was the Vedantic approach that everything, animate and inanimate, had its place in the organic whole, and a spark of the divine impulse, energy or life-force pervaded the universe. So Nehru concluded that India should seek the objective of individual improvement and the lessening of inequalities without forgetting the ethical and spiritual aspects of life; 'and perhaps we might also keep in view the old Vedantic ideal of the life force which is the inner base of everything that exists.'[19] Over a year later he replied to a question about his religious beliefs:

> I am not attracted to the dogmas and conventions of religion, but I have certainly been attracted to the spiritual values in life and to the basis of Indian philosophy. I have no doubt that the great religions of the world contain vital truths. But unfortunately these vital truths are often forgotten and some superstructure is emphasized.[20]

He was impressed by a remark of Vinoba Bhave that the days of politics and religion had gone and the days of science and spirituality had come—understanding by spirituality the basic values common to the great religions. 'I am not exactly', he summed up to a British correspondent, 'a religious person, although I agree with much that religions have to say.'[21] Finally, in one of his last writings two days

[18] C.A. Bayly, 'The Pre-history of "Communalism"? Religious Conflict in India, 1700–1860', *Modern Asian Studies*, 1985, vol. 2, pp. 177–203.

[19] 'The Basic Approach', 13 July 1958, *A.I.C.C. Economic Review*, 15 August 1958.

[20] To J. Higgin, 18 December 1959, Nehru papers.

[21] To J. Cook, 7 April 1964, Nehru papers.

before his death, he emphasized that India should benefit by modern industrial processes and increase production; 'but in doing so we must not forget that the essential objective to be aimed at is the quality of the individual and the concept of *dharma* underlying it.'[22] Nehru was without religious faith but not without religious feeling.

Secularism in India, then, does not follow any definition in a dictionary but has evolved to suit a multireligious society. The ideal secular attitude is also in India the most pragmatic policy. Only secularism of this type, derived from India's past and suited to the present context, can be the cornerstone of an egalitarian, forward-looking society, with religious pluralism, full civil liberties and equal opportunities. It is the only possible social cement for a democratic community and the sole way to enable unqualified efforts at social and economic betterment. It provides every citizen with a sense of partnership and is more than tolerance; it is about equality. It underlay Nehru's thinking and functioning as prime minister. 'We are trying to evolve', he wrote towards the end of his days, 'a modern state within the framework of India's culture.'[23] Secularism coloured even his foreign policy. He could not contemplate transferring Kashmir to Pakistan merely because there was a Muslim majority in that state. Again, while Nehru was prepared on occasions to accept war with Pakistan on political grounds, he was reluctant to do so in 1950 because at that time the cause seemed to be purely communal.

To commit India to secularism and enact its essentials in the Constitution was only the beginning of the struggle. The fact of partition and memories of the migrations and the communal conflicts that came with it could not be easily forgotten. The consequent Hindu revivalism created, in Nehru's words, a crisis of the spirit,[24] and to start, as he hoped, a new chapter in line with India's heritage setting aside recent aberrations, was not going to be easy. Out of tune with the communal mood which seemed to have general acceptance, Nehru at times considered resignation. 'All of us', he wrote sadly, 'seem to be getting infected with the refugee mentality or worse still, the R.S.S. mentality. That is a curious finale to our careers.'[25]

The destruction of Hindu communalism and the establishment of a

[22] 25 May 1964, Preface to Sriman Narain, *Socialism in Indian Planning*, Delhi, 1964.

[23] Nehru to T.A. Nizami, 6 May 1964, Nehru papers.

[24] Nehru to Rajendra Prasad, 7 August 1947, *SW*, Second Series, vol. 3, Delhi, 1985, pp. 189–91.

[25] Nehru to Mohanlal Saxena, 10 September 1949, *SW*, Second Series, vol. 13, October 1992, p. 107. The RSS (Rashtriya Swayamsevak Sangh) is a militant Hindu organization.

secular state and society were therefore vital for the survival of a democratic India. Communalism, apart from its narrow and limited visions, was a cloak for reaction in all forms. To bring religion into politics meant the ruin of both. Throughout his seventeen years as prime minister, except for a few months in 1949 at the time of the Telangana rebellion—when he asserted that there was nothing to choose between communalism and communism in its violent phase—Nehru was never in doubt that Hindu political resurgence was the primary threat to a modern, progressive India. He felt even more strongly than before 1947 that it was the responsibility of the Hindus in India to provide the religious minorities with a sense of security. In particular, they had to make the large number of Muslims, who preferred after the partition to remain in India, feel at home and not see themselves as second-class citizens existing on sufferance. There might be a few Muslims who were communal and out to make mischief; and they would have to be dealt with sternly. But most Muslims in India immediately after 1947 were down and out and on the defensive; and it served no purpose to question their loyalty which could not be produced to order. Winning the Muslims over was a problem of social psychology to be faced by the majority community. They should treat the minorities as a trust rather than as extraneous elements to be crushed or appeased. The test of success is not what the majority community thinks but how the minority communities feel. Full scope for the minorities is as important a criterion of a working democracy as the effective rule of the majority. A sense of grievance on the part of a minority demands self-examination by the majority.

So, when, in December 1949, some images were smuggled into the mosque at Ayodhya in Uttar Pradesh and proclaimed to be the manifestation of the avatar Rama, Nehru recognized the wider implications of this occurrence and urged the Uttar Pradesh government to take remedial action. That government, however, was reluctant to do so and Nehru, in face of this apathy, considered leaving all else and going on a crusade to combat communalism. But the authorities in Uttar Pradesh dissuaded him from proceeding even to Ayodhya, and the consequences of their impassivity are with us still. All that Nehru could do in this particular matter was wring his hands: 'The fact of the matter is that for all our boast, we have shown ourselves a backward people, totally lacking in the elements of culture as any country understands them. It is only those who lack all understanding of culture, who talk so much about it'.[26]

[26] Nehru to G.B. Pant, Chief Minister of Uttar Pradesh, 1950, *SW*, Second Series, vol. 14, Part Two.

However, Nehru took decisive action on the general issue of the creeping paralysis of communalism which seemed to be overtaking even hardened Congressmen. In August 1950, Purushottam Das Tandon, who believed Muslims in India should adopt 'Hindu culture', was elected president of the Congress against Nehru's wishes. Nehru refused to accept this situation. If the argument were that in a democracy the decision of the majority on such an issue as communalism should be respected, 'then I say, to hell with such a democracy'.[27] He forced Tandon's resignation and committed a reluctant Congress to a secular policy. 'If any person raises his hand to strike down another on the ground of religion, I shall fight him till the last breath of my life, both as the head of the government and from outside.'[28]

Despite this ringing declaration, the battle for secularism was far from over. The inauguration of the rebuilt Somnath temple by the president, Rajendra Prasad, made this clear. Secularism demands the disestablishment of all religions. None of them can enjoy a privileged relationship with the state while the government, on its side, should not be, or even thought to be, the agent of any type of religious revival. As prime minister, Nehru was always correct in this matter. He would not associate himself with any function that had a non-secular tinge, and took care to stress that the involvement of the government of India in the 2500th anniversary celebrations of the Buddha in 1956 was not sponsorship of Buddhism but a tribute to the Buddha as India's greatest son. But not all of Nehru's colleagues, even the most senior of them, were as scrupulous in observing the secular ethic that the state should not promote any particular religion. K.M. Munshi, a member of the union cabinet, was the chief patron and promoter of the building of the Somnath temple; the Rajpramukh of Saurashtra wrote to Indian embassies abroad to collect waters and twigs and soil from various countries for the inauguration ceremonies; and the Saurashtra government sanctioned funds. Nor was Nehru able to dissuade the president from being present at the installation.

In promoting the secular idea, Nehru gave attention to all the religious minorities. The Christians created no major problem. While in the years before independence, Nehru shared the general feeling in India that Christianity and imperialism often behaved as partners,[29]

[27] Speech at the Congress session at Nasik, 21 September 1950, *SW*, Second Series, vol. 15, Part One, Delhi, 1993, p. 139.

[28] Speech at Delhi, 2 October 1951, *National Herald*, Lucknow, 4 October 1951.

[29] *An Autobiography*, 1936, pp. 374–5; 'Christian Missionaries in India', 27 February 1940, *SW*, First Series, vol. 10, Delhi, 1977, pp. 430–2.

after 1947 he opposed any hindrance to the practice and propagation of the Christian religion. There was no need to fear evangelical activity and Christians should not be given the impression that they were being suppressed in any way. Such a development, apart from being retrograde and weakening the confidence of a substantial section of the population, ran counter to official policies to integrate the Naga areas and to consolidate popular support in Goa against the Portuguese. He repeatedly pulled up the Congress government in Madhya Pradesh for seeming to be anti-Christian and to be concerned with Christian proselytization, even as later, in 1959 and again in 1962, he publicly disapproved of the interventions of the Christian clergy in the politics of Kerala.

There was, however, a special problem concerning foreign missionaries. Their number nearly doubled soon after 1947. In particular, many American missionaries arrived, spreading out among the villages and projecting, in Nehru's words, 'quietly or aggressively',[30] the American viewpoint in politics at a time when India and the United States differed sharply on various issues. Especially worrying to Nehru and the government was the activity of foreign priests in the north-eastern areas, for they were reported to be fostering ideas of independence and advising the local Christians to keep aloof from the rest of India. Verrier Elwin, himself a British clergyman and Nehru's chief adviser in these matters, wrote that a 'Christian Mahasabha' was being formed.[31] So it was a problem not of missionaries who were foreigners but of foreigners who, though missionaries, were participants in non-religious and anti-national activity. Nehru's approach to the issue was to deal with the principal missionary institutions in India and abroad rather than with individuals and to grant visas liberally to doctors, nurses and specialists. Such missionaries as were asked to leave or were turned away had such action taken on specific political grounds and not because of any general antipathy to evangelical activity. This too was not an approach shared by all those in authority and Nehru had to remind President Rajendra Prasad that, as the symbol of the secular state, he should not have permitted the holding in Rashtrapati Bhavan of a conference where missionaries were generally criticized.[32]

Size and history made the problem of integrating the Muslims more complicated. Aspects of Nehru's policy in this regard were to give

[30] To Amrit Kaur, 25 October 1953, Nehru papers.

[31] V. Elwin, 'Note on Tribal People in Manipur', 24 January 1953, Nehru papers.

[32] Nehru to Rajendra Prasad, 10 August 1953, Nehru papers.

special attention to the recruitment of Muslims in adequate numbers to the armed and civil services, and particularly the police, and to encourage their employment in the private sector. He took much interest in individual cases if they came up before him, and in March 1958 directed the chief ministers to send him quarterly reports of official recruitment, particularly when this was done without examinations.[33] Knowing also that Urdu, while not a monopoly of the Muslims, was a language to which they attached much importance, Nehru pressed his colleagues, especially in Delhi and the United Provinces, to give special consideration to the promotion of Urdu. If this language, which belonged more to the United Provinces than to the whole of Pakistan, were denied its due, the Muslims would begin to feel that they were losing the symbols of their community and there was no honourable place for them in India. So this was more than a matter of language.[34]

Yet, it must be said that certain steps which Nehru, under pressure of circumstances, took, or failed to take, do not fit with his promotion of secularism. Special treatment of minorities and reservations for lower castes, while theoretically a violation of egalitarian principles, can be explained as temporary measures of affirmative action to redress long-standing toleration of injustice. But more serious is the acceptance of communal political parties. In 1948 Nehru committed the government to take action on a resolution of the Constituent Assembly calling for the ban of such parties. This decision, taken in the aftermath of partition, was an obvious aspect of building a secular society. As the state does not interfere with religions, so religious organizations should not meddle in politics. But this resolution has not been implemented to this day. In 1961, Nehru, in the wake of communal riots in several parts of the country, directed the law ministry to examine afresh the matter of banning communal parties but was informed that communal parties were difficult to define and any such attempt might be questioned as an infringement of fundamental rights. But such difficulties could have been overcome more easily in Nehru's time than has proved the case since; and communal parties now flourish vigorously.

Another matter on which Nehru failed to act according to his convictions and in accord with secular principles was the banning of cow-slaughter. Nehru had always been opposed to such a ban. Even in 1923, as mayor of Allahabad, he had persuaded the municipal board to

[33] Nehru to chief ministers, 26 March 1958, G. Parthasarathi (ed.), *Nehru: Letters to Chief Ministers*, vol. v, 1958–64, Delhi, 1989, pp. 34–7.

[34] Nehru to G.B. Pant, Union Home Minister, 9, 10, 12 and 24 June 1958, Nehru papers.

reject a proposal to ban cow-slaughter. In August 1947 he unhesitatingly turned down a suggestion favoured by Rajendra Prasad to ban cow-slaughter as symbolic of the attainment of freedom. He was not prepared to placate Hindu sentiment and viewed the issue as an aspect of the general problem of the breeding of quality cattle.[35] A concern for animal welfare was far more important than any particular measure to prevent the killing of cattle. Yet he allowed the listing of the banning of cow-slaughter as one of the directive principles of state policy in the Constitution. He ensured that nothing came of it in practice. He suggested that any prohibitory legislation should be limited to cows and calves; but even this he discouraged and suggested alternative measures to protect the quality of the breed.[36] Any general ban on cow-slaughter would probably result in the best cattle being killed and the poorest being protected.[37] It would also flare up as a political issue in north-eastern India, where the eating of beef was common. While these valid arguments have ensured that nowhere in India has cow-slaughter been banned, by listing it in the directive principles a blow was dealt to secularism.

An even greater lapse in Nehru's implementation of secular principles was his restriction of the insistence on monogamy to Hindu men and the grant of the rights of divorce and inheritance only to Hindu women. In his keenness to win the confidence of the Muslim community, he failed to provide equality before the law to all Indian women and to sponsor the promulgation of a common civil law code. But there is no room in a secular society for inequalities which claim religious sanction. Religion has to be separated from the law as well as from politics. To deny rights to Muslim women which are available to women of other faiths is a violation of the provision in the Constitution that the state shall not discriminate against any citizen on grounds of religion. The Constituent Assembly had declined, by a resolution in 1948, to accept that Muslim personal law was an inseparable part of the Islamic religion and had rejected attempts to exempt it from the directive principle advocating a uniform civil code. But Nehru felt, in the early fifties, that the time had not yet come to impose on the Muslims in India such decisions taken by what was necessarily a non-Muslim majority. A start should be made with the Hindu code, thereby preparing the ground for the extension of

[35] Nehru to Rajendra Prasad, 7 August 1947, *SW*, Second Series, vol. 3, Delhi, 1985, pp. 189–91.

[36] Nehru to Sri Krishna Sinha, Chief Minister of Bihar, 29 January 1953, Nehru papers.

[37] Nehru to Rajendra Prasad, 30 July 1954, Nehru papers.

its principles to all Indian women. But what Nehru postponed in the fifties has now become even more difficult to carry out.

Nehru's efforts to promote secularism in India, on the basis not of Western ideas but of India's past, were not, therefore, an unqualified or enduring success. He had, in this as in many other matters, the right vision and the correct approach, but the implementation was inadequate and not vigorous enough in the face of entrenched conservatism. Communal rioting occurred throughout the fifties and even increased during the early sixties, and Nehru confessed that a sense of darkness was creeping over him. He had hoped that, as the economic condition of the people improved, religion would recede into the background and cease to be important in public life. He saw a precedent in Europe where the wars of religion, so prominent in the sixteenth century, were rendered irrelevant by economic progress. There was some validity in such an expectation; but he should also have given greater attention to the solvent of education. An educated democracy is synonymous with a secular society, overcoming communalism both of reaction and of fear. It is because of the failure to strengthen the human factor at every level and to foster a robust civil society that the problems which Nehru confronted are now grimmer than ever. But let Nehru have the last word. 'I believe', he wrote soon after independence when the horizon was dark,

> that India can only become great if she preserves that composite culture which she had developed through the ages. I confess, however, that doubts sometimes assail me as to whether this is going to happen or not. And yet at the back of my mind I feel sure that whatever might happen in the present, sometime or other, India will have to tread that path to self-realization and greatness.[38]

[38] Nehru to the Nawab of Bhopal, 9 July 1948, *SW*, Second Series, vol. 7, Delhi, 1988, p. 7.

9

Tradition and Resilience: Mobilizational Energy in the Brahmanical Order*

SATISH SABERWAL

1. RELATIVISM AND CULTURAL APPRAISAL

History and anthropology have both moved towards seeking to comprehend a tradition in terms of its own internal logic, relative to its own totality. This relativism arose in anthropology at an intersection of method and history: the advance in method, associated with Bronislaw Malinowski's immersion in field-work among the Trobrianders during World War I, came as virulent ethnocentrism was spreading in Europe between the Wars. Ruth Benedict's *Patterns of Culture* (1934) argued for the uniqueness of each culture, and respectful curiosity towards other cultures came to mark the subsequent anthropological style. Even when issues are joined comparatively in this way, as by Louis Dumont, the intention is not to pass judgement on the 'other' but to seek to understand the scholar's own through contrast with what is different.

This doctrine of relativism has proved to be remarkably fruitful. It went well with functionalism: that a society's gamut of belief and practice, however bizarre at first encounter, be seen as being functional, if

*Abbreviations: *Contrib.* for *Contributions to Indian Sociology; IESHR* for *Indian Economic and Social History Review; SiH* for *Studies in History*.

Material support has come from a fellowship at Nehru Memorial Museum and Library (1982–4); the Indian Council for Social Science Research; and from my university, including sabbatical leave. S. Bhattacharya, R. Champakalakshmi, and T.N. Madan have commented on earlier drafts beneficially, without pre-empting my accountability.

Indivar Kamtekar has pointed out that the key concept in this chapter, 'resilience', may have aspects which I do not explore here: the caste order did give Indian society a particular kind of resilience. I expect to return to this issue in the future.

only in providing the reassurance of the familiar to those who partake of these beliefs and practices. In comprehending alien societies, this was a useful first principle: minimally, it bound the investigator to a benign curiosity towards the host society, restraining pejorative pre-judgements. Practically, it was an ideology of good manners towards the anthropologist's hosts; and, as research abroad mushroomed, especially from the United States after World War II, the doctrine also began to pervade the other social sciences.

Like anthropologists, historians too seek to reconstruct the past of particular traditions; and therefore they too have tended to work from a relativistic standpoint, especially on traditions other than their own. The more venturesome among them go so far as to intervene in the public domain in relation to the uses and the abuses of that past. Entering the ranks of dissent, the scholar enacts here the citizen's duties towards the present and the future of her tradition.[1]

It seems to me to be part of this responsibility that one be willing to review that past through an appraisal, searching for the historic sources of its weakness and strengths. Such a stance would be consistent with a growing realization—if not within anthropology at least in philosophic reflection on anthropological practice—that the intellectual foundations of relativism are weak and that there are no compelling reasons, in theory or method, to evade the task of appraisals across cultures—and across time.[2] Adequate criteria for appraisal are central to the process, however, and we have to identify criteria that would hold across a variety of traditions and periods. This essay explores the possibility of using *resilience* as a key criterion. Resilience refers to a society's capacity to respond to disturbances and threats, and also to opportunities, external and internal, natural and social, in a way that enables it to maintain its autonomy, i.e. to maintain control over its own fortunes over the long term.

1.1 Elements of Resilience

A society's capacity to respond to ongoing disturbances within its milieu—its resilience—is a complex quality with several components. One element is the ease of association between persons in pursuing purposes both personal and collective. That is to say, how hard are the

[1] E.g. Romila Thapar, 'A Historical Perspective on the Story of Rama', pp. 141–63, *in* S. Gopal (ed.), *Anatomy of a Confrontation: The Babri Masjid-Ram Janmabhumi Issue*, New Delhi, 1991.

[2] S. Lukes, *Essays in Social Theory*, London, 1977, chs 6–8; I.C. Jarvie, *Rationality and Relativism*, London, 1984.

boundaries of the society's constituent groups? Excessively rigid boundaries of a group inhibit its members from relating to outsiders situationally. Furthermore, explore how firm or intractable the groups' internal structures are? How easily, say, could a member distance oneself from one's associates if advantage lay in such a course?[3]

The quality of a society's institutions—i.e. its patterned relationships aimed at particular goals—is an important determinant of its resilience: leadership roles within institutions are central to the mobilization of skills and resources needed for coping with disturbances in the complex, changing milieux of large societies.

However, such disturbances come in various shapes and sizes, and coping with them would involve complex judgements. The quality of such judgement rests upon several elements: on the range and variety of one's experiences, on the quality of one's cognitive apparatus for an appraisal of ongoing experience, and on the quality of learning from experience—lessons which could enter the making of later judgements.

Put otherwise, resilience and quality of judgement are variables. Persons and societies may rate high or low on these variables; their performance may improve or slip over time. The enlarging of experience and of its variety; the methods of recording ongoing experience accurately; the forms of analysis separating the crucial from the incidental in that experience; and the selection from experience—in terms of criteria whose worth, in turn, has been tested against historical experience: these seem to be the mechanisms that contribute to enhancing the quality of judgement—and therefore the resilience—characteristic of a society.

Lessons from particular experiences may enter the societal level variously, in forms which become available to many: changes in the operative concepts, distinctions, theories, and the like, so that the everyday metaphysics is modified; changes in technical devices so that standard procedures become more effective; changes in institutions for improved processing of ongoing experience—to more effectively cope with the environment; and so forth. In the larger cycle of societal learning from experience, this monitoring of the adequacy of operative concepts, technical devices, and institutions—these have to be key steps. Needless to say, some societies have grasped the importance of these processes, and have fitted them into the rhythm of their life ways, more effectively than others.

Appraising a complex tradition for resilience adequately is too large

[3] R.G. Fox, *Kin, Clan, Raja, and Rule*, Berkeley, 1971, p. 159.

a task for a brief essay. Elsewhere I have examined some determinants of the quality of judgement in India and Europe historically, as well as the diverse linkages between ideas, institutions, and experience.[4] This essay has a modest reach: to appraise the Brahmanical tradition for only one element in such resilience, namely its capacities for mobilization. At issue here, I suggested above, is the quality of the society's institutions, the ease with which its members can relate to each other, and the rigidity of its groups' boundaries and internal structures. Such attributes are germane to the mobilization of skills and resources necessary to face up to the threats that ruffle societies continually.

2. MOBILIZATIONAL ENERGY

Confining persons to their segmental spaces may well be taken as the principal, if unintended, theme of the caste order. Yet it has supported a civilization over millennia—with varied achievements that continue to command scholarly as well as lay attention. Furthermore, during the past two centuries, diverse persons and groups have drawn considerable resources from within the caste order for propulsion into the growing, potentially global scale of activities and relationships. If Indians' performances on that stage have been variable in quality, these have not been negligible.

Let us attempt then to identify the settings within the caste order in which social energies have been historically available for mobilization. I shall argue that the caste order allowed for a relatively limited set of institutions or, more generally, types of frameworks in which shared objectives might be set and pursued. The caste order could not sustain open institutions of an impersonal sort, which would ignore the priorities of kinship and *jati*: the kind of impersonal relationships, that is, which began spreading in Europe by the 1100s,[5] and the kind of institutionalization which has given Europe its muscle since Columbus.[6]

Overall, I ask how far mobilization could go in a framework, and why no further.

[4] S. Saberwal, 'Segmentation and Literacy', *Economic and Political Weekly*, 1991 Annual Number, 26: 723–38; 'Ideas, Institutions, and Experience', *Sociological Bulletin*, 1991, 40: 1–19.

[5] Peter Brown, 'Society and the Supernatural: A Medieval Change', *in* his *Society and the Holy in Late Antiquity*, Berkeley, 1992.

[6] S. Saberwal, 'On the Rise of Institutions, or, the Church and Kingship in Medieval Europe', *SiH*, 1991, 7:107–34.

2.1 Kinship and Jati

The Brahmanical social order ensured that ties of kinship and jati would be available to virtually everyone—except perhaps the renouncers. Consequently, one could count on finding some webs of relationships in this framework—and, correspondingly, expect to be able to mobilize at least some resources—in virtually any setting until we get to recent decades. To take measure of this protean resource—its diversity, its malleability, and also its limits—we may consider a variety of domains: physical and social mobility; mobilization for power; commerce; learning; and other specialist occupations, say that of the *devadasis* in the great southern temples.

We begin by noticing several general processes at work historically. The webs of kinship and jati have been crucial: for arranging marriages and, therefore, as fields for social control;[7] for conserving and transmitting attitudes, knowledge, practices, and skills in particular occupational niches; and sometimes sharing a common preceptor and associated ceremonial—anchors for co-operative activity. Indeed, participation in, and the experience of, these webs of relationships contributed to the shaping of shared patterns of personality, characteristic of particular jatis.

The notion of general, public access to various kinds of information is not part of India's indigenous cultural styles. In emergent, changing milieux in such a setting, the capacity to sense and to seize opportunities may depend on recourse to private networks (in the immediate case, largely of kinship ties). In the associated social spaces, good (or not so good!) judgement may be applied, first, to sensing opportunity and, second, to mobilizing skills and resources in moving in for a kill.

In the course of coping with changing milieux, a jati could at times modify its occupational profile markedly, while preserving the jati identity, anchored to durable webs of social bonds and symbols. Illustrtively, some of the Kaikkolar, a Tamil weaver jati, took to itinerant trade and soldiering as opportunity or necessity arose under the Cholas.[8] A similar durability in the web of jati-ties as against other

[7] Stig T. Madsen, 'Clan, Kinship, and Panchayat Justice Among the Jats of Western Uttar Pradesh', *Anthropos*, 1991, 86: 351–65, offers a vivid report.

[8] Mattison Mines, *The Warrior Merchants: Textiles, Trade, and Territory in South India*, Cambridge, 1984, 12ff; Vijaya Ramaswamy, *Textiles and Weavers in Medieval South India*, Delhi, 1985, 14ff. For a twentieth-century case of a jati switching occupations, S. Saberwal, *Mobile Men: Limits to Social Change in Urban Punjab*, New Delhi, 1976, ch. 5.

elements of identity has marked the 'mass movements' of conversion, say to Christianity.[9]

2.1.1 Physical and social mobility: The jati has been a key, elementary, pervasive unit of social organization, and therefore its social field has often provided essential links for both physical and social mobility. Responding to opportunity is one route to such mobility. When the opportunity was sponsored, so that force was not a factor, families could move in small clusters, as with Kessinger's account of demobilized Punjabi soldiers' movement into government-sponsored canal colonies in the 1920s, along with families of artisans and other service groups;[10] though there have been pockets where 'men are not eager to go outside, even for temporary work, unless accompanied by their kinsmen, because the [outside world] is, at best, beset with dangers'.[11]

When the movement took a person some considerable distance away, the importance of access to jati support would be expressed in securing the movement of numerous castemates to the new locality, as with Maratha Desastha Brahmans in South India.[12] Note that the prior presence of numerous other Brahman groups in the host area was of little avail, for connubial arrangements have not been easy with another jati, even of virtually identical status; brides and grooms would commonly be imported from a person's 'home' area.

Where the actors had to sense opportunity on their own, much would depend on the reliability of one's (commonly jati-linked) networks for sensing opportunity and for mobilizing the resources needed for effective access to the opportunity. Illustratively, Sikh carpenters and blacksmiths (the latter-day Ramgarhias) were able to move, in search of opportunity, from Punjab to Assam, to Kenya, and elsewhere in the late 1800s.[13]

Social bonds arising in kinship and jati continue to count among urban professionals too, as Gould[14] reported for Lucknow two decades ago:

[9] E.g. G.A. Oddie, 'Protestant Missions, Caste, and Social Change in India, 1850–1914', *IESHR*, 1969, 6, p. 277.

[10] Tom G. Kessinger, *Vilayatpur 1846–1968*, Berkeley, 1974, p. 93.

[11] W.L. Rowe, 'Caste, Kinship, and Association in Urban India', *in* A. Southall (ed.), *Urban Anthropology*, New York, 1973, pp. 225, 228, *passim*.

[12] R.E. Frykenberg, *Guntur District 1788–1848*, Oxford, 1965, pp. 16, 166f, *passim*.

[13] Saberwal, *Mobile Men*, pp. 90, 97ff; Parminder Bhachu, *Twice Migrants: East African Sikh Settlers in Britain* (London, 1985), reports on the importance of their caste ties both in East Africa and in England after their 'second migration' there.

[14] Harold Gould, 'Some Aspects of Kinship Among Business and Professional Elite in Lucknow, India', *Contrib.*, 1971, n.s. 5, p. 129.

What has deterred greater social structural and interactional homogenization among the business and professional élite is the persistence of the ethnic dimension of caste because it has been functioning as a cooptive structure in the competition for access to and control of modern occupations under conditions of scarcity and slow rates of economic growth.

Physical and social mobility may be aspects of contention for dominance too, as we shall see presently.

2.1.2 Power: Kinship and jati as a field for mobilization is central to the concept of the dominant caste.[15] The jati provided the social field to mobilize variously: aggressively, to secure dominance and rulerships;[16] defensively, to resist the larger states' and empires' attempts to wedge into the dominant jati's domain;[17] and subversively, to take office in one of these larger entities, and use its authority and stature to advance the man's own private interests.[18]

Jati as a field to mobilize force—for attack and for defence—is manifest, for example, in Brenda Beck's analysis of the structure of villages in Kongunadu, the region around Coimbatore. The pattern of the jati-set varies substantially from one cluster of villages to another in this region, and Beck accounts for the variation in terms of the historic routes for the jatis' migrations, their confrontations, and the withdrawal of some into less hospitable hillsides surrounding the Kaveri–Amravati basin. Here the jati, or a segment of it, is the unit of adhesion, of migration, and of confrontation with other jatis.

Elsewhere, the jati has been a field for mobilization: to colonize virgin lands, to fulfil military ambitions, and to resist expansive imperial centres.[19] The latter effort has particularly marked the Rajputs in northern India; and in the continual rise of their states, the linkages of

[15] In M.N. Srinivas's essentially synchronic conception, dominant caste referred to the colonial and the early post-colonial contexts. He did not ask how particular castes came to be dominant over longer time spans. E.g. his *Social Change in Modern India*, Berkeley, 1966, pp. 10–14.

[16] Brenda Beck, 'Centres and Boundaries of a Regional Caste System: A Study of Coimbatore and Neighbouring Districts', *in* her (ed.), *Perspectives on a Regional Culture*, New Delhi, 1979, pp. 54–92; C.A. Bayly, *Rulers, Townsmen and Bazaars: North Indian Society in the Age of British Expansion, 1770–1870* (Cambridge, 1983, p. 18) on Bhumihars and Yadavs in UP and Bihar in the 1700s.

[17] Fox, *Kin, Clan, Raja, and Rule*.

[18] B. Stein, 'The Segmentary State: Interim Reflections', *Purusartha*, 1990, 13, p. 226; Frykenberg, *Guntur District 1788–1848*; S. Subrahmanyam, 'Warfare and State Finance in Wodeyar Mysore, 1724–25: A Missionary Perspective', *IESHR*, 1989, 6: 203–33.

[19] Fox, *Kin, Clan, Raja, and Rule*, 53f, *passim*.

authority—between the royal centre and the localities—would also flow through Rajputs, who were held together by ties both of patronage and of kinship and marriage within the jati's social field.[20] I consider the jatis subversive potential later (Sec. 3.3).

In any discussion of power, especially in northern India, the Rajput category necessarily looms large, for the use of force and power became its forte historically. The point made earlier (Sec. 2.1) concerning the importance of family and jati in transmitting attitudes, knowledge, and skills, and indeed patterns of personality, has been documented particularly well for them.[21] This historic specialization was accompanied by unusual structural features.

The Rajput jati was formed in mid-first millennium AD through association between the then ruling families, dispersed over a large area.[22] Its clans trace their origins back not to common human ancestors but to entities like sun and moon. Over the centuries, the Rajputs everywhere have been effectively open to, i.e. been willing to arrange marriages with, and to assimilate, locally dominant groups, including those in tribal societies hitherto beyond the Brahmanical fold.[23] Furthermore, within the Rajput jati, at least some strata show an exceptional absence of endogamous subgroups.[24] Marital choices could then range over unusually wide spatial and social fields;[25] and the resulting webs of ties,

[20] E.g. N.P. Ziegler, 'Some Notes on Rajput Loyalties During the Mughal Period', *in* J.F. Richards (ed.), *Kingship and Authority in South Asia*, Madison, 1978, pp. 228f; E.S. Haynes, 'The British Alteration of the Political System of Alwar State: Lineage Patrimonialism, Indirect Rule and the Rajput Jagir System in an Indian "Princely" State, 1775–1920', *SiH*, 1989, n.s. 5, pp. 30–44.

[21] Gitel Steed, 'Notes on an Approach to a Study of Personality Formation in a Hindu Village in Gujarat', *in* M. Marriott (ed.), *Village India*, Chicago, 1955; G. Morris Carstairs, *The Twice-born: A Study of High-Caste Hindus*, Bombay (1971, rpt.), 1957; Leigh Minturn and John T. Hitchcock, *The Rajputs of Khalapur, India*, New York, 1966.

[22] B. D. Chattopadhyaya, 'Origins of the Rajputs: The Political, Economic, and Social Processes in Early Medieval Rajasthan', *Indian Historical Review*, 1976, 3, pp. 59–82.

[23] E.g. A.M. Shah, 'Division and Hierarchy: An Overview of Caste in Gujarat', *Contrib.*, 1982, n.s. 16, pp. 10ff. It has been established form, however, to seek to erase the non-Rajput antecedents of these latter groups, partly by providing them with appropriate genealogies and other charters of affiliation. One may add parenthetically that the 'Rajput' identity has been available widely—even without access to established webs of Rajput social relationships, so long as one could call upon brahmana advisers for the distinctive charters of this identity (e.g. Surajit Sinha, 'Tribe–Caste and Tribe–Peasant Continua in Central India', *Man in India*, 1965, 45, p. 74).

[24] Ibid.; see a note of caution in S. Saberwal, *India: The Roots of Crisis*, Delhi, 1986, p. 37n.

[25] Fox, *Kin, Clan, Raja, and Rule*, p. 171.

through kinship and marriage, would provide a Rajput with unusual opportunities: to sense political openings and to mobilize the resources needed to press individual ambitions. Consequently, in the Rajput states of Rajasthan, the primary political relations were intra-familial and intra-caste, within the Rajput jati.

I shall return later to consider questions of power in relations first to kingship and then to the consequences of segmentation.

2.1.3 Commerce: Perhaps the mobilizational potentials within the caste order have in recent decades been demonstrated most strikingly in the merchants' activities: think of the spectacular dispersal of some of the merchant castes into the colonial (and post-colonial) social and economic spaces within India and beyond, together with moves into industrial entrepreneurship.[26] These moves have had long antecedents: during the 1500s, for example, Gujarati merchants—Muslim and Hindu—dominated a vast range of inter-Asian trade all over the Indian Ocean, including east Africa, the Arab coast, and south-east Asia.[27]

I have already noted the importance of family and jati for varied cultural transmissions. It was within this shared occupational milieu,[28] sometimes through apprenticeships,[29] that the variety of commercial skills and the associated attitudes and values were transmitted. I have also noted the importance of these ascriptive ties for sensing and seizing opportunities. These webs of family, kinship, and jati had many uses: they would stretch to fit the available opportunity space, mobilizing such factors as capital, goods, credit, and hospitality; they provided the context to settle such issues as setting the interest rate; and they served also to apply sanctions to the errant and to resolve conflicts within and between merchant jatis.[30]

[26] Kenneth Gillion, *Ahmedabad*, Berkeley, 1968; Thomas A. Timberg, 'Three Types of the Marwari Firm', *IESHR*, 1973, 10:1–36, and *Marwaris: From Traders to Industrialists*, New Delhi, 1978; Raman Mahadevan, 'The Origin and Growth of Entrepreneurship in the Nattukottai Chettiar Community of Tamilnadu 1880–1930', M.Phil dissertation, Centre for Historical Studies, Jawaharlal Nehru University, New Delhi, 1976.

[27] M.N. Pearson, *Merchants and Rulers in Gujarat: The Response to the Portuguese in the Sixteenth Century*, New Delhi, 1976.

[28] Mattison Mines, *Muslim Merchants*, New Delhi, 1972, pp. 109ff, *passim*.

[29] Mahadevan, 'Origin and Growth of Entrepreneurship', p. 53; Timberg, *Marwaris*, p. 6.

[30] Pearson, *Merchants and Rulers in Gujarat*, ch. 5; Timberg, 'Marwari Firm', p. 6; Mahadevan, *Origin and Growth of Entrepreneurship*, pp. 57ff, 90; David Rudner, 'Banker's Trust and the Culture of Banking Among the Nattukottai Chettiars of Colonial South India', *Modern Asian Studies*, 1989, 23, pp. 417–58.

A recent study of two major merchant guilds in medieval South India[31] documents the vast spread of their activities between the ninth and the fourteenth centuries. The guild Ayyavole had members throughout the peninsula and also an overseas reach through Arab and other foreign merchants and, at times, in association with conquering Chola rulers; the guilds maintained close relations with ruling houses generally.[32] Men of various castes belonged to a guild: Brahmans, trading Nattukottai Chettiars, Jains, and others—at times in alliance with the landowning Velala organizations.

They appear to have traded in whatever promised profit—horses, elephants, pearls, spices, dyes, yarn, textiles, iron, camphor, sandalwood, and so forth—and the guild administered a range of trading areas directly: fairs, markets, even towns. Donations for temples indicated the guilds' orientation towards the religious tradition. The sources do not tell us much about the guilds' internal organization; Ayyavole may at times have been a generic name for trade-linked organizations, with particular 'deities of Ayyavole', with which, possibly, any ambitious group of merchants might affiliate. That is to say, the term Ayyavole may have referred not to a unitary organization with anything like central authority but to a congeries of organizations associated loosely—with each other and with royal houses.[33]

During the pre-colonial period, individual merchants had opportunities to move first into managing revenues for the governments and thence into more overt administrative and political roles.[34] The great merchants' services may have been a crucial resource for even the most substantial of regimes.[35] Yet Indian merchants have not had much appetite for openly running the apparatus of government on their own account. Indeed, to pose the issue in these terms is to mis-state the problem: the merchants had difficulties in mutual co-operation even on a much smaller scale; making a bid for something like urban self-government would have been a far cry indeed.

Merchants of Ahmedabad in the 1500s showed a relatively high level

[31] Meera Abraham, *Two Medieval Merchant Guilds of South India*, New Delhi, 1988.

[32] Ibid., p. 75.

[33] Ibid., pp. 68, 74f.

[34] E.g. Pearson, *Merchants and Rulers in Gujarat*, pp. 127, 130; Muzaffar Alam, *Crisis of Empire in Mughal North India: Awadh and the Punjab 1707–48*, Delhi, 1986, pp. 169–75 on Khatris in service to the later Mughals.

[35] Karen Leonard, 'The "Great Firm" Theory of the Decline of the Mughal Empire', *Comparative Studies in Society and History*, 1979, 21, pp. 151–67.

of organization with 'a city-wide [*mahajan*], on which sat representatives of all the occupational *mahajans* and sometimes some of the patels [representing artisanal groups] as well.' It was headed by a Nagarseth, a body which 'regulated general commercial activities in the city, such as rates of exchange and discount, and holidays'. On the other hand, Ashin Das Gupta tells us that, during the 1700s, 'The *nagarseth* of Surat, often compared to the mayor of European cities, was in fact the head of the Hindu and Jain merchants and acted only in emergencies, apart from one annual ceremonial occasion, the opening of the season, when the citizens propitiated the river and the sea'.[36]

Of Surat's seventeenth-century merchants, Das Gupta has elsewhere stressed their being essentially loners, and their inability to build institutions which would stand for their shared interests and 'shield them from sustained adversity. . . . Insecurity was fundamental in the way they worked and the milieu in which they worked, and what little comfort they drew from social support never assured them historical longevity'. The merchants' associational potentials may have varied substantially between localities: Gillion's evidence from Ahmedabad and Bayly's from eighteenth-century Banaras is much more positive in this regard than Das Gupta's from Surat. The difference may arise from the working of the underlying aggregating mechanism which rested on caste and on religious symbols and activities even in Banaras. The merchant body at Surat was exceptionally heterogenous, however; and this may have pre-empted the potentials of co-operation through affiliation with caste groups and particular religious ceremonials. The pressure of European merchants also undoubtedly queered the pitch.[37]

Indian society had been organized in simply too disaggregated a manner, to use Pearson's term,[38] to support any general, widely shared perception of common interests such as might undergird bids from below—by merchants and related groups—to capture the state apparatus. The other face of the coin was that the merchants and others were fairly readily willing to make their peace with whosoever—indigenous or outsider—could establish effective control. Apropos the Gujarati merchants' compliancy towards the Portuguese during the 1500s: 'It was not the business of merchants to go around fighting and getting their

[36] Pearson, *Merchants and Rulers in Gujarat*, pp. 123ff. Ashin Das Gupta, 'India and the Indian Ocean in the Eighteenth Century', *in* A. Das Gupta and M.N. Pearson (eds), *India and the Indian Ocean, 1500–1800*, Calcutta, 1987, p. 135.

[37] Das Gupta, 'Indian Merchants in the Age of Partnership, 1500–1800', *in* D. Tripathi (ed.), *Business Communities of India*, New Delhi, 1984, p. 36. Bayly, p. 175; Das Gupta, *Indian Merchants and the Decline of Surat c. 1700–1750*, Wiesbaden, 1979.

[38] Pearson, *Merchants and Rulers in Gujarat*, p. 154.

ships sunk. Their job was to exchange goods and make a profit, and once the Portuguese had shown them that to continue to do this they would have to accept Portuguese control, they accepted it.'[39]

2.1.4 Learning: Knowledge is important. It gives us orientation—accurately or misleadingly—to the world around us. Also, as Kenneth Boulding noted, the available stock of knowledge is a crucial element in all productive activity.[40] Let us then consider how well the Brahmanical order addressed the processes of learning. Elsewhere I have discussed the implications of the segmentation of Indian society for literacy over the long term.[41]

The long durability of the Brahmanical order attests its ability to transmit its tradition, including its texts. The material resources requisite to this end were secured: endowments for temples; prestations for the masters of particular rites and ceremonies, hospitality for Brahmans generally, and land grants for Brahman communities; endowments for the Hindu monastic institutions too, once Sankaracharya in the 700s had adapted the Buddhist model; and so forth.[42]

The Brahmanical order generated strong motivation to learn the texts and to achieve the psychological states believed to facilitate such outcomes as the 'liberation of the Self'. These motivations tended to arise most often among the Brahmans—and others who took their motivational cues from them. Settings for such pursuits are described for nineteenth-century Kerala by Anand Wood and for the Sankaracharya *mathas* by Cenkner.[43] Access to such institutions has commonly been restricted on jati grounds: teachers and disciples at the

[39] Pearson, *Merchants and Rulers*, p. 116; B. Watson analyses the relative strengths of Indian and English merchants in India, *c.* 1700, 'Indian Merchants and English Private Interests 1659–1760', *in* A. Das Gupta and M.N. Pearson (eds), *India and the Indian Ocean, 1500–1800*, Calcutta, 1987, pp. 301–16.

[40] Kenneth Boulding, *Ecodynamics*, Beverly Hills, 1978, p. 220, *passim.*

[41] Saberwal, 'Segmentation and Literacy'. The skills of literacy overlap with the domain of learning; and we may note the two-way relationship between social mobilization and literacy: the skills of literacy may be pressed into mobilizing social effort, while social energies may be mobilized for literacy and learning. I return to the import of these links in conclusion.

[42] Arjun Appadurai, *Worship and Conflict under Colonial Rule: A South Indian Case*, Cambridge, 1981, pp. 101f, *passim*; William Cenkner, *A Tradition of Traditions: Sankara and the Jagadgurus Today*, Delhi, 1983, pp. 39, 109f; R. Thapar, 'The Householder and the Renouncer in the Brahmanical and Buddhist Traditions', *Contrib.*, 1981, 15: 273–98; S. J. Tambiah, 'The Renouncer: His Individuality and His Community', *Contrib.*, 1981, 15: 299–320.

[43] Wood, *Knowledge Before Printing and After*, Delhi, 1985, chs 1 and 3; Cenkner, *A Tradition of Traditions*, ch. 5.

mathas in Sringeri and Kanchi have been Smarta Brahmans; those in Trichur, Nambudiri Brahmans.[44] These institutions continue to abide by the caste order to this day; and in at least one recent case an otherwise worthy disciple was kept from succession to institutional headship because he was not a Brahman.[45]

The Sankaracharyas are reported to have carried their preaching throughout the subcontinent.[46] This wide reach, however, had its limitations. First, the Sankaracharyas have numbered no more than four or five at any one time—though their disciples have taught on *their* own account, and other orders have had their itinerant preachers too. Second, their objectives, such as noted above, did not include much mobilizing for wider social purposes. To be sure, a body of ideas spread far and wide; but it did so in such way that the intellectual apparata of the literati would rarely scrutinize the stocks of knowledge entering material production, political life, or other areas of experience.[47] Thirdly, their teaching—and the methods of that teaching—strove to maintain and transmit the received corpus; it has been generally disdainful of learning—religious or secular—carried in other social segments within the Brahmanical order, let alone that in alien traditions.

To be sure, the spacious Brahmanical tradition accommodated a matchless diversity of beliefs and practices, owed partly to the numerous orders of ascetics and, historically, there have been numerous innovations too; yet, following N.A. Thoothi's study of the Vaisnava tradition in Gujarat, two cautions apply. One is the strong pull of the doctrinal core:

> . . . though the founder of one *Sampradaya* [sect] or another assures his flock that they are freed from all bonds of *Karma* and that their acceptance of the way, the truth and the life taught by his *Sampradaya* is sufficient in one single span of human life for the achievement of the final beatitude, his successors and their followers persist, with or without reason, in and out of season, in asserting

[44] Cenkner, *A Tradition of Traditions*, pp. 118, 143; Wood, *Knowledge Before Printing and After*, Delhi, 1985, pp. 49ff.

[45] Cenkner, p. 126 on Jyotirmath. Access to institutions such as that at Nalanda in late first millennium AD may have been more open. On the other hand, Nalanda seems to have succumbed to Tantrism long before being sacked by Bakhtiar Khilji in the late 1100s, H.D. Sankalia, *The University of Nalanda*, Delhi (revision of 1932 MA thesis, University of Bombay), 1971, pp. 103, 242, *passim.*

[46] Cenkner, chs 5–8

[47] Wood, *Knowledge*, p. 17; Bhikhu Parekh, 'Some Reflections on the Hindu Tradition of Political Thought', *in* Thomas Pantham and Kenneth L. Deutsch (eds), *Political Thought in Modern India*, New Delhi, 1986, p. 29.

their faith in the infallibility of the hereditary character of [the] social institutions [like *jati, gotra*, and *kula*].[48]

Secondly, while everyone is free to choose his/her own deity, temple, and form of prayer, the social insistence on conformity to jati law in practice is not easy to resist: 'True, individuals and families have always been able to emancipate themselves from [*jati*] control by going over to suitable Sampradayas; but the risks have always been great, the sacrifices involved have always demanded very stout hearts.'[49]

2.1.5 Other specialist occupations: The foregoing illustrates the variety of activities that could find support in social fields arising in kinship, jati, and the like. One could add to the list such commonplace, stable productive activities as metalwork, woodwork, leatherwork, pottery, textiles, transport, and the like.

The protean ties of kinship, jati, and the like could also be adapted to the organization of activity in a range of specialist institutions: for example, the provision of services in a major temple with its priests, temple servants, and diverse services to pilgrims. The idiom served to constitute even the 'jati' of the devadasis. A candidate for acceptance into this 'jati' had to demonstrate modest competence in ritual dancing before the deity. 'Married' subsequently to the deity, the devadasis would maintain more or less stable liaisons with men who might range in status from king to temple servant. Their daughters would have been dedicated to the life of the devadasi in their turn and their sons would marry girls from upper caste families in reduced circumstances—girls whose ties with their natal families would be severed entirely. The social order around the temple sought to generate a jati-like niche for the devadasi too, though with only partial success.[50]

Overall, then, the jati model was available to generate durable social fields, within which specific sets of activities, distributed between jati or jati-like groups, might be pursued, and there were *ad hoc*, situational mobilizations too. More difficult has been the mobilization of diverse

[48] G.S. Ghurye, *Indian Sadhus*, Bombay (2nd edn), 1964; *see also* N.A. Thoothi, *The Vaishnavas of Gujarat*, Calcutta, 1935, p. 111.

[49] Thoothi, p. 365; similarly, L. Dumont, 'World Renunciation in Indian Religions', *Contrib.*, 1960, 4: 33–62; Bhikhu Parekh, *Colonialism, Tradition and Reform: An Analysis of Gandhi's Political Discourse*, New Delhi, 1989, p. 15. *See also* Sec. 2.4.

The segmentive shadow of the caste order falls even over categories whose tradition has been as critical of brahmanism as that of the Jains (M. Carrithers and C. Humphrey (eds), *The Assembly of Listeners: Jains in Society*, Cambridge, 1991, *passim*).

[50] F.A. Marglin, *Wives of the God-King*, Delhi, 1985, pp. 68, 80.

skills, towards the setting and realization of complex, shifting, collective long-term societal purposes. Such an achievement has to build on habits of setting and shaping institutional objectives, overriding particularistic ties and sustaining them over long time horizons. Indian traditions appear not to have nurtured such habits much.

I have been considering the varied potentials of the axis of family and kinship. It is time now to move to other axes, which will continue to echo themes noticed already.

2.2 Locality

Relatively stable patterns of activity across jati boundaries have been common enough in Indian villages and towns. I may make two points here. One, a particular land-controlling family could organize its dependants for the full round of agricultural activity; and collectively the land controllers could command the whole village for their purposes. Secondly, control over land arose ultimately in rights of conquest; and these rights needed continual renewal by way of defence against all comers. This defence needed castemates to stand together for the cause—unless a raja, an imperial power, or an entrenched normative order guarded particular land rights in a locality. In the larger urban settings, the dominance might be general, its reins leading to the king's agents, or to an institution like a major temple,[51] or to the leaders in a key activity, say the great merchants (as in Ahmedabad);[52] the patterns of organized activity would vary accordingly.

2.3 Raja

The raja, head of a kingdom, embodied *legitimate* power by virtue of its consecration by his Brahman *purohit*, who represented sacrality.[53] Depending on the magnitude of force commanded, and the quality of manpower and territory controlled, his resources might enable him to sponsor the construction of palaces and temples and forts, organize raids and campaigns, oversee the temples' management, and provide land grants for Brahmans' settlements. Nevertheless, the polity had its limitations, and Stein is able to concede only the segmentary state in

[51] Appadurai, *Worship and Conflict*, p. 65.

[52] Gillion, *Ahmedabad*.

[53] Ananda K. Coomaraswamy, *Spiritual Authority and Temporal Power in the Indian Theory of Government*, 1942 (Delhi, 1978), pp. 1f; G. Bouchon, 'Sixteenth-Century Malabar and the Indian Ocean', *in* A. Das Gupta and M.N. Pearson (eds), *India and the Indian Ocean, 1500–1800*, Calcutta, 1987, p. 165.

medieval South India.[54] Dumont recognizes the *little* kingdom as the largest effective political unit, as the social totality within which the caste order lay.[55]

Why did the Brahmanical states tend to remain small in their space–time spread, short on the administrative muscle that might have sustained wider range and durability? The European contrast suggests one key element: the agency for legitimation, or two aspects of this.[56] On the one hand, any of the many mobile Brahmans could organize a coronation and other symbols of legitimation at modest cost. No conqueror or pretender appears to have had much difficulty in securing the ceremonies: Bouchon notices a free-for-all in sixteenth-century Malabar, reminiscent of the *Arthashastra*, of Kalhana's Kashmir, and of the Merovingians in Europe.[57]

On the other hand, those who conferred these symbols of legitimation could offer very little by way of reliable resources or institutionalized skills and strengths to underpin state construction. On one hand, they had to fend for their own families and lineages. On the other, they had not devised the complex of ideas, skills, and motivations needed for the institutional nodes that might congeal adequate symbolic, normative, and material resources in aid of larger social visions. Indeed, the ideology they purveyed may have driven kings to divest themselves of resources acquired by other means.[58] Set against medieval Europe, both the Christian church and the Brahmanical order provided for absorbing alien peoples; yet their operative social codes—say the commensal and connubial rules—acted in opposite directions: erasing the differences

[54] B. Stein, 'Eighteenth-Century India: Another View', *SiH*, 1989, n.s. 5: 1–26.

[55] L. Dumont, *Homo Hierarchicus*, 1970 (English trans., Paladin, 1972), Art. 72. The Mughals were scarcely a *little kingdom*, but that is a special case: their state was centred on a conquering group from outside the subcontinent whose dominance owed little to the Brahmanical order (*see* Sec. 3.2). Parenthetically we may recall that the Mughal state began to fall apart in a bare four generations. As empires go, its staying power was not memorable. Pearson offers an interpretation of this empire's rapid folding, 'Political Participation in Mughal India', *IESHR*, 1972, 9: 113–31.

[56] Saberwal, 'On the Rise of Institutions'.

[57] Bouchon, 'Sixteenth-Century Malabar and the Indian Ocean', p. 165; Kalhana, *Rajatarangini* (trans. by Ranjit Sitaram Pandit) [New Delhi, 1968], 1935; I. Wood, 'Kings, Kingdoms and Consent', *in* P.H. Sawyer and I. Wood (eds), *Early Medieval Kingship*, Leeds, 1977.

[58] David D. Shulman, *The King and the Clown in South Indian Myth and Poetry*, Princeton, 1985, pp. 23ff; Bayly (*Rulers, Townsmen and Bazaars*, p. 19) notes that the 'Eighteenth- and early nineteenth-century Hindi genealogies and poems on the duties of kings suggest only a limited set of functions: warfare, the service of the gods, and the

in one case, cysting these in the other.[59] Such elements appear to have been decisive for state construction in India.

The Brahmanical order did generate and regulate a regime of jatis and villages: largely autarchic, effective units at the village—or wider—levels, open to some external cultural influence, principally orally. The units of this social edifice however were rather small, bounded jatis, which were able to resist fluidizing into larger social spaces.

Internal control within a kingship was largely a function of the caste order: to the Brahmanical ideology was added the collective, dispersed dominance of the ruling lineage or jati(s), with recource to force when thought necessary. The society's informational flows were thin, however over such issues as likely threats from outside, or feedbacks—from experience within—for visions for the future. Such ideals as *Ram rajya* furnished little for ongoing agendas.

Accurate knowledge of a society's human and material resources is useful in steering its course closely; yet the skills and routines requisite for such enumeration were not much cultivated.[60] For enumerations comparable with the Domesday Book, ordered for England by William the Conqueror in late eleventh century, India had to wait for the early nineteenth-century colonial efforts.[61]

2.4 Others

Kinship and jati, locality, and raja did not exhaust the possibilities for mobilization within the brahmanical order. Let us review some of the others for the range of possibilities as well as their limits.

First, the deity in a great temple.[62] The deity was defined as being in

---

arbitration between clansmen and castes.' I have reviewed elsewhere the difference made to state construction by the ideology pressed by the Church in medieval Europe: 'On the Rise of Institutions', pp. 110–14, 118–21.

[59] Jostling for status and influence, men of diverse backgrounds did perforce rub shoulders in India too. Bayly (pp. 171ff), considers its limits in one setting.

[60] Kerala's high levels of literacy may have made such enumeration possible there: 'Each village headman and each higher feudal noble was . . . obliged to keep records of the number of able-bodied Nayars he could muster from his village for war.' For the early 1700s, Kathleen Gough estimated that more than half the men and not less than a quarter of the women 'may have been proficient in Malayalam': 'Literacy in Kerala', *in* Jack Goody (ed.), *Literacy in Traditional Societies*, Cambridge, 1968, pp. 147, 151.

[61] E.g. the educational surveys reviewed by P. Radhakrishnan, 'Indigenous Education in British India: A Profile', *Contrib.*, 1990, 24: 1–27, not to mention the later censuses.

[62] E.g. Appadurai, *Worship and Conflict*, on one in Madras or Marglin, *Wives of the God–King*, on the Jagannatha temple at Puri.

a complementary, symbiotic relationship with the king: the king served the deity by protecting the temple and its arrangements for worship, the deity 'protected' the prosperity and well-being of the king and his kingdom. To be sure, a temple became possible by virtue of the resources endowed for building and furnishing it, decorating the deity, maintaining its specialist staff, and performing the rounds of ritual. Managing the endowed resources also called for skill, time, and energy. Around the core temple could arise hospices for the devotees—or a more or less elaborate pilgrimage.[63] Rituals, well performed, would bring the devotees a sense of well-being; and the rigours of pilgrimage or other practice might take the seeker to certain valued psychological states. All this embodied much personal or collective energy, but there is little evidence that these energies could serve any purposes larger than the ones to which these were explicitly directed.

The personal act of *renunciation* would take the renouncer away from kin and jati and from his settled community; yet the renouncer could enter an order of renouncers, finding himself a new community in it. Such orders of sanyasis transmitted a tradition too; and to this end they might maintain mathas, temples and related institutions.[64] In exceptional circumstances, the renouncers' orders have occasionally assumed functions as varied as long-distance trade and warfare.[65]

Securing a personal followership, the renouncer may found a sect. Particular sects, temples, and related institutions may be 'open, at least in principle, to all';[66] but sect membership adds on to, it does not replace, caste membership for lay members. The sect allows a member access to a variant religious course; it does not dissolve the implications of the caste order for a larger, sustained social universe.[67] Even where

[63] E. Alan Morinis, *Pilgrimage in the Hindu Tradition: A Case Study of West Bengal*, Delhi, 1984.

[64] For the Sankaracharya tradition, Çenkner, *A Tradition of Traditions*; for the Sants, Daniel Gold, 'Clan and Lineage among the Sants: Seed, Substance, Service', *in* Karine Schomer and W.H. McLeod (eds), *The Sants*, Delhi, 1987, pp. 305–27.

[65] Bayly, *Rulers, Townsmen and Bazaars*, pp. 28, 142f, 183ff.

[66] Dumont, 'World Renunciation', p. 60.

[67] W.H. McLeod ('The Development of the Sikh Panth', *in* K. Schomer and W. H. McLeod (eds), *The Sants*, Delhi, 1987, p. 229), notes that the 'Sant doctrine, with its strong emphasis upon the interior quality of religious devotion, offers no overt encouragement to the emergence of religious institutions or formally organized communities'. Yet the Sikh tradition did develop such institutions over time.

The wider cultural supports for the process for institutionalization have, however, been weak. Apropos the relatively recent Radhasoamis, Gold ('Clan and Lineage Among the Sants', pp. 321ff), notices that the routines for deciding who should succeed to

a sect has begun in a sharp break with the Brahmanical order, as with the Lingayats, it has tended to settle into a niche within the segmented social universe—though its religious specialists may not be Brahman.[68]

There is also the figure of the political adventurer, drawn to the promise—and the possible payoffs—of conquest. The entrepreneur in this mode would draw other seekers of fortune in his train.[69] His energies might go into freelance marauding, or entering the service of an established power, or competing for dominance on his own account. Success in this latter endeavour would entitle him to claim the status of raja—and all that went with it.

The traditions and institutions of Islam, Sikhism, and the like have offered other nodes for possible mobilization; yet their consideration is unlikely to necessitate much revision of the estimate arising from the foregoing. Missing here, as elsewhere, have been the superordinate institutional resources—of introspection, supervision, and direction—that might have projected an overarching, responsive ideology: one that would build on long-term historical experience, face contemporary choices, and project active, collective visions for the future.

3. CONSEQUENCES OF SEGMENTATION

3.1 For Conflict Resolution

We have noted that the Brahmanical formula for organizing social space gave a jati a substantial area of activity within which it functioned autonomously: it was left to its own devices over such matters as marriages—and the resolution of conflicts over them. Conflict across jati boundaries, if unresolved by the concerned jatis together, could draw in the raja or his representative—whose *ad hoc* intervention would seek to minimize disturbance in the social order. At this wider level, some general ideas of justice would also have prevailed.

What would happen if the ruler did not subscribe to the Brahmanical

---

institutional headship have been ambiguous, and therefore there has been a tendency towards multiple successorships to the *gaddi* with rivalry, litigation, and bad blood—echoing the patterns in kingship.

[68] W. McCormack, 'Lingayats as a Sect', *Journal of the Royal Anthropological Institute*, 1963, 93: 59–71. More generally, R. Thapar, 'Imagined Religious Communities?', *Modern Asian Studies*, 1989, 23, p. 214.

[69] R.E. Frykenberg, 'Company Circari in the Carnatic, *c.* 1799–1859: The Inner Logic of Political Systems in India', *in* R. G. Fox (ed.), *Realm and Region in Traditional India*, New Delhi, 1977, p. 123.

moral order? The establishment of Muslim rule in Bengal in the thirteenth century led to a situation where the various Brahman and Kayastha jatis themselves emerged to take charge, providing authoritative judgements within the local order of jati and kinship—though their power was social and moral, attentive to genealogies, yet lacking the clout of legitimate force.[70]

Europe serves as a foil. By the end of the first millennium, participative, deliberative, and relatively institutionalized procedures for conflict resolution were already at work,[71] and these procedures carried in good measure practices that had come down from Rome. The Church had built up a substantial body of (initially unsystematized) Canon Law. By the twelfth century, the Canon law began to be systematized, while royal courts began to work with formal legal codes. Furthermore, given the formal study of laws from the end of the eleventh century, in Bologna and elsewhere, and given the support of both the Church and kingships, schools and social groups specializing in law and justice emerged during the twelfth century.[72] Compared with India, European societies generated early on a denser institutional complex for resolution of conflicts. Kingships in medieval Europe gave special attention to justice, to securing for disputes authoritative decisions that would be seen to be just. They tried to 'provide enduring legal institutions with a corps of reliable, dependent judges'; and this association with justice helped generate, over the long term, relatively durable loyalties towards the corresponding political communities.[73]

Illustratively, for the late 1200s in France, we read about the judicial arrangements fostered by Philip the Fair (r. 1285–1314). For him 'the basic sign of sovereignty was his right to act as the final and supreme judge in all cases (except those dealing with purely ecclesiastical matters) that arose in his kingdom',[74] and the king sustained the independent standing of the judicial system by submitting even to those of its 'rulings that reduced his income or his jurisdiction'.[75] This is not a case of an exceptional ruler made remarkable by his extraordinary personal

[70] R. Inden, *Marriage and Rank in Bengali Culture: A History of Caste and Clan in Middle Period Bengal*, Berkeley, 1976, pp. 77–9, 137–42.

[71] S. Reynolds, *Kingdoms and Communities in Western Europe 900–1300*, Oxford, 1984, ch. 1.

[72] M.E. Tigar and M. R. Levy, *Law and the Rise of Capitalism*, New York, 1977, pp. 121f, 157.

[73] E.L. Jones, *The European Miracle*, Cambridge, 1981, pp. 128, 233, *passim*.

[74] J.R. Strayer, *Reign of Philip the Fair*, Princeton, 1987, p. 191.

[75] Ibid., p. 210.

deeds of justice. On one hand, these attitudes, procedures, texts, and institutions had notable continuities with those of the preceding seven centuries;[76] on the other, several of Philip's major financial moves were patently unjust, though their beneficiary was the French kingship and state rather than the king personally.[77]

Medieval Europe did continue to display a certain solidarity in kin groups and the like. In the tenth century, 'The extended kin group is the primary unit of society, a fact studiously maintained and defined by the blood feud. Safety and protection still rested on coagulations of kinsmen and dependants in small, intense groups.'[78] Strong lineages or 'related groups of noble families' remained active in the Italian cities for several generations to come,[79] but the scene began to shift by the twelfth century: public authorities (including the Church) were able to improve the conditions for personal security, migration to urban and other areas away from home weakened some kinship bonds, and membership of guilds and of military orders associated with the Crusades could serve as a replacement for kinship ties in some measure.[80]

The rise of contractual relations, which accompanied the growth of commerce in Europe early in the second millennium, also subverted lineage ties and the like over time. As people moved into more differentiated, more impersonal arrangements, they did not get much ideological support for sustaining their kin groups' solidarity. On the one hand, the New Testament had carried the famous passages attributed to Jesus, deprecating the bonds of kinship ties (Matthew x.35; Mark iii.35), a stance the Church had sustained over time.[81] On the other, it was medieval European practice to endow a monastery for its monks to pray for an ancestor's (or for one's own) soul after death. Medieval Europe's

[76] *See* P. Wormald, '*Lex scripta* and *verbum regis:* Legislation and Germanic Kingship, from Euric to Cnut', *in* P.H. Sawyer and I.N., Wood (eds), *Early Medieval Kingship*, Leeds, 1977, pp. 105–38; F.L. Ganshof, *The Carolingians and the Frankish Monarchy*, London, 1971, Ch. 5; J. Nelson, *Politics and Ritual in Early Medieval Europe*, London, 1986, pp. 91–116, 133–71; J.R. Strayer, *On the Medieval Origins of the Modern State*, Princeton, 1970, pp. 23–32.

[77] Strayer, *Philip the Fair*, pp. 142–91.

[78] Brown, 'Society and the Supernatural', p. 311.

[79] F. Schevill, *Medieval and Renaissance Florence*, 2 vols, 1936, New York (1961), p. 70, *passim*.

[80] J. Goody, *The Development of the Family and Marriage in Europe*, Cambridge, 1983, p. 18, n. 8, citing T.F. Glick, *Islamic and Christian Spain in the Early Middle Ages*, 1979.

[81] Goody, *Development of the Family and Marriage in Europe*, pp. 56–64, 194–203; M. Verdon, 'Virgins and Widows: European Kinship and Early Christianity', *Man*, 1988, n.s. 23: 488–505.

monasteries helped meet an anxiety whose pressure has in other societies often provided a core function for descent groups.[82]

3.2 For Secular Mobilization

I noted initially that pre-colonial India offered only a few frameworks in which to set and pursue shared objectives: jati, village, kingship, temple, adventurer's band, etc., and within a locality, neighbours and others would co-operate from day to day. Central to my argument is the proposition, however, that co-operative activities on a relatively large scale can cohere over time only if these can draw adequate support from, (a) shared ideas (and interests), and, (b) legitimate institutions. Such resources were short in this society.

The principle of jati autonomy and the difficulties of secular institutionalization have been interconnected, and we may consider various aspects of this linkage.

(1) *Jati autonomy bred attitudes of embeddedness within the jati and of distantiation from other jatis.* Central to the caste order, this proposition needs no comment. Certain orders of co-operation within this framework have been feasible (Sec. 2). Yet, persons were embedded rather firmly in such groups as the jati; and the skills requisite for—and the tradition of—entering relationships open-endedly have been weak. These characteristics have served to attenuate at least some of the historic possibilities for Indian society.

This general point may be made with reference to the pace of diffusion of technical innovations. A new technique or device commonly arises through a novel combination of elements from diverse sources.[83] Once realized, the pace of its diffusion would depend partly on the absence of impeding social barriers. In the cultural history of large societies, a very large part of 'innovativeness' consists in the extensive diffusion of numerous elements which would otherwise be inconsequential.

Illustratively, the minuscule form of the alphabet came to be developed among monastic scribes in Europe in the late 700s and early 800s in order to speed the writing of texts: demands for them were growing.[84]

[82] The Cluniac monasteries mushrooming in the tenth and eleventh centuries fed on other anxieties too: B.H. Rosenwein, 'Feudal War and Monastic Peace: Cluniac Liturgy as Ritual Aggression', *Viator*, 1971, 2: 129–57; and *Rhinoceros Bound: Cluny in the Tenth Century*, Philadelphia, 1982.

[83] H.G. Barnett, *Innovation*, New York, 1953, chs 2 and 7.

[84] Lynn White Jr., 'The Temple of Jupiter Revisited', *in* his (ed.), *The Transformation of the Roman World: Gibbon's Problem After Two Centuries*, Berkeley, 1966, p. 300.

The minuscule came into general use in subsequent centuries. The idea of some kind of shorthand for rapid writing has been part of Europe's scribal repertoire since the second century BC.[85] It spread to several European languages as their written uses grew. In contrast, though certain forms of abbreviated writing have long been available in some parts of India,[86] their use has been confined to limited occupations only.[87] The social barriers of the segmented society inhibited the circulation of both people and ideas. This was another implication of the disaggregated nature of Indian society.[88]

(2) *This set of attitudes and social embeddedness posed difficulties for secular institutionalization*: Given the firmness of bonds within a particular group, Indian society has not historically provided for a regime of impersonal relationships in relatively specialized institutions: institutions that would recruit their members without reference to kinship and the like, and whose operational logic would follow from the institution's particular functions. Otherwise expressed, in the Indian social framework, the jati and the village—relatively small-scale, bounded social units—were privileged groups, sources of a person's enduring identity from cradle to pyre in a manner quite different from any European social units. This historic difficulty has impeded the general possibility of institutionalizing differentiated activity durably, whether in a bureaucracy (in the strict sense), in scholarship, or in economic activity; it inhibited, too, the kind of organization of force that a state needs to survive on the stage of history for any great length of time.[89]

(3) *The difficulties of secular institutionalization made the jatis' autonomous social spaces less vulnerable.*

[85] B. Bischoff, *Latin Paleography*, Cambridge, 1990, pp. 80–3. I thank Dr Peter Heath of the University of Hull for this reference.

[86] G.W. Leitner, *History of Indigenous Education in the Punjab Since Annexation and in 1882* [Patiala, 1971], 1883, pp. 10, 37, *passim*.

[87] For the larger technological contrast over time between Europe and India, compare I. Habib, 'The Technology and Economy of Mughal India', Dev Raj Chanana Lectures, Delhi, 1970, mimeographed, and 'Changes in Technology in Medieval India', *SiH*, 1980, 2:15–39, with L. White, *Medieval Technology and Social Change*, Oxford, 1962, and *Medieval Religion and Technology*, Berkeley, 1978, and Sylvia Thrupp, 'Medieval Industry 1000–5000', *in* C.M. Cipolla (ed.), *Fontana Economic History of Europe: The Middle Ages*, Collins/Fontana, 1972, pp. 221–73.

[88] Pearson, *Merchants and Rulers in Gujarat*, esp. ch. 6.

[89] *See* Stein ('Eighteenth-Century India', p. 15), for the costs exacted by this situation from Tipu Sultan's kind of eighteenth-century regimes aspiring to centralization.

One may be rather more willing to risk the security of one's natal segment if alternate, sturdier social anchors are available. This had another facet for warrior jatis like the Rajputs. As Fox showed,[90] an ascendant state might subdue the dominant Rajput lineage in a locality for a while; but the state has seldom had either the clout to disrupt these received identities beyond repair, or the ideology to effectively underwrite alternate frameworks for identities: 'there is almost a complete lack of evidence in Indian history of unifying ideological glue'.[91] The prevailing ideologies furnished separative membranes, so to speak, to a greater degree than adhesive social glue.

Temporary loss of power would still leave the framework of identities intact—keeping alive the promise for the lineage to rebound whenever the pressure from above abated, say if troubles elsewhere distracted the imperial centre. For the larger kingship or state, therefore, the normal hazards of weak rulers, succession struggles, external invasion, and the like would be sharpened in India by assertive pressure from below, from lineages entrenched locally and regionally, which may have lain low awhile, awaiting their hour. Between such pincers, the state might well crack up. The autonomous jati endured, holding on to its members—and holding them back from alternate, instituted spaces.[92]

For the course of Indian history, these difficulties have had decisive consequences, including the recurrent weaknesses against force, whether that of alien invaders or of the warriors within. Consider the former first.

The lack of segmentive inhibitions among the invaders from abroad has often overcome their handicap of being alien. 'The basis of the [Mughal] empire, in a measure, had been negative', says Muzaffar Alam, looking back on the empire that was: 'its strength had lain in the inability of the local communities and their systems to mobilize beyond relatively narrow bounds'.[93] The 1500s and 1600s, often celebrated for the varied peaks of achievements in India, were doubly remarkable: even as the Mughals came in to establish their empire centred in Delhi and Agra, Europeans too were establishing toeholds along the coasts. Behind their commerce, there were always the guns; and by the 1700s,

[90] Fox, *Kin, Clan, Raja, and Rule*, ch. 3.

[91] Frykenberg, 'Company Circari in the Carnatic, *c.* 1799–1859', p. 125.

[92] Stein, 'Eighteenth-Century India', p. 15. Once ritual and symbol have gone into hardening group boundaries, such alternate integration would be difficult anywhere. The Christian tradition had withheld support from such groups in Europe very early on.

[93] Alam, *Crisis of Empire*, pp. 5, 305ff.

they were preparing also to take over politically. Both Mughals and Europeans found indigenous allies aplenty.[94]

Furthermore, the Central Asian habits of uninhibited warfare repeatedly worsted the more leisurely habits of conflict within India.[95] The north-western frontier had long been the channel taken by invaders; yet organizing its long-term defence appears never to have been seriously mooted. It would have needed mobilization on a scale—and over a duration—well beyond the reach of North India's fragmented, fragile polities. When the conquerors from abroad came with fresh, sovereign symbols and truths of their own religion—their own 'Great Tradition'—another logic of distancing was piled on to the prior segmentation of society.[96]

Finally, there is the widespread difficulty in India in resisting the armed warriors within; and its consideration takes us to a Weberian theme. For Italian cities between the eleventh and the thirteenth centuries particularly, Weber noticed that the merchant-led city-dwellers, uniting repeatedly, could resist feudal lords even when the latter lived in the same city.[97] At one level, the trading and manufacturing interests were in conflict with hereditary knightly domination. They turned repeatedly to government by autonomous legislation within the city, as against arbitrary knightly rule, which was at times aligned with an external political power, say that of the Emperor in Germany.

These efforts of Italian city-states—Venice, Florence, Genoa, Pisa, etc.—at maintaining their political autonomy had their ups and downs; yet the city of Florence, for example, could keep asserting its autonomy for four centuries, from the late eleventh to the late fifteenth.[98] This

[94] Illustratively, Bouchon, 'Sixteenth Century Malabar and the Indian Ocean', p. 165.

[95] Wink has recently argued that much of the political conflict in seventeenth- and eighteenth-century western India entailed not battlefields and warfare but the sowing of dissension in adversary camps: playing on hurts and rivalries, bribing, and the like. A. Wink, *Land and Sovereignty in India*, Cambridge, 1986, p. 61, *passim*. The model may have greater generality, Irfan Habib's severe castigation notwithstanding: 'Review' [of A. Wink, 1986], *IESHR*, 1988, 25: 527–31; 'Reply' [to A. Wink], *IESHR*, 1989, 26: 368–72.

[96] P. Bhatia, *Paramaras*, c. *800–1315 AD*, New Delhi, 1970, pp. 198f, considers one phase. Did the Sultanate or the Mughal regime perceive its primary threat from potential Central Asian invaders or from the indigenes in India? To ask this question already acknowledges the implications of India's highly segmented socio-political space.

[97] Max Weber, *Economy and Society* (tr. G. Roth and C. Wittich) [Berkeley, 1978, rpt.], 1968, ch. 16, ii.

[98] Schevill, *Florence*.

autonomous assertiveness was expressed in continual participation in warfare, defensive and offensive, under non-monarchical leadership. This possibility rested on a wide-ranging impulse to co-operate within the community.[99]

Insofar as these regimes represented expansive trading and manufacturing interests, they needed to foster a politico–legal order that could resist knightly interference. The capitalist order had its first long innings in cities like Florence under these conditions; but the kind of legal and political regimes that evolved with this urban affluence had corresponding developments in France, England, and also Germany where too similar impulses had been active, leading to similar situations.[100]

The 'urban revolt' option became available in parts of Europe only in a particular historical niche, but the precipitates from this experience were put to more general uses later. For reasons that Weber saw, and which appear to be beyond reasonable dispute, this option could not arise as easily in India.

Overall, in the Brahmanical order, the possibilities of political mobilization were limited by jati boundaries in the first instance. Inside the boundary would be a person's 'own' people; outside it, 'others'. Across these boundaries, there would be the crucial difficulties over trust.[101] Severe factional rivalries even among one's 'own' people have been common however; and the man of political ambition sought to minimize such rivalries in his own camp, and to stoke those in rival camps, hoping thus to enlarge his catchment area for followers. Diverse men might thus converge on the court of a successful ruler, giving it a cosmopolitan appearance. What held them together, however, was their ruler's power and a transient commonality of interests, not an integrative vision or an entrenched ideology.

Nor has the setting been more helpful over the processes of handling information and learning from experience. Observing ongoing experience accurately, recording it for later reference, and cultivating the skills of learning from that experience—these skills and circuits were laid poorly in the Brahmanical tradition, and created difficulties. These

[99] S. Reynolds, *Kingdoms and Communities, 900–1300*, ch. 6, 'Urban Communities', examines the European scene overall for the middle ages.

[100] Ibid., pp. 186ff.

[101] *See* C. von Furer-Haimendorf, *Morals and Merits: A Study of Values and Social Controls in South Asian Societies*, London, 1967, pp. 117, 225ff.

difficulties—over wide-ranging social mobilization, and over the skills of recursive learning—had the combined effect of stunting the capacities to respond to threats and opportunities, in the ever-changing milieu, with adequate foresight and effectiveness.

May I recall in conclusion that a link between Brahmanical values and the relatively weak tendencies to act and to intervene has long been posited. This essay has suggested that this link may have operated, at least partly, through the separativeness in the caste order. That separativeness served to fragment both the normative order and the fields for possible social activity.

V

States and Systems

10

State and Lineage

SHEREEN RATNAGAR

1

When the earliest states known in history emerged in the southern Mesopotamian plains, society saw a profound change in its structure. For now a ruling elite had come into being. Yet it appears that social institutions typical of classless societies are also in evidence. Whether we have a continuity of 'tradition' in the midst of a 'social revolution', and the implications thereof, is the theme of my tribute to Romila Thapar, to whom I owe my interest in such issues. It is offered with gratitude and affection.

In the third millennium BC, over the Early Dynastic, Akkadian, and Ur III periods when political organization moved from several autonomous city–states to incorporation of all Sumer under the close control of the kings of Ur, the evidence for descent groups as recognizable and functioning entities is scattered and often circumstantial, yet striking. The third millennium texts do not refer to tribes by name, except in cases when 'hostile' or 'ravaging' peoples like the Amorites were moving into the plains in large numbers. Neither the royal inscriptions, nor the Sumerian King List, mention the tribal or clan identity of any of the kings. Royal genealogies became important only in the second millennium, after the establishment of Amorite ruling dynasties. There are however references to political institutions which appear very tribal in character, and to kinship groupings and their symbols.

In a seminal article Jacobsen[1] pointed out the existence in the early Mesopotamian states of seemingly anachronistic and 'democratic' institutions such as the Sumerian **guruš.uru** (Akkadian *alum* or *puhrum*, literally 'town' or 'Assembly') and the **ab.ba uru** (*šibutum* or '[Council of] town elders'). They were perhaps, he suggested, remnants of old traditions. The former is attested from the period of the earliest known texts through to the time of Hammurapi, in the early second millennium. From various texts we know that a divine Assembly could raise a deity to rulership of the gods, or a mortal like Sargon to the throne of Akkad; that the Assembly of Kish at least on one occasion raised a particular man to its throne; and that it was a town Assembly that decided to revolt against Naram Sin of Akkad. In Hammurapi's time the Assembly and Council were distinct bodies, settling disputes and meting out punishments. A disputant could 'assemble his city', people 'stood' or 'sat' in the Assembly, and decided on issues by calling out, 'Let it be!' It is likely that attendance in the Assembly was open to all adult males: in the story of Gilgamesh and Agga, when Gilgamesh finds no support from the elders of his city for his proposal of revolt against Agga, he summons the **guruš.uru**. In this context **guruš** means all males capable of bearing arms.

We also know of functioning groups at levels of incorporation larger than the Mesopotamian nuclear family or joint family. The term used for these larger groups is **im.ru.a** (*imrû*), translated 'clan'. An Early Dynastic text about palace personnel in the city–state of Fara enumerates members of named groups and summarizes the total as '539 descendants of 7 **im.ru.a**'. Gudea, a post-Akkad ruler of Lagash, describes how he built and beautified the temple of Ningirsu: he summoned various **im.ru.a** of the land and placed at the head of each contingent, its **šu.nir**. It was this text that provided justification for translating **im.ru.a** as 'clan', and **šu.nir** as its 'emblem' or 'totem'. The **šu.nir** name is written in cuneiform with the semantic indicator of divinity. Gelb[2] points out that if 539 people working for the Fara palace are grouped in 7 **im.ru.a**, i.e. if each of the latter sent on average more than 75 men to labour for the palace, then this group was certainly a large kin group.

When Eannatum, an early king of Lagash, lists his conquests in his

[1] T. Jacobsen, 'Primitive Democracy in Ancient Mesopotamia', *JNES*, 2 (1943), 159–72. *See also* his 'Early Political Development in Mesopotamia', *Zeitschrift fur Assyriologie*, 18 (1957), 91–140.

[2] I.J. Gelb, 'Household and Family in Ancient Mesopotamia', *in* E. Lipinski (ed.), *State and Temple Economy in the Ancient Near East*, Leuven, 1979, pp. 1–97.

inscriptions, he tells us how an enemy ruler 'marched before his **šu.nir**'.[3] On the Stele of Vultures, an inscribed relief commemorating the victories of this king, we see the figure of an enormous deity clasping in his left hand a bird and a huge net filled with enemy corpses, and behind the deity, a soldier carrying a pole surmounted with the figure of a bird.[4] Similarly, an inlay standard from Mari, depicting scenes of war, has in its lower register a man holding in both hands a tall pole surmounted by a bull-like figure. He is followed by a row of bound men and a kneeling figure (defeated enemies).[5]

So we can infer that we have pictorial representations of the **šu.nir**; that people fought in military campaigns in groups identified by their **šu.nir**; that these groups were **im.ru.a** or large descent groups; and that people were recruited for labour in the palace and temple by descent group. Sometimes the term *bitum* (literally 'house') also signifies a large group owning fields and herds, and such units could have attached members, probably of low status, as dependants.[6]

Immensely more significant, however, are more than fifty land sale documents inscribed on stone of the Early Dynastic and Akkadian periods.[7] With the exception of three or four cases, each land

[3] E. Sollberger and J.R. Kupper, *Inscriptions Royales Sumeriennes et Akkadiennes*, Paris, 1971, pp. 58–9.

[4] M.T. Barrelet, 'Peut-on remettre en question la restitution materielle de la Stele des Vautours?' *JNES*, 29 (1970), 233–58.

[5] A. Parrot, *Mari: Capitale Fabuleuse*, Paris, 1974, 46, pl. XIII.

[6] Gelb, 'Household and Family', pp. 2–3, 9. Perhaps if P. Crone ('The Tribe and the State', *in* J.A. Hall (ed.), *States in History*, Oxford, 1986, pp. 48–77) had taken this evidence into account, she would not be so certain that the Sumerians lacked a tribal past. For over a millennium preceding the rise of states, agricultural communities had lived in the southern plains, and if we appreciate the inherent connection between a delayed returns economy based on agriculture and the role of kinship in giving long-term stability and coherence to landholding groups, then we must accept a tribal past. Crone cites the absence of literary references to blood-vengeance; but an important feature of early states is that the ruling elite monopolizes the use of force and local groups can no longer take unilateral action to avenge wrongs. Crone also argues that tribal societies have inbuilt mechanisms to prevent the emergence of inequality; this is true, but it is also known that chiefs having access to extra-kin sources of labour, armed force, or wealth are able to overcome the structural limitations of their kinship obligations. In the case of Sumer we could suggest that the land-use system gave rise to endemic intercommunity warfare, and that as a result a chief could build up a following or militia of clients, dependants, or prisoners-of-war, to whom he did not owe the same generosity as to his own people; moreover, he would have 'external' sources of rapidly incrementing wealth to manipulate for personal gain: booty from raids, as well as the fruits of long-distance trade.

[7] I.M. Diakonoff, 'Sale of Land in Pre-Sargonic Sumer', Papers of the *XXIIIrd International Congress of Orientalists*, Moscow, 1954; and Gelb, 'Household and Family';

transaction involves from 2 to 27 persons as sellers ('men who received the price', 'recipients of silver'). Often the sale document names the ancestors of the sellers, or a group of sellers are called 'descendants of X'. From this we can tell that the sellers of a tract of agricultural land were related to one another and could comprise three generations of kinsmen (women are sellers only occasionally). Thus Diakonoff and Gelb infer that joint title to agricultural land was still being held by descent groups. Take for example a large stone monument (the 'Obelisk of Manishtusu') recording eight land purchases by Manishtusu, king of Akkad. In the first transaction 17 named sellers, 'descendants of Mezizi', belong to 12 nuclear families. According to Gelb, these sellers are a residential clan whose legendary ancestor was Mezizi. The eight land purchases, made in four different regions, involve a total of 98 sellers belonging to 64 families. As 64 families can be expected to have many more than 98 members, Gelb argues, only some members (adult, married men?) had the right to sell these jointly owned lands.

If we consider the order in which sellers are named, the terms by which they are called, and the goods they receive at the sale, these 98 sellers were 'anything but equal'. The first-named seller, 'Lord of the field', receives the most goods. Other 'Lords of the field' also receive goods as price and gift, but in smaller amounts. Sellers who are 'Brother-lords of the field' receive neither price nor gift. Gelb shows that 'Lords' and 'Brother-lords' cannot be distinguished as senior versus junior or branch lineages. Usually the genealogies of the 'Brother-lords' are brief, and it is possible, he suggests, that these persons or their near ancestors were not born lineage members but had become incorporated into the group at some time in the past, so that their approval of the sale was necessary. But in an Early Dynastic sale text where the son of a ruler of Lagash buys four tracts of land, and sellers are distinguished as 'Lords of the field' and 'Sons of the field', the latter are often literally the sons of the former.

Such land sales were legal transactions, not confiscations, and most scholars believe that the quantities of silver, grain, copper, animals, cloth, etc. handed over as recompense were fair in terms of value. But why should a legal sale involve gifts or 'additional payment' (silver, cloth, food items) over and above the price? I am struck by an analogous practice among the Bete people of the Ivory Coast, and the explanation

I.J. Gelb, P. Steinkeller, R.M. Whiting, *Earliest Land Tenure Systems in the Near East: Ancient Kudurrus*, Chicago, 1991.

offered by Köbben[8] for it. Many land transfers among the Bete involve harvest gifts; tension can ensue when sellers repeatedly demand these gifts even after the cash price has been paid. Köbben suggests that this is a residue of the pre-colonial period, when lineage tenure prevailed and there was no private property in land, and outsiders could seek the permission of a local group to open forest tracts to rice cultivation for a specified period. If such were granted, it was customary to present a few baskets of rice to the landholding group at harvest time.

It is tempting to push a similar interpretation for the Mesopotamian practice, namely that it was a relic of times when land was not alienable. There are occasional references in the land sale texts to feasts held for the sellers and/or their witnesses: 20 or 190 or 600 men are said to 'eat bread' together. House sales in the third millennium also involved the giving of both price and gift. And at marriages, gifts were exchanged that were distinct from the bride-price. Renger[9] opines that the *biblum* marriage gift belongs to the realm of custom, whereas the bride-price (*terhatum*) part of the marriage contract belongs to the realm of law. Perhaps the ceremonial marriage gift was also a relic of tribal norms, however transformed in the urban milieu.

To return to the ancient land sales, they do indicate that kin groups continued to own land jointly even after the emergence of ruling elites. Gelb goes so far as to argue that '. . . there may not have been any [agricultural] villages of independent small peasants' in this period.[10] But in some areas descent groups were selling their lands, and often large tracts were involved, perhaps a total of about 3400 hectares in the case of Manishtusu's purchases. The fact that large tracts were often bought by kings or their relatives indicates that lineage land was being incorporated into the palace sector, perhaps to be rented out to cultivators. In a temple statue inscription at Nippur, Sargon, founder of the dynasty of Akkad, narrates that '5,400 men ate bread daily in his presence'; later historical traditions of this king state that 'he let the sons of his palace dwell for five leagues on either side', or that 'five leagues on either side having been cut off, he enlarged his palace, and the

[8] A.J.F. Köbben, 'Land as an Object of Gain in a Non-literate Society', *in* D. Biebuyck (ed.), *African Agrarian Systems*, London, 1963, pp. 245–66.

[9] J. Renger, 'Who are all these People?', *Orientalia*, 42 (1973), pp. 259–73.

[10] Gelb, 'Household and Family', p. 4. Note that the approach is different in Gelb et al., (op. cit., pp. 17–24), published after Gelb's death, where only two alternatives are considered, namely private property as we know it, and temple estates. Kin group tenure is not discussed at all.

[displaced] men stood by him and said to him, 'Where shall we go?'[11] Moreover, on each of the four sides of the Obelisk of Manishtusu the same list of 49 witnesses, all 'sons of Akkad', occurs, and the first-named witness was a relative of the king.

2

If it is clear that in the third millennium descent groups functioned as jural entities holding land and as units of recruitment for war and labour service, the question arises whether they were necessarily a survival from an anterior, tribal, formation,[12] and if so whether lineages continued to enjoy their original functions, but if not, whether lineages were a response to particular historical factors.

When discussing the process of transformation from *Lineage to State* in the Gangetic plains, Romila Thapar observes that lineage groupings survived the emergence of states for centuries. She also makes the point that ruling elites would have been slow to emerge in regions like the upper plains because relative abundance of land would have allowed for lineage flexibility, manouevre, or fission. At the same time, the

[11] C.J. Gadd, 'The Dynasty of Agade and the Gutian Invasion', *Cambridge Ancient History*, I.2, Cambridge, 1971, p. 424.

[12] The very concept of the lineage or clan has recently been called into question. Scholars point out that in some cases groups were identified as 'tribes' by colonial administrators, even when local categories were totally different from the tribe–clan–lineage scheme. A. Kuper (*The Invention of Primitive Society*, London, 1988) argues that lineages are not truly corporate groups and do not neatly coincide with residence groups; that in the Pacific group, membership is fluid and can operate irrespective of descent; that status within a group rarely depends on genealogical position; and so on. One agrees that a descent system does not give us the social structure of a society, and that kinship should instead be studied as the context of social action. But consider the views of A. Strathern ('Kinship, Descent, and Ideology'), and J. La Fontaine ('Descent in New Guinea') (both in J. Goody, ed., *The Character of Kinship*, Cambridge, 1973, pp. 21–33 and 35–51). They show that in New Guinea descent does function as a criterion for group solidarity and inter-group alliances; that entire clans may sometimes contribute to the bride-wealth of a member of a clan section; that by shifting residence an individual does not lose his rights to land in his own descent group. La Fontaine shows that confusion occurs when descent is understood literally, as blood relationship, and Strathern shows that where residence groups incorporate people born outside the local descent group, those who are newcomers become affiliated to those 'born on the land', by eating the food grown on that land. Shared substance therefore involves not only the blood of the lineage but also the food of its land. For F. Barth ('Descent and Marriage Reconsidered', pp. 3–19 in the same volume), however, unilineal descent groups make sense only in their political and economic context: the Middle Eastern patrilineage is certainly a jural entity controlling land, inheritance, and territory, but co-residence of the lineage is a consequence of joint tenure, not of agnatic descent.

corporate character of the lineage may itself be a function of land scarcities: in those parts of Africa where land is abundant it has been found that descent groups are the least corporate. We may argue that lineages will assert their identities and control membership with care only when land is scarce and access to resources needs to be carefully regulated. According to Hayden and Cannon,[13] in the Americas the corporate character of lineages was a function of the onset of land shortages. Meanwhile the Chinese *tsu*, an exogamous corporate descent group, settling its internal disputes and often maintaining a common Ancestral Hall to ritually honour ancestors many generations past, had rich and poor members and was actually 'dedicated to inequality, economic, ritual and political'.[14] Yet it has been understood[15] to prevail in those areas with weak state presence, recent settlement but dense populations, double cropping, and elite control over land: without these elements, the lineage disappears.[16] It is also possible that post-marital residence rules play a part. Patrilocal groups with patrilocal residence have greater opportunity for becoming closely corporate than do matrilineal societies lacking a fixed rule of uxorilocal residence.[17] In other cases it has been found that when agricultural marketing sets in, lineage

---

Then there are arguments that often when small kin groups have made a political alliance, they 'become' a tribe. Such a tribe is obviously not a related group but comprises clans, clan factions, unrelated groups, war chiefs and their clients, and so on. We can also have what Gellner calls the 'typical Middle Eastern tribal quasi-state' where a tribe with external trade and urbanite elites, is controlled by a state power. But none of these refute the tribe as a form of social organization amongst simple agriculturists and pastoralists of the remote past. For one thing, class stratification or private property are not the condition of human existence. As Barfield explains, at lower levels of incorporation common ancestors and kinship are the criteria of membership even if at higher levels, for larger groups, it is military or political alliance that count. *See* P.S. Khoury and J. Kostiner (eds), *Tribes and State Formation in the Middle East*, London, 1991, especially T. Barfield on pp. 153–82.

[13] B. Hayden and A. Cannon, 'The Corporate Group as an Archaeological Unit', *Journal of Anthropological Archaeology*, 1 (1982), pp. 132–58.

[14] M. Fried, 'The Classification of Corporate Unilineal Descent Groups', *Journal of the Royal Anthropological Institute*, 87 (1957), pp. 1–29; M. Freedman, *The Study of Chinese Society*, Stanford, 1979, esp. pp. 334–50.

[15] R.N. Anderson, 'Lineage Atrophy in Chinese Society', *American Anthropologist*, 72 (1970), pp. 363–5, and Freedman, op. cit.

[16] If we consult R. McC. Adams' survey maps (in his *Heartland of Cities*, Chicago, 1981 (fig. 27) we find that the Kish and Marad areas, two regions where Manishtusu bought up land, were relatively sparsely settled in the Akkad period.

[17] *See* D. Biebuyck, 'Introduction', and J. Vansina, 'Les Regimes Fonciers Ruanda et Kuba', *in* D. Biebuyck (ed.), *African Agrarian Systems*, pp. 28–9 and 348–63, respectively.

groupings become important (land and labour are necessary in large enough units to ensure adequate profits)[18] or the reverse, that lineage tenure continues for subsistence cropping, but cash crops are grown on individually owned plots.[19]

The point that lineage organization need not be an old social form but can re-emerge under particular conditions is forcefully made by Rosenfeld[20] for Palestine under Ottoman rule. Under the *masha'* system agnatic kin groups held collective usufruct, fields were allocated to members every two years, and taxes were shared by members at the threshing floor. But Rosenfeld does not see this system as a survival from a tribal past. He says it was 'instigated' by the Ottoman fiscal–administrative system; that the state 'imposed a structured autonomy on the village itself'. Instead of being a 'historically self-sustaining collective in its own right', the patrilineage was very vulnerable to political vicissitudes.

Rosenfeld then asks whether the ancient Sumerian lineages were not also responses to state structures. We are here reminded of the fact that our early kings never recorded their clan or tribal origins in their inscriptions. Even so, there is a crucial difference. In ancient Sumer there is little evidence for independent peasant households, whereas in Ottoman-ruled Palestine it was lineage *usufruct* that prevailed, and only on state-owned lands; there was also land privately owned by officials and merchants, as well as tenant farming. Indeed, Rosenfeld does discuss the contradictions between descent-group collectivities and an economy based on private property.

For Diakonoff[21] Sumerian lineage members were free persons in terms of their rights to land, their access to the labour of their kin, and their rights to participate in local affairs. Membership in kin groups kept persons independent of the ruling elite, even if they had to surrender labour. The landholding lineage could therefore have been a mechanism

[18] Hayden and Cannon, 'The Corporate Group'.

[19] R.G. Cooper, 'Dynamic Tension: Symbiosis and Contradiction in Hmong Social Relations', *in* J. Clammer (ed.), *The New Economic Anthropology*, London, 1978, pp. 138–75.

[20] H. Rosenfeld, 'The Problem of Arab Peasant Kinship', *in* J. Mencher (ed.), *The Social Anthropology of Peasantry*, Delhi, 1983, pp. 154–76. *See also* R. McC. Adams, 'Property Rights and Functional Tenure in Mesopotamian Rural Communities', *in* M. Dandamayev et al. (eds), *Societies and Languages of the Ancient Near East* (Diakonoff Festschrift), London, 1982, pp. 1–14.

[21] I.M. Diakonoff, 'The Rural Community in the Ancient Near East', *JESHO*, 18 (1975), pp. 121–33.

of self-preservation outside the state sector.[22] While we may thus infer that this situation was one inherited from a preceding social formation, Diakonoff also considers the likelihood that kin organization emerged afresh when new rural settlements were founded, for example in the Ur III period.

This last point is significant. We learn from Adams' surveys[23] that third millennium settlement was constantly shifting. Centres like Uruk grew to immense size over a period of a century or two, but then collapsed to a fraction of their former size. So too rural settlement enclaves. This ebb and flow of population was a response to chronic warfare, pastoral nomad incursions, canal silting, rapid stream avulsion, and related factors. Thus it is very likely that local groups were periodically moving, splitting, and re-forming, and their territorial boundaries likewise.

However fluid such groups, it appears that they performed a very important function. Fernea[24] has demonstrated the suitability of tribal tenure to the pre-modern land-use system of southern Iraq. Tribes were landholding groups, feasting groups, and warrior groups, with a *mudhif* or 'guest-house' as a common meeting place. In Iraqi history irrigation systems did not decay with the collapse of central governments. It was fully within the capabilities of local kin groups to provide and maintain their irrigation canals. Also, tribal tenure, with reallocation of fields to families according to need, common stores, commons for pasturage, and co-operation in labour, ensured a flexible man–land relationship and the observance of alternate-year fallows so crucial to the long-term success of agriculture in the region.

We are reminded of Wolf's observation[25] that complex societies may have resources 'too costly or too difficult to bring under direct control'; resources left to 'interstitial structures' to manage. Third millennium Mesopotamian states were not providers of irrigation in any major way—they could not have had the organizational capacity to do so for

[22] To this Adams (*Heartland*, p. 250) adds the rider that in any case, given continuous flux between agriculture and herding in the countryside, the persistence here of 'essentially defensive formations of semi-sedentary, tribalized peasantry' is the other side of the coin of Mesopotamia's precocious urban development.

[23] Ibid.

[24] R.A. Fernea, *Shaykh and Effendi: Changing Patterns of Authority Among the El-Shabana of Southern Iraq*, Cambridge, Mass., 1970.

[25] E. Wolf, 'Kinship, Friendship and Patron–Client Relations in Complex Societies', *in* M. Banton (ed.), *The Social Anthropology of Complex Societies*, London, 1966, pp. 1–22,

all rural communities. Only a few royal inscriptions refer to irrigation works as royal enterprise; from the Early Dynastic to the Ur III periods there are references in administrative texts to a fee being charged for irrigation water, but this is on temple lands and payable by tenants of the temple; it is only in the later old Babylonian period that landowners pay irrigation fees to a state authority.[26]

While kin groups had a crucially important function to perform in agricultural production, we should not forget that the land sale texts reveal a marked social change taking place. Lineage tenure includes a complex bundle of rights: the rights of individual members to cultivate, the group's rights to fallow, rights ensuing on political allegiance, and so on—but *not* rights of disposal. It is the entire lineage which is land-owner, and the lineage in the pristine sense is a perpetual entity even as its members die and new members are born. Its land is inalienable in the sense that neither ancestors nor future members are present to validate an act of land disposal.[27] When our land sale deeds mention the rite of 'nailing the nail into the wall and pouring oil', perhaps they are referring to the ratification of deeds that in former times could have caused offence to the ancestors. So we have our first clue that 'tradition' itself had undergone an important change in the third millennium. This was in the context of the emergence of the state and the state sector of production.

It was Diakonoff who first conceived of third millennium society as comprising the 'state sector', or the public households of the temple and palace, under the rulers' direct control, and the 'private and communal sector' of kin groups controlling lands and agricultural production on them.[28] The state sector comprised the temples, the palace, certain production units within them such as mills or smithies, and the incorporated households of state officials. These were staffed by a hierarchy of officers (priests heading the temple hierarchies) as well as workers. Owning fields, houses, storehouses, animals, pastures, and orchards, a public household was 'a full socio–economic unit'[29] and operated on the mobilization of labour for its various activities. Often Iraqi tribal chiefs have had disproportionately large landholdings, but

[26] P. Steinkeller, 'The Renting of Fields in Early Mesopotamia', *JESHO*, 24 (1981), pp. 113–45.

[27] This comes through in several contributions to D. Biebuyck (ed.), *African Agrarian Systems*, London, 1963.

[28] I.M. Diakonoff, 'Socio–economic Classes in Babylonia', *in* D.O. Edzard (ed.), *XVIIIeme Rencontre Assyriologique Internationale*, Munich, 1972, pp. 41–8.

[29] I.J. Gelb, 'The Arua Institution', *Revue d'Assyriologie*, 66 (1972), 10.

this was justified as necessary for the social activities of the mudhif. As the Sumerian temple so the mudhif was the place where oaths were taken. Originally the temple must have been tribally owned.

Up to the end of the Ur III period a large proportion of archival texts have to do with ration distributions. Standard amounts of grain and wool are handed out to named individuals, either monthly or annually; oil less regularly. These are not wages, as they can be allotted to infants and the blind, and the amounts given depend on the age and sex of the worker and not on the amount or skill of work. Wage disbursements appear in Ur III but are less extensive. Those who received rations were called **gemé** ('woman') and **guruš** ('man').

According to Gelb, these terms have a status or class connotation. He distinguishes the **guruš** from slaves (for whom different terms are used, and whose rations are listed separately in the temple and palace accounts) and from independent agriculturists (again distinct terms and separate ration lists).[30] He considers that the **guruš** were the major workforce of the third millennium. (According to current opinion, however, the term has no status connotation.) **Guruš** labour worked in groups under foremen at agriculture, herding, oil-pressing, milling, weaving, and leather production. In Early Dynastic records reed mat-makers, boat-builders, metallurgists, and stone-cutters also receive rations. If we pursue particular personal names in the ration lists, which were dated, we see that some persons received rations through the year (that is, they worked only for the temple or palace), whereas others received them for say four months in the year (they would have had other means of support).

The state sector had reached truly gigantic proportions under the Third Dynastic of Ur. In a much cited list of contingents of labourers recruited from various cities for harvest work in the north, the total number of men is about 21,800, so that the area of state land involved must have been many hundreds of square kilometres. Again, the total animal wealth under state management in Ur III, according to Adams' calculations, was 53 per cent higher than the animal population of the same area in 1952, although the human population in Ur III was less than one-third that of 1952![31]

Tablets in the Mari archives refer to the responsibility of certain palace officials for the procurement of metal, the organization of

[30] I.J. Gelb, 'The Ancient Mespotamian Ration System', *JNES*, 24 (1965), pp. 230–43.

[31] Adams, *Heartland*, pp. 144–9; K. Maekawa, 'Cereal Cultivation in the Ur III Period', *Bulletin on Sumerian Agriculture*, vol. I, Cambridge, 1984, pp. 73–96.

metallurgical production, and storage of the end product. There is evidence also in the second millennium from Mari for the occasional flight of palace craftsmen, searches for them, their capture, and their reinstatement.[32] Texts from one room in the Nanna temple at Ur (Ur III period) represent not part of the main temple archive, but concern goods allotted by the palace as monthly offerings to the gods, raw wool sent by the palace and disbursed for spinning and weaving, and raw materials for leather-work, seal-cutting, carpentry, and metallurgy. The texts also incorporate attendance lists of palace craftsmen. Thus this archive shows that temple and palace functions were closely interdigitated.[33]

Gelb sees a substantive difference in the labour force of temple and palace: a larger proportion of women and children in the temple, and a greater number of war captives working for the palace. After the Early Dynastic period, palace workmen could be called **erin**, 'men in gangs', a word which originally meant the 'yoke' used to transport prisoners of war. But for Maekawa these were detachments distinct from those menial workers or craftsmen working regularly for the palace only in that they performed compulsory labour in alternate months, when alone they received rations. A major point of interest is that often people gave ex-voto (**a.ru.a**) individuals, mainly women and children, to the temple, and they joined the workforce. Rich and poor alike seem to have given people, the latter perhaps due to distress. Thus Gelb, 'The temple apparently served as a collecting centre for all these poor, unwanted, and rejected people. . . .'[34]

What immediately comes to mind is that unless these people were only the urban riff-raff, one important function of the corporate kin group, succour to the bereaved, impoverished, or disabled, seems to have been lost. In any case, the entire population certainly did not now have rights to sustenance in its native patrilineage. We need not romanticize the city Assembly institution either, for there are any number of injunctions in the literature that to go and stand in the Assembly is just asking for trouble. Moreover, Bayliss[35] finds that rituals (food offerings, the pouring of water, and 'calling the name') for

[32] C. Zaccagnini, 'Patterns of Mobility Among Ancient Near Eastern Craftsmen', *JNES*, 42 (1983), pp. 245–64.

[33] T. Jacobsen, review of L. Legrain, *Ur Excavation Texts II: Business Documents of the Third Dynasty of Ur*, in *American Journal of Archaeology*, 57 (1953), pp. 125–8.

[34] Gelb, 'The Arua Institution'; I.J. Gelb, 'Prisoners of War in Early Mesopotamia', *JNES*, 32 (1973), 81; K. Maekawa, 'Collective Labour Service in Girsu–Lagash', *in* M.A. Powell (ed.), *Labour in the Ancient Near East*, New Haven, 1987, pp. 49–71.

[35] M. Bayliss, 'The Cult of Dead Kin in Assyria and Babylonia', *Iraq*, 35 (1973), pp. 115–25.

the dead were incumbent more on the heirs of the deceased than on kin in general. This obligation was 'closely bound up with the process of inheritance', and we do not know of rites being performed for ancestors farther removed than grandparents. Even more significant is one of the laws promulgated by Urnammu, founder of the Third Dynasty of Ur. This law specifies the rate at which a cultivator must pay compensation if he allows irrigation water to flood the sown field of his neighbour.[36] What one would expect to have been the routine sort of matter with which a corporate lineage could cope, is now a matter of state decree. (It is possible, however, that this law refers only to tenant fields on state lands.) We can also guess that state and kinship interests would eventually become incompatible in some spheres of life, e.g. in the case of a person who was both a palace office holder and a member of his own descent group. And if rural communities came to be treated increasingly as territorial or administrative units, and their elders came to depend more and more on state recognition rather than on the support of their own kinsmen, the corporate character and function of the kin group would have been further eroded. We must therefore conclude that by the end of the third millennium the Mesopotamian lineage had come to play very restricted—though important—social functions.

3

At the theoretical level we are dealing with a society at a transition between a kinship structure and a class structure, for we cannot suggest that the schism between rulers and the ruled was *based* on private property. The temple estates, community wealth in the earlier periods, were by the Early Dynastic period the de facto property of the ruler and his family (a late Early Dynastic ruler of Lagash, Urukagina, instituted 'reforms' to change the state of affairs but did not succeed), and large palace estates had also been carved out; excavated palace structures are immensely larger than known contemporary temple structures, incidentally, and palace architecture often incorporated a strong defensive element. But for the rest, communal land tenure still prevailed, and the populace at large retained effective control over its basic resources. The question then arises whether the model of the Asiatic Mode of Production can help us understand early Mesopotamia.[37]

[36] J.J. Finkelstein, 'The Laws of Ur-nammu', *Journal of Cuneiform Studies*, 22 (1968–9), no. 28.

[37] For references *see* A.M. Bailey and J.R. Llobera (eds), *The Asiatic Mode of Production*, London, 1981.

Perhaps so, if we take the key feature of the AMP to be communal tenure, the low level of the division of labour in rural communities which combine agriculture and crafts, and marginal commodity production—but not large-scale state irrigation projects or despotic rule (which were causally connected in the original model). When the state mobilized mass labour it was not for canals but town walls or temples or pyramids. If rural communities are self-sustaining and self-reproducing, they are (or their form is) more stable than the ruling dynasties which rise and fall. This is the only sense in which the feature of 'stagnation' is acceptable. Even if the concept of the AMP took form in an attempt to comprehend the absence of capitalism in some parts of the world, Marx in one context placed the AMP in a sequence of historical stages, so that it may be viewed as a level of development rather than a geographically specific kind of society. ('The Asiatic system is not yet class society, or if it is, then it is the most primitive form of class society'.)

A variant of the AMP has been suggested for African state societies[38] with their simple technologies, communal landownership, little commodity exchange, remnant tribal political structures, and inchoate administrative machinery. In this 'tributary' mode, class formation is inchoate; ruling elites feed on warfare and external trade, but are not direct exploiters of their own rural populations except as mobilizers of labour or tribute, and sponsors of diverse crafts for export or sumptuary consumption at court. While tribal structures persist, state structures are relatively fragile. While rural output is contained, the elite exhibit at court their sumptuary trade wealth. In the Mesopotamian case the slave and arms trade are not relevant, but here too we may suggest that the spurt in craft production and technology in the early third millennium was under state auspices, and that elites relied heavily on warfare and on external trade. This model however has no place for mass recruitment of unskilled labour. Perhaps contrasting agricultural techniques and output, and population densities, may explain the difference.

But the problem remains of where urbanism fits in. Urban development was 'hypertrophic' in early Sumer: in Early Dynastic I, Uruk was a 400-hectare settlement, and by the Early Dynastic III phase, settlements of 40 ha. or more in size comprised 78 per cent of the total settled area.[39] Yet for Marx cities do not really belong to the Asiatic economies

[38] C. Coquery-Vidrovitch, 'Research on an African Mode of Production', *in* D. Seddon (ed.), *Relations of Production*, London, 1978, pp. 159–69; D. Seddon, 'Approaches to Pre-Capitalist Formations in the Maghreb', *in* J. Clammer (ed.), *The New Economic Anthropology*, London, 1978, pp. 61–109.

[39] Adams, *Heartland*, pp. 84–5, 138.

unless their location was favourable for external trade, or, quite significantly, 'where the head of the state and his satraps exchange their revenue for labour'. This prompts the question whether urbanism was in some way an outgrowth of an expanding state sector.

The answer will of course depend on how we define urbanism in the bronze age. The point has often been made that the ancient Near Eastern city housed a larger portion of food producers than craftsmen, traders, and administrators. But Adams points out[40] that if Early Dynastic Uruk was inhabited by 40,000 to 50,000 people, an agricultural area of 14 km radius would have been required to feed the city; we do not expect farmers to regularly commute between home and field for distances greater than 4 km; so there is a strong possibility that only a fraction of Uruk's population engaged in agriculture. For Andreev, however,[41] the Sumerian cities were 'unnaturally vast concentrations of agricultural populations', not unlike the Yoruba 'cities' of recent times, whose inhabitants spent long spells at their farms.

Excavated artefacts reveal exceptionally advanced techniques of craft work, especially in metallurgy, in ancient Sumer. Texts give us incidental information on the organization of craft production. The amount of archaeological data on craft loci or workshops however is dismal. Thus we can make few confident inferences about specialization and the division of labour as essential to the economy of the Sumerian city. At the same time I would suggest that it would be dangerous to assume that specialization involved full-time and exclusive engagement in one craft activity in the city throughout the year. In the Ur III period the chief temple at Ur received huge quantities of raw wool from the palace, and disbursed this to villages around Ur for spinning and weaving; and craftsmen here were apparently regularly 'set free for the harvest'.[42]

For the Sumerians the name 'Lagash' meant the urban centre as well as the state of Lagash. In both Sumerian and Akkadian just one word was used for 'city', whereas diverse descriptive terms were used for features of the countryside. The Mesopotamians appear to have had a very definitive conception of city-ness. It was in the city that the largest temples, the most prolific scribal output, the administrative institutions, and the greatest inflows of goods were to be found. The city was primarily a political and ritual centre, and a node of military defence.

[40] Ibid., pp. 85ff.

[41] Y.V. Andreev, 'Urbanization as a Phenomenon of Social History', *Oxford Journal of Archaeology*, 8 (1989), pp. 167–77.

[42] Jacobsen, review of Legrain.

And it is in this context that we must consider the role of craft 'specialization': it is not unreasonable to assume that the major craft output was organized by the temple and palace, even if the written evidence is biased (in the sense that small-scale and independent craft work would not have required the maintenance of written records). What one is trying to suggest is that craft production was not fostered primarily by increasing demand and economies of scale in the urban centres, but by the motivations of the ruling elite and the structure of the public households.[43] Yet the entire economy of a city like Uruk or Lagash could not have been reducible to the state sector. Kin identities may have survived in the cities,[44] but any number of transactions (loans between individuals, sales of house plots, the accounts of independent merchants in the Ur III period) are documented which have nothing to do with kinship networks; they reveal, rather, the impersonal and sporadic dealings with non-kin that are typical of urban life. We can suggest neither the kin group nor the temple/palace as the source of the bronze knives or pottery or cylinder seals used in the residence of a merchant at Ur. Did an over-extended state sector and urban hypertrophy themselves pave the way for social and economic transformation towards individual enterprise, private property, and increased commodity production for developing market systems after 2000 BC?

The reader will have guessed that this kind of question makes little sense when we know so little about the earliest urban centres. At this stage it is more useful to ask if the coexistence of class and kin, state and lineage, gave a particular form to the earliest states. In other words, was this duality structurally connected with other aspects of the states?

The first correlation I would suggest is with the form of the economy. No market system economy prevails. As Meillassoux points out,[45] the rise of the market economy opens the way for the transformation of the output of a kin group into merchandise. 'Once a product can be sold, the producer can be bought.' Kinship then 'loses its actuality' as relations of production begin to 'revolve around the means of material production'.

[43] V. Gordon Childe (*Social Evolution*, New York, 1951, pp. 144–5) perhaps pre-empts G. Balandier (*Political Anthropology*, Harmondsworth, 1970, pp. 99ff, 130–2) when he suggests that when in the ancient past one kin group had acquired dominance over its neighbours, its leaders could claim sacral powers and only then begin to concentrate wealth.

[44] J.N. Postgate, *Early Mesopotamia*, London, 1992, pp. 81–2, 89–91.

[45] C. Meillassoux, 'The Social Organization of the Peasantry: The Economic Basis of Kinship', *in* D. Seddon (ed.), *Relations of Production*, London, 1978, pp. 159–69.

Second, the state sector as principal agent for the development of crafts and trade, the persistence of tribal institutions, and the absence of fully developed class distinctions, all, according to Andreev, militate against a total separation between food production and crafts and trade.

The kin–class duality and lack of market systems in turn are connected with the fact that surplus is in the main mobilized as labour exactions and not as tax on village produce. On one section of temple lands, those which were allocated to functionaries, tenant cultivators did pay rent. But in the thousands of third millennium administrative texts, as pointed out by Diakonoff, there is no reference to a universal harvest tax. When Gilgamesh persuades the people of Uruk to revolt against Kish, the argument goes, 'To continually stand at attention, to be continually assigned to a post, to go on raids with the king's son, to continually urge on the donkey, who has breath [enough] for that?'[46] Taxes find no mention in the argument.

The levy of a universal harvest tax may have been beyond the capabilities of the earliest kind of state. It would require a heavy investment by the state in transportation, mechanisms to guard against fraud, ensuring collections on schedule, and salaries or reimbursement of the large number of personnel involved. Moreover, to increase its wealth, a state would either have to use coercion, or encourage the extension of cultivation, or actively promote higher productivity.

It may be more to the point that direct control by the state over all land is not compatible with lineage tenure and community economy. Significantly, Romila Thapar sees in the ancient Gangetic basin a coincidence between the decline of lineages, the rise of individual landownership, and the appearance of agricultural taxation. Theoretically it would appear that taxation on individual families would, as plots were now individually measured, encourage increasing independence of the household, its disengagement from the descent group collectivity, and adjustments of labour to land at the household level. Owners would derive decreasing benefits from attachment to their natal group. When in the second millennium in Mesopotamia there is a great increase in documentation on independent households with their own small plots, we also have evidence for increased use of wage labour, loans, indebtedness, land sales, and tenancies.[47]

[46] S.N. Kramer, 'Gilgamesh and Agga', *American Journal of Archaeology*, 53 (1949), pp. 1–16. See commentary and alternate translation of lines 25–8 by T. Jacobsen, pp. 16–18.

[47] H. Klengel, 'Non-Slave Labour in the Old Babylonian Period', *in* M. Powell (ed.), *Labour in the Ancient Near East*, New Haven, 1987, pp. 159–66.

Surplus mobilization in the form of labour levies is an early, indirect, and perhaps disguised form of exploitation. Mesopotamian warrior–kings were also stewards of the gods' earthly estates, builders of temples and installers of statues, and appointing priests and priestesses. Kings were participants in the New Year's day ritual of the Sacred Marriage, which took place in the temple, and which, involving the king in the role of Dumuzi (deity of the rejuvenating vegetation), and a chosen priestess in the role of Inanna (the goddess of fertility), ensured the prosperity of the land in the coming year. On New Year's day the populace was feasted; and there is a rare reference to a feast in a royal inscription: the king Urnanshe, after completing the building of the temple of Ningirsu at Lagash, provided 70 **gur** (an enormous amount) of barley for a feast.[48] Service in the state sector was probably understood as service to the gods, a formally reciprocal relationship between ruler and ruled blurring the connection between labour and the final disposal of the product of that labour.[49] Sacrality would also have masked the militarist foundation of kingship: Mesopotamian kings were first and foremost military leaders, as royal titles and inscriptions, city defence, palace architecture, and the epics about early kings amply testify.

Fifth, our earliest states have a very rudimentary administrative organization, with little specialization of tasks. For example, it is a priest who writes to a king about the surprise and defeat of 600 Elamites and their detention in his temple.[50] Bureaucratic structures were undeveloped in the third millennium.[51] Bureaucratic organization means that each office has its own field and jurisdiction, specifically delegated, and therefore special sets of expertise; a hierarchy of command; an organization based on written records and communications; officials acting according to norms ('rules and regulations'); and a separation between state funds and the private wealth of officials. Even in the highly centralized Ur III state with its plethora of administrative records, we find instead that individuals held multiple offices; all holders of high office were not literate; marriages were arranged between the families of high officials and the king; the carvings on standardized seals presented to

[48] Sollberger and Kupper, *Inscriptions Royales*, 46.

[49] This point was made by C. Morris, 'Reconstructing Patterns of Non-Agricultural Production in the Inca Economy', *in* C.B. Moore (ed.), *Reconstructing Complex Societies*, New Haven, 1974, in the context of the Inca state which also functioned on labour levies—the state could not acquire goods directly, but mobilized people to produce them.

[50] Sollberger and Kupper, *Inscriptions Royales*, pp. 75–6.

[51] M. Gibson and R.D. Biggs (eds), *The Organization of Power*, Chicago, 1987.

high officials clearly indicate the subservience and personal dependence of the official on the king; and not only the official in charge of a temple, but also members of his family secure doors of the temple or conclude contracts on its behalf.

If the third millennium Mesopotamian state was structured on lineage tenure, sacral kingship and formal reciprocity, labour levies, and 'patrimonial' rather than bureaucratic organization, we can suggest that elites exercised power over people rather than over productive resources. This appears enormously paradoxical, for the state was by the end of the millennium controlling truly vast agricultural and herding resources. Yet we can see that such resources would have had no significance without political institutions and ideology directing the labour of the populace to make them productive.

> Blood will I form and cause bone to be;
> Then will I set up *lullu*, 'Man' shall be his name!
> Yes, I will create *lullu*, Man!
> Upon him shall the services of the gods be imposed that they may be at rest.

[From *Enuma Elish, the Babylonian 'Epic' of Creation.* Note that in some contexts *lullu* means a lout or a fool.]

11

'Peripheral Regions' and 'Marginal Communities': Towards an Alternative Explanation of Early Iron Age Material and Social Formations in Sri Lanka*

SUDHARSHAN SENEVIRATNE

'It is now a truism to say that significant new evidence on early periods of history is more likely to come from archaeological than from literary sources. This makes the collaboration between the historian and the archaeologist imperative. Whereas the method of data collection may differ between the two, the final process, that is, the interpretation of the data is similar in both disciplines. In short, the process of change and transition from one type of society to another can be better culled from historical sources if there is a general framework from archaeology with which it can be correlated or at least

*This study attempts to provide some answers to issues raised on institutional formation in the course of my Doctoral research carried out under the supervision of Professor Romila Thapar, to whom I am grateful for the insight provided on this aspect. Much of the field and other research work was carried out at the Department of Archaeology, University of Peradeniya and subsequently at the Institute of Fundamental Studies, Kandy under the project on Ancient Materials and Technology. I am thankful to my departmental colleagues Piyatissa Senanayake, Chulani Rambukwella and D.K. Jayaratne for their research support; to Professor C.B. Dissanayake and Dr Martha Prickett for all the stimulating discussions and infrastructural support; to Priyantha Karunaratne at the Postgraduate Institute of Archaeology for unpublished information from his ongoing research.

I wish to thank Tamara, Dayasisira and Harshani at the Institute of Fundamental Studies for their technical assistance in the preparation of this paper.

compared . . . Archaeology can thus assist in answering the question relating to 'how' and 'why' of cultural change . . . If precise evidence on material culture is available it enables the historian to discuss institutions with greater clarity. Human institutions emerge as a result of many factors and material culture together with ideology join in varying proportions to evolve an institution. Archaeology can at least provide the data for the former.'[1]

1. INTRODUCTION

The Early Iron Age in the history of Sri Lanka may be identified as the Formative Period and is broadly located within the Proto and Early Historic Periods. This essay seeks to advance an alternative explanation of the early material and social formations, shifting the perspective away from linear and symmetric views which are represented in nineteenth and twentieth-century writings more specifically on the early history of the island. An investigation of the material and social formations of the Early Iron Age is the central focus of this essay.

The backdrop to this essay is that it is now imperative—in view of post-colonial and contemporary ideological adaptations which reflect the dialectical contradictions inherent within a post-colonial dependent economy—to argue from a fresh perspective. While a large segment of the Sinhala as well as the Tamil-speaking population has been progressively alienated from the decision-making process, the state is in search of alternative measures of sustaining its hegemony. In this context, one has to view ethno-religious history emanating from the written and oral traditions, including material evidence drawn from archaeological sources, as critical factors which provide a basis for community identity on the one hand, and an ideology of domination and legitimation on the other.

The significance of ethno-religious history as a powerful undercurrent within the contemporary political structure, and its impact both on the masses and on intellectual writing, has not received serious attention from students of history or political systems. There appear to be two problems in this area. The first is a lack of understanding about community and the cultural origins of this island society, and second the inability to take cognizance of interacting ideological forces associated with socio–political change during different epochs. Therefore I look at some historical implications associated with the Early Iron Age

[1] Romila Thapar, 'The Historian and Archaeological Data', *in* D.P. Agrawal and A. Ghosh (eds), *Radiocarbon and Indian Archaeology*, Bombay, TIFR, 1973, pp. 378–90.

community and cultural origins, focusing on the ecological base of its material and social formations.

2

The core of the problem lies in understanding the 'past' as transmitted to the present in the form of written and oral history as well as material remains, and the treatment of that past within the present context, with special reference to the formative period. The priest–scholars, who composed and maintained chronicles, documented their version of the peopling of this island and 'the emergence of civilization', essentially attributing it to 'elite' groups arriving from North India, as a consequence of the *janapada* settlements they established in north and south-east Sri Lanka. This fourth-century projection was uncritically accepted by the Orientalists, the Antiquarians, the colonial administrators, and the twentieth-century Nationalists. Most of their studies documented a series of 'historical events' based on conjectural myths of origin, invasion and confrontation. The bulk of the extant data in such studies has been retrieved from Middle and Late Historic textual sources, utilizing at the same time oral tradition, inscriptions and archaeological sources to present an ethno-religious history with a sectarian bias.[2] Conversely, contemporary attempts at deconstructing colonial and nationalist historiography, and the efforts by several Western scholars to 'anthropologize' historical texts (especially the *Mahāvaṃsa*), have added a third dimension to the treatment of the past. This position is ironically enmeshed in the historicity of the very sources it set off to negate.

Better insights into this process are possible by understanding the ideological duality and its role in synthesizing past and present: at the one end there is a codification of history carried out by Middle Historic scholar–monks, and at the other end is the formation of the nineteenth- and twentieth-century ideological matrix.

The codification of history carried out by scholar–monks is found in a series of texts and their commentaries, though the best representation is depicted in the organization of 'events' in the *Mahāvaṃsa*. This was the role model for most subsequent compositions of religious as well as religio–political texts. The *Mahāvaṃsa* operates at two levels: the horizontal and the vertical.

[2] For a comprehensive presentation of versions in the *Mahāvaṃsa* and the *Dīpavaṃsa*, *see* H.C. Ray (ed.), *University of Ceylon History of Ceylon*. Colombo, 1959, Section I.i. *Also see* H. Ellawala, *Social History of Early Ceylon*, Colombo, 1969; Tilak Hettiarachchi, *History of Kingship in Ceylon*, Colombo, 1972; Ananda Guruge, *Asoka, the Righteous: A Definitive Biography*, Colombo, 1993; Ananda Guruge, *Anagarika Dharmapala: Return to Righteousness*, Colombo, 1965.

Mahāvaṃsa Synthesis

At the horizontal plane there are links between places, events and personalities in North India with particular individuals and events in Sri Lanka. The *Mahāvaṃsa* chapterization is a conscious effort at maintaining this link, without forgetting the functionally important

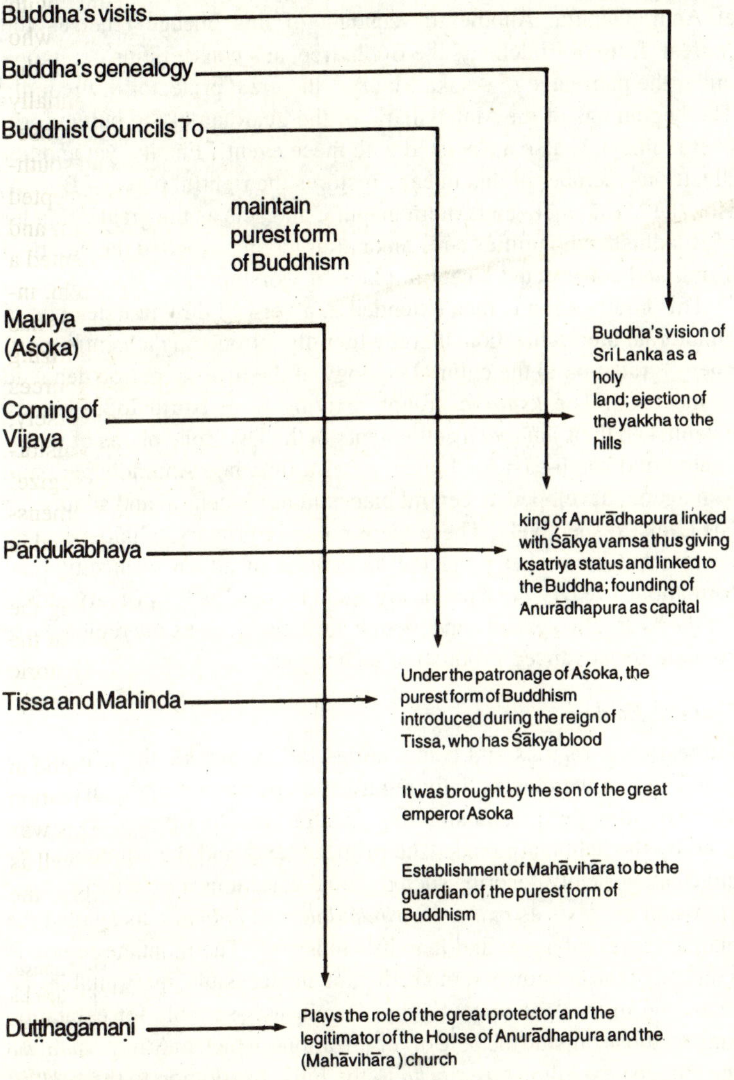
Buddha's visits
Buddha's genealogy
Buddhist Councils To
maintain purest form of Buddhism
Maurya (Aśoka)
Coming of Vijaya
Buddha's vision of Sri Lanka as a holy land; ejection of the yakkha to the hills
Pāṇḍukābhaya
king of Anurādhapura linked with Śākya vamsa thus giving kṣatriya status and linked to the Buddha; founding of Anurādhapura as capital
Tissa and Mahinda
Under the patronage of Aśoka, the purest form of Buddhism introduced during the reign of Tissa, who has Śākya blood
It was brought by the son of the great emperor Asoka
Establishment of Mahāvihāra to be the guardian of the purest form of Buddhism
Duṭṭhagāmaṇi
Plays the role of the great protector and the legitimator of the House of Anurādhapura and the (Mahāvihāra) church

Figure 1. Mahāvaṃsa Synthesis

hierarchy. At its apex is the Buddha, who personally visits the island and endeavours to make it habitable for the 'civilized' and a sanctuary for the righteous doctrine. With the demise of the Buddha, the arrival of Vijaya from North India symbolizes the continuity of this process. Following this, *kṣatriya* groups arriving from North India are linked to the genealogy of the Buddha. One of its members inaugurates the capital at Anurādhapura. Another descendant of this lineage receives the 'purest' form of Buddhism, the Bodhi tree, at a consecration ceremony under the patronage of Aśoka Maurya, the great protector of the faith. The beginnings of the Mahāvihāra, or the guardian of the purest form of Buddhism, is also associated with these events. Finally, yet another illustrious member of this lineage restores the rightful place of Buddhism, the Mahāvihāra and Anurādhapura, and acts as the great defender of Buddhism who unifies Sri Lanka after having expelled the heretical Tamil and constructed a central place of worship.

This codification is then extended in a vertical direction, leading to an internal hierarchization, thereby literally introducing a 'centre–periphery' gradation to the cultural ecology of the historic period depicted in the texts. The *kṣatriya* groups arriving from North India mainly established their *janapada* settlements in the Dry Zone plains of north-central and south-east Sri Lanka. After a time lag, Anurādhapura and Mahāgāma developed as central places in north-central and south-east Sri Lanka respectively. These were not only primary religio–political centres but were also projected as centres of advanced institutional formation. The Dry Zone plains are again focused as the primary region for the hydraulic systems and plough agriculture, or as the region more suitable for advanced production techniques.

Cultural Ecology

Interestingly, regions and communities falling outside the pale of the 'core' region were essentially regarded as peripheral and marginal in the texts, thereby juxtapositioning 'centre' and 'periphery' as envisaged by the scholar–monks. The primary texts and the commentaries quite categorically describe such regional variations. For instance, hills known in the texts as *malaya, girimanḍala* and *pabbata*, as against the plains, represent a wet and marshy landscape. The montane region is a terrain of the unknown, remote, distant, inaccessible, inhospitable and restricted to the 'outsider'. Such a terrain was suitable for habitation only by those outside the pale of 'civilization', which may have justified the Buddha expelling the *yakkha* to the hills. In addition to the *yakkha*,

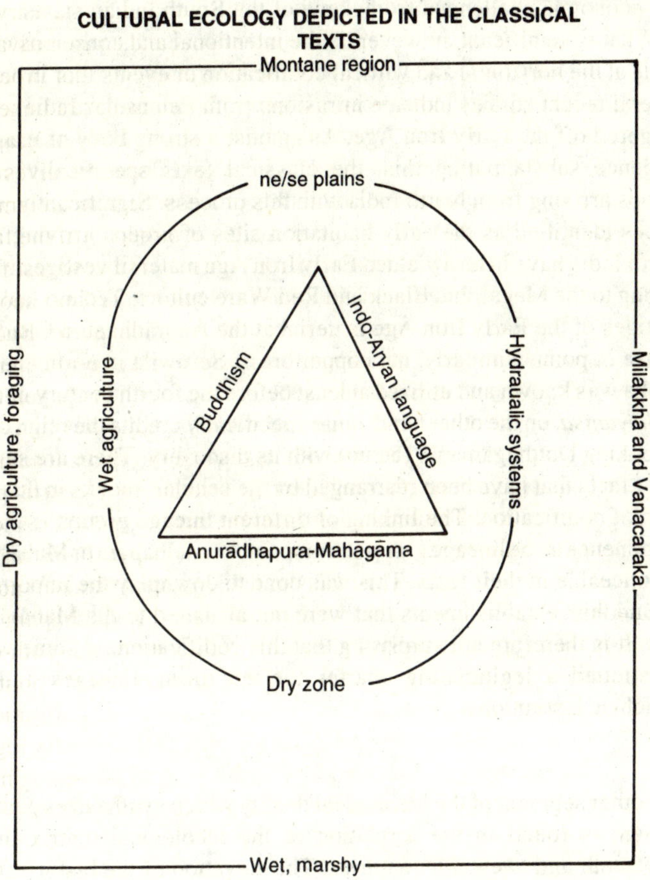

Figure 2

the forest-dwellers or the *vanacaraka* consisted of the Pulinda and the *milakkha manussa*, to mention two. They were largely hunter–gatherers who thrived on the montane-forest ecology. They possessed no advanced farming or irrigation systems, though subsistence farming was not unknown. Such regions were necessarily retreat areas, suitable for use during famines, plagues or political chaos.

It is quite obvious that the scholar–monks who codified the classical texts legitimizing a particular faith, lineage, political and ritual centres in a pan-island context, carried out their task during the period of the evolved state system of Sri Lanka, when it consistently faced political and economic challenges from some of the South Indian states.

What is significant, however, is the intentional and conscious effort made at the horizontal and vertical codification of events. For instance, several recent studies indicate intrusions from Peninsular India which triggered off the Early Iron Age. As against a strong body of material evidence substantiating this, the classical texts specifically credit groups arriving from North India with this process. Significantly, most places identified as the early habitation sites of groups arriving from North India have in turn yielded Early Iron Age material vestiges which belong to the Megalithic Black and Red Ware culture. Techno–cultural vestiges of the Early Iron Age material at the Anurādhapura Citadel is a case in point. Similarly, the copper ore at Seruwila in north-east Sri Lanka was known and utilized at least before the fourth century BC. The *Mahāvaṃsa*, on the other hand, quite specifically credits the reign of the hero–king Duṭṭhagāmaṇi (150 BC) with its discovery. There are several other facts that have been rearranged by the scholar–monks in this process of codification. The linking of different lineage groups ascribing prominence to the lineage group or groups at Anurādhapura or Mahāgāma is noticeable in their texts. This was done to downplay the importance of Buddhist establishments that were not affiliated to the Mahāvihāra sect. It is therefore not surprising that this codification, in some ways, constituted a legitimating charter for the ruling lineages and the Buddhist institutions.

3

The other segment of the ideological duality which synthesizes past and present is found in the formation of the ideological matrix in the nineteenth and twentieth centuries. The elevation of the historical and oral traditions almost to a legitimating charter of a functionally stronger ideological force in the late-colonial and post-colonial periods has multiple orientations. 'The need to discover and study the past' had qualitatively different meanings to the Orientalist and the Antiquarian, the Colonial administrator and the Nationalist. It is significant however that they all retrieved their information from a common group of sources, namely the classical texts of Sri Lanka, the oral history, the historical monuments—including artifacts and irrigation works.

When reading the past, the Orientalists and the colonial administrators who were nourished within the classical schools of art in Europe, and within an imperial political culture, transferred symbols associated with a metropolitan ethos to South Asia and other colonies. While various monumental constructions of the past such as royal capitals, religious edifices, palace art and gigantic hydraulic works fired their visual imagination, several heroic personalities (not forgetting 'Oriental Despots') responsible for the 'Golden Era' were discovered in the classical texts. This late-nineteenth-century synthesis—of material remains and the textually recorded religio–political history—provided the basis for what was to emerge as '*Mahāvaṃsa* Archaeology' in Sri Lanka. It is clear that the initial work of the Orientalist, the Antiquarian and the colonial administration provided useful information to the anti-colonial sentiments of the Nationalists. However, the structural and long-term ideological implications it developed were far more complex in nature and have been little understood to this day.

The Ideological Matrix

The late-colonial and post-colonial ideological matrix emanating from the nationalist school may be formulated schematically (see Figure 3). The aspiration towards group distinctiveness, both at the macro and the micro levels, was enhanced by the national movement. At the macro level, a common language basis and religion, including a 'racial' selection as Aryan and Dravidian, provided an affinity with groups within the broader region, i.e. India. At the micro level, an overarching group identity was spread over a relatively heterogeneous socio–cultural group on the basis of a common territory, religious symbolism, a common language and a vague notion of common biological characteristics. A natural consequence of this process is seen in the 'we–they' distinction, which was initially maintained *vis-à-vis* the colonialists, and which subsequently came to represent the Sinhala–Tamil dichotomy in this island society. Also significant is the way in which the majority community has utilized the concept of marginalization, found in the texts, not only against the Tamil-speaking people but also on Vedda aboriginal groups, gypsies and even caste groups, as a mechanism of alienation.

It is apparent that a greater awareness about the historicity of ethno-cultural origins provided a substantial impetus towards a higher degree of ethnic consciousness, which in turn had an anti-colonial, nationalist perspective which interlocked with a communal as well as racist ideology. Each group has tended to have, among other things, an origin myth, folk heroes, genealogies, mythical ancestors, the concept of an original homeland, and even a mother language. This ideological expression, therefore, essentially remained within the narrow confines of ethnocentricism, cultural implantation and the compartmentalization of

THE IDEOLOGICAL MATRIX

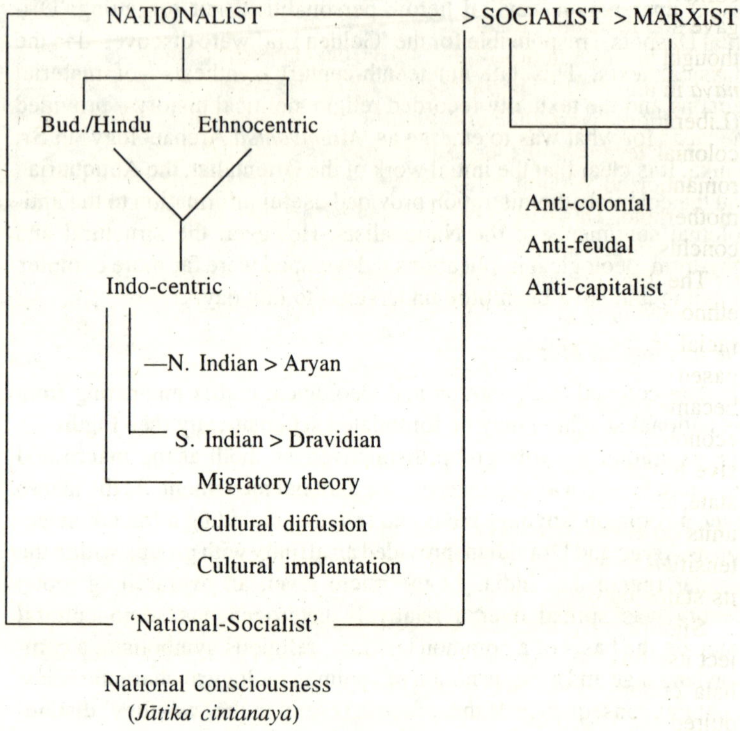

Figure 3

language–cultural zones along imagined racial lines. All this ultimately gave vent to the acceptance of a mono-cultural and single belief system within a pan-island context both in the past and in the present.

It is significant that the emergence of the socialist movement from the national movement during the late colonial period did not provide a long-term remedy either. Both, being products of the colonial period, faced a conceptual crisis and were unable to advance a social explanation of post-colonial adaptations in the face of the social polarization between ethnic groups within a dependent economy. This may be identified as one of the major factors that contributed to the failure of the traditional left in Sri Lanka. While the Marxist school of thought, which evolved out of the socialist stream, maintained its anti-feudal, anti-capitalist and anti-imperial stance, it remained in an isolated corner, away from the mainstream. Ironically, it is socialist thinking that gave sophistication to an ideological synthesis with ethno–nationalist thought in the evolution of 'National Consciousness', or the *jātika cintanaya* in the 1980s. The JVP (Janata Vimukti Peramuna) and the LTTE (Liberation Tigers of Tamil Elam) of the 1980s, both products of the colonial legacy and the post-colonial dependent economy, shared a romanticized version of socialism as well as common ideals of the motherland. This had to be defended with blood, epitomizing a logical conclusion towards a social fascist ideology.

The three decades following 1948 witnessed a rapid polarization of ethno–cultural groups which became increasingly chauvinistic and racial in their attitude. The self-perpetuation of sectional ideologies based on ethno–cultural lines, causing both group and spatial affiliation, became critical in the face of an unstable political structure, socio–economic alienation, and a state increasingly intolerant of and repressive towards dissent. As opposed to the colonial legacy of a unitary state, centrifugal forces have been threatening to carve out geo-political units on ethno-cultural or more specifically racial lines, which has intensified on account of a protracted war waged by the state to maintain its status quo.

Significantly, the state made far greater efforts in the 1980s to project itself as the defender of Buddhism, and as the chief patron of Sinhala culture, these being an alternative socio–political ideology required for hegemony and domination over the majority community. Dissent was brutally suppressed and some of the rhetoric of national consciousness was incorporated into the ideological framework of the state. These ideas percolated to the mass base of the majority community through the state infrastructure—into the fields of art, literature, and other intellectual activity, very specifically through some of the state-sponsored archaeological programmes. In fact the mid-twentieth-century romanticization of 'the golden era of the past,' expressed through the tank–*stūpa*–village synchronism, came to be reviewed and popularized as the roots of a 'national culture' which required preservation and perpetuation.

4

It is evident that any study of Sri Lanka's past must bear in mind the ideological implications of the scholar-monks' codification of texts as well as colonial and post-colonial ideological adaptations. The dilemma is whether the ideology of classical historiography resulted in contemporary ethno-nationalism or the nineteenth- and twentieth-century ideological adaptations introduced ethno–cultural and religio–political symbols in understanding meanings transmitted through such texts and archaeological monuments. The dialectic process synthesizing past and present has therefore to be seen as a part of this ideological duality. Significantly, there is still a deterministic bias towards locating historical and archaeological studies within the *Mahāvaṃsa* rubric. This persistence is explained by two factors: first, a continued acceptance of the time and space codification adhered to in the texts which results in the second condition, namely a refusal to accept an alternative perspective to that which was codified by scholar–monks.

This situation has resulted in the adherence to a linear and symmetrical view of history by a large section of historians and archaeologists, and consequently led to biases and prejudices on the history of this island. For instance, North India, Indo-Aryan languages, Gautama Buddha, monastic Buddhism, and emperor Asoka loom large in the background, inspiring the documentation of historical developments and influencing interpretations of the past. The social historian tends to adhere to the caste system of Early Historic North India when explaining social formations of the parallel period in Sri Lanka. An exclusive adherence to the Indo-Aryan language base in deriving meanings for particular terms found in the inscriptions is another example.[3]

This linear and symmetric view envisages blanket developments in Sri Lankan history, leaving little room for *uneven* and *parallel* developments. That the spread of North-Indian culture via immigration and the spread of Buddhism were both rapid and pan-islandic in horizontal spread may be cited here. A similar view is expressed on the 'unification' of the island by hero–kings, and on the extension of a 'metropolitan religio-political' ethos over the island. Naturally, periodization comes to be identified not on a techno-cultural or chrono–cultural basis, but is named after a capital city, e.g. the 'Anurādhapura Period', or after 'hero kings'. This perspective also negates unevenly distributed resources

[3] For some critical studies on the Sri Lankan sources, *see* The Social Scientists Association, *Ethnicity and Social Change in Sri Lanka*, Colombo, 1984; Sudharshan Seneviratne 'The Archaeology of the Megalithic Black and Red Ware Complex in Sri Lanka', *Ancient Ceylon* 5, 1984, pp. 237–307; Bardwell L. Smith (ed.), *Religion and Legitimation of Power in Sri Lanka*, Anima Books, 1978. For India, *see* Romila Thapar et al., *Communalism and the Writing of Indian History*, New Delhi, 1977; Romila Thapar, *The Past and Prejudice*, New Delhi, 1975; Sarvepalli Gopal (ed.), *Anatomy of a Confrontation*, New Delhi, 1991; D. Mandal, *Ayodhya. Archaeology After Demolition*, New Delhi, 1993. Also Benedict Anderson, *Imagined Communities*, London, Verso, 1990.

and the uneven development of institutions, as well as the coexistence of different production techniques, especially during the Formative Period. It is also evident that this view may have been responsible for the alienation and elimination from history of physical regions and their resident communities which were situated away from the 'centre' both in the present and in the past.

It is this idealized picture, largely based on historical texts and very little on material evidence, that has been taken up for study by several scholars who tend to read history through anthropology. These studies have used a range of symbols, drawn from the Greek myths to Freud, for insights into the events and characters narrated in the texts. Their chief sources being texts and the information codified by scholar–monks, this leaves serious doubts about the authenticity of the real situation in different ecological zones of this island over different epochs. This methodology also throws up several problems. With texts as the primary source, little attention is given to the inscriptions, coins, and the artifacts and ecofact assemblage retrieved by archaeology. The dependence on texts also means adherence to the sequence of events narrated in the chronicles and commentaries, which results in reading meanings into events and relating events to contemporary behaviour patterns. A large segment of such scholars quite honestly hold the view that the contemporary ethno-nationalism of the majority community has its roots in the *Mahāvaṃsa* tradition. In fact the *Mahāvaṃsa*-bashing carried out by such scholars is a direct consequence of historical determinism emanating from their ignorance of the concepts of time, event and history as understood by earlier societies. By giving greater weightage to the role of the individual and elite groups, they negate the significance of substratum groups and regions situated away from political and ritual centres in the 'core' regions. These studies have strengthened a generalized view of time and space and perpetuated the notion of blanket developments within a pan-island context.

5

Against this background, this essay seeks to understand the material and social formations of the Early Iron Age. In a previous study, 'The Archaeology of the Megalithic Black and Red Ware Complex in Sri Lanka' (*Ancient Ceylon*, no. 5, 1984: 237–307) using information derived primarily from archaeological and Brāhmī inscriptional sources, I discussed the dynamics associated with the peopling of Sri Lanka during the Early Iron Age. There I looked at techno–cultural composition, with special reference to the indigenous Mesolithic culture and the intrusive Proto Historic Black and Red Ware culture from Peninsular India as well as Early Historic cultures from Eastern India.

Nearly a decade after this, a series of field studies carried out in the montane zones, the intermediary zones, and in particular the lowland resource zones, all situated outside the north-central and south-east 'core' regions, has provided us with a far better understanding of the anatomy of the Early Iron Age techno–cultural and social milieu. The present essay attempts a synthesis of some published and unpublished material from the textual and inscriptional sources, along with data retrieved from environmental archaeology, Early Iron Age archaeology, and ancient materials and technology. It goes without saying that the progressive transition of archaeological studies in Sri Lanka from antiquarianism to a problem-oriented multidisciplinary science in the last two decades has provided a whole range of material evidence for the study of Early Iron Age social archaeology of Sri Lanka,[4] an area that cannot possibly be studied with textual sources alone.

I am therefore in a position to question some of the historical assumptions associated with the Formative Period and the 'emergence of civilization' in Sri Lanka. As opposed to the lowland–hydraulic agrarian eco-zone that is said to have sustained the momentum towards civilization, I will focus attention on a different topographical and ecological system that threw up equally important parallel material and social formations which, in the long run, contributed to the very survival of the 'core regions'.

Resource Use and Cultural Ecology

Environment and human society have little meaning if they are seen as distinct entities.[5] Discussion of resource use, especially minerals, has no significance unless it is related to social context. This is even more true when we deal with resource use during the Formative Period of a particular society. Often, such societies had to reach, discover, extract, and move resources without pre-existing knowledge or infrastructural

[4] For a summary of views, *see* Eva Myrdal-Runebjer, *Archaeo Lanka*, Tryckeri, Riksantikvarieambetet, 1990.

[5] For a useful range of studies, *see* Timothy K. Earle and Jonathon (eds), *Exchange Systems in Prehistory*, New York, 1977; David R. Harris and Gordon C. Hillman (eds), *Foraging and Farming*, London, 1989; Henri J.M. Claessen and Pieter van de Velde (eds), *Early State Economics*, New Jersey, 1991; Joan M. Gero and Margaret W. Conkey (eds), *Engendering Archaeology*, London, 1991; Emilio F. Moran (ed.), *The Ecosystem Approach in Anthropology*, Michigan, 1990; Karl W. Butzer, *Archaeology as Human Ecology*, Cambridge, 1990.

support which would facilitate these activities, i.e. the movement of resources from source areas to their places of consumption.

The symbiotic relationship between early societies and their natural environment was carried through several mediums, i.e. technology, subsistence pattern, resource use and settlement pattern. Consequently, the mental and physical response to this process of material interaction culminated in the formation of institutions that may be broadly identified as social, economic, political and religious. This scenario presents the total cultural ecology of a society at a given time and place in history.[6] While one has to take note of the uneven development of such formations, the scale of transition, both quantitative and qualitative, from simple to complex societies, for instance, provides a better understanding about material conditions and human behaviour patterns leading to institutional formation, and ultimatel[illegible] its long-term historical legacy.

The momentum [illegible] processes associated with form[illegible] largely depended upon certain preconditions which led to a viable utilization of mineral resources. The utilization of a particular raw material in the production of a luxury, prestige, utilitarian or ritual item was conditioned by variations in demand, based on factors such as the functional value of the item, the level of material development of that society, direct or indirect access to strategic resources, the possession of a suitable technology for resource extraction and production—including the existence of an exchange mechanism and route networks facilitating the movement of raw material and finished products.[7] (see Figure 4).

The Mesolithic 'Balangoda' culture has been identified as the earliest techno–cultural formation in Sri Lanka, though a possible presence of the Upper Paleolithic is not ruled out.[8] The Mesolithic culture essentially functioned within a hunting–gathering–fishing economy and

[6] Sudharshan Seneviratne, *Ordering the Past: Decoding Ancient Cultural Ecology through Archaeology*, Kandy, 1994; *also see* Maurice Godelier, *The Mental and the Material*, Verso, 1988.

[7] Sudharshan Seneviratne, 'Iron Technology in Sri Lanka: A Preliminary Study of Resource Use and Production Techniques during the Early Iron Age', *The Sri Lanka Journal of the Humanities*, xi (1 & 2), 1985, pp. 129–78; Sudharshan Seneviratne, 'The Ecology and Archaeology of the Seruwila Copper-Magnetite Prospect: Northeast Sri Lanka'. To be published in the George Dales Volume. Mark Kenoyer and Richard Medow eds, Madison.

[8] For the best detailed study of the prehistoric environment, subsistence pattern and technology, *see* S.U. Deraniyagala, *The Prehistory of Sri Lanka: An Ecological Perspective*, Memoir Volume 8, pt I and pt II, Colombo, 1992; Kenneth A.R. Kennedy et al., 'Biological Anthropology of Upper Pleistocene Hominids from Sri Lanka: Batadomba

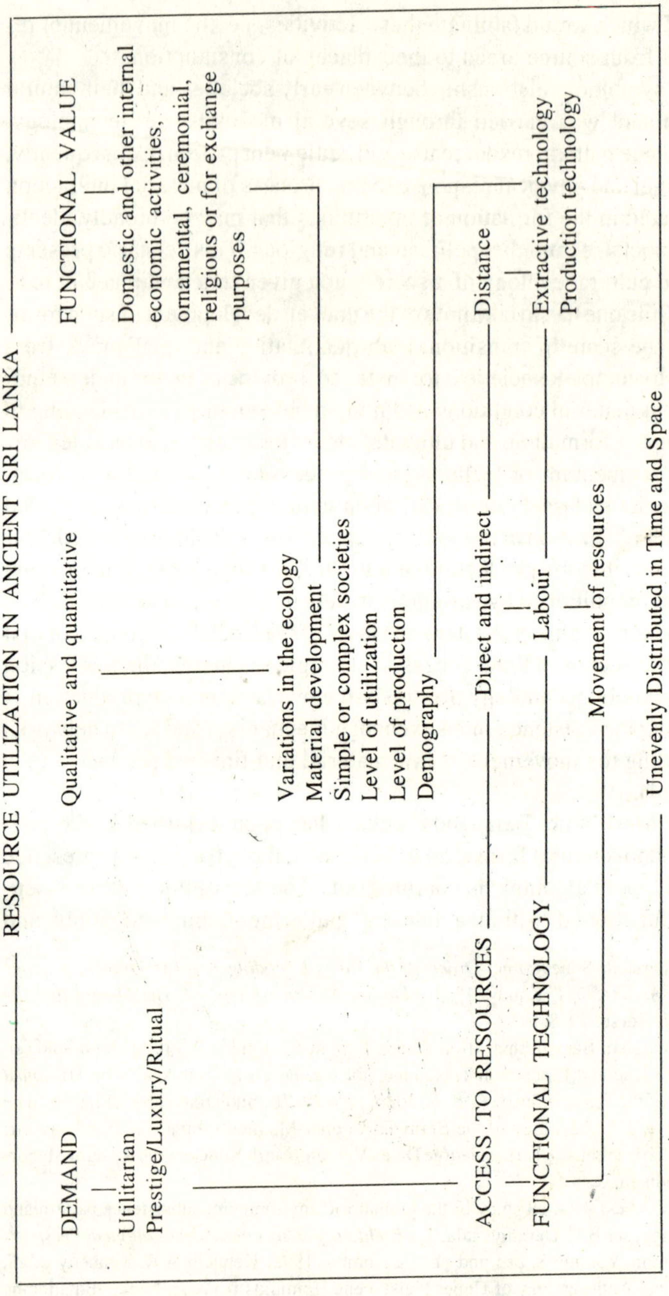
RESOURCE UTILIZATION IN ANCIENT SRI LANKA
DEMAND
Utilitarian
Prestige/Luxury/Ritual
Qualitative and quantitative
FUNCTIONAL VALUE
Domestic and other internal economic activities, ornamental, ceremonial, religious or for exchange purposes
Variations in the ecology
Material development
Simple or complex societies
Level of utilization
Level of production
Demography
ACCESS TO RESOURCES
Direct and indirect
Distance
FUNCTIONAL TECHNOLOGY
Labour
Extractive technology
Production technology
Movement of resources
Unevenly Distributed in Time and Space

Figure 4

utilized certain mineralized stones such as haematite, limonite, molybdenum, mica, graphite, blue clay and kaolin as pigments for ritualistic purposes and cave art.[9] The total rhythm of life, its momentum, perpetuation and symbolic expressions, were set in motion within the natural environment of the island, with the exception of the Jaffna peninsula and the lower Mahaweli plains where the presence of this culture is very remote. Radiometric dates now indicate an early date for the Mesolithic as 28,000 BC as well as later dates around 5000 BC.[10]

The Stone Age was succeeded by the Early Iron Age (more commonly known as the Proto Historic and the Early Historic Periods).[11] Conclusive evidence on an intervening Neolithic or Chalcolithic is not yet established. The Early Iron Age may be identified as the Formative Period in Sri Lanka. There is for the first time a recognizable formation of institutions and also a coincidence between the dominant techno-cultural zone and the physical zone.

For the convenience of our study the Early Iron Age is divided as the Proto Historic Period (900 to 400 BC) and the Early Historic Period (300 BC to *c.* 1st century AD). A broad chronological context is envisaged due to the difficulty of a pan-island blanket chronology for the Early Iron Age.[12] Archaeological investigations at Proto Historic habitations and burial sites indicate that Sri Lanka formed the southernmost sector of the broader Early Iron Age Peninsular Indian techno–cultural complex. The ecofact and artefact assemblages from these sites in Sri Lanka have established that rice cultivation, animal domestication, the horse, small-scale metallurgical operations involving iron and copper, bead production, village settlements, the 'megalithic' burial ritual, the ceramic industry involving the production of Black and Red Ware and Black Ware, and post-firing graffiti symbols were introduced to Sri Lanka from Peninsular India, or more specifically from South India.

Lena and Beli Lena Caves', *Ancient Ceylon* 6, 1986, pp. 67–168; Kenneth A.R. Kennedy, 'Palaeodemography of Sri Lanka and Peninsular India: A Crossregional Survey', *in* Sudharshan Seneviratne et al. (eds), *Perspectives in Archaeology*, University of Peradeniya, Department of Archaeology, 1990, pp. 29–37.

[9] S.U. Deraniyagala, 'Prehistoric Ceylon: A Summary in 1968', *Ancient Ceylon* 1, 1971, pp. 3–46; B.D. Nandadeva, 'Rock Art Sites of Sri Lanka: A Catalogue', *Ancient Ceylon* 6, 1986, pp. 173–208.

[10] S.U. Deraniyagala, *The Prehistory*, pp. 865–706; *also see* Gregory L. Possehl, *Radiometric Dates for South Asian Archaeology*, Philadelphia, 1994.

[11] Sudharshan Seneviratne, op. cit., 1984.

[12] For the most recent radiometric dates from the Proto and Early Historic Periods in Sri Lanka, *see* S.U. Deraniyagala, *The Prehistory*, pp. 707–59.

This chronological context (largely obtained in the form of radiometric dates), the techno-cultural elements and their region of origin, does not in any way agree with the descriptions of the peopling of Sri Lanka narrated in the Middle Historic chronicles of Sri Lanka.[13]

The coincidence between the techno–cultural zone and the physical zone during the Proto Historic Period is essentially seen with micro eco-zones. The habitat now came to be associated with localities possessing strategic resources, a broad spectrum subsistence pattern coinciding with functional technology in the hands of these resident communities. Archaeo–zoological and archaeo–botanical studies from the Proto Historic levels at Anurādhapura amply establish the existence of hunting and pastoral activity along with rice cultivation.[14] The Ibbankatuwa habitation site yielded large quantities of faunal remains and little indication of rice cultivation.[15] Field investigations revealed the existence of these Proto Historic micro eco-zones in the littoral zone, along fertile pockets of the alluvium and mineral-bearing locations in the plains. These Early Iron Age habitats continued through the Proto and Early Historic transition, and well into the Early Historic Period. The association of the earliest Brāhmī inscription-bearing cave shelters in and around Proto Historic burial as well as habitation sites indicates the continuation of the descendants of the Proto Historic communities into a new cultural milieu.[16]

There are two significant developments related to the eco-zones during the Proto Historic–Early Historic transition. One is the expansion of the techno–cultural zone beyond the original micro ecological

[13] For an overall discussion, *see* Sudharshan Seneviratne, op. cit., 1984; Kenneth A.R. Kennedy, *The Physical Anthropology of the Megalith-builders of South India and Sri Lanka*, Canberra, 1975; For a recent discussion, *also see* S.U. Deraniyagala, *The Prehistory*, pp. 707–59.

[14] S.U. Deraniyagala, 'The Citadel of Anuradhapura 1969: Excavations in the Gedige Area', *Ancient Ceylon*, 2, pp. 48–169; Sudharshan Seneviratne and R.M.M. Chandraratne, 'Flora and Fauna Resources in Antiquity: The Study of Archaeobotany and Archaeozoology in Sri Lanka', *IFS: Kandy School Science Course Notes*, Kandy, IFS, 1992, pp. 12–16; R.M.M. Chandraratne is currently completing his Doctoral Thesis, at the Deccan College, on a study of the faunal remains from the Anurādhapura Citadel excavations. He is a Faculty Member of the Department of Archaeology, University of Peradeniya.

[15] Information from Priyantha Karunaratne, 1994.

[16] This connection was first indicated in Sudharshan Seneviratne, op. cit., 1984, App. I, 'The Megalithic-BRW Sites and Early Brahmi Inscriptions', pp. 294–5; *also see* Sudharshan Seneviratne, 'Pre-State Chieftains and Servants of the State: A Case Study of Parumaka', *The Sri Lanka Journal of the Humanities*, XV (1 & 2), 1992, pp. 99–131.

THE NORTH CENTRAL PLAINS: EARLY IRON AGE SITES

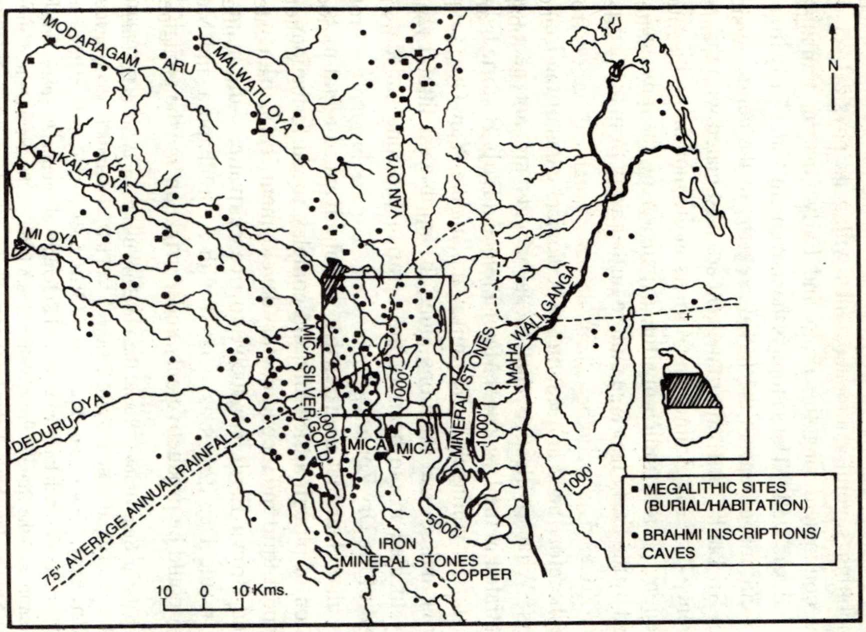

Figure 5

niche. This development is seen in the formation of macro eco-zones incorporating several micro eco-zones within its physical region, a pattern common during the Proto and Early Historic transition in South India as well.[17] The second is the movement of the Early Iron Age techno–cultural groups to the foothill regions of the central montane zone of Sri Lanka, at least around 600 BC. Associated with this is the occurrence of Early Brāhmī inscriptions in the montane region in the subsequent period, indicating the expansion of the physical area covered by the Early Iron Age culture further away from the plains and the Dry Zone.

We therefore need to question the ecological basis of the Iron Age habitats. What is clear is that these habitats are not necessarily concentrated in the Dry Zone. Major Proto and Early Historic habitats in the Jaffna peninsula,[18] Vavuniya, the middle Yan Oya valley,[19] Seruwila and several locations along the north-west littoral are not exactly located in the heart of the agrarian eco-zone and the 'tank country' of the Dry Zone.[20]

It is also clear that an extensive use of advanced metal tools, the extension of plough agriculture and complex social formations were more a post-third and second-century development. It is also known that Red and Brown Earth, conducive to rice cultivation—the main soil region in the Dry Zones associated with Anurādhapura and Mahāgāma— could be productive only under irrigation and the plough. The

[17] Sudharshan Seneviratne, 'Social Base of Early Buddhism in South East India and Sri Lanka, Third Century BC to Third Century AD', Ph.D. dissertation, 1985, Jawaharlal Nehru University, New Delhi; 'Pre-State to State Societies: Transformations in the Political Ecology of South India with Special Reference to Tamilnadu', paper presented at the 'Seminar on the State in Pre-Colonial South India', 1989, New Delhi, Centre for Historical Studies, Jawaharlal Nehru University; Sudharshan Seneviratne, 'The Twilight of Perumakaṇ: South Indian Polity Restructured and Incorporated', *in* Martin van Bakel et al. (eds), *Pivot Politics*, 1994, Amsterdam, pp. 161–79; Sudharshan Seneviratne, 'From Kuḍi to Nāḍu: A Suggested Framework for the Study of Pre-state Political Formations in Early Iron Age South India', *The Sri Lanka Journal of the Humanities* (in press).

[18] Ponnampalam Raghupathy, *Early Settlements in Jaffna: An Archaeological Survey*, Madras, 1987.

[19] Sudharshan Seneviratne 'Proto and Early Historic Investigations Along the Yan Oya Valley', *Second South Asian Archaeological Congress*, Colombo, 1987.

[20] Sudharshan Seneviratne, op. cit., 1984, pp. 242–7 for north-west sites; *also see* V. Begley, 'Archaeological Explorations in Northern Sri Lanka', *Expedition*, 9(4), 1969, pp. 21–9; V. Begley, 'Excavation of Iron Age Burials at Pomparippu 1970', *Ancient Ceylon* 4, 1981, pp. 49–95; Sudharshan Seneviratne, 'Marine-littoral Ecology and Archaeology', paper presented at the Seminar on the Maritime Heritage of Sri Lanka, 1987, Colombo, Department of Archaeology.

EARLY IRON AGE SITES: UPPER KALA OYA REGION

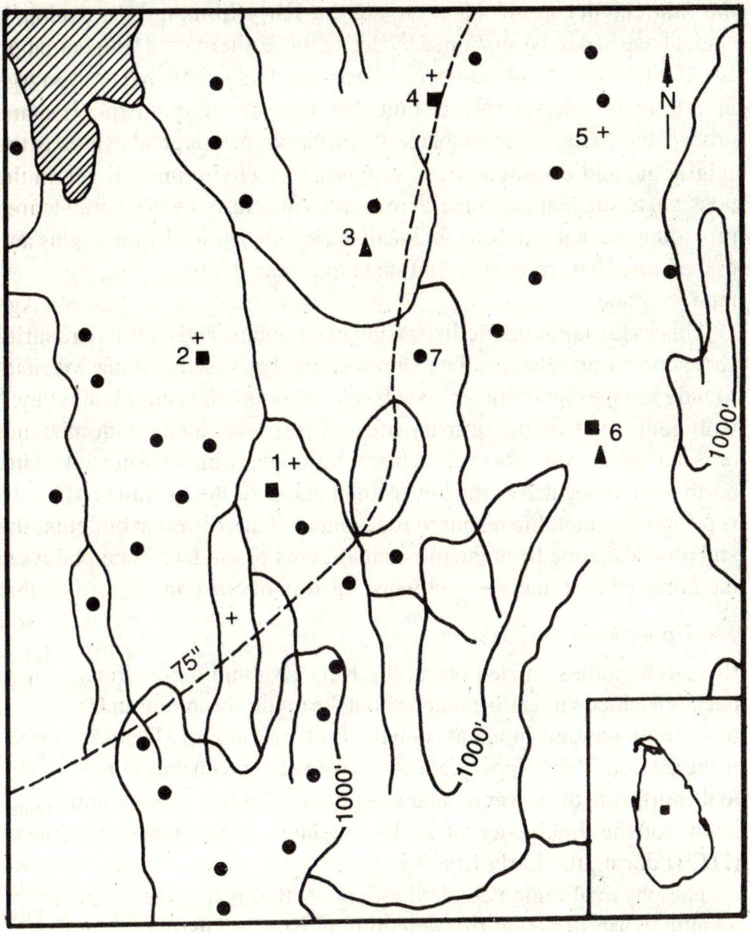

Sites 2 to 6 information from Priyanta Karunaratne
Postgraduate Institute of Archaeology (1994)

0 5 kms

■ Megalithic burial (cists)
\+ Proto Historic habitation
▲ Early Historic habitation
● Early Brāhmī inscriptions and drip-ledge caves

1 Ibbankatuwa
2 Anakatava
3 Malasna
4 Rotawewa
5 Sigiriya
6 Kandalama
7 Dambulla

Figure 6

establishment of more complex irrigation systems certainly post-dates the first century BC. If that were so, the Early Iron Age material and social base had to be sustained by one or more alternative sources. This is more true of a large number of Early Iron Age sites that are located in relatively inhospitable terrain and natural environment. Having probed the material assemblage from the archaeological record, and epigraphic and textual sources supported by environmental data, it is possible to suggest that mineral resources may have been such a source providing the material base for localized specialization by the beginning of the Early Historic Period, and sustaining social formations away from the Dry Zone.

This essay takes up for discussion two regions, and a third region for short comparative study. The Upper Kala Oya system, along with the Matale hills, essentially represents a lower montane–sub-plain region, with gemstones as the primary mineral resource, along with metallic ores and other minerals such as mica. Seruwila, which is situated in the north-east, is located in the lower flood plains of the Mahaweli river. It is primarily a metallic resource zone, situated in a different bio-climatic and physical zone from the montane regions or the Dry Zone plains of the north-central and the south-east sectors of Sri Lanka.

The Upper Kala Oya System

Research studies carried out in the Kala Oya and its environs over a decade yielded vital information about the cultural ecology and the scale of institutional development from the Proto to the Early Historic Period in that region.[21] The Upper Kala Oya, taken along with the plains situated to its north and the lower montane region to its south, offers a good case study for the emergence of an Intermediary Transitional Ecosystem (ITES) during the Early Iron Age.[22]

The physical region covered in this section is an area extending in a south–north direction from the hills of Matale District to the Upper

[21] Sudharshan Seneviratne, 'The Locational Significance of the Ibbankatuwa Cist Burial Site', paper presented at the First National Archaeological Congress, 1986, Postgraduate Institute of Archaeology.

[22] Sudharshan Seneviratne, 'The Locational Significance of Early Iron Age Sites in Intermediary Transitional Eco-system: A Case Study of the Upper Kala Oya Region', *in* Senake Bandaranayake et al. (eds), *The Settlement Archaeology of the Sigiriya–Dambulla Region*, Colombo, 1990, pp. 121–40. Utilizing this model a similar study was carried out subsequently for the Deduru Oya Upper Valley by Piyatissa Senanayake, 'The Social Base of North-western Sri Lanka during the Early Historic Period: An Analysis of the Early Brahmi Inscriptions', paper presented at the Annual Congress of the Epigraphical Society of India, 1991, Tamil University, Thanjavur.

Kala Oya valley. These represent two contiguous topographical zones in the same geological formation, or the Highland Series which is formed of quartzites, marbles, calcgneisses, granulites, varieties of charnockites, quartz-feldspar, and garnet-silimanite-graphite-schists. The southern formation, better known as the knuckles range, the Laggala range and the Matale plateau, has a sharp contour variation, clustered hills, dense forests and water bodies including marshes, clearly representing a difficult and inhospitable terrain.[23] This region is known to the early texts as the Malayarattha or Malaya and Giriman-ḍala, where the Pulinda, Vyāda, *milakkha manussa, upacaraka*, and *vanacaraka* inhabited the montane forests that are full of hazards and where accessibility is limited.[24]

A contrasting picture is visible further north, in the region centring around Dambulla in the Upper Kala Oya valley, which is also a part of the northern peneplains of the island. The landscape here is marked with several inselbergs that had both religious and politically strategic locations. In addition, the fan-like spread of the ridge and valley formation of the southern hills determined the general drainage pattern in this area, for both perennial and non-perennial streams. Water and soil became major factors determining the Early Iron Age settlement pattern. While the soil cover in the elevated areas is low due to erosion, pockets of the fertile Red and Brown soils are found in the lower areas. The major belt of this soil type is located further north in the Kalawewa–Mahaalagamuwa region.[25]

The geological formation, the topography, and the drainage pattern provided the Upper Kala Oya region with its status as a link zone. The Early Iron Age site distribution pattern points to a route network of three river valleys converging into one route in the Upper Kala Oya, gaining access to the central hills, especially during the Early Historic Period. The process of Early Iron Age institutional formation could be understood within a time-and-space framework and scales of expansion

[23] P.G. Cooray, *An Introduction to the Geology of Sri Lanka*, Colombo, 1984, The National Museum of Sri Lanka.

[24] *Mahāvaṃsa* (*MV*). vii. 68; *Cūlavaṃsa* (*CV*). 70.3–5; *DhV*. 33–6; *Sahassa*. 83, 94.

[25] U.A. Chandrasena, 'The Geographical Landscape of Dambulla', *in* H.T. Basnayake (ed.), *Dambulla Project First Archaeological Excavation and Research Report* (April–December, 1983), Colombo, 1988, Central Cultural Fund, pp. 105–9; A. Liyanagamage, 'Sigiriya: Military Fortress or Pleasure Resort?—A Historical Perspective', *Kalyani*, III & IV, 1984/1985, pp. 67–81; Seneviratne Epitawatte, 'The Physical Environment of the Study Area', *in* Senaka Bandaranayake, *The Settlement Archaeology*, pp. 40–8; L.H. Cramer, *A Forest Arboretrum in the Dry Zone*, Kandy, 1993.

incorporating the Proto and Early Historic cultures, indicating a transition from simple to complex societies.

The earliest Iron Age techno–cultural intrusion into this region is represented by the cist burials of the Proto Historic Period located at Ibbankatuwa, Anakatava, Kandalama and Rotawewa.[26] While the Ibbankatuwa cists have yielded radiometric dates up to the seventh century BC,[27] its habitation site has lower radiometric dates up to the fourth century BC.[28] The other three burial sites are also associated with habitation vestiges, while at Mapagala, near Sigiriya, habitation remains yielded Proto and Early Historic BRW.

The palaeo–human ecology in this region may indicate some of the recognizable dynamics associated with the earliest phase. In this connection, palaeo–environmental studies carried out in the micro region housing the burial-cum-habitation site at Ibbankatuwa revealed some interesting features about the soil regions.[29] The cemetery and the settlement sites are situated on the Yellowish Brown soils. This soil type is not suitable for wet agriculture as it has low water retention, a wilting point that is reached fairly rapidly, and high acidity levels. Similarly, the Dark Grayish Brown soils are unsuitable for wet agriculture due to the high percentage of silt in them. The Red soils in this area are less favoured for wet agriculture due to their high gravel content.[30]

Our investigations at the Idamoluwa weva, located immediately to the south of the habitation and the burial sites, revealed that it is situated within a depression in the natural topography, and therefore is the catchment for run-off rain water from the nearby inselberg, known as the Punchi-Dambulla hill. The existing dam, which is a man-made

[26] Information on Kandalama from Priyantha Karunaratne, 1994. The habitation site near the Ibbankatuwa burial site was recorded by the present writer in 1988 while the excavations were in progress at the burial site; also, for an overview study of the burial sites at Ibbankatuwa and its neighbouring burial site at Anakatava, *see* D.K. Jayaratne, 'The Environmental Archaeology of an Early Iron Age Habitation cum Burial Complex: Ibbankatuwa and its Environs', 1993, M.Sc. thesis submitted to the Postgraduate Institute of Archaeology, University of Kelaniya.

[27] S.U. Deraniyagala, *The Prehistory*, p. 734.

[28] Ibid.

[29] D.K. Jayaratne, 'Preliminary Investigations of the Soil Regions at the Ibbankatuwa Megalithic Burial-cum-Habitation Site', paper presented at the World Archaeological Congress-3, New Delhi, 1994.

[30] Ibid.; S.N.U. Fernando, *Ceylon Soils*, Colombo, 1967; C.R. Panabokke, 'The Nature of Soil as a Governing Factor in the Regional Settlement Pattern in Ancient Ceylon', *Ancient Ceylon* 3, 1979, pp. 231–6.

construction, post-dates the Early Iron Age. A similar situation is seen at the Pomparippu urn burial site and the large cist burial complex in the middle Yan Oya valley, where the megalithic burials pre-date the artificial reservoirs situated in their vicinity.

At present this region receives an annual rainfall of around 1500–1200 mm. This comes mostly from the short north-east monsoon, which is the only other source of water for natural ponds and water-holes, other than springs found in the limestone belt. Crystalline limestone is not conducive to wet agriculture. Kandalama and Sigiriya are in fact located on this limestone band. When water was available following the monsoon rains, the inhabitants could consume tubers and other aquatic resources available in these natural water bodies. In addition, pastoral activity (in an area that has excellent pasture land) and hunting went into sustaining these subsistence farmers, who may have depended less on irrigated rice cultivation and more on dry farming. It is significant that the micro region at Ibbankatuwa indicated only 300 hectares of fragmented land, composed of the Reddish Brown, Grayish Brown and Dark Brown soils, along with the loam, as soil region conducive for both wet and dry cultivations.[31] The Red soils, in particular, are productive only under irrigation and plough agriculture. Both these aspects were intensified in the early Christian period and later. In view of this, it can hardly be suggested or accepted that the requirement of new agricultural land triggered off community movements to the foothill regions during the Proto Historic Period.

It is possible therefore to suggest resource requirements, especially minerals, as an alternative factor determining the locational pattern of the Proto and Early Historic sites in this region. The whole region, extending from the Matale hills to the Upper Kala Oya system, is situated within the Highland Series, which is rich in alumina and marbles. Conditions of high pressure and temperature provided the basis for the formation of these rocks, and the crystallization of many gem minerals. It is now known that almost all gem deposits in Sri Lanka are found within the Highland Series and with a few formation in the South-west Group. What is important however is the occurrence of the source as well as the correct topography. It is pointed out that a relatively flat topography—drained by wide meandering streams—is most conducive to the formation of gem-bearing alluvial deposits. The source areas of the Highland Series are supplied with a network of radial drainage

[31] D.K. Jayaratne, 'Preliminary Investigations'.

systems, and these rivers transport the sediments deriving from the gem-mineral source rocks.[32]

Table 1
Mineral (stone) occurrences from Early and Middle Historic Sites

Mineral (Sri Lanka)	A'pura	Ibb.	Kanta.	Tissa.	Man.	Dam.	Clas. Lit.
Amethyst	*	*	*	*	*		*
Beryl	*			*			*
Chalcedony	*			*	*		
Chert	*	*	*		*		
Citrine					*		*
Coral			*		*		
Cordierite					*	*	
Corundum (Yellow Sapp.)						*	*
Corundum (Ruby)					*		*
Feldspar						*	
Fluorite						*	
Garnet	*						*
Jasper	*				*		
Orthoclase (Moonstone)	*				*		*
Salenite				*			
Spinel			*				
Quartz (Crystal)	*	*	*	*	*	*	*
Topaz							*
Tourmaline	*			*	*		*
Zircon						*	

(cont.)

[32] *See* C.B. Dissanayake and M.S. Rupasinghe, 'A Prospector's Guide Map to the Gem Deposits of Sri Lanka', *Gems and Gemmology*, 29 (3), 1993, pp. 173–81; P.G. Cooray, *An Introduction*, pp. 241–9; J.W. Herath, *Mineral Resources of Sri Lanka*, Colombo, 1975, pp. 60–5.

Table 1 (*cont.*)

Mineral (Sri Lanka)	A'pura	Ibb.	Kanta.	Tissa.	Man.	Dam.	Clas. Lit.
IMPORTED							
Agate	*	*	*	*	*	*	
Carnelian	*	*	*	*	*	*	
Jadeite				*			
Jet	*				*		
Lazurite (Lapis)	*				*		
Amazonite	*				*		
Onyx	*				*		
Red Coral	*			*	*		
Glass	*		*		*		
Pumice Stone				*			

A'pura : Anurādhapura (includes the Citadel, Jetavana and Abhayagiri)
Ibb. : Ibbankatuwa
Kanta. : Kantarōḍai
Tissa. : Tissamahārāma
Man. : Māntai (Information from Dr Martha Prickett)
Dam. : Dambulla
Clas. Lit.: : Western classical literature

In addition to gemstones, the Upper Kala Oya system and the Matale hills contain some of the richest deposits of mica and graphite, including metallic resources such as silver, copper and iron. The montane bio-climatic region is also extremely conducive to the growth of spice plants, and as a habitat for elephants.[33]

The earliest Iron Age intrusions into the Upper Kala Oya region may have occurred around the seventh century BC, and were carried out perhaps by semi-sedentary groups which adhered to a multi-resource subsistence pattern. Their intrusions may have been sporadic and were conditioned by the ability to procure mineral resources. Our investigations revealed that gem prospecting was carried out around the

[33] *See* Herath, *Mineral Resources*; Sudharshan Seneviratne, 'Mica Zones and Early Iron Age Sites in Sri Lanka: An Exploratory Study', *The Sri Lanka Journal of the Humanities*, XII (1 & 2), 1988, pp. 121–32.

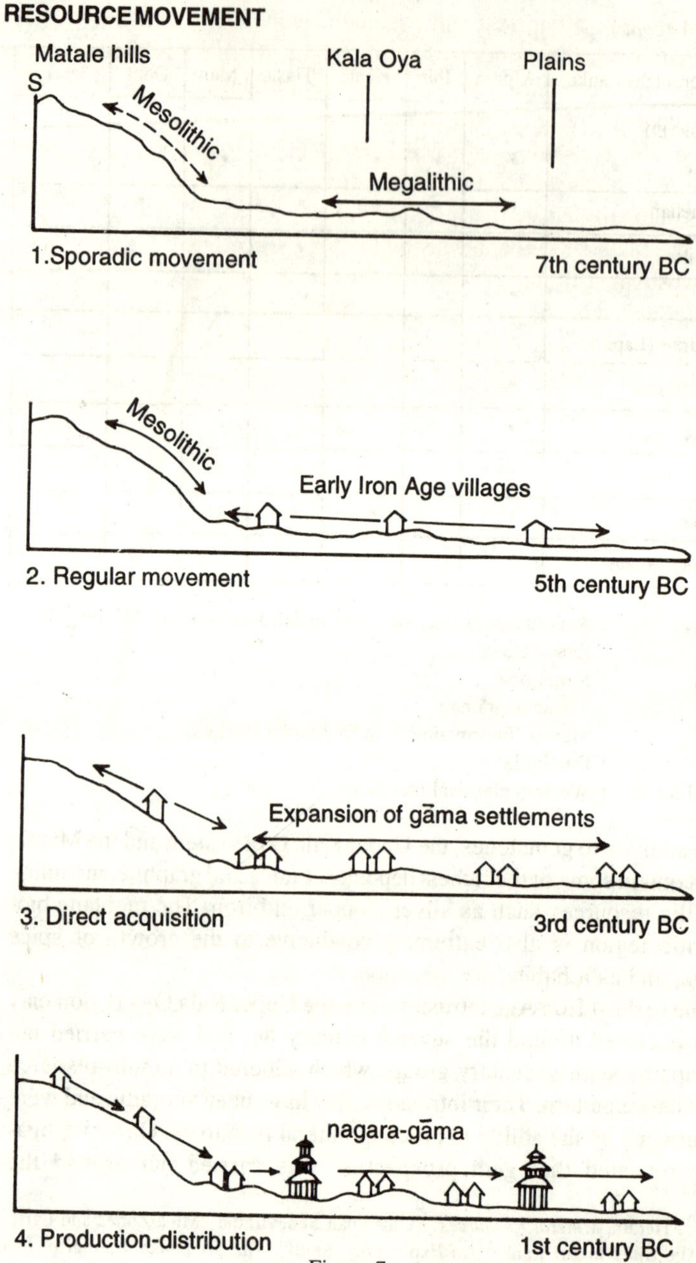
RESOURCE MOVEMENT
Matale hills
S
Mesolithic
Kala Oya
Plains
N
Megalithic
1.Sporadic movement
7th century BC
Mesolithic
Early Iron Age villages
2. Regular movement
5th century BC
Expansion of gāma settlements
3. Direct acquisition
3rd century BC
nagara-gāma
4. Production-distribution
1st century BC

Figure 7

Ibbankatuwa site until the mid-twentieth century. It is also known that good quality topaz stones are easily obtained from the land around Sigiri. It may be suggested that the megalithic folk may have carried out exchanges with the Mesolithic people in the montane area. The Matale hills have been identified as a potentially rich region for future Stone Age studies. Surface investigations at Ibbankatuwa yielded remains of quartz and chert. The latter is an import to this region, probably from the Matale hills. The Mesolithic–Megalithic interaction needs to be investigated further.

The second phase of this process may be seen in the beginnings of more permanent settlements in the Upper Kala Oya, which is attested by the founding of village sites. Judging by the habitation vestiges in the Upper Kala Oya, a more planned exploitation of localized resources seems to have taken place during this phase, indicating a better understanding of the micro and macro environment. The Ibbankatuwa habitation site has been radiometrically dated to the fourth century BC. A greater sedentation may have been conditioned by a regular demand for raw material from several Iron Age habitats in the plains. It is significant that the Citadel excavations at Anurādhapura revealed that, around *c.* 500 BC a wider range of minerals (e.g. evidence of lapidary work, gold, copper, etc.) moved into that site.[34]

The occurrence of large quantities of carnelian beads in the Ibbankatuwa cists points to another significant feature. This stone, which was considered a prestigious object within the Early Iron Age culture complex of Peninsular India and Sri Lanka, had to be imported as raw material from the Deccan. Industrial remains of bead production from layers datable to the sixth century BC at Anurādhapura indicate that this stone was turned into beads at that site. The carnelian beads found at Ibbankatuwa most probably originated from the north-central plains; they may have been an exchange item between two or more ecological zones.[35] It is therefore not surprising that the burials of Ibbankatuwa represent a range of minerals such as amethyst, feldspar, gold, mica and copper. The raw material most obviously moved down from the Matale hills to the Iron Age habitations (see Figure 8).

What is also significant is the social archaeology of this resource acquisition. While it is evident that the Early Iron Age society was a

[34] S.U. Deraniyagala, 'Excavations in the Citadel of Anuradhapura: Gedige 1984, a Preliminary Report', *Ancient Ceylon* 6, 1986, pp. 42–3.

[35] For details on carnelian, *see* Seneviratne op. cit., 1984, pp. 276–7; Seneviratne, *Intermediary Transitional Eco-systems*, p. 126.

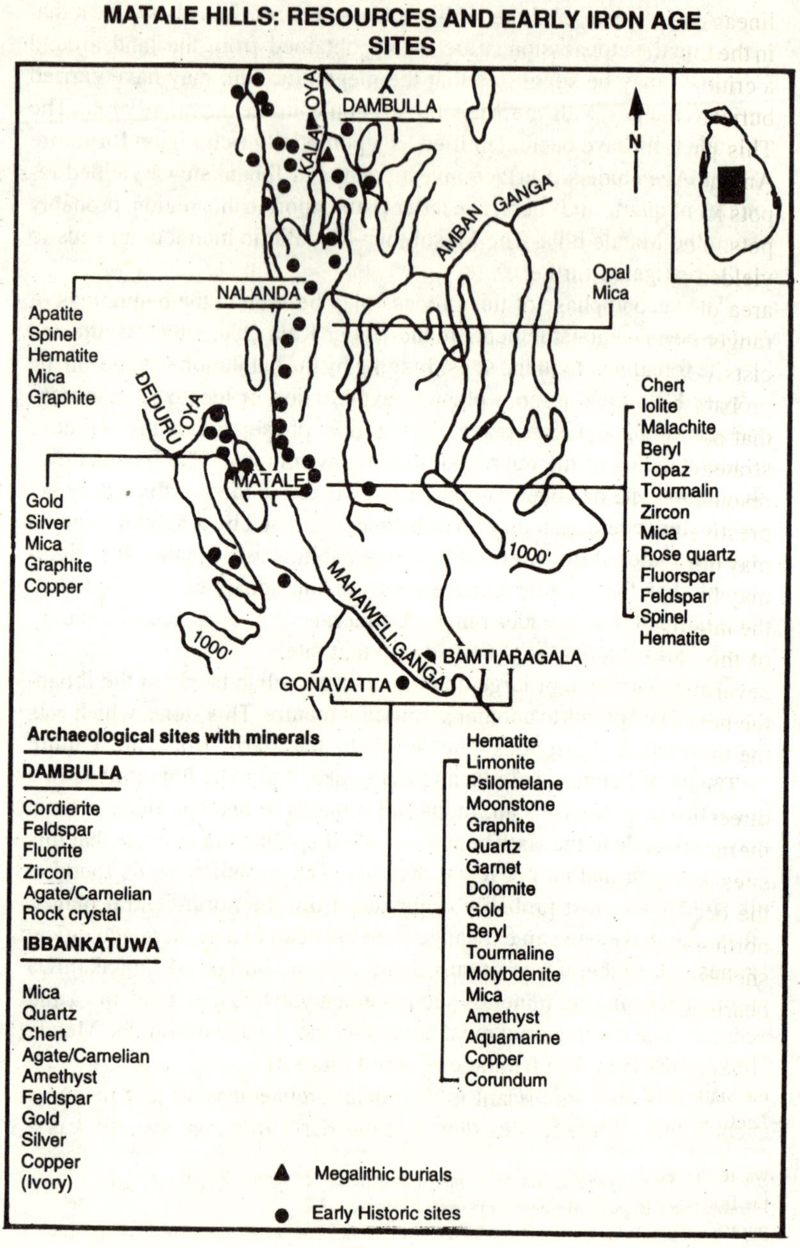
MATALE HILLS: RESOURCES AND EARLY IRON AGE SITES
DAMBULLA
KALA OYA
N
AMBAN GANGA
Opal
Mica
NALANDA
Apatite
Spinel
Hematite
Mica
Graphite
DEDURU OYA
MATALE
Gold
Silver
Mica
Graphite
Copper
Chert
Iolite
Malachite
Beryl
Topaz
Tourmalin
Zircon
Mica
Rose quartz
Fluorspar
Feldspar
Spinel
Hematite
1000'
MAHAWELI GANGA
1000'
BAMTIARAGALA
GONAVATTA
Archaeological sites with minerals
DAMBULLA
Cordierite
Feldspar
Fluorite
Zircon
Agate/Carnelian
Rock crystal
IBBANKATUWA
Mica
Quartz
Chert
Agate/Carnelian
Amethyst
Feldspar
Gold
Silver
Copper
(Ivory)
Hematite
Limonite
Psilomelane
Moonstone
Graphite
Quartz
Garnet
Dolomite
Gold
Beryl
Tourmaline
Molybdenite
Mica
Amethyst
Aquamarine
Copper
Corundum
Megalithic burials
Early Historic sites

Figure 8

lineage-based one, the lineage chieftains, i.e. *perumakan*, or *parumaka*, in the Early Brāhmī inscriptions during the next phase, may have played a critical role in this exchange mechanism. In one instance a large cist burial at Ibbankatuwa revealed a gold fillet along with carnelian beads. This particular cist carried two megalithic symbols on the capstone. Another three-chambered cist had several copper objects in the offering pots located around it, and also large sheets of mica placed under BRW pots. Yet another burial to the north-east of the three-chambered cist yielded more carnelian beads. All these cists are located in the central area of the ten-hectare burial site at Ibbankatuwa, and the spatial arrangement indicated that some of them were surrounded by smaller cists, perhaps establishing a higher status to the larger and richer burials probably associated with lineage chieftains. I have already suggested that not only were these lineage chieftains located at regions yielding strategic resources, they also extended some form of control over such resources and resource movement.[36] In its southward movement, a prestige item such as carnelian, which was turned out at Anurādhapura, may have been acquired by lineage chieftains in the foothill areas. They may have in turn moved mineral resources acquired from the hills and the intermediary zone towards the plains. The long-term consequences of this interacting process, involving more than one ecological zone, several techno–cultural groups and a network of habitations surfaced by the next phase, with the beginning of the Early Historic Period around the third century BC in the Upper Kala Oya system.

The third and fourth phases in this process may be identified with the direct acquisition of resources from the source area, mainly situated in the montane region and the development of larger production–distribution sites in the foothill area. This movement is best demonstrated with the occurrence of Early Brāhmī inscriptions for the first time in the northern montane region, where they are found in drip-ledge cave shelters located along a natural route moving into several resource-bearing localities along its path (see Figure 8).[37] In spite of the difficult

[36] Seneviratne, *Parumaka*, pp. 113–16; *also see* R.A.L.H. Gunawardana, 'Prelude to the State: An Early Phase in the Evolution of Political Institutions of Sri Lanka', *The Sri Lanka Journal of the Humanities*, VIII (1 & 2). 1985, pp. 1–39.

[37] It is significant to note that recent excavations at the Citadel of Anurādhapura yielded waste as well as finished products of garnet and amethyst from layers firmly datable to the first quarter of the third century BC, at the latest. *See* Robin Coningham, 'Anuradhapura Citadel Archaeological Project: Preliminary Results of the Excavation of the Southern Rampart 1992', *South Asian Studies*, 9, 1993, pp. 120–1.

terrain we not only find the occurrence of inscriptions recording donations by *gahapati, gāmika, bata, aśa*, *parumaka*, but also the existence of guilds, specialist craftsmen and production–distribution centres, and even a strong evidence of more systematic exchange patterns being introduced into this region.

It is amply clear that the Iron Age communities of the Early Historic Period gained access from one ecosystem to another through mountain passes. The Early Brāhmī inscriptions record the existence of a series of settlements having the suffix *kaḍa*. The early texts also carry several references to places in the foothill areas having the suffix *kaḍa*. The etymology of the term *kaḍa* and the possible location of such sites suggest the following.[38] In a broader spatial situation *kaḍa* implied a specific physical area linking up with other environmental, physiographic or resource zones. At the micro situation, initially, *kaḍa* may have implied a hill or mountain pass. Gradually, by the Early Historic Period, such points may have evolved into settlements that functioned as centres receiving or collecting resources, subsequently funnelling these to centres of production and consumption. Such *kaḍa* settlements are mentioned in inscriptions of the Early Historic Period, from Matale to Dambulla. The transfer of goods from one ecosystem to another not only expanded settlement zones into the montane region, but this economic activity also introduced new techno–cultural elements and social formations of the Early Historic Period into a new physical and environmental zone.

The earliest references to the northern montane and its foothill areas in the early Pali chronicles of Sri Lanka coincide with the Early Historic Period. What is also interesting is that most references are associated with natural resources, and mineral resources in particular. The texts refer to Girikaṇḍa, and lower montane regions yielding minerals such as mica, silver, gemstones and gold, during the period of Devānāmpiyatissa and Duṭṭhagāmaṇi.[39] More specific information however is available from both archaeological and inscriptional sources of the Early Historic Period.

It is evident that the lineage chieftains exercised control over resource areas and over routes as well. For instance, the names of two *parumaka* Abijhi and Tiripala are found at Sigiri and at Neluvakaṇḍa,

[38] *Kaḍa, kaḍai, kaṭai, kaṇḍa*—to pass through, traverse, proceed, pass; end, limit, boundary, entrance, gate, shop, market, shop located in a place', *DED* 958; *PPTI* 205; for example Dhānyakaḍa in Andhra. For details, *see* Seneviratne, *Intermediary Transitional Eco-systems*, pp. 127–9.

[39] *MV*. XI.10–14; XXVIII.18–35.

in the hills located south of Matale.[40] It may be noted that Tiri is the Dravidian form of the Indo-Aryan personal name Śrī. At least two other sites bearing Brāhmī inscriptions near Matale carry non-Brāhmī symbols or those identified as megalithic symbols. The descendants of the Proto Historic lineage chieftains intruded into these regions and this is even better documented from the other sectors of the lower montane in north-west Sri Lanka.[41]

A second example is seen with a lineage group that originally occupied the foothill area overlooking the Upper Kala Oya plains and subsequently extended its hegemony after a few generations across the Matale hills, all the way up to the resource areas in the central hills, touching the middle valley of the Mahaweli river. Their lineage ancestor is known as Pocunika *rāja*.[42] The term *pocuni* or *pocani* may derive from *pacina*, or 'ancient'. It is not altogether impossible that this lineage group may have had its origins in the *parumaka* group which introduced elements of the Iron Age culture into the montane region. It is also significant that in listing their genealogy this group has adhered to the practice of taking up the grandfather's name, or what is known as *peyaran* in the South Indian Sangam texts.[43] This particular lineage group, at one point of time, may have controlled the complete resource network extending from the middle Mahaweli through the Matale hills to the foothills near Dambulla.

It is also possible that the lineages may have exercised some control over production and distribution. The recent discovery of globular shaped burnt clay seals at Udupihilla near Matale carry a ladder symbol and Tiśa in the early Brāhmī script. It is not impossible that this Tiśa may refer to *aya* Tiśa or Gamaṇi Tiśa recorded in the genealogical table of the Pocani lineage.[44]

Additional information for this control over routes, resource zones and production–distribution centres in the montane region by other lineage groups is available from the Brāhmī inscriptions datable to around 50 BC from Gonavatta (middle Mahaweli region) and Demada Oya near Nālanda.[45] It is not altogether impossible that the chieftain

[40] S. Paranavitana, *Inscriptions of Ceylon*, vol. I, Archaeological Survey of Ceylon, 1970 (*IC*) 819 and 968. Hereafter the number indicated against *IC* refers to the number of the inscription given in that publication.

[41] For the technological and social aspects of this process, *see* Seneviratne, *Parumaka*, pp. 113–19.

[42] *IC*. 814, 831–3.

[43] Seneviratne, *Social Base of Early Buddhism*, p. 415.

[44] Seneviratne, *Intermediary Transitional Eco-systems*, p. 127.

[45] *IC*. 813, 830.

Mahā Cuḍika, may have undermined the authority of the Pocani lineage. The personal name Mahā Cuḍika, means the 'bearer of the great gem', indicating his primary interest over minerals. His inscription from Demada Oya very specifically records the arrival of *maṇikara* (lapidarists) under the service of this chieftain to procure blocks of stone.[46] It is not certain whether this is a reference to the exploitation of gemstones, the crystalline limestone or 'books' of mica. The Nālanda area is well endowed with all these three resources. Inscriptions datable from the same period at Bambaragala records a Kolagāma, which we interpret as the 'village of the metalsmith'.[47] Recent geological studies confirmed copper occurrences in and around Bambaragala.[48] The same inscription also records the existence of Cita-nagara, and another settlement called Kalata. This information confirms that by the second century BC and after, specialized craft producers were quite definitely functioning in the montane region, and sometimes their labour was under the authority of local lineage chieftains. Craftsmen often resided close to resource areas and formed themselves into villages (*gāma*) which were situated adjacent to *nagara* or production–distribution centres. Several inscriptions from elsewhere in the montane region refer to some of these *nagara* in relation to corporate bodies, equating the status of the *nagara* to that of the *nigama*.[49] There are also references to specific corporate bodies such as the *puga* at Kudagala near Matale,[50] pointing to the existence of specialized commercial bodies along this route network to the plains.

Archaeological evidence retrieved from Anurādhapura, the north-western coast, Māntai and Kantarōḍai points to this resource movement through the plains and on to coastal port sites. For instance, in the *Naturalis historia*, Pliny (AD 50), probably referring to mica, records that a 'marble which resembles tortoise-shell' was exported from Taprobane, the social prestige of which he equates with gold, silver, pearls and precious stone.[51] Another inscription dated to around 50 BC,

[46] *IC*. 830; *also see* Seneviratne, op. cit., 1984, pp. 278–9; Seneviratne, *Mica Zones*; Seneviratne, *Intermediary Transitional Eco-systems*, p. 126.

[47] While Paranavitana has read the name of this village as Koligāma, the estampage clearly shows Kolagāma, *IC*, Plate LXXXIX.

[48] David C. Almond, *Solid-Rock Geology of the Kandy Area Sri Lanka*, Kandy, 1994, pp. 61–2.

[49] For some *nagara* centres in the montane region, *IC*. 786, 794, 796a.

[50] Malini Dias, *Epigraphical Notes*, Colombo, 1991, Department of Archaeology, no. 5, p. 3.

[51] J.W. McCrindle, *Ancient India as Described in Classical Literature*, Westminster, 1901, p. 106.

situated on the hill pass at Galagedara near Kandy, overlooking the Mahaweli river, mentions a *parumaka* who travels to Barukaca.[52] Similarly, the existence of *bata* individuals, in the montane region of Matale,[53] bears testimony to the direct link this region had established with the coastal port sites exporting mineral resources to external regions, more specifically with the intensification of the 'Roman trade' in South India.[54]

This brings us to a discussion of the Early Historic developments in the Upper Kala Oya valley.

Contrary to its identification as a 'retreat area' in history, the upper Kala Oya witnessed a relatively rapid pace in new social formations, receiving its main impetus from economic activity related to mineral resource use. The occurrence of minerals originating in the montane region at several coastal and inland habitation sites, including the demands made by the Peninsular Indian and the West Asian market, is indicative of an expansion in resource extraction and its movement in the post-third century BC. A natural consequence of this was an expansion in the volume of resources moving out of the source areas. An increase in the demand for 'weight-gaining material', such as mineral stones, and to a lesser extent metallic resources found in the montane region, and the outflow of a larger volume of resources in contrast to the Proto Historic Period, had a bearing on the emergence of a major production–distribution zone in the Upper Kala Oya region. This situation saw either the marketing of raw material in this region or the

[52] Bagavalena inscription *IC.* 1183.

[53] Sudharshan Seneviratne, 'The Baratas: A Case Study of Community Integration in Early Historic Sri Lanka', in *James Thevatasan Rutnam: Festschrift 1985*, A.R.B. Amarasinghe and S.J. Sumanasekare Banda (eds), Colombo, 1985, pp. 49–56.

[54] The occurrence of second century BC Hellenistic Black Slipped Ware and Arikamedu pottery type together with Rouletted Ware in the same stratigraphic context dated to the second or first century BC at the Citadel of Anurādhapura is noteworthy. *See* Robin Coningham, 'Anuradhapura Citadel Archaeological Project: Preliminary Report of the Second Season of Sri Lankan–British Excavations at Salgahawatta, June–August 1990', *South Asian Studies*, 7, 1991, pp. 171–2; *also see* S.U. Deraniyagala, *The Prehistory*, pp. 712–13; M. Prickett, 'Sri Lanka's Foreign Trade before AD 600: Archaeological Evidence', *in* K.M. de Silva et al. (eds), *Asian Panorama: Essays in Asian History, Past and Present*, New Delhi, 1990, pp. 151–80. A recent study on the waste flakes of stone working carried out at Māntai in antiquity revealed the following types: rock crystal, carnelian, amethyst, onyx, sardonyx, moonstone, amazonite, garnet, cordierite, corundum, tourmaline and lazurite—*see* M. E. Prickett-Fernando, Sudharshan Seneviratne and H.W.S. Siritunga, 'Stone-working Waste from Mantai and Evidence for Production, Technology, and Trade', *Annual Review*, Kandy, 1992, Institute of Fundamental Studies, pp. 63–4, 66–7.

transfer of material, semi-finished and finished products ultimately to port sites and inland habitation sites for consumption or redistribution (see Figure 9).

The situation outlined above required better organized units of specialized production and a socio–economic infrastructure sustaining this development. Both archaeological and inscriptional sources point to the founding of new settlements, a demographic expansion, the spread of the primary habitation nucleus in the major Red and Brown soil region, which is more suitable for wet agriculture, the development of a settlement hierarchy and a stratified society.[55] The continuation of Proto Historic habitation sites to the Early Historic Period, e.g. Ibbankatuwa, and the emergence of new and larger habitation sites in the Red and Brown soil region, e.g. Malasna,[56] including the development of a *nagara* or major production–distribution centre and several tank or *vāpi-gāma* (village) settlements indicates a relatively stable settlement situation. It is, however, important to note that *vāpi* or man-made reservoirs and their associated settlements are first mentioned in inscriptions datable to the first century AD in this region. In fact settlements with larger tanks, or *mahāvāpi*, in the same region are mentioned in post first- and second-century AD inscriptions. The table listing village settlements in the Upper Kala Oya region in Early and Later Brāhmī inscriptions gives credence to this assumption.[57]

Early Brāhmī	*Later Brāhmī*
Uparikaḍa	Abalavi
Rakitagāma	Maladavi
Garadiḍagāma	Nakadavi
Kolagāma	Mayāviya
Maṭukagāma	Tiyavikahavāvi
Caṇigāma	Mahavāvi
	Matukaṭaka
	Dubalagāma
	Kaḍapivāpi
	Paḍagāma

[55] R.A.L.H. Gunawardana, 'Social Function and Political Power: A Caste Study of State Formation in Irrigation Society', in Henri J. M. Claessen and Peter Skalnik (eds), *The Study of the State*, The Hague, 1981, pp. 133–54.

[56] Information from Priyantha Karunaratne, 1994.

[57] For inscriptions see *IC*. 218, 837, 841, 842, 873, 1151, 1152, 1185, 1187–8; Dias, *Epigraphical Notes*, pp. 30–1, no. 7, p. 47, no. 10; Ranawella, in Senake Bandaranayake *Sigiriya Project*, p. 203, no. 8, p. 202, no. 7.

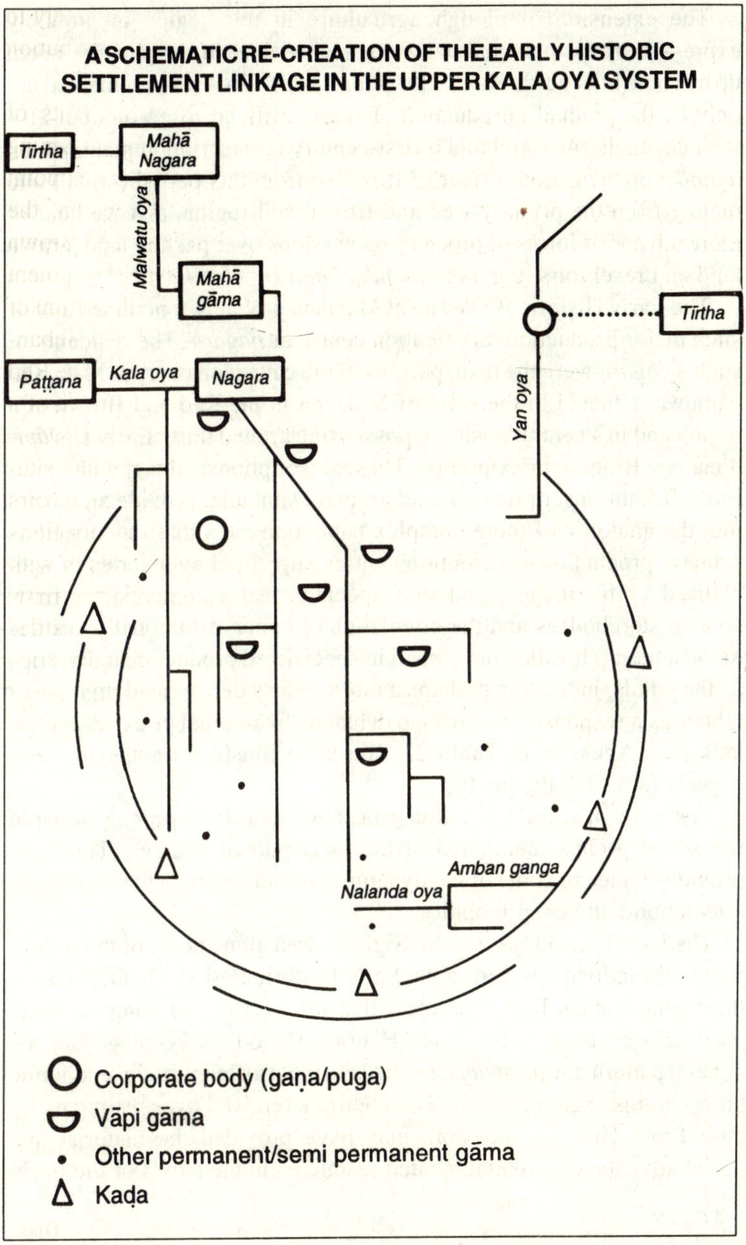
A SCHEMATIC RE-CREATION OF THE EARLY HISTORIC SETTLEMENT LINKAGE IN THE UPPER KALA OYA SYSTEM
Tīrtha
Mahā Nagara
Malwatu oya
Mahā gāma
Tīrtha
Paṭṭana
Kala oya
Nagara
Yan oya
Amban ganga
Nalanda oya
Corporate body (gaṇa/puga)
Vāpi gāma
Other permanent/semi permanent gāma
Kaḍa

Figure 9

The extension of plough agriculture in this region is probably expressed by the personal name *naguli*, 'wielder of the plough', taken up by some lineage chieftains, the parumaka'.[58] This was augmented not only by the gradual introduction of small artificial reservoirs but also with channels. At Dambulla a first-century BC inscription mentions an *aṇaṇika* or 'irrigation officer'.[59] It is also from this period (AD 50) and mainly from the primary Red and Brown soil region, that we hear of more advanced forms of property ownerships over pasture land, arable land and reservoirs, e.g. *taṇa būmika bhojaka, vāpi hamika.*[60]

The Early Historic BRW site at Malasna probably functioned as one such major production–distribution centre or *nagara*. The residents of such a *nagara* were the main patrons of the cave monastery at Mahaalagamuwa, situated to the west of Malasna in the Red and Brown soil region and in a central position, possessing around thirty Early Historic donative Brāhmī inscriptions. These inscriptions, along with other Early Brāhmī inscriptions in and around Dambulla, provide an insight into the anatomy of more complex habitation sites that functioned as primary production–distribution centres supported by a series of specialized craft villages, and into specialists at commercial activity; so also storehouses and the circulation of coins. Additionally, around AD 50 a hierarchization developed in specialized production units, such as the guilds, indicating perhaps a more clearly demarcated division of labour as a response to increased demands by internal or external markets (see Avukana in Table 2). The table illustrates some of these aspects (see also Figure 10).

The scale of social formation is best understood by probing some of the social groups mentioned in the inscriptional sources. This may provide an idea of some of the dynamics associated with the process of interaction and social mobility.

The Upper Kala Oya and the Sigiriya area alone boast of thirty-four *parumaka* individuals during the Early Historic Period. On the basis of their genealogical lists, it is clear that the ancestry of some of these *parumaka* go back to the Proto Historic Period. In keeping with the general pattern, the *parumaka* formed the most affluent socio–economic group in this region as well. The control exercised over resources by their Proto Historic ancestors may have provided the material and social advantage of retaining such resources in the hands of the Early

[58] *IC.* 869.

[59] *IC.* 846.

[60] *IC.* 1149, 1151, 1153.

Table 2

Nagara, Crafts and Commerce

Site	*Reference*	*Function*
Mahaalagamuwa	*IC.* no. 230	*Nagara guta* (citykeeper)
	IC. no. 241	*Koṭagārikà* (keeper of stores)
	IC. no. 215	*Koṭagārika* (keeper of stores)
	IC. no. 226	*Koṭagārika* (keeper of stores)
	IC. no. 212–13	*Gaṇaka* (keeper of accounts)
	IC. no. 217	*Dhaniya* (banker/creditor)
Vanasimha vihāra	*IC.* no. 201	*Gaṇa* (corporate body)
Panikkan kuḷam	*IC.* no. 209	*Maṇikara* (lapidarist)
Pidurangala	*IC.* no. 873	*Kolagāma* (village of the metalsmith)
Sigiri	Ranawella no. 8	*Barasala* (storehouse)
Kandalama	*IC.* no. 860	*Toṭa-bojaka* (controller of ford)
Dambulla	*IC.* no. 857	*Śatada dhana* (fifty coins)
Avukana	*IC.* no. 1152	*Puka* (corporate body); *jeṭa* (alderman); *mahatavara* (president)

Historic *parumaka*. The following table may give an insight into some sectors of the economy associated with this group. It indicates their influence over labour, settlement units, fords, agricultural production and mineral resources in the Upper Kala Oya region.[61]

Parumaka	Maṭukagama *bujika*
Parumaka	naguli (wielder of the plough)
Parumaka	*toṭa bojika* (controller of the ford)
Parumaka	nagara guta (city-keeper)
Parumaka	'*padagaḍa-kama kārapita*' (the step has been caused to be done)
Parumaka	Cuḍa
Parumaka	Cuḍa
Parumaka	(son of) gaṇaka (accountant)
Parumaka	Kaḍapi vāpi hamika
Parumaka	Gajadabutaka *vāvi hami*

Some of the *parumaka* may have acquired this title not by descent but as a designation indicating rank or official status, which is relatively

[61] *IC.* 203, 206, 212–13, 230, 837, 856, 860, 869, 1151, 1153.

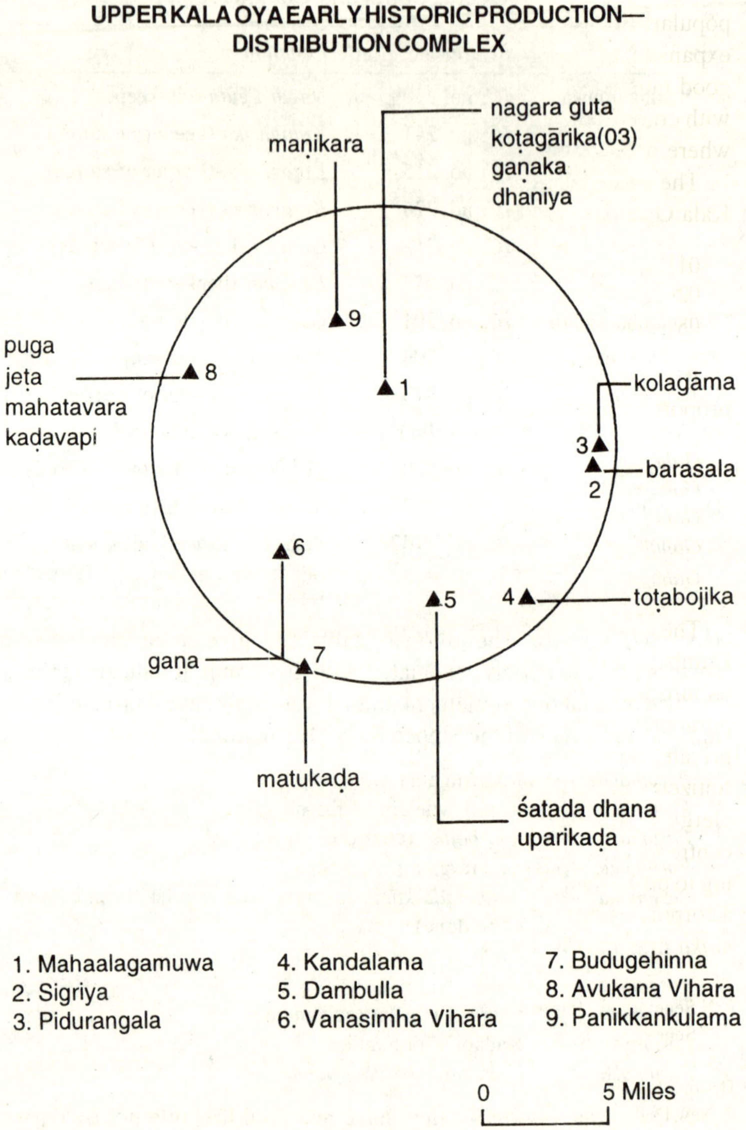
UPPER KALA OYA EARLY HISTORIC PRODUCTION—DISTRIBUTION COMPLEX
nagara guta
koṭagārika(03)
gaṇaka
dhaniya
maṇikara
9
puga
jeṭa
mahatavara
kaḍavapi
8
1
kolagāma
3
barasala
2
6
5
4
toṭabojika
gaṇa
7
matukaḍa
śatada dhana
uparikaḍa
1. Mahaalagamuwa
2. Sigriya
3. Pidurangala
4. Kandalama
5. Dambulla
6. Vanasimha Vihāra
7. Budugehinna
8. Avukana Vihāra
9. Panikkankulama
0
5 Miles

Figure 10

clear elsewhere in the island.[62] Such individuals often had their social origins in other affluent groups within the Early Historic society. Some of these groups may be identified as the aśa, gahapati and *gāmika*. The popular view that these groups emerged primarily due to the rapid expansion of the agricultural economy has to be partially modified.[63] A good number of individuals from these groups are identified directly with crafts and commerce in the Early Historic inscriptions found elsewhere in Sri Lanka.

The entire macro zone extending from the Matale hills to the Upper Kala Oya system indicates a relative paucity of the following groups.

01 *aśa* from an all-island total of 27
02 *gāmika* from a total of 143
08 *gahapati* and *kuṭumbika* from a total of 91.

It is significant that even among this limited group, a significant proportion had some association with resources and commerce.[64]

Gahapati	(son) *koṭagārika*
Gahapati	Cuḍa
Gahapati	Cuḍa
Gahapati	Cuḍatara
Gahapati	(of) Rakitagāma

The *gāmika* in this area indicate similar traits. Donative records from Dambulla and Ranagiramada, located in two different valleys, provide us information to this effect. *Gāmika* Vahaba's daughter, married to a *parumaka*, made a donation of a cave at each site. While she made her private endowment at Dambulla, she was joined at Ranagiramada by the 'citizens' or the corporate body of Aba-nagara in donating a cave to the clergy.[65] Aba-nagara was another important production–distribution centre located in the Upper Deduru valley system. It would be interesting to probe the connection between the *gāmika* family and members of a corporate body. It is not altogether impossible that the *gāmika* or *parumaka* may have wielded some authority over this corporate body.

[62] Seneviratne, *Parumaka*.

[63] Seneviratne, *Social Base of Early Buddhism*, pp. 493–505.

[64] *IC*. 215, 828, 842; *also see* Piyatissa Senanayake, 'Notices on Coined Money in Early Historic Inscriptions of Sri Lanka', paper presented at the World Archaeology Congress-3, New Delhi, 1994. I am thankful to my colleague Piyatissa Senanayake for providing me the map on coined money for publication.

[65] *IC*. 330, 962.

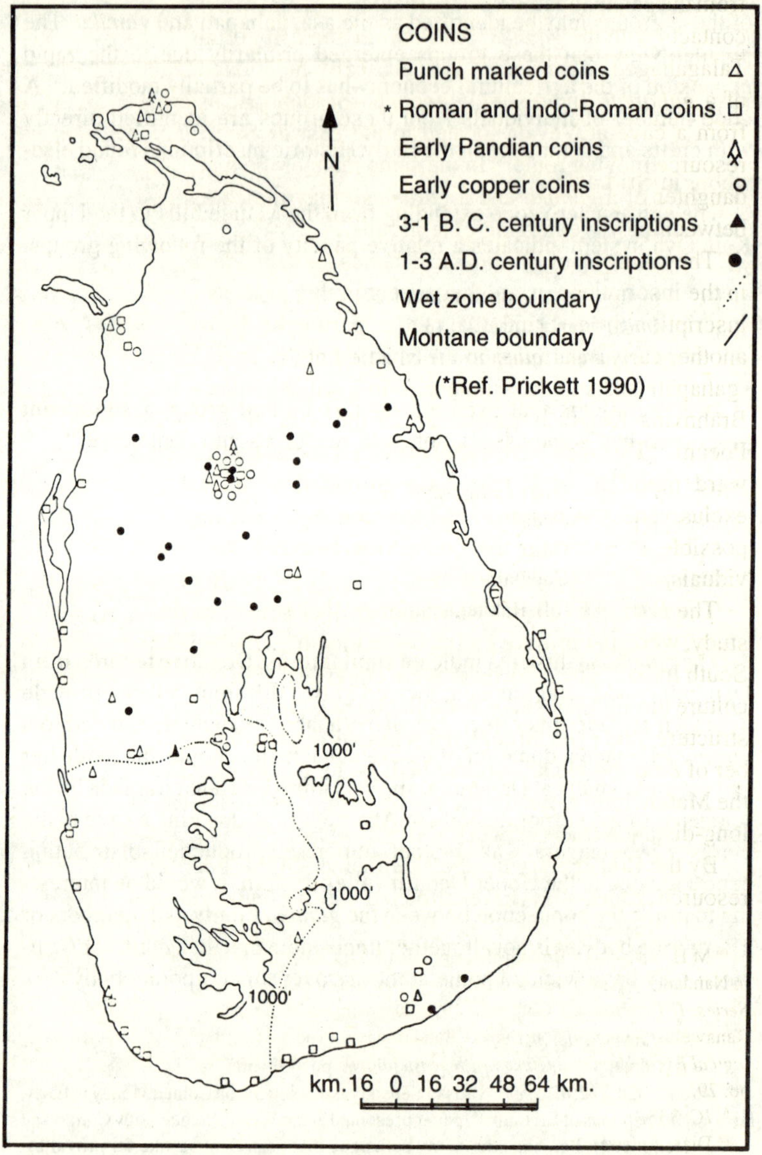
COINS
Punch marked coins
* Roman and Indo-Roman coins
Early Pandian coins
Early copper coins
3-1 B. C. century inscriptions
1-3 A.D. century inscriptions
Wet zone boundary
Montane boundary
(*Ref. Prickett 1990)
N
1000'
1000'
1000'
km.16 0 16 32 48 64 km.

Figure 11

It is significant that some of the new *parumaka* title holders emerged from the gahapati families in particular, and had marriage or other social contacts with the *gāmika, bata-barata* and *aśa* groups. For instance, at Talagahagoda a *parumaka* is specifically mentioned as the eldest son of a *gahapati*. Interestingly enough, an identical inscription is found from a cave at Vevala located to the east of Sigiri, along a primary resource moving route.[66] In the same manner the marriage between the daughter of a *gāmika* and a *parumaka* may indicate social interaction between newly emerging elite groups.

The taking up of Brahmanical names, or to be identified as a *bamaṇa* in the inscriptions, is another aspect in this process. An Early Brāhmī inscription from Dambulla reads 'parumaka bamaṇa tiśa',[67] while another early inscription in the Matale hills at Talagahagoda mentions 'gahapati kośikaputa' Śumana.[68] In a third instance the daughter of Brāhmaṇa Kojara is mentioned as the wife of a descendant of rāja Pocuni.[69] This may have either provided social legitimation gaining upward mobility, or it may have provided a ritual status for class exclusiveness. A bamaṇa kośika is mentioned at Yangala,[70] and it is not possible to ascertain the connection between the two kośika individuals.

The *bata* individuals, who number over fifteen in the region under study, were an intrusive group, being members of the affluent Barata of South India.[71] They, however were integrated with the local society and culture through a positive assimilation into the existing socio–economic structure, and even through the religious establishment. The high number of *bata* individuals spread both in the Upper Kala Oya system and the Matale hills indicates their involvement in linking this region to the long-distance trade network.

By the first century BC, the significance of these regions as primary resource zones may have attracted the attention of major political

[66] M.H. Sirisoma, 'Brahmi Inscriptions of Sri Lanka from 3rd Century BC to AD 65', *in* Nandadeva Wijesekera (ed.), *Archaeological Department Centenary Commemorative Series. II Inscriptions*, Colombo, 1990, Department of Archaeology, p. 45, no. 41; S. Ranawella, 'Epigraphy', *in* Senake Bandaranayake (ed.), *Sigiriya Project, First Archaeological Excavation and Research Report*, Colombo, 1994, Central Cultural Fund, p. 211, no. 29.

[67] *IC*. 838.

[68] Dias, *Epigraphical Notes*, p. 7, no. 9.

[69] *IC*. 814.

[70] *IC*. 205.

[71] Seneviratne, *Barata*.

centres such as Anurādhapura. The earliest inscription from a major state system in the island in this region cannot be dated beyond 100 BC. Following this period, more specifically during the early Christian era, there are several inscriptions bearing the titles of kings, ministers and army commanders, including terms used for revenue and administrative units associated with this region.[72]

The Upper Maha Oya System

This river system has been 'peripheral' to the extent that, until recent years, it did not even merit basic historical studies. The following summary is derived from a largely unpublished research corpus collated from several years of research studies carried out in this area.[73] This brief survey is introduced here as a comparative study, substantiating the dynamics of Early Iron Age social formations associated with mineralized regions and settlement zones elsewhere, more specifically with the lower montane region.

The upper valley and sections of the middle valley of this 74-mile-long river has now revealed nearly a hundred Early Iron Age sites, the majority of which belong to the Early Historic Period. There are three megalithic burial sites, two cave sites bearing megalithic symbols, pre-Christian stūpa and Early Historic Black and Red Ware sites, and drip-ledge cave shelters with or without Early Brāhmī inscriptions representing the main body of archaeological vestiges for the period under study.

It is now known that the Proto Historic iron-using communities reached the Upper valley around the sixth century BC, by traversing the main river and its tributary system. It is not known to what extent the pre-existing Mesolithic communities were absorbed into the fold of the Early Iron Age culture. The unbroken sequence of rock paintings from the Mesolithic to the Early Iron Age at Doravakakanda is an interesting one.

During the next few centuries the Early Iron Age culture diffused within the valley and seems to have developed several nuclei. The micro

[72] Dias, *Epigraphical Notes*, p. 46, no. 4.

[73] Sudharshan Seneviratne and Chulani Rambukwella, 'The Locational Pattern of Early Hisoric Sites in the Plateau of Kandy', paper presented at the Second National Archaeological Congress, Colombo, 1987, Postgraduate Institute of Archaeology; Chulani Rambukwella, 'The Early Iron Age Socio-political Landscape of the Mahaoya River Valley: A Suggested Model for the Montane Region of Sri Lanka', paper presented at the World Archaeology Congress-3, New Delhi, 1994.

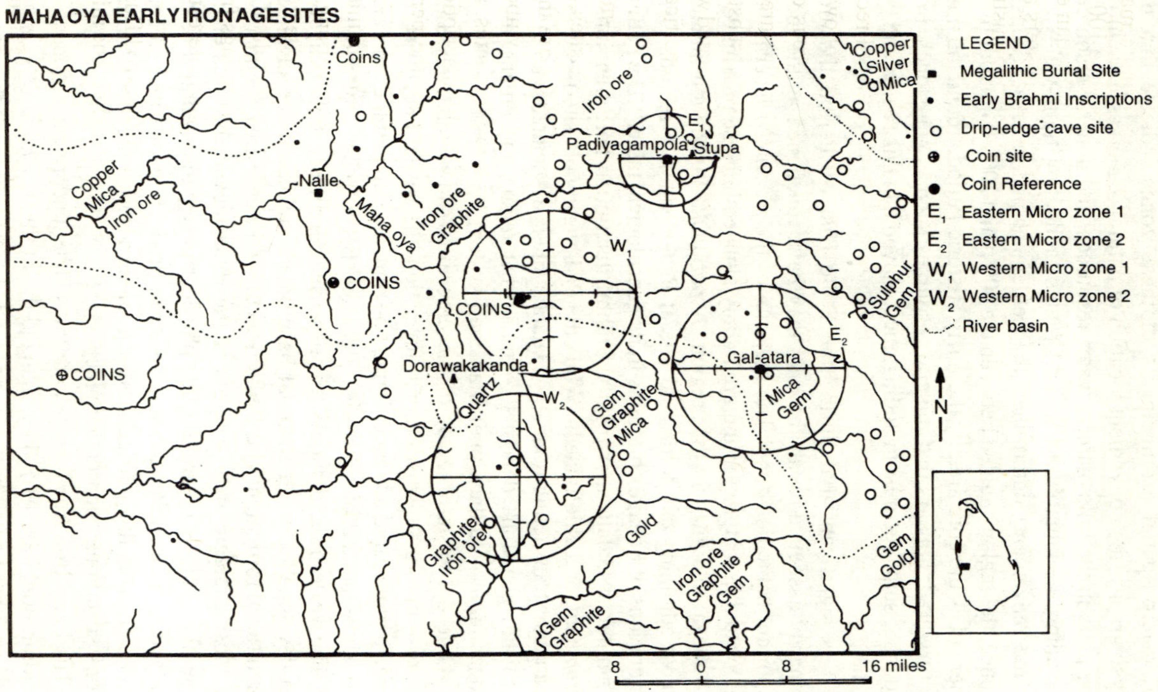
MAHA OYA EARLY IRON AGE SITES
LEGEND
Megalithic Burial Site
Early Brahmi Inscriptions
Drip-ledge cave site
Coin site
Coin Reference
E_1 Eastern Micro zone 1
E_2 Eastern Micro zone 2
W_1 Western Micro zone 1
W_2 Western Micro zone 2
River basin
N
Coins
Copper
Silver
Mica
Iron ore
Padiyagampola
Stupa
E_1
Nalle
Copper
Mica
Iron ore
Maha oya
Iron ore
Graphite
COINS
COINS
W_1
Sulphur
Gem
E_2
Gal-atara
Mica
Gem
COINS
Dorawakakanda
Quartz
W_2
Gem
Graphite
Mica
Graphite
Iron ore
Gold
Iron ore
Graphite
Gem
Gem
Gold
Gem
Graphite
8
0
8
16 miles

Figure 12

and macro spatial arrangements of these zones indicate that the physiography, the convenient location of natural resources, i.e. cultivable plots in the hills, natural water resources, and mineral resources (including the situation of natural routes facilitating trans-valley resource movement) determined the settlement pattern. As a consequence, the region situated between the 500 ft and 1000 ft contour lines emerged as the core area by the Early Historic Period around the third century BC. It appears that mineral resources such as gemstones, iron and other sulphide ores, including mica, moved into this region and out of it.

It is significant that during the Proto Historic Period the area primarily associated with the hills may have functioned as the most important habitation zone. The majority of the *parumaka* inscriptions are located in that sector and are mainly situated in close proximity to two megalithic sites in that region. A *parumaka* inscription situated almost adjoining the dolmenoid site at Padavigampola records three generations of lineage chieftains in its genealogical table.[74] The pattern is similar at Galatara. An Early Brāhmī inscription here mentions a *parumakaḷ*, or a chieftainess. While the Padavigampola site is situated on a major transacting route, the Galatara site is associated with major mica and gemstone deposits found in that region and on the route connecting it with the Upper Mahaweli system.

While the eastern sector of the core area shows relatively slow progress in terms of institutional formation, the western sector maintained a more rapid advance. It must be remembered that the core area as a whole had a Proto Historic megalithic–BRW techno–cultural matrix. The western sector, however, possessed the correct ecological base and developed a better material base which entailed more advanced institutional formation. The western sector of the core area commanded the most strategic area in terms of the route movement transferring mineral resources to various other physical and environmental zones in the island. As a consequence, a series of production–distribution centres emerged in this particular sector, along with parallel social formations sustaining such developments.

The Early Iron Age lineage chieftains either underwent a process of acculturation, i.e. where they changed their titles to *rāja, aya*, *gāmaṇi*, or were subordinated by a new political elite intruding into this region. We hear of only three *parumaka* in the western sector as against thirteen in the east. It is however significant that one of the consorts of *aya* Śiva

[74] *IC.* 801.

is referred to as *upāśika* Vēḷ.[75] This lady in fact had the economic and social status to make an individual donation of a land allotment (*paṭaka*) to the clergy. The Vēḷir formed an important segment within the Proto Historic *perumakan* group in Sri Lanka and in the pre-state political structure in South India as well.[76]

Settlement units and land allocations made by the political elite[77]

From Batasanagara and Anudigama, one lot each.
Donated by aya Duhatara.

From Upaligama and Kacaragama, one lot each.
Donated by gāmaṇi Śiva.

From Dusataragama and Patalagama, one lot each.
Donated by gāmaṇi Śiva.

From Niliyanagara and Salivaya, one lot each.

From Cemagama, one lot.
Donated by upāśika Vēḷ, consort of aya Śiva.

From Cemagama, another lot.

From Śivanagara, one lot.
Donated by gāmaṇi Śiva.

A spatial analysis done for the Early Historic sites in this sector revealed that all Early Brāhmī inscriptions mentioning political titles (not *parumaka*), *bata*, gahapati, *amati*, *nagara*, *gāma*, *maṇikara*, and the earliest reference to *kahavaṇa* (punch-marked coins) and even an officer in charge of canals (*aḍika*) are all situated in two clusters centring around the *nagara* locations (see Figure 13).[78] Another critical factor is that within the core area (which covers thirty miles from west to east) and during the same chronological context of the Early Historic Period, there is a sharp unevenness represented in the formation of institutions in the Upper Maha Oya valley.

It is evident therefore that the Upper Maha Oya evolved its social stratification, specialized economic production, new elements in landownership and labour organization, and even the use of coined money in this lower montane region situated at a considerable distance from the

[75] *IC*. 795

[76] Seneviratne, *Parumaka*, pp. 108–12.

[77] *IC*. 786, 792–96a.

[78] These maps are from the paper presented at the WAC. I am grateful to my colleague Ms Rambukwella for providing me with the same for publication.

SCHEMATIC PRESENTATION OF CORE AREA—MAHA OYA

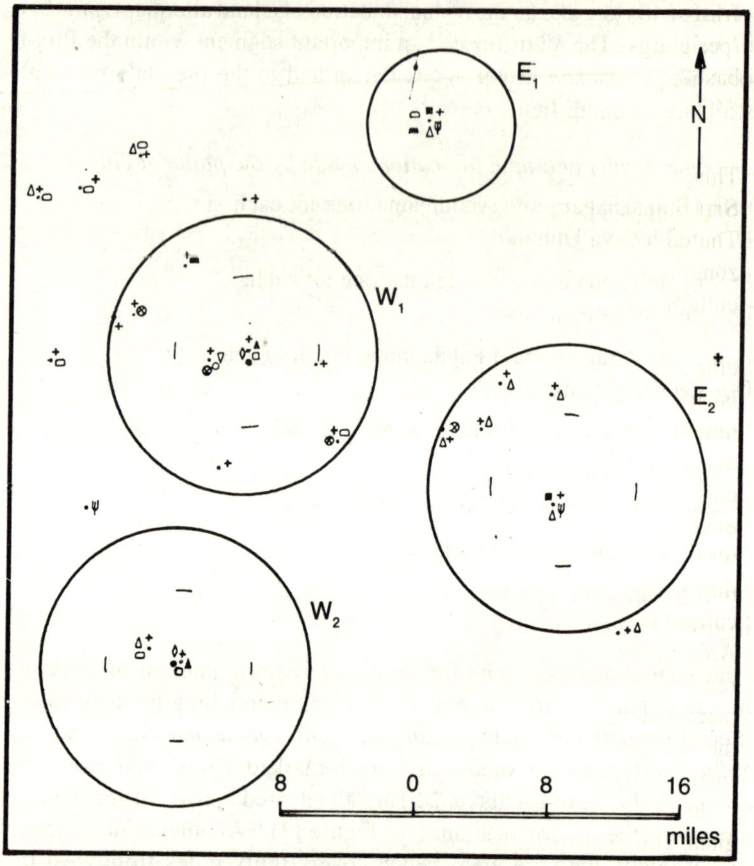

LEGEND

- ■ Megalithic burial site
- Ψ Megalithic symbol site
- + Early Brāhmī inscriptions,
- Δ Parumaka
- ● Royal titles
- ⊗ Administrative titles
- ▬ Gahapati
- ⊂ Bata
- ▲ Nagara
- □ Gāma
- ∇ Craftsmen
- ○ Coin reference
- ⊕ Coin site
- ◊ Share donations
- · Site location

Figure 13

primary agricultural zone of the dry bioclimatic region. This forms the fringe area of the Early Historic settlement zone, and, far from being a 'peripheral' region, it carried the potential for social formation largely based on minerals and production–distribution, less on agriculture.

CONCLUSION

This essay demonstrates that the earliest institutional formation in Sri Lanka was quite different from that described in the classical texts. The developments outlined also entailed a physical and bio-climatic zone far removed from the Dry Zone plains suitable for irrigated agriculture.

Contrary to the view expressed in classical texts on North-Indian elite groups instrumental in introducing advanced institutions to an island largely populated by backward forest dwellers, the argument here is that intrusive techno–cultural elements from South India introduced the earliest recognizable social, economic, political and religio–cultural institutions to different ecological zones in Sri Lanka. There is evidence to indicate that some of the pre-existing Mesolithic groups were absorbed into the fold of the Early Iron Age culture. In fact during the period coinciding with the demise of the Buddha, the Early Iron Age culture had already reached the lower montane region of this island. Around the third century BC and later, the settlements expanded in such regions and there is an intensification of activities carried out by commercial and craft guilds, the use of coined money, long-distance trade, the development of new property relations in land, the emergence of relatively large chiefdoms, and quite certainly social stratification.

Institutional formation in the 'peripheral' regions involving 'marginal' communities of the Early Iron Age certainly had its material base beyond the confines of an agrarian economy and the Dry Zone centring around Anurādhapura and Mahāgāma. It is clear that during the Formative Period, mineral resources played a critical role in transforming the social base into a complex one in particular regions. Little attention has been paid both in South India and Sri Lanka to the role of craft production and trade, and more to agriculture, for having played a more critical role in social change, especially during the period of Proto and Early Historic transition. The demand made by both local and external markets was responsible for reaching out to the mineralized zones on the one hand and gradually establishing the Early Historic culture through a series of habitation, religio–cultural centres and interacting route networks on the other.

An increase in the quantitative level of exploitation and utilization of mineral resources could be associated with a relative improvement in the extractive, production and transport technology, a demographic expansion and the structural transformation in the political institutions leading to the emergence of the pristine state. Post-first-century BC developments are mainly seen as attempts at a greater integration of natural resources, more control over labour, and even over distribution by the state and elite groups. The emergence of the developed state and the gradual hierarchization of ecosystems, on the basis of the relative functional status within the state system, gradually witnessed the emergence of the agricultural hinterland sustained by complex hydraulic systems as areas of attraction, while mineralized regions were destined to play the role of repository zones. The scholar–monks who composed Sri Lanka's chronicles were residents of political and ritual centres that dominated this political and economic landscape of the evolved state system of the post-first and second centuries AD. A larger segment of colonial and post-colonial historiography conveniently based itself only on the codified history of the classical texts and rarely probed substratum developments. The rest was history.

12

Towards a New Discourse: Discursive Processes in Early South India

RAJAN GURUKKAL

In South Indian historiography, religion is the central focus of ideological history, the object of the study being conceived as having been completed rather than as an ongoing process. Ideology, though predominantly manifest in religion, is never exclusively confined to it. As a leavening substratum it pervades every intellectual and cultural practice of a society. Religion-centred analysis of ideology not only fails to capture this leavening substratum, but also loses sight of its historical context of social totality. The most useful framework that transcends these limitations is the social formation paradigm, in which a society is perceived as a system resulting from the coexistence and interaction of diverse forms of subsistence.[1] This provides the conceptual prerequisite for the present attempt to understand the discursive processes of society in early South India.[2] In South Indian historiography, discourse analysis is a relatively new exercise both in terms of the perception of

[1] The concept of social formation is developed in Nicos Poulantzas, *State Power Socialisms*, London, 1980. For ideas about mode of production as a combination of several forms of subsistence, *see* Emmanuel Terray, *Marxism and Primitive Societies*, London, 1972. *Also* Godelier, *Perspectives of Marxist Anthropology*, London, 1977, pp. 33ff; Barry Hindes and Paul Hirst, *Pre-capitalist Modes of Production*, London, 1975, pp. 45ff. The overall perspective here is that of the structuralist reading of the mode of production paradigm.

[2] The concept is borrowed from Michel Foucault, *Archaeology of Knowledge*, New York, 1972, but used here within the framework of the materialistic theory of history, the central instrument of analysis for the study. The concept is adopted here, notwithstanding the 'radical' uses to which the post-structuralists have put it. Structuralist Marxists from

ideological phenomena and analysis of their historical context. The attempt here is to view the breakdown of a discourse and the emergence of another in the wake of the deliverance of a new social formation from the pre-existing one. To be specific, the attempt is to discuss the dissolution of the heroic discourse and the emergence of *bhakti*, in terms of how one episteme is supplanted by another.

Early South India, as used here, represents almost a millennium from about the third century BC, as the sources indicate. Spatially it comprises the landmass between the hills of Vēnkaṭam and the tip of Kanyākumāri. The temporal extent subsumes the long duration of the emergence and dissolution of a social formation. The regional specificity, as expressed in the term Tamiḻakam, rests on historically contingent factors such as the linguistic identity and cultural homogeneity of its inhabitants.

History begins in the region with the diffusion of iron technology through the different strands of the Black and Red Ware (BRW) tradition, the widespread prevalence of which dates back to the mid-first millennium BC. Yet very little source material for this early phase exists. From the third century BC onwards we have epigraphical material, however meagre. As we come closer to the turn of the Christian era there are other categories of sources such as Graeco–Roman writings, old coins and the Tamil heroic poems. It is through a methodical and appropriate integration of clues from these various categories of sources that the early historic social formation of South India is reconstructed and its discursive processes made out.

The social formation, as reconstructed from the clues in the sources, was a system combining various forms of subsistence, such as hunting/gathering, herding, shifting cultivation, and wetland agriculture.[3] Adapted to the various ecological systems, these diverse economies, despite the iron technology, were not uniform in terms of the level of productive forces and productivity of labour. This ensemble of unevenly evolved

Althusser to Poulantzas have drawn this crucial distinction between the 'dominant' instance and 'determinant' instance in any mode of production. For them the 'economic' is both dominant and determinant only under capitalism, while in pre-capitalist forms, non-economic instances may be dominant. This opens up the space for using insights derived from discourse analysis.

[3] This has been discussed at length in Rajan Gurukkal, 'Forms of Production and Forces of Change in Ancient Tamil Society', *Studies in History*, vol. V, no. 2, 1989. *Also see* K. Sivathamby, 'Early South Indian Society and Economy: The Tinai Concept', *Social Scientist*, no. 29, 1974.

forms of subsistence is perhaps best represented in the concept of *aintiṇai* comprehending Tamiḻakam as a physiographical conglomeration of five micro eco-zones: the hilly backwoods (*kuṟiñci*), the parched areas (*pālai*), the pastoral tracts (*mullai*), the littoral (*neital*), and the wetland (*marutam*), inhabited respectively by hunters/shifting cultivators (*vēṭar* and *kuṟavar*), cattle lifters (*maṟavar*), pastoralists (*iṭaiyar*), fishing-salt-manufacturing people (*paratavar*), and wetland agriculturists (*uḻavar*). This is a semiotic representation of reality about the ecosystems, their inhabitants and modes of human adaptation. There is a further conceptualization of the physiographic features into a binary between the relatively small agrarian wetland (*menpulam*) and large non-agrarian tracts (*vanpulam*) in the Tamil heroic poetics. What the poetic concepts signify through this semiotic web is the broad scenario of the ecosystems and modes of human existence in a milieu of interaction and shared cultural practices.

The peoples of the micro eco-zones, irrespective of the forms of subsistence, were descent groups dispersed into domestic segments (*kuṭi*) around the respective clan settlement (*ūr*). Each *ūr* was a self-sustaining system made up of *kuṭis* that were independent production units based on the kin labour of the concerned descent group (*kuṭimakkaḷ*). Each descent group had its headman called *kiḻār* who pooled and redistributed the resources of the *ūr*. This elementary structure of chiefdom acquired varying degrees of complexity in terms of the nature and extent of redistributive social relationships. This in turn depended upon the ecosystems and the productive relations within them. There were three categories of chieftains in the ascending order, namely *kiḻār*, *vēḷir* and *vēntar*, the redistributive social relationships of which involved a corresponding increase in complexity. Interspersed with the kin-based production units of the clan settlements of the various chiefdoms, there existed *brāhmaṇa* households with a different system of productive relations devoid of kinship. Prestations and predatory exactions were the usual modes of chiefly appropriation of resources, and gifts and redistribution their instituted channels of social sharing. Plunder was the principal means of exacting the resources and was beyond the control of clan ties for all categories of chieftains.

This did not preclude other formal means of circulating the resources. The early forms of exchange, as ascriptive and customary practices, date back to the late Stone Age. Formal exchange became more extensive with the Iron Age, the closing phase of which overlaps with the period of the Tamil heroic poems. The punch-marked coins that reached from the Gangetic region, the names of specialist merchants seen in the Tamil Brāhmī label inscriptions, the Roman coins brought by the long-distance traders, and the writings by the Graeco–Roman geographers provide evidence of mercantile circulation of resources.[4] We start getting coins of the *vēntar* chiefdoms and pottery graffiti shedding more light on the extent of local participation in organized exchanges. However, the overall nature of contemporary internal exchanges, as depicted in the heroic poems, was by and large that of reciprocity based on use-value. The influx of gold and silver as coins and bullion that characterized the period thus provides insufficient proof to argue for the existence of a monetized economy. The coins and bullion seem to have functioned as part of valuables rather than as money.[5] What emerges is the picture of a social formation dependent on multiple forms of economies, kin-based relations of production, redistributive system of social appropriation, and predatory political control.

As chiefdom-level societies of prestations, gifts and redistribution maintained through the politics of frequent raids for plunder, the production and circulation of heroic discourse was central to their cultural practices. The Tamil heroic poems that are amazingly extensive vouch for this. These were primarily bardic compositions embodying knowledge based on the discursive practices of the heroic society. The bardic form of communication and dissemination of knowledge dominated the prevalent culture of redistributive economy and discursive social relationships. The social conditions of the realization of the familial labour of

[4] The labels refer to specialist merchants such as *pon-vaṇikan* (gold merchant) *koḻu-vaṇikan* (ploughshare merchant or ironmonger), *aruvai-vaṇikan* (textile merchant), *uppu-vaṇikan* (salt merchant) and *panita-vaṇikan* (beverage merchant probably dealing with toddy). See the interpretations in I. Mahadevan, *Tamil Brahmi Inscriptions*, Madras, 1970. *See*, for the details of Graeco–Roman writings, W.H. Schoff, *The Periplus of the Erythraean Sea*, New York, 1912; McCrindle, *Ancient India as Described in Classical Literature*, rpt. Westminster, 1975; K.A. Nilakantha Sastri, *Foreign Notices of South India*, Madras, 1939. For details about the numismatic evidence, *see* W. Elliot, *Coins of Southern India*, Trubner, 1886; H. Mattingly, *Roman Coins*, rpt., London, 1960. Details of places and their coin hoards are given in K.V.S. Aiyar, *Historical Sketches of the Dekhan*, vol. I, Madras, 1917, pp. 86–7. *Also see* P.L. Gupta, *The Early Coins from Kerala*, Trivandrum, 1965, p. 65.

[5] In a society of kin-based redistribution and of gifts and prestations, profit-oriented exchange would be unlikely. *See* M. Sahlins, 'On the Sociology of Primitive Exchange', *in* M. Banton (ed.), *The Relevance of Models for Social Anthropology*, London, 1968, pp. 139ff. Also, Mac Adams, 'Anthropological Perspectives on Ancient Trade', *Current Anthropology*, no. 15, pp. 239–58. Another point is that in such a society money does not make any sense. Money enters its exchange systems as a valuable and forms part of the

the *kutis* that were interlocked through the clan ties of the *ūr*, were obviously discursive. This would suggest that the role of discourse in the relations of production was decisive.

The discursive processes of a society are best represented in its literature which is a domain of innovative expressions linked to the power–knowledge praxis. In this context the Tamil heroic poems derive enormous importance as a collection of socially symbolic texts. Projecting chieftains and warriors as heroes and glorifying their might, mien, and munificence, the poems legitimize raids for plunder, capture of booty, redistribution and gift-giving. Articulated under the structural imposition of the social formation and facilitating the reproduction of redistributive social relationships, the form and content of the heroic poems were discursive.

Collected, classified, and redacted at a relatively later date, the Tamil heroic poems are now available to us in the form of anthologies. *Eṭṭuttokai* (the eight anthologies) and *Pattuppāṭṭu* (the ten idylls) are the two major collections of anthologies whose classificatory norms transcend our notion of chronology and history. With a few exceptions, most of the anthologies belong to a period roughly from the third century BC to the third century AD, which is the most intelligible phase of ancient social formation in South India. Scholars have considered the Tamil grammatical treatise entitled *Tolkāppiyam*, the didactical texts grouped as *Patineṇkīḻkkaṇakku*, and the twin epics known as *Cilappatikāram* and *Maṇimēkalai* as part of the corpus of 'Sangam literature', which is a misnomer applied to designate the ancient Tamil texts.[6] Besides their baffling problem of chronology, the ancient Tamil texts pose a variety of other problems for historians attempting to derive evidence from them. Following the diction of heroic compositions, they use formulaic expressions, stock phrases, and symbols representing underlying meaning, preventing us from taking them literally. The task of decoding the real meaning of the texts thus involves arduous exercises, ranging from syntagmatic analysis of morphology to paradigmatic, psycho–analytical and semiological analyses.[7] The absence of precise chronology or

treasure. *See* the relevant concepts in C. Meillassoux (ed.), *The Development of Indigenous Trade and Markets in West Africa*, London, 1971, pp. 67ff.

[6] K. Kailasapathy, *Tamil Heroic Poetry*, London, 1968, pp. 3–4.

[7] For the details of syntagmatic analysis, *see* F. Saussure, *Course in General Linguistics*, New York, 1959. *Also see* the demonstration of the method of syntagmatic structural analysis in V. Propp, *Morphology of the Folktale*, New York, 1979. For the method and concepts of paradigmatic structural analysis, *see* Claude Lévi-Strauss, *Structural*

symbolism is not a serious impediment since the focus here is essentially on what is discursively significant in the poems, and this scarcely requires the specific date of each poem to be established. What I attempt to chart is the discursive internality of literature and its relation to the social formation.

The discursive constituents, as clusters of semantic signs of the heroic poems, are encapsulated in a series of poetic codes in the Tamil heroic poetry. What is fundamental to the Tamil heroic poetics is the dual concept of *tiṇai* and *tuṟai*, denoting the situation and context respectively, for the presentation of specific moods in the poems.[8] The concept of *tiṇai* has a wider connotation in the sense that it articulates the reality about the man–nature situation of the times. Beyond this apparent reality, it has a realm of interpretive meaning that transcends its formal structure and function. Similarly, the concept of *tuṟai* which denotes the thematic context of the poems has a regime of interpretive meaning hidden beneath its apparent meaning and formal function as defined in poetics. Both *tiṇai* and *tuṟai* bear within their form a series of enunciative codes that help us delve into their semantic world of signs and paradigms.

There are about nine enunciative codes in the poetics, around the concept of *tiṇai*, as listed here: (a) *tumpait-tiṇai*, versifying the situation of warriors getting ready for a raid; (b) *vañcit-tiṇai*, of warriors arriving for raiding the enemy's territory; (c) *kāñcit-tiṇai*, of defending against a raid; (d) *noccit-tiṇai* of warriors guarding the wall; (e) *veṭcit-tiṇai*, of raiding cattle; (f) *karantait-tiṇai*, of raid for recovering the cattle; (g) *vākait-tiṇai*, of devastation and martial rejoicing after killing enemies in a raid; (h) *uḻiññai-tiṇai*, of warriors returning after a raid; and (i) *pāṭāṇ-tiṇai*, of the situation of a bard singing the hero's fame, might, mien, and munificence. Among these, all except the last are based on flower symbolism according to which the flowers such as *tumpai, vañci, kāñci, nocci, veṭci, karantai, vākai*, and *uḻiññai* are considered symbolic of the respective situations. In poetics these constituted distinct thematic situations, but in the hermeneutics with which we are concerned they constitute the diverse codes of a single discourse.

Anthropology, London, 1963. Aspects of symbols and unconscious meaning analysed in psychoanalytical studies are discussed in Alan Dundes, 'The Study of Folklore in Literature and Culture: Identification and Interpretation', in his *Analytic Essays in Folklore*, The Hague, 1975.

[8] See discussions in Kamil Zvelebil, *The Smile of Murugan*, Leiden, 1973, pp. 9–22; K. Kailasapathy, op. cit., pp. 16ff.

There are about thirty-five enunciative codes around the concept of *turai*, which may be grouped here into five clusters of closely related meanings:

(a) *turais* extolling individual heroism, for instance, *tānainilai*, versifying the context of the kind of heroism exalted both by the fighters and the fought; *nallicai* vañci, the context of a hero's march with an intrinsic potential of devastation; *alilattu*, the context of a hero destroying the enemies with a spear pulled out from his own chest; *pillaippeyarcci*, the courage of a hero ignoring evil omens; *makatpārkañci*, a hero's courage to deny his daughter even to a *vēntar* seeking to marry her; and *erumaimaram*, the context of a hero fighting the enemies single-handed;

(b) *turais* extolling the family tradition and heritage of heroes, for instance, *ērāṇmullai*, versifying the context of praising the family tradition of a hero; *kuṭinilaiyuraittal*, of praising the heroic tradition of a warrior family; *mutal vañci*, of praising a warrior's ancestral tradition of heroic exploits; *vallanmullai*, of praising the place and family of a hero; and *mūtinmullai*, of praising the warrior families by depicting even their womenfolk as innately courageous;

(c) *turais* extolling the virtues of raids for plunder, for instance, *malapulavañci*, versifying the context of raid and devastation of settlements; *korravallai*, of expressing grief in the plight of the devastated as an indirect way of praising the might of the hero; *cerumalaital*, of praising a hero shedding horror through his cattle raid; and *vāṇmankalam*, of praising the power of a hero's sword;

(d) *turais* extolling the collective passion of the communities for raid, for instance, *uṇṭāṭṭu*, versifying the context of collective drinking and dining by the warrior folk before setting out for a raid; *peruñcōrrunilai*, of rice feast offered to the warrior folk; *talaittōrram*, of collective rejoicing at the news of a hero bringing cattle as booty; *uvakaikkalulcci*, of a wife shedding tears of joy at the sight of her husband's chest covered with wounds; and

(e) *turais* extolling the act of gift-giving, for instance, *iyanmolivālttu*, versifying the context of praising the boundary of a chief; *pāṇārruppaṭai*, of a bard directing another to a chief by praising his generosity; *virali-yārruppaṭai*, of a *virali* (female bard) persuading another to go to a chief by singing his bounty; *pulavarārruppaṭai*, of a poet praising a chieftain's bounty in order to secure a specific gift.

All these distinct enunciative codes of poetics are signifiers of the same discursive formation. They signify the discursive formation behind the dominant mode of organizing and recognizing contemporary thought and action. Beyond their functional meaning as distinct classificatory elements of poetics, they project the message of the primacy of the values and passions of a heroic society. They signify the various intrinsic notions of a society based on raids for plunder and redistribution of booty. It is quite natural that the enunciative categories of heroic poetics do so.

This would suggest that generalizations about the hegemonic status of the heroic discourse made solely on the basis of clues from heroic poetics need not invariably be true since we cannot expect the heroic poems to represent all aspects of the society. The heroic compositions do however also contain allusions to the non-martial aspects of life. Indeed, several anthologies among the corpus of heroic narratives are entirely devoted to non-martial, non-heroic themes, though their diction clearly exhibits the link with the heroic literature. Even the compositions that are exclusively about martial exploits do maintain a resonance of the other dimensions of contemporary society. What is brought to bear in all compositions is, however, the hegemony of the heroic discourse. It is quite unlikely to be otherwise in a society of plunder-based redistributive economy.

All institutional forms and cultural practices of the period vouch for the hegemony of the heroic discourse. The institution of *vaṭakkiruttal*, which was a ritual of self-immolation by a hero wounded on his back, through fasting, seated in penance facing the north, is one example. To be wounded on the back was the most ignominious thing for a warrior who always would cherish death by wounds to his chest. Cultural practices such as *uṇṭāṭṭu*, the collective drinking and dining of the warriors; *tuṇankai-kūttu*, dance performed by female bards, and *kuravai-kūttu*, dance by the womenfolk of the warriors, are direct manifestations of the heroic discourse. The nature of deities and modes of worship in the various *tiṇais* is another pointer to the hegemony of the heroic discourse. Cēyōn or Murukan of the *kuṟiñci*, hero stones of the *pālai*, Māyōn of the *mullai*, Vēntan of the *marutam* and Varuṇa of the *neital* are the deities or objects of worship prescribed in the poetics.[9] The cult of heroism was central to the worship of all these deities despite their distinct functional meanings in relation to the economic processes of the respective *tiṇai*. Thus we see Cēyōn as a deified hunter hero, Māyōn as the deified cowherd hero, and so on, all exhibiting, though in varying degrees, the effects of the heroic discourse. However, an agriculturist not

[9] For details of the concept of deities in each tiṇai, *see* N. Subrahmanian, *Sangam Polity*, Bombay, 1966, pp. 352ff. *Also see* R. Champakalakshmi, 'Vaisnava Concepts in Early Tamil Nadu', *Journal of Indian History*, vol. L.XX, pt III, 1972.

being a warrior by himself, the deity of the farming communities, i.e. Vēntan, the rain god, hardly had a context to incarnate as a hero. Though often taken as the counterpart of Indra, the warrior image of the Vedic deity is absent in Vēntan. It is significant that he is largely celebrated in later works such as *Paripāṭal, Cilappatikāram*, and *Maṇimēkalai*. However, the system of worship among the agriculturists too had to function within the broad social unity of shared cultural practice.

This does not mean that there was no dissenting voice within the overarching hegemony of heroic discourse. The discursive content of contemporary cultural practices, institutional structures, and political operations could never have been univocal since the social formation was an ensemble of different economies with contradictory interests. The coexistence of antagonistic voices with the hegemonic is attested to by the enunciative codes in poetics. They are grouped into three categories of discursive prescriptions.

(a) The category of the *tuṟai* codes stressing the importance of peace and security as exemplified by *ceviyarivūru*, versifying the context of offering advice to chieftains regarding the maintenance of peace, order, and security in society.

(b) the category of the *tuṟai* codes stressing the importance of asceticism and other-worldly life as exemplified by *porunmoḻikkāñci*, versifying the context of advising a chieftain about what gives strength in this and the other worlds; and *perunkāñci*, the context of appraising a chieftain about the transient nature of the worldly life; and

(c) the category of the *tuṟai* codes stressing the importance of *brāhmaṇas* and the Vedic, Purāṇic and Śāstric discourses as exemplified by *pārppanavākai*, versifying the context of praising *brāhmaṇas* and brahmanical rituals; *mutumoḻikkāñci*, of conversing on *dharma, artha* and *kāma*; and *manaiyaṟam*, of distinguishing between the ascetic and family life.

These are obviously discursive signs transmitting values and passions antagonistic to what was hegemonic in the social formation. Emphasis on values of peace, spirituality, and order was antagonistic to the discursive milieu of raids for plunder and redistribution of booty. Some of the poems of these *tuṟais* advise the chieftains to offer protection to agriculturists from the raids and to hold themselves aloof from the instigators of raids. They exhort the chieftains to refrain from predatory campaigns that lead to the destruction of agricultural settlements. This is a reflection of the voice of dissent against the heroic discourse which was reproducing the conditions of its perpetuation through various institutions and practices.

The coexistence of the antagonistic voices with the hegemonic was rooted in the contradictory dynamic of the social formation. The contradictions were being generated through the process of the coexistence of conflicting forms of production and their collective functioning as a system. The plight of plough agriculture, as enmeshed in the institutional structures and strategies of primitive agriculture and pastoralism, shows perhaps the most glaring of all the contradictions. The institutions, ideas, and other forms of culture generated and maintained by the society of cattle-breeders and primitive agriculture were altogether inimical to the growth of plough agriculture. The former was the dominant form of production despite the fact that the latter was superior in terms of both technology and productivity. The political practices and institutional forms were the result of articulations at the economy of agro–pastoralism.[10] The instituted practices like raids for plunder, gifts, redistribution, bardic compositions, and so on dominated the social life of the period. Predatory marches of chieftains, their destruction of agriculture and agrarian settlements were extremely detrimental to the development of plough agriculture. Burning of crops and settlements referred to in the poems as *eriparantetuttal* was routine to all kinds of raids.[11] There is an echo of the helpless voice of agriculturists in certain poems that characterize them as defenceless people who knew no weapon other than plough and no bow other than the rainbow.[12] Kallāṭanār gives in *Puṟanāṉūṟu* (Pn) 23 a representative instance of agrarian settlements devastated by a raid. Pāṇṭaran Kaṇṇanār alludes in Pn. 16 to the burning of agricultural fields which knew no forest other than fields of sugar-cane. Nettimaiyar describes in Pn. 15 another instance of burning fields of crops as part of the atrocities of a raid. The raids of predatory chieftains that swept through the agrarian tracts caused far wider destruction of grain than was exacted.

Being stereotypical and formulaic, these poetic allusions are hardly

[10] The political practices point to a chiefdom-level society. Institutions and ideas such as plunder raid, redistribution and heroic poems signify the economic milieu of agro-pastoralism. The conceptual scenario invoked here is that of the processes of the political evolution of early society as discussed in Hindes and Hirst, *Pre Capitalist Modes of Production*, pp. 26ff. See the characterization of pre-state societies in Claessen and Skalnik (eds), *The Early State*, The Hague, 1978. *Also* R. Thapar, *From Lineage to State*, New Delhi, 1984, pp. 24ff.

[11] See the songs of Vañcittiṇai in *Puṟanāṉūṟu*.

[12] See *Puṟanāṉūṟu*, poem 20. Empirical details of the problem are given in Rajan Gurukkal, 'Aspects of Iron Age Economy: Problems of Agrarian Expansion in Tamilakam', *in* B.D. Chattopadhyaya (ed.), *Ancient Indian Economic History*, Delhi, 1987.

historical as regards social life *per se*. They are only conventional poetic motifs. However, these conventional motifs should be historicized in the sense that they signify the collective reality of contemporary society, albeit not in terms of their apparent meanings. The cry for the protection of agriculturists and the exhortations for abstaining from raids and encouraging peace emerge as a voice of dissent from this collective reality.

At the same time, however, the importance of plough agriculture was also a matter of social recognition. Its overall significance and primacy is reflected in the poems. The poetics has a specific enunciative code under the *tuṟai* concept, namely *ērkaḷuruvakam* dealing with constructs based on imagery from the labour processes of plough agriculture. All poems belonging to this *tuṟai* draw upon a hero's fight in a language of metaphors relating to the activities of plough agriculture, equating him with an agriculturist, his weapon with the plough, fighting ground with the agricultural field, fighting with the act of ploughing, and so on.[13] This would suggest that though the significance of plough agriculture was tacitly recognized in the social rhetoric, the contradiction involved in the reproduction of institutional forms and cultural practices impeding the growth of agriculture was not realized. There is nothing unnatural about this since the dominant form of production was agro–pastoralism which generated and perpetuated the politics of plunder as fundamental to the maintenance of the complex system of redistributive social relationships.

Elsewhere it has been argued that plough agriculture was the dominant economic form during the period and the totalization on the basis of heroic poems could be misleading.[14] This argument makes no sense however since theoretically a society with such an enormous volume of heroic compositions could only have been a system structured by the dominance of the heroic discourse. The antagonistic voices that we have identified from the enunciative codes of heroic poetics themselves are clear indicators of the subordinate status of agriculturists in comparison to that of the warriors. Moreover, the overarching political structure of

[13] See Ērkaḷuruvakam tuṟai songs in *Puṟanāṉūṟu*.

[14] There are studies characterizing the society in an entirely different way. For instance, a well-developed civilization has been attributed to the society in question in V. Kanakasabhai, *Tamils Eighteen Hundred Years Ago*, Madras, 1904. Indeed, almost every nationalist historian of South India conceived the society more or less in the same way. The perspective also recurs in certain modern works. N. Subrahmanian, op. cit.; Singaravelu, *Social Life of the Tamils*, Kuala Lumpur, 1966.

the period is strong evidence of the domination of the redistributive economy in which sedentary agriculture was struggling to secure its conditions of development.

The contradictions at the economic level were being regenerated continuously through the coexistence and interaction of the conflicting forms of production. An outstanding consequence of the economic process of resource redistribution in the discursively realized pattern of social relationships, was intensification of the contradictions. Raids involved capture of *ūr* (settlement) and its redistribution among warrior chiefs which would mean imposition of predatory right of alien chiefs over descent groups.[15] Though not in the form of actual land grants, *brāhmaṇas* as scholarly bards and Vedic priests, seem to have been given gifts of *ūr*, obviously as a part of the redistribution system. Such gifts must have given rise to individual holdings against communal holdings. In the case of gifts of *ūr*, probably the right of exaction to warrior chiefs beyond the clan kinship must have given rise to the formation of chiefly lineages branched off from clans. But the gifts of *ūr* to *brāhmaṇas* would mean formation of their households involving far-reaching changes in terms of relations of production, because it was much more than the superimposition of an alien right of exaction. The *brāhmaṇas* being a non-cultivating group by themselves had to depend upon the familial labour of neighbouring clans for the cultivation of their land. This meant making some permanent arrangement for the supply of labour in the *brāhmaṇa* households, obviously a system transcending kinship. The *brāhmaṇa* land with his household thus emerged as an independent unit of production with working clansmen families attached to it. The centre of *brāhmaṇa* households is referred to in the poems as *pārpanac-cēri*, which in the present context signifies the alternative system of agrarian relations counterposed to what was dominant. The development of the alternative system was itself a process aggravating systemic contradictions.

The *brāhmaṇa* household as a nexus of new relations reverberated with the anticipatory traits of a new discourse through the Vedic, Purāṇic and Śāstraic texts. They inevitably emitted the values and norms of *brāhmaṇa* households as the antagonistic voice struggling to be heard in the heroic society. Discursive formations broadly akin to the brahmanical ones in terms of their antagonism to the heroic discourse were

[15] Such evidence is examined at length in M.G.S. Narayanan, 'Warrior Settlements in the Sangam Age', *Proceedings of the Indian History Congress*, 1982, pp. 102–9.

gradually beginning to appear also with the spread of the heterodox religions. Though there is no reason to assume that the Jains and Buddhists were concerned about the values of agrarian society, their interest in social peace can indeed be assumed. The Jains and Buddhists had always been in favour of the communities engaged in exchanges whose operations required peace and order as an essential prerequisite. This circumvents the discursive needs of agriculturists and the social groups engaged in exchange of goods. It must be remembered here that the new discursive formation that was yet to secure dominance in the social formation of the Tamil south had already become the dominant discourse in the Deccan and further north even before the close of the first millennium BC. In the Deccan the society contemporaneous with the Tamil heroic society was structured enough to constitute a full-blown state apparatus while the latter was weltering in the presages of state formation.[16] The concept of a king, kingdom, and kingly authority does exist at the level of the rhetoric of heroic Tamil poetry as bardic implantation for the glorification of the status of chiefdoms. Ideas on periodic exactions, patronage of agriculturists, and intensification of production as opposed to predatory campaigns do reach the ears of chieftains, but to fall flat as dissonant impulses within a pre-state society.

Similarly, the brahmanical discourse of social differentiation and stratification does seek to express itself through the changing conditions around the brahmanical households themselves. But stratification was primarily confined to the binary between the *uyarntōr* (the high-born) and *iḻipiṟappāḷar* (the low-born), primarily differentiating the *brāhmaṇas* and patrons from the clansfolk. Though the beginnings of caste system can be made out as implicit within the social nexus of *brāhmaṇa* households, the larger society remained casteless.[17] At the same

[16] The processes of state formation in South India are examined in Seneviratne, 'Pre-State to State Societies: Transformations in the Political Ecology of South India with Specific Reference to Tamil Nadu', *in* R. Champakalakshmi (ed.), *State in Pre-Colonial South India* (forthcoming). Also Rajan Gurukkal, 'Social Formation and Political Processes in Early Tamilakam', ibid.

[17] Scholars have sought to argue that four castes existed in Tamiḻakam that were different from the castes under the varṇa order. *See* N. Subrahmanian, 1966, op. cit., pp. 255ff. But this argument is not sustained by evidences. What is often considered is a poem in *Puṟanāṉūṟu* (335) that mentions the four *kuṭis* of the settlement. The poem obviously talks only about the particular village. Moreover, the term *kuṭi* acquired the meaning of caste only later.

time it was not entirely classless either, albeit without an objectively identifiable level of class domination. As the contradictions immanent in the social formation and the voices emitting values exotic to the heroic discourse would indicate, the process of class differentiation was continuing and the strategies of domination were in the making. An impending crisis was implicit in the contradictory dynamic of the social formation that could hardly sustain itself for long with its low labour productivity and limited scope of economic reproduction.[18]

There is however no direct evidence for a total crisis leading to the dissolution of the Tamil heroic society. A disjunction is explicit in the sources, both archaeological and literary, which in terms of their existing chronology and historical context would have us believe that the principal chiefdoms went into oblivion by the close of the third century AD. None of the heroic poems sing the exploits of a chieftain belonging to the period after the third century nor can the historians clearly identify any chieftain of the well-known chiefdoms reigning during that period. The heroic compositions of typical bardic diction too seem to have been discontinued by this time. There is a corresponding discontinuity also of the institution of raids and booty redistribution. This is synchronized by a marked decline in the post-third century layers of the major archaeological sites. The sites with Buddhist association, however, provide evidence for continued development.[19] Historians have been associating the period with the inroads by a predatory people known as Kaḷabhras who belonged to the uplands of Karnataka.[20] They seem to have swept through the domains of the Tamil chieftains and caused their eclipse. However, the Kaḷabhra episode can hardly be so fundamental as to usher in major changes and the disappearance of the chiefdoms calls for an alternative explanation that can account for substantial socio–political changes.

[18] Following the studies on complex redistributive societies, one can conceptualize the internal economic dynamic of the early historic Tamil society. The contradictory dynamic as an ever-mounting problem of complex redistributive societies is discussed in E. Terray, op. cit., pp. 53ff. Also Godelier, op. cit., pp. 81ff. A conceptual generalization about the problem of low labour productivity and limited prospects for economic reproduction as features immanent in the redistributive society is given in Hindes and Hirst, op. cit., pp. 42ff.

[19] *Indian Archaeology: A Review*, 1964–5 and 1970–1.

[20] Almost all historians of South India who had to discuss the early history have referred to the Kaḷabhras, and many have attempted to identify them. The generally accepted view is that they were a marauding tribe from the uplands of Karnataka. For a specialized study on the period, *see* M. Arunachalam, 'The Kalabhras in the Pāṇḍya Country and Their Impact on the Life and Letters There, Madras University, 1979.

What is to be considered fundamental here is the contradictory dynamic of the social formation that matured over the years and culminated in a rupture. It is not unlikely that the predatory marches of the Kaḷabhras accentuated the culmination process which seemingly had evil effects on the *brāhmaṇas* whose hardships of that time have gone down as the memories of the Kali age in a few copper plates of the eighth and ninth centuries.[21]

The historical process of the maturing of the contradictory dynamic and the consequent dissolution of the social formation can only be understood as a theoretical construct and not as empirical reality, for the characteristic frailties of the sources seldom bear directly upon what is investigated. The question therefore of direct evidence in matters concerning the transformation of Tamil heroic society into a new system of relations and values does not arise. One could only search for indirect clues. Those suggesting the discontinuity of ideas and institutions typical of the heroic society are our most valid clues. The discontinuity explicit in the existing chronological understanding of the heroic poems need not be accidental. Both the present state of knowledge about the poems and the absence of evidence for the continuation of the chiefdoms go well with the ever-intensifying contradictory dynamic immanent in the heroic society of prestations, gifts, and redistribution, making systemic dissolution inevitable. This would at once confirm the alleged discontinuity and account for the absence of evidence which is not altogether accidental.

A much greater and more substantive factor that stresses discontinuity is the presence of a new class of literature and inscriptions datable about a century later and radically different from the heroic compositions and the cave labels. Their objects, contexts, and strategies bear no comparison with those of the heroic texts and cave labels.

It is the *Kīḻkkaṇakku* texts belonging to the fourth to fifth centuries AD, that constituted the new class of literature significantly separated from the diction of the heroic tradition, albeit without moving away from the domain of oral compositions.[22] Most of these texts are didactic, specializing in the social ethic and personal conduct. Even in others which are not avowedly ethical, there is a stress on the importance of peace,

[21] The Vēḷvikkuṭi plates of the Pāṇḍyas provide us with direct allusions to the period of the Kaḷabhras as equal to that of the Kali, but it is a relatively later record referring to the earlier period. As a recurring motif the Kaḷabhra–Kali terms of evil social experiences appear in a few other copper plates belonging to the Calukyas and Cōḷas.

[22] There are eighteen texts in *Kīḻkkaṇakku* literature. Most of them deal with ethical postulates. *The Tirukkuṟaḷ* may be the most popular.

loyalty, and social morality. The existence of a body of literature emphasizing such values presupposes a situation desperately in need of them. They all seemingly address themselves to a society of transitional complexities ranging from general disorder to specific problems of new relations and values replacing the old. The texts are not directly concerned with the ethical task of highlighting the social imperative to establish order in collective life that is incidental to their central thematic concerns. But as discursive impulses generated under the influence of social processes, their ethical postulates are more important in the context of discourse analysis. They constitute the running thread across the texts that draw upon diverse themes. In certain cases the didactic elements are explicit and direct, while in others they are implicit and succinct. Those that are explicit and direct are in the forms of exhortations for obedience, hard work and loyalty in the society.[23] All those that are implicit and succinct exude the values of agrarian society organized into relations transcending kinship. In sum, the new class of literature seems to take the form of statements of a new discursive formation transcending the semantic regime of the heroic discourse.

The other category of a radically different source indicating the breakdown of the heroic discourse is a set of two rock inscriptions in Tamil Brāhmī characters of the fifth-sixth centuries AD.[24] The date of one inscription is given in the beginning as 192nd year of an unspecified era. The inscription refers to a certain king Cēntan Kūṟṟan, who is not seen in any of the known royal genealogies. He could probably be the father of Kūṟṟap-Perum Cēntan of *Muttoḷḷāyiram*, a work not far removed from the period. Unlike the earlier label inscriptions, they document a land transaction for the creation of an agrarian settlement under the *brāhmaṇas* and set down the rights, privileges, and obligations of landholders, leaseholders, and actual tillers. The records represent the transactional relations of an asymmetrically structured society composed of diverse categories of people grouped on the basis of their rights over land. This is a social structure almost entirely alien to the heroic society. The records registering the orders of the ruling powers voice an echo of a political authority that bears no comparison with that of predatory chiefdoms.

[23] *Tirukkuṟaḷ*, verses 731ff.

[24] See the particulars of the inscription in R. Nagaswamy, 'An Outstanding Epigraphical Discovery in Tamil Nadu', *Proceedings of the Fifth International Conference Seminar on Tamil Studies*, Madurai, 1981. Also, Y. Subbarayalu, 'A Note on the Socio-economic Milieu of the Pulankurichi Rock Inscription', *Avanam-3*, 1993.

One might feel sceptical about the assumption of the alleged discontinuity as it is grounded on the availability of certain new types of sources whose data are different. But, as has already been pointed out, the availability of new types of sources only at a relatively later date is not accidental in the sense that they represent a social formation that is altogether new. A document like the Pūlānkurichchi rock inscription registering a land transaction and land rights is anachronistic to the heroic period that was characterized by co-operative farming and collective appropriation. Though gift-giving played a very crucial role in the maintenance of the status, ranking and authority of chieftains, it did not seem to have developed into the institution of land grants during the heroic period.

It is true that the colophons of the heroic anthologies do refer to land grants to bards, particularly the *brāhmaṇa* bards who also officiated at Vedic rituals.[25] But there is a time lag of three or four centuries between the poems and their colophons, which accounts for their presence.[26] Landholding by the *brāhmaṇas* as distinguished from communal holding was known to the heroic society, but it was, as has already been noted, the beginnings and rights over land were yet to be evolved through the emergence of intermediaries. The *brāhmaṇa* households of the heroic period were in fact anticipatory constituents of the evolving social system that manifested itself with its institutional structures by the time of the Pūlānkurichchi records. Despite the linkage in terms of mode of production, the earlier *brāhmaṇa* households and the subsequently structured brahmanical society were two different entities, the former as part of the social formation dominated by primitive agriculture and animal husbandry and the latter dominated by irrigated agriculture. What appears therefore as disjunction between the old and new sources is the distance of the evolutionary process between two social formations.

The treatment of the *Kīḻkkaṇakku* texts as a new class of literature representing discontinuity of heroic society can be controversial since their existence as a single corpus owes to their compilation and not to their origin. There is no uniformity of theme nor chronology for these texts which are classified as *Kīḻkkaṇakku* on arbitrary criteria adopted by the compilers. In addition to their thematic diversity, the texts had different religious affiliations through their brahmanical, Jain, and Buddhist authors. Above all, what is important is the thread of social ethic

[25] N. Subrahmanian, op. cit., pp. 275ff.

[26] K. Kailasapathy, op. cit., p. 4.

running through the diversity of their themes and religious affiliation. Even if no uniform chronology for them exists, they all fall within a comprehensive period during which their appearance amounts to a spate of didactical compositions. It is this spate of ethical texts during the fourth–fifth centuries that makes the assumption of discontinuity reasonable. The intellectual construct of one social formation dissolving into another accounts for the crowding of works on social ethic during a specific span of time. It is not the potential of discursive breakthrough in their ethical postulates that enables these texts to represent the discontinuity of heroic tradition, but their potential for domination.

The discursive content of the *Kīḻkkaṇakku* texts had its rudimentary beginnings in the heroic society itself, as we have shown while discussing the enunciative codes of certain *tuṟais* like Ceviyaṟivuṟu, Poruṇmoḻikkāñci, Mutumoḻikkāñci, Pārppana-Vākai, and Manaiyaram, stressing the values of peace, order and security of social life. These enunciative codes emitting antagonistic impulses have to be viewed as anticipatory constituents of the discursive formation taking shape in the *Kīḻkkaṇakku* texts. Despite this linkage, there is a distance of two social formations between them. One was part of the dissonant voice counterposed to the heroic discourse of the ancient social formation where it lacked the potential for domination. The other represented the initial statements of the emerging hegemonic discourse with the potential for domination.

What is reflected in the ethical postulates of the *Kīḻkkaṇakku* texts and the transactions of the Pulankurichchi records is the developmental process of a new-born social formation structured by the dominance of agrarian relations. It was a long process witnessing the development of a complex system of hierarchical social relations of production and distribution out of an essentially simple system of production relations evolved in the earlier *brāhmaṇa* households. In the background were the waning trails of the dissolving heroic society, concomitant to which a dialectical process of discursive transformation was also taking place. What was the voice of dissent in the heroic society subsequently becomes a new discourse and the voice of dominance in the agrarian society. Here the contours of the new discourse are not complete and final since they were augmented further through the process of subjectification within the new social formation. Just as the social relations were yet to acquire greater complexity, the discursive domain was also very much in the making.

The social relations began to be further structured during the sixth–seventh centuries with the steady expansion of plough agriculture across the wetland. A perceptible feature of agrarian expansion was the proliferation of *brahmadeya* villages throughout the fertile tracts of the major river valleys in the region. It was a complex process of differentiation, stratification, and political formation leading to the development of a state system and authority structures. Discursive development was inextricably woven into the process and the formation of institutions was part of it. The new political formation represented by the Simhavarman line of the Pallavas and the Kaḍungon line of the Pāṇḍyas owed itself to the developing agrarian society whose expansion was linked to royal patronage.[27] Expansion of agrarian settlements through the creation of *brahmadeyas* often involved the superimposition of the superior rights of the *brāhmaṇas* over the communal holdings and the clan families of the locality. It must have been an intricate process of transformation of primitive agriculture and clan settlements into advanced agriculture and farmer settlements, respectively.

Discourse played the crucial role, probably as the coercive instrument in transforming and organizing people for the labour processes of wetland agriculture. The ethical didactics of the *Kīḻkkaṇakku* works stemming from the discursive elements of Vedic, Purāṇic and Śāstric texts provided the foundation for social organization. It was an extremely intense process of reification that filled the discursive domain, offering prescriptions, explanation, meaning, and legitimacy to the variety of rights, ranks, positions, privileges, entitlements, and obligations binding the hierarchical social relationships. The most potent discursive instrument that stabilized the relations of production was caste, accommodating in its fold a variety of economically stratified functionaries of hereditary trades. As agrarian expansion advanced, human settlements (*ūr*) originally bound by kinship got integrated as agrarian localities (*nāḍu*) which subsequently acquired great political significance in the monarchical system.[28] The role of caste in the integration of the agrarian society whose mechanisms of appropriation were based

[27] These kings represented the *cakravartin* model of consecrated monarchy. See the discussions in B. Stein, 'All the Kings' Maṇa: Perspectives on Kingship in Medieval South India', *in* J. F. Richards (ed.), *Kingship and Authority in South Asia*, Wisconsin, 1977.

[28] The process has been discussed in the light of inscriptions in Y. Subbarayalu, 'The Place of ūr in the Economic and Social History of Early Tamil Nadu', Madras, 1977. Also his *Political Geography of the Cola Country*, Madras, 1973. The evolution of ūr/kuṭi into nāḍu as implicit in certain place names figuring in the early Pāṇḍya inscriptions is discussed in Rajan Gurukkal, 'The Agrarian System and Socio-Political Conditions in the Early Pandya Period, AD 600–1000', Ph.D. dissertation, Jawaharlal Nehru University,

on extra-economic coercion, was extremely crucial. In sum, the realm of ideology became enormously complicated through reification and discourse production catered to the changing functional requirements of the expanding agrarian society.

The formation of agrarian localities was an ongoing process, and everywhere it accomplished a uniform structure of social relations irrespective of whether they were *brāhmaṇa* settlements (*brahmadeyas*) or *veḷḷān-vakai* settlements (*ūr*). The social structure was a hierarchy with landholders (*brahmadeya*-kiḻavar in the case of *brahmadeyas* and ūrār/nāṭṭār in the case of *veḷḷān-vakai* settlements) at the apex and the large number of leaseholders (*kārāḷar*) who were mostly artisans and craftsmen, in the middle, placed over the primary producers (*aṭiyāḷar*) who were at the bottom. Almost parallel to the leaseholders there were many who held small strips of land as hereditary holdings (*kāṇi*) which were also tilled by the primary producers. The circulation of the produce in given shares thus took a structured path through all these categories enjoying differing levels of entitlement. The most benefited were the landholders who were ensured goods and services by the settlers in their land while the most exploited were the primary producers. As part of the social mechanisms of ensuring goods and services to the landholders through the notion of obligation, all artisans and craftsmen were subjected to immobility. The conditions of subjection together with the objective reality of the producers being stripped off their produce constituted the major contradiction in the system. Perpetuating relations of domination through the reproduction of the contradictory dynamic, the discursive regime became distinct by the breakdown of the heroic discourse and the emergence of the alternative.

The most powerful discourse born out of the contradictory dynamic that began to develop during the sixth to seventh centuries was *bhakti*. As a new religious sensibility, it gradually made its appearance in the invocatory stanzas of the heroic anthologies before being institutionalized through the Āḻvār and Nāyanār hymns.[29] The *Paripāṭal*, one of the collections under Eṭṭuttokai introduces the concept of *bhakti*, placing it at the beginning of the new discourse, i.e. the *bhakti* of the Āḻvār/Nāyanār hymns.[30] However, the historical context of *bhakti* as a discourse

1984, pp. 105ff. The place-names with *ūr-kūṟṟam, kuṭi-nāḍu* and *ūr-nāḍu* as suffixes exemplify the process.

[29] See the detailed study on the problem in M.G.S., Narayanan and V. Kesavan, 'Bhakti Movement in South India', *in* S.C. Malik (ed.), *Dissent, Protest and Reform in Indian Civilization*, rev. edn, Simla, 1980.

[30] See the discussion in Kamil Zvelebil, *The Smile of Murugan*, Leiden, 1973, pp. 23ff.

whose genealogy goes far back in time, was the expansion of structured agrarian society of contradictory relations. There it mirrored the way the subjected and exploited lived, the relation between themselves and the objective conditions of their existence. It glossed over the material reality of the conditions of domination by inventing other-worldly explanations for the social contradictions. The discourse provided a psychological basis for social acceptance of the explanation of the plight of the oppressed in the agrarian society. The psychological basis took the form of a cult of complete surrender at the feet of gods as the final refuge, acting as an illusary solace to the miserable. It gained momentum as a cult of personal gods housed in temples that grew up as the nerve centre of agrarian settlements more or less as a sequel to the expansion of agriculture. The hymns of the Āḻvārs and Nāyanārs were composed in praise of these personal gods of temples whose distribution and sacred geography corresponded to the course of agrarian expansion.[31] With the manifestation of the *bhakti* discourse as a temple-based movement in the seventh and eighth centuries, the formation of the dominant ideology of the agrarian society was complete.

Within the mystifying discourse of *bhakti*, voices of dissent against the hegemonic were not precluded. Since it was a social formation of contradictory relations involving the tension of subjection and exploitation, voices of protest were inevitable.[32] The hegemonic discourse was so imposing that the elements of protest and dissent could be articulated only through its discursive practices that neutralized them through the strategy of containment.[33] A detailed analysis of the process is not within the scope of this essay, which stresses the emergence of the voice of dissent in a social system of contradictory relations.

To conclude, what is perceptible about the discursive processes across the two social formations in early South India are: the breakdown of the heroic discourse along with the redistributive social relationships

[31] Veluthat Kesavan, 'The Temple Base of the Bhakti Movement', *The Proceedings of the Indian History Congress*, Delhi, 1979.

[32] How the elements of dissent were absorbed as part of *bhakti* is discussed in M.G.S. Narayanan and V. Kesavan, op. cit.

[33] The concept of the strategy of containment is developed in Lukacs, *History and Class Consciousness*, Berlin, 1971. For an elaboration of the concept by postulating ideology in terms of the strategy of containment, whether intellectual or formal, *see* Frederick Jameson, *The Political Unconscious*, op. cit., pp. 53–4. For an insightful demonstration of the historical process in which one may discern the operation of the mechanisms of containment, *see* Romila Thapar, 'Renunciation: The Making of a Counter Culture', in her *Ancient Indian Social History*, New Delhi, 1978. Also her 'Dissent and Protest in Early Indian Tradition', *Studies in History*, vol. I, no. 2, 1979.

enchained by it; the dissemination of the Vedic, Purāṇic and Śāstric prescriptions as the dissonant impulses; enlargement of the dissonant impulses into the ethical postulates of didactic texts; reification and discourse production within the hegemonic framework in response to the expanding agrarian relations of domination; emergence of *bhakti* as the mitigating force within the social contradictions of subjection and exploitation; and their convergence into a new discourse.

Appendix: Romila Thapar—A Bibliography

BOOKS

Asoka and the Decline of the Mauryas, Oxford, 1961 (updated second edition, 1997).
(Edited), *Problems of Historical Writing in India*, Delhi, 1963.
A History of India, vol. 1, Penguin Books, 1966.
Ancient India, NCERT, New Delhi, 1966 (Model Text-Book for Middle School).
Medieval India, NCERT, New Delhi, 1967 (Model Text-Book for Middle School).
The Past and Prejudice (Sardar Patel Memorial Lectures), New Delhi, 1975.
Exile and the Kingdom: Some Thoughts on the Ramayana, Bangalore, 1978.
Ancient Indian Social History: Some Interpretations, New Delhi, 1978.
From Lineage to State, New Delhi, 1984.
(Edited), *Situating Indian History*, New Delhi, 1986.
The Mauryas Revisited (Deuskar Lectures), Calcutta, 1987.
Cultural Transaction and Early India (Qureishi Memorial Lectures), Delhi, 1987.
Interpreting Early India, Delhi, 1992.
(Edited), *Recent Perspectives of Early Indian History*, Bombay, 1995.
Time as a Metaphor of History: Early India, Delhi, 1996.
Śakuntala: Texts, Readings, Histories, Delhi, 1999.
Cultural Pasts: Essays in Early Indian History, Delhi, 2000.
Narratives and the Making of History: Two Lectures, Delhi, 2000.

PAPERS

The following papers were published in academic journals. Those republished in the collections entitled *Ancient Indian Social History: Some Interpretations, Interpreting Early India* and *Cultural Pasts* are not listed below.

1959: 'The Later Mauryas', *Journal of the Bihar Research Society*, xxxxv, 1–4, pp. 1–15.

1960: 'Asoka and Buddhism', *Past and Present*, 18, pp. 43–51.

1962: 'The Study of Indology: A Case for Reorientation', *The Journal of University Education*, I, 1, pp. 1–9.

1963: 'The Writing of a General History of Ancient India: Some Problems', *in* S. Gopal and R. Thapar (eds), *Problems of Historical Writing in India*, IIC, Delhi, pp. 90–6.

1966: 'The Impact of Trade *c.* 100 BC–AD 300, in India', *in* H. Kruger (ed.), *Kunwar Mohammad Ashraf—An Indian Scholar and Revolutionary (1903–62)*, Akademic Verlag, Berlin, pp. 30–8.

1973: 'The Historian and Archaeological Data', *in* D.P. Agrawal and A. Ghosh (eds), *Radiocarbon and Indian Archaeology*, TIFR, Bombay, pp. 378–90.

1974: 'History of the Indian Sub-continent, 1500 BC–AD 1200', *Encyclopaedia Britannica*, 14th edn (revised in 1992).

1975: 'Asokan India and the Gupta Age', *in* A.L. Basham (ed.), *A Cultural History of India*, Oxford.

1977: 'The Punjab under Emperor Asoka', *in* M.L. Joshi and Fauja Singh (eds), *History of the Punjab*, vol. I, Punjab University, Patiala, pp. 282–99.

1977–78: 'Some Aspects of the Economic Data in the *Mahabharata*', *ABORI*, pp. 993–1007.

1978: 'A Possible Identification of Meluhha, Dilmun and Makan', *JESHO*, XVIII, 1, pp. 1–42.

1979: 'The Historian and the Epic', *ABORI*, LX, i–iv, pp. 199–213; 'Dissent and Protest in the Early Indian Tradition', *Studies in History*, I, 2, pp. 177–96.

Co-authored with M.H. Siddiqi, 'Chota Nagpur: The Pre-colonial and Colonial Situation', *Trends in Ethnic Group Relations*, UNESCO, Paris, pp. 19–64.

1980: 'Durkheim and Weber on Theories of Society and Race Relating to Pre-colonial India', in *Sociological Theories: Race and Colonialism*, UNESCO, Paris, pp. 93–116.

'State Formation in Early India', *International Social Science Journal*, XXXII, 4, pp. 655–70.

1981: 'The Householder and Renouncer in the Brahmanical and Buddhist Traditions', *Contributions to Indian Sociology*, n.s. 15, 1, and 2, pp. 273–98; 'The State and Empire', *in* H.J. Claessen and P. Skalnik (eds), *The Study of the State*, Mouton, The Hague, pp. 409–26; 'Death and the Hero', *in* S.C. Humphreys and H. King (eds), *Mortality and Immortality: The Anthropology and Archaeology of Death*, Academic Press, London, pp. 293–316.

'The Dravidian Hypothesis for the Identification of Meluhha, Dilmun and Makan', in *JESHO*, XXVI, ii, pp. 178–90.

Review article of H. Alahakoon, 'The Later Mauryas', in *The Sri Lanka Journal of the Humanities*, VII, 1 & 2, pp. 153–65.

1982: 'The *Ramayana*: Theme and Variation', *in* S.N. Mukherjee (ed.), *India: History and Thought*, Subarnarekha, Calcutta, pp. 221–53.

'The Evolution of the State in the Ganges Valley in the Mid-first Millennium BC', in *Studies in History*, IV, 2, pp. 181–96.

1983: 'The Archaeological Background to the Agnicayana Ritual', *in* F. Staal (ed.), *Agni*, Asian Humanities Press, Berkeley, pp. 1–40.

1984: 'The Mouse in the Ancestry', *in* S.D. Joshi (ed.), *Amrtdhara*, Ajanta Publications, New Delhi, pp. 427–34; 'Legitimation politique et genealogie en Inde du Nord', in *Annales*, 39, 4, pp. 783–97.

'Milenarismo, religion y sociedad en la India antigua', in *Estudios de Asia y Africa*, XIX, 4, pp. 457–76.

'The Problems of Human Rights in Hindu and Buddhist Traditions', in *Human Rights Teaching*, IV, Paris, pp. 34–8.

'The Oral and the Written in Early India', Bose Memorial Lecture, C.I.E., Delhi University.

1985: 'Asoka', in *Epochen der Weltgeschichte in Biographien*, Band I, Fischer Taschenbuch Verlag, Frankfurt, pp. 159–78.

Presidential Address: Historiography, Section V in *Proceedings of the Andhra Pradesh History Congress*, Kurnool, pp. 178–83.

1986: 'Society and Historical Consciousness: The *Itihasa-purana* tradition', *in* S. Bhattacharya and R. Thapar (eds), *Situating Indian History*, OUP, New Delhi, pp. 353–83.

'A Response to Professor A.M. Shah', in *Contributions to Indian Sociology*, n.s. 20, 2, pp. 289–95.

'State Formation in Early India', *in* A. Kazancigil (ed.), *The State in Global Perspective*, UNESCO, Paris.

1987: 'Religion and the Social Order', *Contributions to Indian Sociology*, 21, 1, pp. 157–64.

'State and Empire: An Attempt at a Definition', *Teaching Politics*, XIII, 3 & 3, pp. 139–48.

'Epigraphic Evidence and Some Indo-Hellenistic Contacts during the Mauryan

Period', *in* S.K. Maity and U. Thakur (eds), *Indological Studies*, Abhinav Publications, New Delhi, pp. 15–19.

'Indian Views of Europe: Representations of the "Other" in History', University of Heidelberg.

'Archaeological Artifacts and Literary Data: An Attempt at Co-relation', *in* B.M. Pande and B.D. Chattopadhyaya (eds), *Archaeology and History*, Agam Kala Prakashan, Delhi.

1988: 'The Social Role of Craftsmen and Artists in Early India', *in* M. Meister (ed.), *Making Things in South Asia: The Role of Artist and Craftsman*, University of Pennsylvania, pp. 10–17.

1989: 'Epic and History: Tradition, Dissent and Politics in India', *Past and Present*, 125, pp. 3–26.

'The Early History of Mathura: Up to and Including the Mauryan Period', *in* D.M. Srinivasan (ed.), *Mathura*, AIIS, New Delhi, pp. 12–18.

1990: Co-authord with M. Gadgil, 'Human Ecology in India: Some Historical Perspectives', *Interdisciplinary Science Reviews*, 15, 3, pp. 209–23; 'Communalism and the Historical Legacy: Some Facts', *Social Scientist*, 18, 6 & 7, pp. 4–20.

1991: 'A Historical Perspective on the Story of Rama', in S. Gopal (ed.), *Anatomy of a Confrontation*, Penguin India, New Delhi, pp. 141–63; 'Genealogical Patterns as Prceptions of the Past', *Studies in History*, n.s. 7, 1, pp. 1–36.

'Sakuntala: The Bardic and the Courtly View', *in* C. Margabandhu, et al. (eds), *Indian Archaeological Heritage*, Agam Kala Prakashan, Delhi.

1992: 'Clan, Caste and Origin Myths in Early India', Niharranjan Ray Memorial Lecture, IIAS, Shimla.

'Patronage and Community', *in* B. Stoller Miller (ed.), *The Powers of Art: Patronage in Indian Culture*, OUP, New Delhi, pp. 19–34.

'Black Gold: South Asia and the Roman Maritime Trade', *South Asia*, n.s. xv, 2, pp. 1–28.

'The Aryans Ride Again', *Indian Historical Review*, 1991–92, XVIII.

1993: 'Archaeology and Language at the Roots of Ancient India', *Journal of the Asiatic Society of Bombay*, n.s. 64–6, pp. 249–68.

1994: 'Asoka and Buddhism as Reflected in the Asokan Edicts', *in* A. Seneviratne (ed.), *King Asoka and Buddhism*, BPS, Kandy, pp. 11–26.

'Sacrifice, Surplus and the Soul', *History of Religion*, pp. 305–24.

1995: 'The First Millennium BC in Northern India', *in* R. Thapar (ed.), *Recent Perspectives of Early Indian History*, Popular Prakashan, Bombay, p. 80–141.

'The Theory of Aryan Race and India: History and Politics', *Transactions of the International Conference of Eastern Studies*, Tokyo, XL.

'The Search for a Historical Tradition: Early India', ibid., Kyoto.

1997: 'Early Mediterranean Contacts with India: An Overview', *in* F. De Romanis and A. Teherina, *Crossings*, Manohar, Delhi.

1998: 'Aufe der Suche nach einer historischen Tradition: Das Fruhe Indien', *in* J. Rusen et al. (ed.), *Die Vielfalt der Kulturen*, Frankfurt.

1999: 'Some Appropriations of the Theory of Aryan Race Relating to the Beginnings of Indian History', *in* Daud Ali (ed.), *Invoking the Past: The Uses of History in South Asia*, OUP, Delhi.

'History of Science and the Oikoumene', *in* S. Irfan Habib and Dhruva Raina (eds), *Situating the History of Science*, OUP, Delhi.

'Einige Uberlegungen zum fruhen Indischen Geschichtsdenken', *in* J. Rusen (ed.), *Westliches Geschichtsdenken*, Gottingen.

'Historical Interpretations and the Secularising of Indian Society', Visthara, Bangalore.

2000: 'Perceiving the Forest: Early India', Sontheimer Memorial Trust, Pune.

Index

Abalavi 298
Aba-nagara 303
'Abd-ul-Malik Qidwa'i 179
'Abd-ul-Qādir Badāoni 175n
'Abd-ur-Rahman Ibnal-'Arabi 176
Abraham, Meera 225n
Abu'l Fazl 165n, 172, 173
Ācāryas 123, 140, 146, 150
Achal Singh 172
Acyuta 74
Adams, R. McC. 251n, 252n, 253n, 255n, 258n, 259n
Adeeb, Masud Husain Rizvi 183n
Ādicittanātar 133
Aditi 14
Advaita 140, 153, 204
Afghans 166, 168n
  Bagash Afghans 167
Africa 89, 91, 224, 251, 258
Āgama 118, 138, 141, 145, 149, 152
Agashe, R.P. 15n
Agga 246
Agni 14
Agni Purāṇa 61
agnihotra 16
Agnivetāla 83n
Agra 239
Agrawala, V.S. 72n
Ahirs 184
Ahmadnagar 203
Ahmedabad 179, 225, 226, 230
Āin-i-Akbarī 91, 165n, 166n
Aitareya Brāhmaṇa 15n
Aiyar, K.V.S. 316n
Ājīvikism 57
Akappēy cittar 113, 118
Akappēy cittar *pāṭal* 118n
Akbar 205
Akkad 246, 248, 250
dynasty of 249
Akadian period, the 245, 247, 251n
Akuvana 301
Al Sirajiyyah: Or the Mohamedan Law of Inheritance 23
Aḻakarmalai *see* Irunkunṟam
Alaler Gharer Dulal 95
Alam, Muzaffar 166n, 167n, 169n, 171n, 172n, 173n, 184n, 239.
Alavi, Muhammad Ali Haider 166n
'Ali 179
'Ali, M. Rahman 176n
Allahabad 173n, 175, 182, 213
Almond, David C. 296n
Althusser 314n
Aḻukaṇi/Aḻukuṇi cittar 113, 119
Āḻvārs 121, 122, 123, 135, 136, 137, 138, 139, 140, 141, 142, 143, 146, 148, 151, 155, 156, 161, 162, 332, 333.

Ambarakośa 60
Amarāvati, R. 222
Amballa 45
Amethi 166, 176
Amorite period, the 245
Anakatava 286n
Anderson, Benedict 274n
Anderson, R.N. 251n
Andhra 79, 128, 294n
Andhras 57
Andreev, Y.V. 258n, 261
Angas 71, 74, 144
Anglicists, the 92, 93
Ansari, M.A. 199
Ansari, Muhammad Raza 170n, 177n, 186n, 187n, 188n
Āṇṭāḷ 140n, 141, 146
Anudigama 309
Anurādhapura 268, 270, 274, 282, 288–9, 291, 293n, 296, 197n, 306, 311
Āpastamba Dharma Sūtra 56
Appadurai, Arjun 163n, 227n, 230n, 232n
Appar *see* Tirunāvukkaraśar
Arab coast 224
Āraṇyakas 125, 127
Arthashastra 231
Arunachalam, M. 326n
Aruṇagirināthar 117
Asia 89, 90n, 91
  Central Asia 240n
  South Asia 89, 271
  South East Asia 89, 224
Ashoa 167
Aśoka Maurya 268, 274
Assam 62, 63, 64, 221
Aśvaghosha 203
aśvamedha 16, 17
Atharva Veda 55
Atma Ram 173n
Aurangabad 177n
Aurangzeb 167, 169, 170, 171, 172, 175, 176, 177n, 178
Awadh/Ayodhya 165, 166, 167, 168n, 170, 171, 172, 173n, 174, 175, 176, 177, 178, 179, 182, 185, 187, 188, 189, 191, 210
Ayyar, C.V. Narayana 158n
Ayyāvole 225
Badakshan 178
Baden-Powell 31n
Bagavalena inscription 297n
Bāhlika 58
Bahmanis 190
Bahraich 165, 170
Bailey, A.M. 257n
Bairagis 185, 191
Baiswara 165, 167, 171, 172
Bakhtiar Khilji 228n
Bāla-gopāla 83n
Balakrishnan, P.K. 107
Balandier, G. 260n
Balangoda 277
Balasubramaniam, S.R. 150n
Bambaragala 296
Banaras *see* Vāraṇāsī
Bandaranayake, Senaka 285n
Bandopadhyaya, Suresh Chandra 59n
Bannu 34, 35
Bannuchis, the 34, 35
Bansa 178, 179, 185, 188, 191
Barabanki 174
Barata 305
Barfield 251n
Barnett, H.G. 237n
Barrelet, M.T. 247n
Barth, F. 250n
Barukaca 297
Basel Mission (school) 96
Batasanagara 309
Bayliss, M. 256n
Bayly, C.A. 208n, 222n, 226n, 231n, 232n, 233n
Beaconsfield (Lord) 97
Beck, Brenda 222n
Begley, V. 282n
Bedekar, V.M. 78n, 79n
Bendict, Ruth 216
Benett, W.C. 172n
Bengal 21, 23, 25, 27, 32, 48, 59n, 162, 63n, 64n, 69, 70, 71, 72, 73, 74, 76, 80, 81, 82, 84, 85n, 87, 88, 90, 141, 200, 201, 235
Bengal Presidency 94
Bentham, Jeremy 23, 24, 29
Bentinck, William (Lord) 92, 93
Bete, the 248, 249

Bhabha, Homi K. 49n
Bhachu, Parminder 221n
Bhagavad Gītā 139, 175
Bhāgavata Pāñcarātna 61
Bhāgavata Purāṇa 58, 140, 141n, 144n
Bhāgavataśāstra 70
Bhārgava 146
Bhartṛhari/Bhadragiri *see* Pattiragiriyar
Bhatia, P. 240n
Bhatnagar, Bahadur Singh 173n
Bhatta, Balam 28
Bhattacharya, N.N. 19n
Bhave, Vinoba 208
Bhopal, the Nawab of 215n
Bhumihars 222n
Bhyachara 45
Biardeau, Madeleine 77, 78n, 79n, 80n
Biebuyck, D. 251n
Biggs, R.D. 262n
Bihar 201
Bilgram 166, 173n
Bilgrami, Murtaza Husain Ilahyar Usmani 166n
Bilgrami, Rafat 167n–168n
Bischoff, B. 238n
Bisens, the 165
Bodhi tree, the 268
Bologna 235
Boman-Behram, B.K. 92n
Bombay Presidency 94
Bonazzoli, Giorgio 68
Boswell, James 20
Bouchon, G. 230n, 231n, 240n
Boulding, Kenneth 227n
Boulnois, C. 25n
Bourdieu, Pierre 34n
Bradlaugh, Charles 105
Brahmā 70, 81, 83n, 152
Brahman 66, 67, 125, 126, 153
brāhmaṇa (Brahman) 18, 25, 56, 58, 61, 67, 68, 69, 70, 71, 72, 77, 78, 79, 80, 81, 82, 84, 85, 86, 87, 90n, 101, 112, 116, 122, 123, 125, 133, 140, 142, 143, 144, 145, 146, 147n, 148, 152, 154, 155, 156, 163, 170, 175, 181, 221, 225, 227, 228, 230, 231, 235, 328, 329, 332
  Maratha Deśastha Brahmans 221
Brāhmaṇa Kojara 305
Brāhmaṇas, the 10, 11, 16, 125
Brahmāṇḍa Purāṇa 58n
Brāhmaṇism 57
Brahma Purāṇa 61
Brahmavaivarta Purāṇa 63n, 64, 67n, 69n, 71n, 72n, 76n
Brāhmī 280, 295
  Early Brāhmi inscriptions 293, 294, 300, 305, 306, 308, 309
  Later Brāhmi inscriptions 298
  Tamil Brāhmi inscriptions 315
Braj 174
Brandreth, E.L. 32, 33n
Bṛhadāraṇyaka Upaniṣad 14n, 55, 125n
Bṛhaddharma Purāṇa 64, 76n
Bṛhannāradīya Purāṇa 63, 70n, 71n, 74, 75n
Britain 23
British, the 21, 22, 25, 27, 28n, 30, 31, 32, 35, 40, 44, 47, 48, 89, 105, 106, 107, 108
Brown, C. Mackenzie 73n, 79n, 80, 81n
Brown, Peter 219n, 236n
Buddha (Gautama), the 57, 203, 206, 211, 268, 274, 311
Buddhacharita 203
Buddhism 57, 114, 121, 123, 126, 147, 153, 268, 273, 274
Buddhists 120, 121n, 126, 127, 128, 143, 148, 149, 150, 157n, 160, 324, 329
Buddhist Sahajīya Yogin 124, 126, 129
Burhan-ul-Mulk 171, 173
Burke, Peter 20n
Butter, Donald 172n
Butzer, Karl W. 276n
Buxar 172

Calcutta 27, 103, 207
Calicut 97
Caliph 169
Cāḷukyas 327n
Camayakkuravar Nālvar 147
Campantar 113n, 121, 128n, 142, 146, 147, 149, 150n, 151, 152n
Caṇḍikā 83n
Cand Sadagar-Lakhindar, story of 87
Canigama 298

Cankam/Sangam texts 127, 136, 137, 138, 141, 155, 156, 295, 317
Cannon, A. 251n, 252n
Cāṉṟōr 146
Canṭīśa 146
Carrithers, M. 229n
Carstairs, G. Morris 223n
Cārvāka/Lokāyata 83n, 126
Caturvedin 143, 144, 145
Cīkkiṭār 148, 162
Cemagama 309
Cenkner, William 227n, 228n, 233n
Cēntan Kūṟṟan 328
Cēra 120, 121, 146, 147, 157
Cēramān Perumāḷ 147
Ceviyaṟivūṟu *tuṟai* 321, 330
Cēyōn 320
Chait Rai 171
Chait Ram 185
Chakrabarti, Purna Chandra 87n
Champakalakshmi, R. 137n, 139n, 140n, 141n, 145n, 153n, 154n, 155n, 158n, 161n, 162n, 320n, 325n
Chandra, Satish 170n, 188n
Chandraratne, R.M.M. 230n
Chandrasena, U.A. 285n
Chartier, Roger 94n
Chatterji, Bankim Chandra 95
Chattopadhyaya, B.D. 223n
Chhabele Raṃ 167n
Chidambaram temple 162
Childe, V. Gordon 260n
China 112
Chishtiya Ashrafiya k͟hānqāh 81
Chishtiya silsilā 176, 179, 189
Choudhuri, U. 12n
Chowdhry, Prem 46n
Christian Mahasabha 212
Christian missionaries 94
Cilappatikāram 137, 157, 317, 321
Cita-nagara 296
Citrapati 28
Citraśikhaṇḍin Ṛṣis 74
Claessen, J.M. 276n, 322n
Cluniac monasteries 237n
Coburn, Thomas B. 79n, 80
Code of Gentoo Laws, the 22, 23, 28
Coimbatore 222
Cōḷa 120, 121, 122, 147n, 148, 150, 154, 155, 156, 157, 160, 161, 162, 163, 220, 225, 327
Cōḷanāḍu 161
Colebrooke, H.T. 23, 24, 26, 28, 29n
Columbus 219
Coningham, Robin 293n, 297n
Conkey, Margaret W. 276n
Constituent Assembly, the 213, 214
Cook, J. 208n
Coomaraswamy, Ananda K. 230n
Cooper, R.G. 252n
Cooray, P.G. 285n, 288n
Cornwallis 21
Cramer, L.H. 285n
Crone, P. 247n
Crusades, the 236
Cūlavaṃsa 285n
Cuntarar 113n, 146, 147n, 149, 155
Cust, R.N. 21n
Customary Laws of Punjab 22
Cutler, Norman 136n, 151n

Dakṣa 83n, 87
Dalhousie 25, 36, 37, 40
Dalmau 167
Dambulla 285, 286, 288–9, 294, 295, 300, 301, 303, 305
Dara Shukoh 175
Dārāsuram 161
Darnton, Robert 97n
Darwin, Charles 105
Daryabad 166, 167n, 178, 179
Das, Shiv 167n
Das, Sisir Kumar 95n
Daśāvatāra 87
Das Gupta, Ashin 226n, 227n
Dasgupta, Shashibhushan 124n, 125n, 126n
Dattaka-candrika 27n, 28n
Davis, Natalie Zemon 93n
Davy, William 91
Dayabhaga 27n, 28
Dayakarma/Sarigraha 27n
Dayà-tattva 27n
Deccan 128, 178, 179, 180, 186, 190, 291, 325
Deduru Oya, R. 284n

Deduru Oya Upper Valley 284n, 303
Delhi 168, 171, 177, 178, 188, 213, 239
  Qutb of 188
Demada Oya, R. 295, 296
Deraniyagala, S.U. 277n, 279n, 280n, 286n, 291n, 297n
Derrett, J.D.M. 22n, 23n, 27n, 28n, 29n, 30n, 48n
Desai, P.S. 157n
Devānāmpiyatissa 294
Devī 84
Devībhāgavata Purāṇa 64, 69n, 70n, 71, 75, 77n
Devī Purāṇa 63n, 76n
Dewey, Clive 31n
Dewey, John 203
Dhānyakaḍa 294n
Dharmaśāstra 30n, 65, 66, 156
Dharmasūtras 56
Diakonoff, I.M. 247n, 248, 252n, 253, 254n, 261
Dias, Malini 296n, 298n, 305n, 206n
Digby, Simon 184n, 190n
Digest of Hindu Law 23
Dīpavamṣa 266n
Dissanayake, C.B. 288n
Diwali 184
Divyaprabandam 139n, 141, 151
Domesday Book, the 232
Dondia Khera 172
Doravakakanda 306
Dorson, Richard 20n
Dow, Alexander 89
Drāviḍa Sangha/Jain Sangha 157
Drāviḍa Veda 151
Dubalagama 298
Duhatara, aya 309
Dumergue, W. 97n
Dumont, Louis 216, 229n, 231n, 233n
Dumuzi 262
Duncan, J. 57n
Dundes, Alan 317n
Durgā 138, 156, 160
Durgeshnandini 95
Dusataragama 309
Dutch, the 89
Duttaka-mimansa 27n
Duṭṭhagāmaṇi 270, 294
Dvāpara age 70

Earle, Timothy K. 276n
East India Company 21, 28, 89, 90, 92, 98, 172
Eaton Richard, M. 190n
Egypt 112
Ekādaśi *vrata* 63n
Elamites, the 262
Eliade, Mircea 112n, 113n
Ellawala, H. 266n
Elliot, C.A. 165n, 166n, 171n, 172n
Elliot, W. 316n
Elwin, Verrier 212n
England 232, 241
Enuma Elish 263
Ērkaḷuruvakam *tuṟai* 323n
Eṭṭuttokai 136, 317, 332
Europe 101, 196, 215, 216, 219, 231, 232, 235, 236, 238n, 241, 270

Faizpur 200
Fara (city state of) 246
Farrukhabad 167, 172
Farrukh Siyar 165, 188
Fernando, S.N.U. 286n
Fernea, R.A. 253n
Filliozat, Jean 151n, 152n
Finkelstein, J.J. 257n
Firoz Tughlaq 190
Firshori, Ghulam Husain Siddiqi 166n
Florence 240, 241
Foucault, Michel 313n
Fox, R.G. 218n, 222n, 223n, 239n
France 235, 241
Freedman, M. 251n
French 89, 236
Freud, Sigmund 275
Fried, M. 251n
Friedmann, Yohnan 169n, 190n
Frykenberg, R.E. 90n, 221n, 222n, 234n, 239n
Fuller, C.J. 145n
Fuṣūṣ-ul-Ḥikam 176

Gadd, C.J. 250n

Gajadabutaka *vāvi* 301
Galagedara 297
Galatara 308
Gaṇas 81
Gaṇḍarāditya 147
Gandhi, Mahatma 198, 199, 203, 207
Gaṇeśa 83n, 87
Ganga, R. 167, 172, 174
Gangetic plains/region 250, 261, 315
Ganeshof, F.L. 236n
Garadiḍagāma 298
Garh Amethi 180
Gautama Dharma Sūtra 56
Gayā 61
Gelb, I.J. 246n, 247n, 248n, 249n, 254n, 255n, 256n
Genova 240
Gentoos, the 23, 90
George, K.M. 95n
Germany 20, 240, 241
Gero, Joan M. 276n
Ghani, Ashraf 190n
Ghaus-i-A'zam 187
Ghāzi Miyān 170
Ghiyas-ud-Din Tughlaq 189
Ghurye, G.S. 229n
Gibson, M. 262n
Gilgamesh 246, 261
Gillion, Kenneth 24n, 226, 230n
Gilmartin, David 47n
Girdhar Bahadur 167n
Girikaṇḍa 294
Girimaṇḍala 285
Gladwin, Francis 91
Goa 212
Godelier, Maurice 277n, 313n, 326n
Gokul 174
Gold, Daniel 233n
Gonattva 295
Goody, J. 236n
Gopal, Sarvepalli 274n
Gopalakrishnan, P.K. 97n
Gopamau 166
Gorakhnath 174
Gorakhnāthi Yogi 124
Gorakhpur 165
Gough, Kathleen 232n
Gould, Harold 221n
Gṛhya rites 58
Grimm, Brothers 20
Gros, Francois 141
Gudea 246
Gujarat 86, 87, 228
Gujarati merchants 224, 226
Gunawardana, R.A.L.H. 293n, 298n
Gupta, A.S. 78n, 79n, 80
Gupta, P.L. 316n
Guptas, the 59
Gurgaon 46n
Guru Gorakhnāth 124
Guruge, Ananda 266n
Gurukkal, Rajan 314n, 322n, 325n, 331n

Habib, Irfan 169n, 238n, 240n
Haimendorf, V. von Furer 241n
Halbfass, Wilhelm 22n
Halhed, Nathaniel 23, 91
Hama Ūst 174, 175
Hammurapi 246
Ḥaqā 'iq-i-Hindī 174n
Hardy, Friedhelm 137n, 138n, 139n, 140n, 141n, 143n, 144n, 146n, 148n, 149, 151n, 155n, 156n, 161n
Harha 167
Hari 74, 76, 86n, 133
Har Narayan 173
Harris, David R. 276n
Harrison, R. 23n
Hart, George L. (III) 137n, 145n
Hasan, Mushirul 201
Hasan, S. Nurul 169n
Hastings 22n, 23, 90, 91
Haṭhayoga 124
Hayden, B. 251n, 252n
Haynes, E.S. 223n
Hazra, R.C. 56n, 57n, 58n, 59n, 60n, 61n, 62n, 63n, 64n, 71, 64n, 84n
Heesterman, J.C. 60n, 68n
Henrietta Temple 97
Hearth, J.W. 288n, 289n
Herder 20
Hettiarachchi, Tilak 266n
Higgin, J. 208n
Hillman, Gordon C. 276n

Hindes, Barry 313n, 322n, 326n
Hinduism 65, 66, 67, 68, 71, 72, 74, 77, 88, 122
Hindu Mahasabha 198
Hirst, Paul 313n, 322n, 326n
Hitchcock, John T. 223n
Hume, L.J. 23n
Humphrey, C. 229n
Husain of Karbala 189
Hutton, J.H. 65n, 66

Ibbankatuwa 280, 286n, 287, 288–9, 291, 293, 298
'Id 168
Idamoluwa weva 286
Iltutmish, Sultan 189
Inden, R. 235n
India 89, 106, 235, 237, 238n, 239, 240n, 241
Indian National Congress 103, 105, 106, 107, 199, 200, 201, 202, 207, 211
Indian Ocean 224
Indra 11, 12, 13, 14, 18, 321
Indradhvaja 76
Indulekhā 96, 97n, 98n, 99n, 100n, 101n, 102n, 103n, 104n, 105n, 106n, 107, 108
Indulekhā (of *Indulekhā*) 99, 100, 101, 102, 103, 107
Institutes of Hindu Law: Or the Ordinances of Manu 23
Iraq 253
Irumbayam, George 99
Irunkuṉṟam/Mālirunkuṉṟam/Tirumāliruncōlai/Aḻakarmalai 136
Isakhels, the 35
Ishaq, M. 176n
Ishwaran, K. 159n
Ism-i A'ẓam 182, 187
Iṭaikkāṭṭuccittar 113, 118
Iṭaiyar 118
Italian city-states 240
Ivory coast 248
Iyer, A.V. Subramanya 117n, 120n

Jacobsen, T. 246n, 256n, 259n, 261n
Jaffna 279, 282
Jafri, S.Z.H. 169n
Jagadeesan, N. 139n
Jagat Narayan 173
Jahangir 169, 178
Jainism 57, 114, 121, 123, 126, 128, 150, 158
Jain 120, 121n, 127, 128, 141, 143, 148, 149, 150, 157n, 158, 160, 162, 225, 229, 324, 329
Jain Purāṇas 147
Jais 172
Jameson, Frederick 333n
Janata Vimukti Peramuna (JVP) 273
Janmāṣṭami vrata 63n
Janwars, the 165
Jarvie, I.C. 217n
Jats, the 172
Jaunpur 176
Jayaratne, D.K. 286n, 287n
Jesudasan 111n
Jesus 236
Jha, D.N. 122n
Jhansi 195
Jinnah, M.A. 200, 201, 202n, 207
Jīvakacintāmaṇi 162
Johnson, Samuel 20
Jonathon 276n
Jones, E.L. 235n
Jones, Sir William 23n, 24n, 28, 29, 91n
Juma 168
Justice Plowden 45n

Kabir 127, 174, 186, 187
Kacaragama 309
Kacci Ēkampam 149
Kaḍapivāpi 298, 301
Kaḍungōn Pāṇḍya 331
Kaelber, Walter O. 15n
Kaikkōḷar 220
Kailāsanātha temple 156
Kailasapathy, K. 111n, 112n, 113n, 317n, 318n, 329n
Kakori 166
Kaḷabhras 121, 157, 326n, 327n
Kālāmukha 128, 129, 159
Kālan *see* Yama
Kala Oya, R. 284
Upper Kala Oya 284, 285, 287, 289,

291, 293, 295, 297, 298, 300, 301, 303, 305
Kalata 196
Kalwewa-Mahaalagamuwa region 285
Kalhaṇa 231
Kali age 58, 62, 70, 327n
Kālikā Purāṇa 62, 63, 81, 82n, 83n, 84n, 85n, 86n, 87
Kalittokai 137n
Kallāṭanār 322
Kaḷvar 146
Kāmākhyā 81
Kāmarūpa 81, 82, 83
Kanakasabhai, V. 323n
Kanchi *see* Kāñcīpuram
Kāñcīpuram/Kanchi 139n, 153, 156, 157, 158, 161, 162, 228
Kandalama 286n, 287, 301
Kandy 297
Kaṇṇappa/Kaṇṇappar 146, 148
Kaṇṇi 113
Kaṇṇi-nuṇ-ciṟu-t-tāmpu 144n
Kantarōḍai 288–9, 296
Kanyākumāri 314
Kapālakuṇḍalā 95
Kāpālin 83n
Kāpālikā 124, 128, 129
Kapila 105
Karachi 197, 199, 207
Kāraikkal Ammaiyār 147
Karan Ghelo 95
Kaṛnataka 159, 162, 326n
Karuvūr Tēvar 147
Karve, Irawati 66n
Kashmir 62, 129, 209, 231
Katesar 167n
Kathakaḷi 102
Kāṭuveḷiccittar 111n, 115n, 119
Kātuvēḷiccittar *Pāṭal* 119n
Kauṇḍinya 147n
Kaur, Amrit 212n
Kaveri, R. 140, 150, 161, 222
Kāvērippaṭṭiṇam/Puhār 157
Kāyasthas 173, 235
Kāyāvarohaṇa/Kārōṇam temple 128
Kejariwal, O.P. 22n, 23n, 90n, 91n
Kennedy, Kenneth A.R. 277n, 280n
Kenya 221
Kerala 96, 212, 227, 232n
Kessinger, Tomb 221n
Khairabad 165, 167, 168n
Khan, Iqtidar Alam 190n
Khan, Munshi Muzaffar-ud-Din 168n
Khatris 173
Kheri 167n
Khoury, P.S. 251n
Khusrau Khan 189
Khwaja 'Ali Akbar Maududi Chishti 184, 185n
Khwaja Nasir-ud-Din Chiragh-e-Delhi 189
Kīḻkaṇakku texts 327n, 329n, 330, 331
Kish 246, 251n, 261
Klengel, H. 261n
Köbben, A.J.F. 249n
Kōccenkaṇ 146, 147
Kōlagāma 296n, 298, 301
Kongunāḍu 222
Kooij, K. R. Van 82n, 83n, 84n
Korān/Quran, the 22n, 24, 90, 177, 201
Koṟṟavai 138, 156
Kosambi, D.D. 72n
Kōstiner, J. 251n
Kramer, S.N. 261n
Kriyāyogasāra 63
Kṛmikaṇṭha *see* Kulōttunga II
Kṛṣṇa (Krishna) 67, 71, 140, 174, 180, 183, 185, 186, 187
kṣatriya 57, 58, 87, 268
Kudagala 296
Kuiper, F.B.J. 11n
Kulacēkara 139, 140, 146
Kulacciṟai 147
Kulōttunga II 148, 161, 162
Kummi 113
Kundalatā 95, 97n
Kuper, A. 250n
Kupper, J. 247n, 262n
Ḳureshi, Badr-ud-din 47n
Kūrma Purāṇa 60, 61
Kūṟṟap-Peṟum Cēntan 328
Kutampai(y) 118
Kutampaiccittar 113, 118
Kutampaccittar *Pāṭal* 119n

Lachmi Narayan 173

La Fontaine, J. 250n
Lagash 246, 248, 257, 259, 260, 262
Laggala range 285
Laharpur 167n, 168n
Lakshman 186
Lakulīśa 128
Lalji 166n
Latin America 89, 91
League of Nations, the 202
Leitner, G.W. 238n
Leonard, Karen 225n
Lévi-Strauss, Claude 317n
Levy, M.R. 235n
Liberation Tigers of Tamil Elam (LTTE) 273
Lingayats, the 234
Liyanagamage, A. 285n
Llobera, J.R. 257n
Logan, William 97
Lokāyata *see* Cārvāka
Lomaharṣaṇa, *sūta* 55
Lorenzen, David N. 114n, 128n, 153n, 159n
Lucknow 165, 166, 168, 178, 185, 186, 221
Ludhiana 35, 46n
Lukacs 333n
Lukes, S. 217n
Lyall, J.B. 34n

MacAdams 316n
Macnaghten, W. 26, 28n, 30n
Macaulay 92, 93
Madan, T.N. 195
Madana 87
Mādhava 71, 76
Mādhavan (of *Indulekhā*) 98, 99, 100, 101, 102, 103, 104, 105, 106, 107
Madhya Pradesh 212
Madras 98, 232n
Madras Presidency 94
Madsen, Stig T. 220n
Maekawa, K. 255n, 256n
Mahaalagamuwa 300, 301
Mahābhāgavata Purāṇa 64
Mahābhārata 56, 58, 74, 77
Mahā Cūḍika 296
Mahādeva 81, 82, 175
Mahadevan, I. 316n
Mahadevan, Raman 224n
Mahāgāma 268, 270, 282, 311
Maha Oya, R. 306
Upper Maha Oya system 306, 309
Mahāpurāṇas 60, 61, 62, 73, 80, 84
Maharashtra 126
Mahāvamṣa (*MV*) 266n, 267, 270, 271, 274, 275, 285n, 294n
Mahāvihāra 268, 270
Mahāvratas 128
Mahāvāvi 298
Mahaweli, R. 284, 295, 297
Mahaweli plains 279
Upper Mahaweli system 308
Mahendravarman Pallava 121, 128, 149
Maheśvara 74, 75, 125
Mahmud of Ghazni 205
Mahmud, Syed 196n
Mahomedans 90
Maine, Henry 24n, 26n, 28n, 31n
Maitreyī 125
Majeed, Javed 22n, 23n, 29n
Majumdar, R.C. 55n, 64n, 73n
Māl/Māyōn 136, 137, 138, 320
Malabār 96, 98, 99, 100, 101, 102, 107, 231
Malabar Manual 97
Malabar Marriage Commission 101, 102
Maladavi 298
Malasna 298, 300
Malayaraṭṭha/Malaya 285
Malfūẓ-i-Razzāqi 178n, 179n, 180n, 183n, 184n, 185n, 186n, 187n
Malihabad 166, 168
Malik Muhammad Jaisi 180, 181
Malik, Z.U. 188
Malinowski, Bronislaw 216
Malirunkuṉṟam *see* Irunkuṉṟam
Mallai/Māmallapuram 139n, 156
Mallick, S.C. 123n
Maloney, Clarence 157n
Māmallapuram *see* Mallai
Manaiyaṟam *tuṟai* 321, 330
Manāqib-i-Razzāquiya 178n, 180n, 182n
Manasā 87
Manasā Maṅgala 87
Manāẓir-i Akhaṣṣ-ul-Khawāṣ 176

Mandal, D. 274n
Mani, Lata 27n, 48n
Māṇikkavācakar 142, 147
Maṇimēkalai 157, 317, 321
Maṇipravāla 153
Manishtusu 248, 249, 251n
Mannoni, O. 93n
Māntai 288–9, 296, 297n
Manu 24n, 25n, 27n, 55, 57n
Manusmṛti 57
Mapagala 286
Marad 251n
Marathas, the 172
Marglin, F.A. 229n, 232n
Mari 247, 255, 256
Mark 236
Mārkaṇḍeya Purāṇa 61
Marr, J.R. 161n
Marshall, P.J. 22n
Mārtāṇḍa-bhairava 83n
Marx, Karl 196, 258
Marxism 204
Matale 294, 295, 296, 297
Matale hills 284, 287, 289, 291, 295, 303, 305
Matale plateau 285
Mathura 61, 141
Mathurakavi 140, 143, 144, 146
Mātṛs 81
Matsya Purāṇa 57n, 61
Mattavilāsa prahasana 128
Matthew 236
Mattingly, H. 316n
Maṭukagama 298, 301
Matukaṭaka 298
Maturai/Madurai 136, 157, 158, 161
Maulavi 'Abd-ul-Qadir 181n
Mauryas 57
Mayāviya 298
Max Mueller, F. 12n
māyā 13, 14
Māyāmoha 83n
Mayilai 139n
McCormack, W. 234n
McGindle, J.W. 296n, 316n
Mclennan 24n, 26n
McLeod, W.H. 233n
Medhātithi 57
Meenakshisundaram, T.P. 113n, 128n
Mehendale, M.A. 55n, 56n, 61n
Mehta, Nanda Shankar Tiliya Shankar 95
Meillasoux, C. 260n, 317n
Melkote 162
Menon, Govindan Kutty (of *Indulekhā*) 103, 104, 105, 106
Menon, Oyyarath Chandu 96n, 97, 99, 100, 101, 102n, 103, 105, 107
Menon, Panchu (of *Indulekhā*) 98, 103
Merovingians, the 231
Meru (mount) 74
Mesopotamia 245, 246, 249, 253n, 257, 258, 259, 261, 263
Meyñānappulampal 117
Mezizi 248
Middle East, the 250n, 251n
Mill, James 23n, 29n
Mīmāṁsā (system) 67
Mines, Mattison 220n, 224n
Mir 'Abd-ul-Jalil Bilgrami 189
Mir 'Abd-ul-Wahid Bilgrami 174n
Mir 'Abd-us-Samad Khuda-numa 179
Mir Muhammad Isma'il 183
Mir Saiyid Ghulam 'Ali Azad Bilgrami 189n
Mir Saiyid Muhammad Qannauji 177
Mir'āt-i-Mas'ūdī 170
Mir'āt-ul-Maḇhlūqāt 175
Mirza 'Abd-ul-Qadir Bedil 189n
Misra, B.B. 90n
Mitakshara 27n, 28
Mitra, Pearey Chand 95
Mlecchas 81, 82
Montgomery, M.R. 25n
Montgomery (dt) 32, 34
Moosvi, Shireen 166n
Moran, Emilio F. 276n
Moranwan 167
Morinis, E. Alan 233n
Morris, C. 262n
Moses, the Prophet 184
moulavis 90
Mudaliyar, Ramalinga 112
Mudaliyār Santāna 162
Mughal 165, 166, 167, 169, 170, 171,

172, 173, 175, 177, 179, 180, 188, 189, 190n, 231n, 239n, 240n
Muhammad, the Prophet 174, 189
Muhammad Ashraf Simnani 174
Muhammad bin Tughlaq 189
Muhammadu, Piru 112
Mujaddid-i-Alf-i Sani 175
Mujeeb, M. 176n
Mukherjee, S.N. 91n
Mulla Kamal-ud-Din 184, 185
Mulla Mahmud 176n
Mulla Muhammad Raza 185
Mulla Nizam-ud-Din 182, 183, 184, 185
Multan 46n
Mulla Nizam-ud-din Firangi Mahalli 178n
Munshi, K.M. 211
Muntakhāb-ut-tawārikh 175n
Murukan 136, 137, 138, 152, 156, 160, 320
Muslim League, the 199, 200, 201, 202
Muttoḷḷāyiram 328
Mutumoḻi kkāñci *tuṟai* 321, 330
Myrdal-Runebiger, Eva 276n
Mysore 128

Nācciyār Tirumoḻi 140n
Naga 212
Nagarseth 226
Nagaswamy, R. 122n, 156n, 328n
Nair/Nayar 96, 98, 99, 100, 101, 102, 103, 232
Nakadavi 298
Nālanda 228n
Nalanda (Sri Lanka) 295, 296
Nambi Āṇḍār Niambi 148
Nambūdirī 99, 103, 228
Nambudiripad, Suri 99, 102, 103
Nammāḻvār 139n, 141, 143, 144, 146
Nandadeva, B.D. 279n
Nandanār 123
Nandas 57
Nandi 149
Nandi, R.N. 128n
Nandy, A. 195
Nānmukan Tiruvantāte 121n
Nanna, temple of 256
Nantan 148, 158
Naqshbandi silsilā 169, 175, 190n
Nāraḍa 69
Narasiṁha 79, 80, 83n, 183
Nārāyaṇa 69
Nārāyaṇakkōnār 118
Narayana Ayyar, C.V. 128n
Narayanan, M.G.S. 123n, 155n, 324n, 332n, 333n
Narmadā, R. 61
Nāthamuni 146, 161
Nāth Yogin 124, 127, 129
Nattukottai Chettiar 225
Naturalis historia 296
Nawab Muhammad Khan Shahjahanpuri 178n
Nawal Rai 173
Nāyanārs 122, 123, 128, 135, 136, 138, 141, 142, 143, 146, 147, 148, 154, 155, 160, 162, 332, 333
Nedungaddi, Appu 95, 97n
Nehru, Jawaharlal 195, 196n, 197, 198, 199, 200, 201, 202n, 203, 204, 205, 206, 207n, 208, 209n, 210n, 211, 212n, 213n, 214n, 215n
Nelson, J. 236n
Neṭṭimaiyār 322
New Guniea 250n
New Testament, the 236
Nilkantha Sastri, K.A. 21n, 138n, 148n, 162n, 316n
Niliyanagara 309
Ningirsu 246, 262
Nippur 249
Nizaṃi, K.A. 169n, 190n
Nizami, T.A. 209
Nizamiya silsilā 179
North West Provinces 94
North West Frontier Province 200
Nyāya (system) 67

Oddie, G.A. 221n
Oḍra 86
O'Malley, L.S.S. 65n, 66
Orientalists, the 22n, 23n, 26, 27, 29, 30, 49, 91, 92, 266, 270
Orissa 61, 63
Ottoman rule 252

Paḍagama 298

Padavigampola 308
Padmanji, Baba 95
Padma Purāṇa 61, 63
Pakistan 207, 209, 213
Palestine 252
Pāli chronicles 294
Pali 168
Paḷḷankōyil plates 157
Pallava 121, 122, 123, 137, 149, 156, 157, 160, 161, 331
Pāmpaṭṭicittar 111n, 112, 114, 118
Pāṇa 146
Panabokke, C.R. 286n
Pāṇāḷvār 144
Pañcāla 86
Pāñcarātras, the 57
Pāñcarātra Saṁhitā 59
Paṇḍāram 116
Pāṇḍināḍu 161
Pāṇḍya *see* Pāṇṭiya
Panikkam kuḷam 301
Panikkar, Govinda (of *Indulekhā*) 103, 104, 105, 107
Panikkar, K.N. 98n
Paṉṉiru Tirumuṟai 116
Pant, G.B. 210n, 213n
Pāṇṭaran Kaṇṇanār 322
Pāṇṭiya/Pāṇḍya 120, 121, 122, 137, 147, 149, 150n, 156, 157, 161, 327n, 331
Pantulu, Kandukuri Viresalingam 95
Paramaśiva 124
Parameśvara Viṇṇagaram 156
Paranavitana, S. 295n, 296n
Parāntaka I 160
Parappanangadi 97
Paras Ram 185, 187
Parekh, Bhikhu 228n, 229n
Paripāṭal 136, 137, 152, 156, 321, 332
Pārppanavākai tuṟai 321, 330
Parrot, A. 247n
Pārśvanātha 141
Pārvatī 71, 76, 81, 175
Pāśupata 57, 114, 128, 159
Patalagāma 309
Pātañjala 67
Patiṉeṇkīḻkkaṇakku 317
Paṭṭinappālai 138n
Paṭṭinattār 111n, 114n, 117
Pattuppāṭṭu 317
Pattiragiriyār 117
Paul, M.P. 107
Pearson, M.N. 224n, 225n, 226n, 227n, 231n, 238n
Peishkar, Dewan 100
Periyāḷvār/Viṣṇucitta 140, 146
Periyāḷvār Tirumoḷi 140n
Periya Ñānakkōvai 112
Periya purāṇam 146, 147, 148, 161, 162
Periya Tirumaṭal see *Tirumāṭal*
Periya Tirumoḷi 121n, 147, 156n
Perunkāñu *tuṟai* 321, 330
Peterson, Indira Viswanathan 141n, 142n, 145, 149n, 150n, 151n, 152n, 153n
Pēy 139n
Philip the Fair 235, 236
Pidurangala 301
Pillai, Samuel Vedanayakam 95
Piratapa Mutaliyar Carittiram 95
Pisa 240
Pliny 296
Pocock, D.F. 86n
Pōkar 114
Pocani lineage 295, 296
Pocunika rāja 295, 305
Pomparippu 287
Portuguese, the 89, 212, 226, 227
Porunmoḷikkāñci *tuṟai* 321, 330
Postema, J. 23n, 24n, 29n
Postgate, J.N. 260n
Poulantzas, Nicos 313n, 314n
Poykai 139n
Prahlāda 79, 80
Prajāpati 14, 15, 16, 18
Pramathas 81
Prasad, Rajendra 201, 209, 211, 212n, 214n
Pratap Narayan 173
Prayascitta-tattva 27n
Prickett, M. 297n
Prickett-Fernando, M.E. 297n
Prinsep 33
Propp, V. 317n
Puhār *see* Kavēripaṭṭnam
Pulānkurichchi inscription 329, 330
Pulinda 269, 285

Puli Pani 114
Punjab, the 21, 24n, 25n, 26n, 27n, 30, 31, 33, 36, 37, 38, 40, 41, 43, 46, 48, 200, 201, 221
purāṇa 55
Purāṇas, the 55, 56n, 57, 58, 59n, 60, 61, 62n, 64, 65, 66, 67, 68, 69, 70, 71, 72, 73, 74, 75, 76, 77, 78, 79, 80, 81, 82, 84, 85, 96, 87, 88, 105, 138, 141
Purāṇa Saṁhitās 70, 77
Puṟanāṉūṟu 138n, 322n, 323n, 325n
Purāṇārtha Prakāśaka 64n
Purāṇasāra 64n
Purāṇa-sarvasva 64
Puri 195, 228n
  Jagannatha temple at 288n
  Sankaracharya of 195
Purser, W.E. 32n, 34n
puruṣa 18
puruṣasūkta 16, 18
Pūrva Mīmāṁsa 125
Puṣkara 61
Pūtam 139

Qadiri silsilā 178, 179, 191
Qazi Maudud 167
Qazi Shahab-ud-Din Daulatabadi 176

Rādhā 71, 76
Rādhākavaca 69
Radhakrishnan, P. 232n
Radhasoamis 233n
Raghumani 28n
Raghunandana 59n
Raghupathy, Ponnampalam 282n
Rai, Bhupat 167n
Rai, Sahib 167n
Raikwars, the 165
Raj (the British) 198
rāja 17
Rajamanickam, M. 153n
rājanya 18
Rājarāja I 147n, 148, 161
Rājaśekhara Charitra 95
Rājasimha Pallava 156
Rajasthan 224
rājasūya 16, 17
Rājataranginị 231n
Rajputs 165, 166, 167, 168, 169, 170, 171, 172, 173, 178, 179, 180, 181, 190, 191, 222, 223, 224, 239
  Basis Rajputs 165, 167, 168, 172
  Bais Rajputs 165, 167, 168, 172
  Gaur Rajputs 165, 167
Rakitagāma 298, 303
Rāma 185, 186, 210
Rāma bhakti 187
Ramanathan, Aru 112n
Rāmānuja 143, 153, 159, 161, 162
Ramanujan, A.K. 136n, 139n, 151n, 159n
Ramaswamy, Vijaya 163n, 220n
Rambukwella, Chulani 306n
Ramgarhias 221
Ram Narayan 173
Ranagiramada 303
Ranawella, S. 298n, 305n
Ranbirpur 167
Randall, Susan C. 85n
Ranganātha 140n
Rashtrapati Bhavan 212
Rashtriya Swayamsevak Sangh (R.S.S.) 209n
Rasul Khan 178
Rasulpur 178
Rattigan, H.A.B. 35n
Renger, J. 249n
Revolt of 1857 90
Reynolds, S. 235n, 241n
Ṛg Veda 10, 11, 13n, 14n, 15n, 16n, 18n, 58, 65
Rieu, Charles 175n
Risāla Tasuriya 175, 176
riwaj-i-ams 33, 36
Rizvi, S.A.A. 170n, 174n, 175n, 176n, 178n
Rocher, Ludo 69n
Roe, Arthur R. 35n
Rocher, Rosanne 23n
Rolland, Romain 203
Roma Rịshi 114
Rosen, F. 23n
Rosenfeld, H. 252n
Rosenwein, B.H. 237n
Roshniyas 190n
Rotawewa 286

Rowe, W.L. 221n
Rudauli 166, 174, 175, 179, 187
Rudner, David 224n
Rudra 15
Rukmani, T.S. 140n
Rupasinghe 288n
Rushd Nāma 174
Russell, Bertrand 196

Saberwal, S. 219n, 220n, 221n, 223n, 227n, 231n
Sabhā 154
Sabiriya silsilā 179Sadr Diwani Adalat 27
Safdar Jang 167, 171, 172, 173
Sahassa 285n
Sāhitya Akademi 95
Sahlins, M. 316n
Said, Edward 91n
Sainpur 167
Śaiva Āgamas 59, 156
Śaivas 59, 82, 121, 128, 135, 138, 141, 142, 145, 146, 147n, 148, 150, 151, 152, 153, 154, 156, 158, 159, 160, 161, 162, 163
  Ādi Śaivas 145, 147, 148
Śaiva brāhmaṇas 145
Śaiva Pāśupata 61
Śaivism 57, 121, 138, 149, 155, 160
Śaiva Siddhānta 148, 151, 152, 162
Saiyids 166, 167, 168, 188
Saiyid Brothers 167n, 188, 189n
Saiyid 'Abd-ullah 188
Saiyid 'Abd-ur-Rahim 178
Saiyid Husain 'Ali Khan 188, 189
Saiyid Jahangir Ashraf 167
Saiyid Salar Mas'ud Ghazi 170
Saiyid Shah 'Abd-ur-Razzaq Bansawi 178, 179, 180, 181, 182, 183, 184, 185, 186, 187, 188, 189, 190
Śaka 58
Śākta (system) 61
Śāktas 82
Śāktism 57
Śakti worship 84
Śalākapuruṣas 147
Salivaya 309
Salon 169, 172
Sāma Veda 58, 132
Saṁhitās, the 125
Sāṁkhya (system) 67, 105
Sandhyācala 81
Sandi 168
Sandila 168
Sangam see *Cankam*
sangha 58
Sankalia, H.D. 228n
Śankara/Śankarācārya 67, 140, 153, 154, 227
Sankaracharyas 195, 228, 233n
Sant 126, 127, 129, 233n
Sanyal, Hitesh Ranjan 86n
Śāradātantra 87
Sarasvati 83n
Sargon 246, 249
Śastras/(Shastras), the 22, 23, 24, 69, 90, 132
Sastri, A.C. 18n
Śatapatha Brāhmaṇa 13n, 14n, 15n, 16n
Satguru 124
Śaura (system) 61
Saurashtra 211
Saussure, F. 317n
Saxena, Mohanlal 209n
Schevill, F. 236n, 240n
Schoff, W.H. 316n
Schomer, Karine 126n
Schwab, Raymond 22n
Scotland 20
Scott, C. James 51n
Seddon, D. 258n
Sena 149
Senanayake, Piyatissa 284n, 303n
Seneviratne, Sudharshan 274n, 277n, 279n, 280n, 282n, 284n, 291n, 293n, 294n, 295n, 296n, 297n, 303n, 305n, 306n, 209n, 325n
Seruwila 270, 282, 284
Shah, A.M. 223n
Shah Daula 187
Shah Dosi 187
Shah Ghulam Dost Muhammad 183
Shah 'Inayat-ullah 181
Shah Muhammad Ishaq Khan 183
Shahabad 166, 168n
Shahjahan 170, 178

Shaikhs 166
Shaikh 'Abd-ul-Jalil Siddiqi 169n
Shaikh 'Abd-ul-Haq Muhaddis Dehlavi 169n, 176
Shaikh 'Abd-ul-Quddus 174
Shaikh Abd-ur-Rahman Chishti 170, 175, 177
Shaikh 'Abd-ur-Rashid 170n
Shaikh Ahmad 'Abd-ul-Haq 174, 175
Shaikh Ahmad Sirhindi 169n, 175, 176, 177
Shaikh Muhammad Ashraf 169
Shaikh Muhammad Yusuf 179
Shaikh Muhammadi 177n
Shaikh Muhibb-ullah 175, 176
Shaikh Nizam-ud-Din Aulia 189
Shaikh Nizamuddin of Amethi 176
Shaikh Pir Muhammad 169
Shaikhazadas 166, 172, 179, 188, 189
Shaikhzada Ruh-ul-Amin Khan 173n
Shāradātilaka 87
Sharma, Krishna 140n, 141n
Sharp, H. 93n
Shills, Edward 93n
Shiv Narayan 173
Shujā-'ud-Daulah 171, 172
Shulman, David 142n, 159n, 231n
Siddha/Citta 111, 112, 113, 114, 115, 116, 117, 118, 119, 120, 123, 124, 125, 126, 127, 128, 129, 147, 148, 159, 160
Siddha medicine 114
Siddhism 115, 117, 129, 159
Siddiqi, Muhammad Suleman 190n
Sigiriya 286, 287, 291, 300, 301, 305
Sikander Lodi 176
Siṁhācalam 79
Simhavarma Pallava 331
Singaravelu 323n
Singha Gaur 167n
Sinha, Sri Krishna 214n
Sinha, Surajit 223n
Sinhala, the 265, 271, 273
Sirisoma, M.H. 305n
Siritunga, H.W.S. 297n
Sīrkāḻi 147n
Sirrah 168
Sirsa 43, 44, 46n
Śiva 81, 83n, 115, 116, 119, 121, 131, 132, 133, 137, 138, 142, 145, 147n, 149, 150, 151, 152, 153, 155, 156, 160, 161
  forms of
    Bhikṣāṭana 152
    Dakṣiṇāmūrti 152
    Lingodbhava 152
    Naṭarāja 152
    Rāvaṇānugraha 152
    Yogi 152
Śiva, gāmaṇi 309
Śiva, aya 309
Śivanagara 309
Śiva brāhmaṇas 145
Sivaramamurti, C. 151n
Sivathamby, K. 314n
Śivavākkiyar 111, 115n, 116, 117, 119, 120, 129
Śivavākkiyar *Pāṭal* 116, 119n, 120n
Śivayogi 116
Skalnik, P. 322n
Skanda Purāṇa 79, 80
Smārta (religious movements) 57, 153
Smārta brāhmaṇas 145, 228
Smārta Śaivas 58
Smārta Vaiṣṇavas 58
Smith, Bardwell L. 136n, 274n
Smith, Brian K. 67n, 68n, 69n
Smṛti 56, 57, 58, 63, 64, 68, 69, 72, 75, 77, 153
Smṛti nibandha 59n
Smṛti Saṁhitā 59
smṛti 78, 145
Sollberger, E. 247n, 262n
Soma 14
soma 13
Somaskanda 156
Sombansis 165
Somnath temple 205, 211
Spencer, George W. 161n
Śrauta (religious movements) 57
Sri Lanka 112, 264, 265, 266, 267, 268, 270, 271, 272, 274, 275, 276, 277, 279, 280, 282, 284, 287, 291, 294, 295, 303, 309, 311, 312
Sringeri 228
Srinivas, M.N. 222n

Srinivasan, K.R. 158n
Srīrangam 140, 161, 162
Śrī Śrī Padma Purāṇa 87
Śrīvaiṣṇava 79, 80, 139, 150, 151, 161
Śrī Vaiṣṇavism 140, 153
Srivastav, A.L. 173n
Śruti 69, 77, 150
śruti 78, 80
Steed, Gitel 223n
Stein, Burton 123n, 152n, 153n, 155n, 222n, 230, 231n, 238n, 331n
Steinkeller, P. 248n, 254n
Stele of Vultures 247
Sthalapurāṇa 80
Stokes, Eric 23n
Strange, T.A. 26, 28, 30n
Strasser, Hermann 85n
Strathern, A. 250n
Strayer, J.R. 235n, 236n
Subbarayalu, Y. 328n, 331n
Subrahmanian, N. 157n, 320n, 323n, 325n, 329n
Subramanian T.N. 156n, 157n
Subrahmanyam, S. 222n
Suddhi-tattva 27n
śūdra 17, 57, 58, 59, 70, 86, 144, 146
Sufi 165, 167, 174, 176, 177, 178, 179, 182, 183, 184, 185, 186, 187, 188, 189, 190, 191
Śuka 70
Sukhtankar, V.S. 77, 78
Śumana (gahapati kośikaputa) 305
Sumer 245, 247n, 252, 258, 259
Sumerian King List, the 245
Sumerians the 247n
Sunni 169
Surajbansis 165
Surat 226
Sūrya 83n
sūta 55
Sūtras, the 56
Swamy, B.G.L. 156n

Talagahagoda (parumaka) 305
Tambiah, S.J. 227n
Tamiḻakam 120, 135, 139, 155, 157n, 314, 315, 325n
Tamil Nadu 121, 124, 128, 129, 154
Tamil Veda 144
Tandon, Purushottam Das 211
Tāṇḍya Mahābrāhmaṇa 18n
Tañjāvūr 147n, 161
Tāṇṭavarāya kkōnār 118
Tantras 59n, 60n, 82, 84, 85, 152
  Buddhist Tantras 125
  Hindu Tantras 125
Tantric Siddhayoga 114, 116, 129
Tantrism/Tantricism 58, 59, 84, 228n
Taprobane 296
Tarikh-i-Jā'is 181n
Tarkapancanana, Jagannath 23, 28
Taylor, W. 116
Telangana 210
Tellichery 96
Temple, Richard 26
Tēraiyar 114
Terray, Emmanuel 313n, 326n
Tēvāram 141, 142, 146, 147, 149, 151, 152n, 161
Tēvāram aṭankanmuṟai 128
Thanesvar 61
Thapar, Romila 60, 159, 217n, 227n, 234n, 245, 250, 261, 265n, 274n, 322n, 333n
Thoothi, N.A. 228n, 229n
Thorburn 34, 35, 36
Thrupp, Sylvia 238n
Tigar, M.E. 235n
Tiloi 181
Tillai 147n
Timberg, Thomas A. 224n
Tipu Sultan 238n
Tirukkōvaiyār 142n
Tirukkōvalūr/Tirukkoyilūr 139
Tirukkuṟaḷ 327n, 328n
Tirumālai 121n, 143, 144n, 149
Tirumāḻicai/Tirumāḻisai Āḻvār 121, 146
Tirumāḻiruncōlai *see* Irunkuṉṟam
Tirumankai 121, 139, 146, 147, 148, 156n, 161
Tirumantiram 113n, 115n, 116n, 148
Tirumaṟaikanta Purāṇam 147
Tirumāṟpēru 145
Tirumaṭal 139, 148
Tirumūlar 112, 113n, 115, 116, 117, 129, 147, 159

Tirumuṟai 147
Tirumurukāṟṟuppaṭai 137, 156
Tirunāḷaippōvār 147
Tiruñānacampantar *see* campantar
Tirunāvalūr 147n
Tirunāvukkaraśar/Appar 121, 128, 142, 143, 145, 146, 147n, 149, 150, 151, 152n, 159n
Tirunīlakaṇṭa Yāḻppāṇar 142
Tirupati *see* Vēnkaṭam
Tiruppallāṇṭu 140n
Tiruppaḷḷiyeḻucci 140n
Tiruppāṇāḻvār 123, 143, 146
Tiruppāvai 140n
Tiruppukaḻ 117
Tiruttomṭar tiruvantāti 146
Tiruttoṇṭattokai 146
Tiruvaiyāṟu 149
Tiruvāmūr 147
Tiruvārūr 149, 159n
Tiruvāymoḻi 144, 146
Tiśa 295
  Gāmaṇi Tiśa 295
Tissamahārāma 288–9
Tithi-tattva 27n
Tiyavikahavāvi 298
Tolkāppiyam 138, 317
Toṇḍaināḍu 161
Toṇḍaraṭippoṭi/Toṇṭaraṭippoṭi 121, 139, 143, 144, 146, 149
Trichur 228
Tripathi, D. 226n
Tripura-bhairavi 83
Trobrianders, the 216
Tucci, Guisseppe 113n
Tupper 22, 24n, 25n, 26n, 27n, 31n, 33n, 34n, 37n, 38n, 39n, 40n, 43n
Tūzuk-i-Jahāngirī 169n, 170n

Udupihilla 295
Ugraśravas, souti 55
Ugratārā 81, 82
United provinces, the 200, 201, 213
United States of America, the 212, 217
  missionaries of 212
Unnao 168
Upaligāma 309
Upaniṣad 70, 71, 114, 125, 126, 127
Upapurāṇas, the 60, 61, 62n, 69, 80
Uparikaḍa 298
Ur 245, 253, 254, 255, 256, 257, 259, 260, 262
Urnammu 257
Urnanshe 262
Uruk 253, 258, 259, 260, 261
Urukagina 257
Uttar Pradesh 145

Vadamas 145
Vāgbhairavi 83n
Vahaba, gamika 303
Vaiśeṣika (system) 67
Vaiṣṇavas 59, 67, 82, 86n, 121, 127, 128, 135, 136, 138, 139n, 141, 142, 150, 151, 153, 156, 159, 160, 161, 162, 174, 228
Vaiṣṇavism 86n, 153, 161, 162
Vaiṣṇava poet-saints 126
Vaiṣṇavism 57
vaiśya 18, 58
vājapeya 16
Vālmīki Purāṇa 88
Vāmana Purāṇa 61
Vaṁsidāsa, Dvija 87n, 88
Vanasimha vihāra 301
Vañcittiṇai 322n
Vaṇigar 122
Vansina, J. 251n
Varāha Purāṇa 61
Vārāṇasī/Banaras 27, 61, 226
varṇa 17, 18, 75, 81, 82, 146
varṇāśramadharma 57, 58, 123, 125, 126, 159
Varuṇa 13, 15, 320
Vaśiṣṭha 81
Vaudeville, Charlotte 124n, 126n, 127n
Vavuniya 282
Vāyu Purāṇa 58n
Vedānta 67, 74, 151, 153, 204, 205, 208
Vedavedāngaśāstra 71
Vedda (aboriginal groups) 271
Vēḷ, upāśika 309
Vēḷir 309
Vēḷāḷas 112, 146, 147n, 148, 152, 153, 154, 155, 163, 225
Velde, Pieter van de 276n

Vellaivaranan, K. 142n, 148n
Veluthat, Kesavan 122n, 123n, 128n, 155n, 332n, 333n
Vēḷvikkuṭi plates 327n
Venice 240
Venkatachari, K.K.A. 150n
Vēnkaṭam/Tirupati 139, 162, 314
Vēntan 320, 321
Venugopal, C.N. 159n
Venugopalapillai, M.V. 112n
Verdon, M. 236n
Vevala 305
Vidhātā 81
Vidrovitch, C. Coquery 258n
Vijaya 268
Vijayanagar 154, 163
Vinogradoff, P. 24n
Virāj 18
Vīraśaiva 159
Vīraśaivism 159
Viṣahārī 87
Viṣṇu 70, 74, 81, 82, 83n, 121, 136, 137, 138, 139, 140n, 144, 149, 152, 153, 156
Viṣṇucitta *see* Periyāḻvār
Viṣṇudharmottara Purāṇa 62
Viṣṇu Purāṇa 58n, 61
Viswanathan, Gauri 51n
Viṭṭhala/Viṭhōba 126
Vivadabhangarnava 23, 28
Vivada-cintamani 27n
Vivadarnava-setu 23, 28
Voltaire 203
Vṛtra 11, 12, 13
Vyāda 285
Vyāsa/Vedavyāsa 55, 60, 70, 71, 77, 78

Wāḥdat-ul-Wujūd 174, 176, 190, 191
Wāḥdat-ush-Shuhūd 175
Wajib-ul-arz 33
Walker, Gordon 35n, 36
Weber, A. 13n
Weber, Max 240n, 241
White, L. 238n
White Jr., Lynn 237n
Whiting, R.M. 248n
Wilkinson, J. 43n
William the Conqueror 232
Wilson 30n, 41n, 42n, 43, 44n
Wilson, H.H. 74n
Wink, A. 240n
Wolf, E. 253n
Wood, Anand 227n, 228n, 231n
Wormald, P. 236n
Wynyard 45

Yadavs, the 222n
Yājñavalkya 125
Yajur Veda 58, 151
Yama/Kālan 81, 131
Yamuna R. 174
Yamunācārya 159
Yamuna Paryattan 95
Yangala 305
Yan Oya R.
  middle Yan Oya Valley 282, 287
Yasin, Mohammad 169n
Yaśodā 140
Yavana 58
Yoga 124, 125, 126
Yogin 124
Yoruba, the 259

Zaccagnini, C. 256n
Ziegler, N.P. 223n
Zvelebil, Kamil 111n, 113n, 115n, 116n, 117n, 118n, 137n, 145n, 146n, 147n, 148n, 159n, 318n, 332n